Venus to the Hoop

Sara Corbett

DOUBLEDAY New York London Toronto Sydney Auckland

Venus to the Hoop

A Gold-Medal Year in Women's Basketball

PUBLISHED BY DOUBLEDAY
a division of Bantam Doubleday Dell Publishing Group, Inc.
1540 Broadway, New York, New York 10036

DOUBLEDAY and the portrayal of an anchor with a dolphin
are trademarks of Doubleday, a division of
Bantam Doubleday Dell Publishing Group, Inc.

Book design by Bonni Leon Berman

Library of Congress Cataloging-in-Publication Data
Applied For

ISBN 0-385-48025-3

First Edition

10 9 8 7 6 5 4 3 2 1

CONTENTS

Contents

Venus to the Hoop

The less she thinks, the better her game tends to be. Thus she begins each night just shooting the ball to clear her mind. Like most basketball players, each time she steps onto the court she must take a few minutes to relearn the weight of the ball, recalibrating the relationship of hoop to ground, ground to body, body to ball. For Sheryl Swoopes, shooting to warm up has become ritual, a gradual draining of the mind that each evening as daylight fades over Lubbock takes her out of one world and deposits her unshakably into another.

She starts close to the basket, moving through her arsenal of inside shots, a quick turnaround jumper, the same with her left hand, then a soft hook from inside the foul line. Slowly her shots grow longer, her body edging farther from the hoop, the ball suspended in the air for another heartbeat. She is six feet even and solid, with her dark hair cut short in such a way that it puffs gently over her forehead. Her legs are planed with muscle, her arms, extending as she puts up a shot, drift together like beams on a cathedral. When the ball drops into the hoop, she doesn't smile. She's been around far too long to let one shot or another, even if it's a gloriously articulated left-hander on an otherwise glum day, affect her mood. Instead, her face bears a prim, don't-mess-with-me expression that seems to quiet the guys starting to mass on the sidelines, waiting somewhat impatiently for pick-up.

There was a time when the shift came automatically, when a single jump shot was enough to obliterate the mundanities and frustrations of daily life. But back then she was untouchable, the surest shot in college hoops, her emergence like a lightning bolt that lit up women's basketball and made it, if even briefly, something that people talked about, not just in West Texas, but all over the country. They called her the female Jordan, a point-scoring machine. She earned every Player of the Year award in the book and more or less single-handedly won the national championship for Texas Tech. People would drive hundreds of miles across the plains to see her play. She could hardly cross a street in Lubbock without somebody asking for an autograph. In the end, they retired her number, 24, hoisting it high into the rafters at the Municipal Coliseum.

But the white-hot intensity of those days comes less easily now. When she trains, it's in a crowded gym at the Texas Tech rec center, an aerobics class going full blare through the wall. When she plays, it's with part-time students who come in the form of out-of-shape insurance agents and car dealers and ranch hands who don't shower and any number of the other guys who show up for pick-up, intent on disavowing the roll of fat around their middles. Sometimes, gathering on the court, they look at her as if to say: How the hell did you get here? There is an answer to this question, but she doesn't often offer it. She's not particularly looking for friends out here. Anyway, if she were to answer it, it might come out sounding like an apology.

Backing up until her toes touch the three-point line, she bounces the ball once, boosts herself a few inches into the air, and *blam*, her jump shot cuts a sharp parabola and collapses neatly into the hoop.

"You got it now," says her companion, a round-faced guy with a freshly shaved bald head, stepping beneath the hoop. "You're right there." She shoots again, on the mark, and he feeds the ball back to her. Part of the ritual.

This is Eric Jackson, fiancé to Sheryl Swoopes. He calls himself her high school sweetheart, though according to Sheryl they started dating just two weeks before she went to college. There were plenty of boys in that high school, says Sheryl, though in the end there was only Eric, the most persistent of them all, who at the time he finally captured her heart was just sixteen years old.

Each time Sheryl shoots, Eric, who is now twenty-one, registers it, successful or not, with an almost imperceptible nod. He's not a coach and he knows it. But the thing he knows better than anyone is Sheryl Swoopes, her moods, her frustrations, and the small things that can set her mind adrift, sometimes resulting in a half-cocked wrist or feet that are planted just a bit too wide.

"Think about your shoulders," he says, watching keenly as she misses one then two shots from the perimeter, his brow furrowing slightly. "Get your stance right and then shoot. No hurry now."

They have come here to the rec center, she and he, nearly every night for nine months straight, Sheryl to play, Eric to look after Sheryl. At the local bank, where by day Sheryl is a teller, Eric works security in the vault. In less than two months, their friends and family will drive out from Brownfield for Sheryl and Eric's wedding.

Brownfield is a community of ten thousand set down in the wide-open plains southeast of Lubbock, built by the men who worked on outpost ranches and oil fields that cover much of West Texas, the kind of place where people raise their families modestly, sitting together on Sundays at the Baptist church downtown, praying for no tornadoes and no layoffs and the kind of faith it takes to live under the cumbersome white wall of Texas sky. Girls have babies in high school, boys get the same jobs as their daddies. People in Brownfield stay in Brownfield, says Sheryl, though her own daddy took off in 1971, when she was just three months old, never to come back. But those who stay are good to one another, they like things simple, and this is something Sheryl says she remembers when she looks at Eric.

As a girl, even unconsciously, it seems she was intent on leaving. From the gravel of her backyard, she watched the airplanes crossing the sky, on their way from Dallas to L.A., flashing in the sun. She'd seen the stewardesses on TV, their burgundy skirts and lipstick and little caps on their heads, the perfect ladies, and she dreamed someday of becoming one, of living her life high in the air above Brownfield. Out in the gravel with James and Earl, her two older brothers, she would toss a basketball through the rim of an old bicycle wheel they'd nailed to a post. She played each day until the sky got dark and the taillights from the planes blinked red above her. Sometimes one of the boys would give her a hard shove and she'd run sweating inside to find her mother cooking dinner, who, hugging her, would say, that's all right baby, you belong here with me.

In the end, however, where she belonged was on the basketball court. At Brownfield High they'd never seen anyone play the way Sheryl Swoopes did. She was lean and graceful and could shoot the ball from anywhere on the court. Beyond that, she was fast, hustling past defenders so quickly that they could hardly turn around before she'd made her move to the basket. Her junior year, Brownfield beat Comanche, Slayton, and Ingleside, and finally on the strength of 26 points from Sheryl, they beat Hardin-Jefferson for the state championships in Houston. James and Earl drove down and watched their kid sister dance on the court with both hands raised in the air. Everyone in Brownfield knew it then: Sheryl Swoopes would soon be leaving.

She was offered a scholarship to return to Austin and play for the University of Texas Lady Longhorns, then one of the top three women's basketball programs in the country. But when she flew there after her graduation, she found it to be big and disorienting and she missed her mother and she missed Eric and no amount of great basketball—no promise of a high-profile NCAA future—was worth that. She was home after a week, enrolled at the local junior college, where she stayed and played basketball until Eric finished up at Brownfield High. Nobody called her a quitter exactly, but sometimes it was suggested in the way people spoke to her that she'd done a dumb female thing and traded a career for a man.

When finally after two years at junior college Sheryl packed up and drove thirty-eight miles across the buffalo grass and sage to play ball at Texas Tech, there were awards and accolades and plenty of nights when she could do no wrong. Little boys and little girls tried to imitate her famous jump shot, so effortless that the ball seemed to lift from her fingertips of its own accord, arcing over the heads of opponents and teammates alike before dropping delicately into the hoop. Attendance at the Municipal Coliseum nearly quadrupled. And in 1993, her second and final season at Tech, Sheryl Swoopes brought home the national championship.

It's a day that Eric still sees when he closes his eyes. The numbers rattle easily off his tongue. She scored 47 points, a record. Her tournament statistics were all records too: most points (177), most field goals (56), and most free throws (57). When it was over and Sheryl was dancing on the court, Eric, from his place in the stands, danced with her.

But the problem with having the best day of your life is that there's always a day after and more days and weeks and even months that will never be as good as that one day. Two years after cutting down the net in Atlanta, the female Jordan is back in Lubbock, working behind the teller window at South Plains National Bank of West Texas, biding her time at the rec center and nursing one last dream.

Some nights she runs and dribbles and jumps until the sweat rivers off her body and her legs lose their spring, her last shot at greatness seeming utterly in reach. Other nights she can't find it inside herself—the day at the bank was too long, the last workout hurt too much—and instead she sits at home and reads in the newspapers about this kid Lobo who's come after the last kid, Leslie, the new sensations, and suddenly the impossible seems possible: Swoopes is old and basketball is on the verge of passing her by. Never mind that Nike has said it wants to name a shoe after her, that she still gets autograph requests from little kids. If she's only as good as her last game, then she's good enough to play the insurance salesman and car dealers and she's a Lubbock bank teller and not a lot more.

And thus there is an urgency to the way she plays these days. Tryouts for the U.S. national team, the one that will play in the 1996 Olympics in Atlanta, are a week away in Colorado Springs at the Olympic Training Center. The place seems jinxed to her. She's got a disaster story for nearly every trip up there she's made. There was a sprained ankle one year, a concussion the next, and finally a busted knee that dashed her hopes for the 1992 Olympics. When finally she did make a U.S. team, last summer, she went to Australia to play in the World Championships, and she blew it, shooting poorly and tiring easily, unable to keep pace against the stronger and tougher international competition.

When on the plane home from Australia, Sheryl asked the world championship coach, the hard-nosed Tara VanDerveer of Stanford, how she could bring her game up to par, VanDerveer said, "I don't know, Sheryl, but playing with guys is not the answer."

Yet on a Thursday night in Lubbock, with team trials looming, the guys are all Sheryl Swoopes has. When the battered-looking wall clock lurches to seven, the group collects itself at center court. Sheryl throws up one last shot, then tosses Eric her ball and joins them as they divide into teams. Several of the men nod hello to her, gestures she acknowledges coolly. The sunbeam smile that was her trademark in college is kept firmly in check. Instead, she stands with eyebrows arched, lips set in a firm line, hands on hips, waiting finally to play.

As the game gets under way, Eric monitors it gravely from the sideline, bent over at the waist like a baseball ump. From time to time he offers a directive, though Sheryl seems hardly to hear him. She hadn't wanted to come at all tonight, having plunked herself on the couch after work and flipped on the TV, but he'd stood in front of the couch and reminded her maybe a bit grumpily, this was the home stretch. On the way there, they'd quibbled over the fact that Sheryl had forgotten her ankle braces. For a second they considered turning back to get them, but Sheryl waved it off. It was just another night of practice. What was the difference?

At its best, pick-up basketball upholds a certain egalitarian ideal, governed by an open-acceptance policy that allows the worst to play side by side with the best, the fit to meet the unfit, strangers to become teammates. The rule being that whoever shows up plays. By extension, pick-up play tends to be rough, catering to the lowest common denominator of skill, a breeding ground for bad habits. Egos flare, passing is kept to a minimum, rules concerning double-dribbling, traveling, and camping out beneath the basket are often abandoned, and in the end even the most polite of games can quickly devolve into a thrashing free-for-all.

"Watch yourself there!" Eric calls out as one player, an older white guy, charges his bride. When the man misses his layup, Sheryl grabs the offensive rebound and tosses the ball back out, then while her teammate tangles with the ball, she accelerates expertly in and out of the under-the-hoop traffic until she's found an open patch of court. "Here!" she calls out, her voice rising above the others, her right hand flipped high in the air. "Right here!" The ball flies in her direction and she jumps to catch it just as a defender bears down. She spins out of his way and comes up in shooting position, lofting the ball into the net.

The perspiration is beginning to drip from Sheryl's forehead. Several of the guys are huffing hard as they thunder up and down the court, chasing the ball through nearly continuous turnovers.

"Finish your shot," Eric calls to an awkward kid of about fourteen, unable to help himself. "See it through now." The kid's shot bounces out. He reaches for the rebound, but Sheryl is there first, her body sixteen inches in the air, her fingers wrapping neatly around the ball as she drops back to earth. But somewhere in that moment the kid has slid himself beneath the hoop, inadvertently undercutting Sheryl as she comes down. Eric knows it's coming before he even sees it. Her feet land crookedly, thrown off by the boy's foot; her knees buckle and she thumps to the floor, the ball skittering away.

Then there is silence. Suddenly Eric comes storming, and before anyone knows it he has a hand on the guy's shoulder, his other hand curled in a fist, but when he sees the apologetic face he pulls back—it was a mistake, he knows it immediately—and then he catches sight of Sheryl, strewn on the floor and screaming as her ankle balloons grotesquely, and he wheels around and takes off running. Some of the guys think he's gone for help or ice, but he doesn't come back. They try to help her, but she's barely able to breathe, letting loose with great hiccuping sobs.

"Breathe, Sheryl. C'mon, girl."

"I'm fine, leave me alone, don't touch it. I'm *fine*," she's saying, her voice a barely concealed wail.

"Just . . . please, leave me alone for a sec. Somebody get Eric. Don't worry about me, just go get him. Tell him . . . tell him I'm okay."

Nearly an hour later they drive home in silence. Sheryl's ankle is packed in bags of ice and swaddled in an Ace bandage. Her eyes are puffed from crying. She chews on a thumbnail and stares morosely out the window. Eric can't think of a thing to say to her. What is there to say? He simply lost it, running out into the hallway and up the stairs that led outside, needing a few minutes just to calm himself down before returning to piggyback her off the floor. Maybe it's not right, pouring so much of himself into her, taking on the weight of her dream, even as she herself seems to falter under it. He steers the car gently, easing it around corners and into stoplights, as if that somehow could make it easier on her. Outside, the streetlights seem to glare, their frank white light blotting out the vast Texas plains in the distance.

She'll have to stay off the ankle for at least a day or two. She won't play hard for a solid week. But at least it's not her knee. It doesn't mean surgery or rehab or anything more than easing up a little. In a week she'll still be able to play, anyway, even if it's not at top form.

At home, he will rewrap her ankle, maybe fix her a chocolate milk shake, rub her shoulders. "It's going to work out," he says quietly. "You're going to be okay."

Five days later Sheryl is back on the basketball court, both ankles wrapped tightly in athletic tape, working her way stiffly around the three-point line, banking on the one shot she knows might distinguish her from the other women going to Colorado Springs. Eric stands off to one side, chasing the occasional loose ball but mostly remaining quiet as the once-great Sheryl Swoopes works to resurrect herself. The indifference that once calmed her is gone. Instead, there is a prayer to accompany every shot, not particularly a fully formed prayer but a hope that borders on the religious, a silent request that things will work out.

As her muscles begin to warm up, she tests her ankle gingerly, dribbling the ball slowly down the passing lane, throwing up an easy set shot, which bumbles on the rim and then bounces away. With two quick, pained steps she recaptures the ball near the foul line. Grimacing, she sizes up the basket and then almost in anger breaks into an instinctive run, dribbling the ball ahead of her, favoring her right leg just slightly as she charges beneath the basket and lets the ball fly, a looping hook shot she sends off into the air with a single desperate thought: *please.*

1

Team Trials

       Colorado Springs lies seventy miles south of Denver, located precisely where the flats of the eastern part of the state escalate abruptly into the boulder-strewn front range of the Rocky Mountains. The city itself is laid out at the foot of the mountains in a quiet grid of broad, tree-lined streets, with a sleepy but vaguely corporate downtown area and a large, landscaped park that fronts the Monument River on both sides. On a spring evening the park overflows with joggers, dog walkers, and Frisbee throwers, while brilliantly colored flocks of cyclists zip through the streets, past well-dressed men and women floating down Cascade Avenue, headed for the evening symphony.

Life in "the Springs," as it's known in Colorado, is generally prosperous. Drawn by a combination of mild weather, a low cost of living, and an influx of relocating businesses, people have moved to Colorado Springs in droves recently, making it one of the country's fastest-growing communities. The population is overwhelmingly white and mostly middle class, lending the city a comfortable if unstimulating homogeneity as well as a decidedly conservative bent. The U.S. Air Force Academy sits on the bluffs north of town, while the right-wing Christian organization, Focus on the Family, has its headquarters nearby. Local radio broadcasts daily Christian call-in shows led by former University of Colorado football-coach-turned-evangelist Bill McCartney, who not too long ago relocated himself and his fundamentalist men's coalition, the Promise Keepers, to town.

Set on a nondescript street about a mile behind the stately mountain-view homes on Cascade is the Olympic Training Center, situated conveniently next to a hospital and across from a Taco Bell. The center is perhaps best described as the Pentagon of American athletics, home to a brain trust of physiologists, trainers, sports psychologists, and coaches whose sole purpose is to boost the strength, speed, and competitiveness of elite U.S. athletes. Helped along by small stipends from the U.S.

Olympic Committee, athletes of all stripe—wrestlers, fencers, cyclists, swimmers—come here for training residencies of various length, housed in several unsightly concrete dormitories that were once barracks in the compound's former incarnation as an Air Force base. As the center has grown over the years, it's been supplemented with a mixture of new buildings and hastily thrown-up modular cubes that serve as trainers' rooms and sports science labs. Today, with its cheery industriousness and bric-a-brac buildings, the training center bears the aura of part college campus, part trailer park. A large digital sign on a grassy lawn counts down the days to the next summer and winter Olympics.

On a Thursday in late May, the day that twenty-four female basketball players came to try out for the U.S. national team, the sign registered 425 days before the 1996 Summer Olympics in Atlanta. The last of the winter's snow lay patchworked across the mountains, the Monument River was fast and bloated with spring runoff, a touch of the passing season's brusqueness still hung in the air. For the women who checked in at the training center's front desk, receiving dormitory keys in exchange for their signature, Atlanta seemed immeasurably far away. The colorful six-foot-high Olympic rings that festoon a large wall in front of the gym seemed to signify only a distant and evanescent place in time, an abstraction rather than an actual event. Yet it was for this abstraction, the promise of it, that they had come.

They brought with them little more than what it would require to get through the next week: gym bags, basketball shoes, mouth guards, piles of freshly laundered white socks, an outfit or two to wear to the movies or the mall or the Japanese restaurant near the mall. Packed into their bags, too, were the small individual things—amulets, distractions, baubles they could return to in quieter moments. Lisa Leslie, a lanky forward from southern California, brought a thick paperback romance novel. Pint-sized point guard Dawn Staley packed two decks of cards for acey-deucey in the dorm; Nikki McCray, a young guard for whom singing was the ultimate anodyne, brought her Whitney Houston CDs and a portable player; Val Whiting packed a worn-looking teddy bear and a bag full of vitamins; Jennifer Azzi brought a Bible; Ruthie Bolton arrived from Florida with little to help her but the memory of her mother, who had recently died of cancer.

Each one of them had been to Colorado Springs before, auditioning for the various teams that USA Basketball, the sport's nonprofit governing body, sends on the yearly rotation of summer tournaments, including the Goodwill Games, Pan Am Games, and World Championships. More often than not, they'd made every team they tried out for. They had been NCAA Players of the Year and All-Americans, forces who had led their college teams to national championships. They'd played professionally all over the world—from Brazil to Japan to Sweden—and garnered every award that basketball had to offer a woman. Two of them had Olympic medals already; others weren't even out of college. They ranged from five foot five to six foot six, from twenty to thirty in age. They hailed from Oregon and Illinois and Mississippi and Massachusetts and all parts in between. Fourteen of them were black; ten were white. Four had their college numbers retired. Some of them were friends, others nodding acquaintances, still others were rivals from years before. But what they would have in common, at least for the next week, were the same two hoops and a ball filled with eight pounds of air.

Whether the athletes fully understood it or not, women's basketball had reached a new threshold in terms of popularity that year. Three weeks earlier, led by senior star Rebecca Lobo, the University of Connecticut Huskies had capped off an undefeated season by winning the national championship at the Target Center in Minneapolis. As the final point was scored in front of 19,000 rambunctious fans and a national television audience of 5.4 million, one thing became clear: America was paying unprecedented attention to the women's team from Connecticut.

Perhaps it was fortuitous that the Huskies had their home court in the media-rich Northeast, near the well-to-do suburbs of New York City where a number of influential marketing executives made their homes. Surely it helped that they went undefeated in a season during which it was announced that women were outbuying men in the athletic shoe market, when *BusinessWeek* was reporting that women's hoops attracted "well-educated, family-oriented fans," i.e., demographic dreams for television advertising. It was significant, too, that cooperative, humble stars like the Huskies' Rebecca Lobo leapt into the limelight just as a *Sports Illustrated* cover story was bellyaching about the "pouting prima donnas" of the NBA, and polls showed that the 1994 baseball strike had rendered Americans disenchanted with the millionaire celebrity culture created by men's professional sports. A more recent hockey strike had left sportswriters with empty columns to fill, and because of this, women's basketball had gotten more coverage lately than ever before. Given what seemed to be a harmonic convergence of factors, at the finish of the 1995 college season, women's basketball was poised to bust into the mainstream.

If anyone had been paying attention to all of this, it was Teresa Edwards, a guard with broad, rounded shoulders, cornrowed hair, and a half-inch scar between her eyebrows, the result of a childhood mishap long forgotten. For her, basketball had become political. It went beyond the totaling of wins and losses, of gold medals and bronze medals and the arcane math of statistics; basketball was instead about discipline and tenacity and, above all, fairness. She had grown up poor, the child of a single mother who had left high school to work in the vegetable fields outside Cairo (pronounced kaý-ro), Georgia, when she got pregnant with Teresa at the age of sixteen. For Teresa, the basketball court had become an equalizer, the place where with something as simple as determination she could transcend the circumstances that by a sociologist's measure were most likely to doom her. She went to college and became the first in her family ever to graduate. She traveled the world playing basketball, her athleticism and control on the court making her one of the best guards in the world, her career growing into one of the longest and most distinguished in the history of the women's game. She was the grande dame of the international scene, a player who could not let go of the game of basketball, even as nearly every one of her contemporaries had retired. Eventually, she had earned enough money to go home to Cairo and buy her mother a car and a three-bedroom house with a deck in the nice section of town. This, Teresa liked to say, meant more than any shot she could ever take.

Still, she was thirty years old, and having played in the last three Olympics, her wisdom was tempered by a sober pragmatism. She'd read in the papers about UConn and Rebecca Lobo and all the attendant hoopla, but she had also seen basketball brilliance flare and then fizzle in the past, with Sheryl Swoopes, for example, or back in the eighties, when Cheryl Miller's prolific scoring had briefly captured the country's imagination. She'd seen pro leagues for women come and go, most of them defeated by what she felt to be the misguided, almost surreal perception that women's play needed to be accessorized with things like colored balls, lowered hoops, and players wearing shiny, body-hugging spandex unitards.

In fifteen years of basketball, she had seen a whole lot, and while the victories stood out like mountain peaks, in particular the gold medals in the '84 and '88 Games, the defeats made her feel shallow and a touch bitter. The U.S. team had settled for bronze in Barcelona, soundly beaten by the Russians and the Chinese. They had lost again at the World Championships in 1994, this time to a feisty, trash-talking Brazilian team. Over the course of Teresa Edwards's unusually long career in basketball, the once-preeminent U.S. women had been overthrown, toppled. The worst part of it all was that back in the States, nobody outside the insular world of coaches and players had really seemed to care one way or the other about post-college women's basketball. While on the college level women's basketball was starting to grow a following, the American sports machine, fueled as it was by shoe companies and television contracts and salary wars, male sportswriters and the star-making wizards of the NBA, was still built to support men and not women. Given what Teresa had seen in her lifetime—the empty coliseums and practices scheduled late at night in order not to interfere with the men's teams, the unitards and all—that was pretty clear.

Perhaps as a result she had learned to trust people just as much as she needed to, letting them in only by increments, meeting the world with an even gaze that revealed little emotion, her brown eyes frank and at times intentionally intimidating. While a basketball team was a good place to find at least a tenuous racial equity, stepping off the court into the masses of mostly white coaches, mostly white media, mostly white marketing people, and even the mostly white fans, the powerful imbalance of the world came rushing back. More than once she had done interviews only to have the interviewer forget her name and inadvertently substitute the name of another black player instead.

"You gonna remember me tomorrow?" she once asked a television producer before agreeing to an interview, one eyebrow cocked doubtfully. On a number of occasions she simply refused to give interviews at all.

Years had passed and international tournaments had come and gone and each season the faces got younger, the women Teresa played with seemed more resilient, shaped by a different kind of basketball—a quick and more privileged version of what she had known in college, back when Division I programs were cash poor and uncelebrated. Beyond that, the young players had a new optimism, a fresh-faced eagerness that in turns eased and aggravated her sagging spirit.

In the moments following the U.S. loss in the semifinals at the 1992 Olympics in Barcelona, a television reporter had caught Teresa and one of her teammates, both still shining with sweat, as they left the court and asked whether they'd be back in 1996. "Not me, I don't think so," announced Teresa without hesitation, punctuating the declaration with an emphatic shake of her head. ". . . I'm getting too old for this."

But four years later, having returned home to her house in Atlanta from a draining season in France, Teresa was reading the sports pages and half believing that this time things could change for real. Attendance at women's games was up all around the country, women were getting more press. The shoe companies had been giving women free gear for years, but now they were starting to *pay* female players to wear their shoes.

And then there was this national team. The bronze in Barcelona had been enough of a debacle that USA Basketball had decided to make changes: In the past, Olympic teams had been chosen just six weeks before Opening Ceremonies, thrown together under a good deal of pressure to learn plays, scout the competition, and adjust to the various personalities and styles within the team. This year, USA Basketball, with the help of the NBA, had lobbied companies like Sears, State Farm, Tampax, and Champion to finance a women's national team, paying twelve top U.S. players to spend an unprecedented fourteen months preparing for Atlanta under the direction of one of the country's most renowned coaches, Tara VanDerveer of Stanford. With a $3 million budget and the marketing muscle of the NBA's merchandising department behind it, the team would embark on a barnstorming world tour, complete with public appearances, nationally televised games, and a movable feast of reporters following along.

Understanding this, Teresa Edwards had started thinking. She thought about what she'd given to basketball and what basketball had given her back, about the long hours of practice and all the travel and how it could make her feel strong and weak at the same time. Then she considered the future, the day that would come when her body would start resisting the workouts, her joints stiffening and her reflexes slow-ing. She would become a coach or an administrator, someone close to the court, for basketball would always be there for women, though the question was to what extent and how and where and in front of whom. Thinking that here was her chance to shape the answers, she arrived at a thought that four years earlier she couldn't have conceived of: She had one comeback left.

The creation of a national team had infused a new hope in many American players. While male college stars graduated (or, as was increasingly the case, didn't graduate) to the happy excesses of the NBA draft, their female counterparts faced the ignominious choice between early retirement or a career playing for the largely substandard club and corporate teams in Europe, Asia, and South America, places where professional women's basketball had been around for years, drawing modest crowds and varying amounts of corporate sponsorship, but thriving enough to give certain teams budgets to bring in two foreign players, usually Americans, each season. Life abroad was far from glamorous, however. Female players routinely complained of loneliness, racism, and professional mistreatment. In Japan, where higher salaries lured many American athletes, male coaches often kicked and punched their female players, even during time-outs in a game.

In the three years since she'd finished her NCAA career at Virginia, Dawn Staley had rotated through six different teams in France, Italy, Brazil, and Spain and was quick to admit she was tired of it. ("I'm not going back to Europe ever," she declared. "Not even on vacation.") Sheryl Swoopes had signed on with a team in Italy following her final season at Texas Tech, but it was only three months before a dispute over her paycheck had brought her home. Shanda Berry had a lawyer write a "no abuse" clause into her contract before going to play in Japan. Twenty-seven-year-old Ruthie Bolton had left her husband of three years each fall for nearly six months in order to compete in the European season, and Val Whiting had logged two unhappy seasons abroad in order to save money for medical school. As rumors of a national team had floated across Europe early on in the 1994–1995 season, they were met by exiled American players with a uniform joy.

The only exception was Katrina McClain, a soft-spoken black twenty-nine-year-old forward from Georgia who happened to be Teresa Edwards's best friend. She had played on USA Basketball teams nearly every summer for the last thirteen years and had won a gold medal already, in the 1988 Olympics. On the ill-fated '92 Olympic team, she had been the top rebounder, and when the U.S. lost the World Championships to Brazil in '94, it had been despite the best efforts of Katrina, who scored more points per game than any other American. She was widely considered one of the best female players in the world, a dynamic six-foot-two power forward who could hurl herself into the rowdiest tussle under the hoop and emerge, a foot and a half in the air, with the ball in hand. She had weathered years of highly physical basketball with hardly an injury to speak of. Now, pushing thirty, she was at the pinnacle of her game. Playing for a corporate team in Japan, she was making more than $200,000 a season, over twice the average salary of an American player abroad.

To Katrina's way of thinking, the invisibility that went along with playing women's basketball was just fine. Or maybe she was simply used to it, having been right there in '92 as the women's team vanished in the shadow of Michael Jordan and the rest of the men's Dream Team. Either way, returning home from Japan in late February, she had little interest in trying out for the national team. First, the physical exhaustion of the last season, of seven years of nearly continuous basketball, pushed her to say no. Then there was the money. She'd had an offer of $300,000 to play for a Hungarian team next season, while USA Basketball could pay just $50,000 and wanted over a year of her life. Then, of course, there were all those obstacles, she said, all the ways the women got treated worse than the guys, all the attitudes people had about female players. When the 1992 team had returned from Barcelona, *The Washington Post* published a story by staff writer Tom Callahan entitled "The (Lesser) Games Women Play," which criticized the female basketball players, observing that "They walked like men, slapped hands like men. They played like junior high school boys. No, to be fair, high school boys, the junior varsity." The attitude was familiar and infuriating. Sometimes, said Katrina, you could feel it in the way people looked at you, as if being tall and strong and female to boot made you some kind of mannish freak.

Beyond that, playing for Tara VanDerveer last year at the World Championships had been no piece of cake. VanDerveer was a saturnine coach with a work ethic that bordered on the maniacal. Her teams won—and they usually did win—because they outworked their opponents, running the ball up and down the court fast and hard enough to leave the other team breathless and spent. The superior conditioning of VanDerveer's teams could be attributed to her fondness of lengthy "two-a-days," morning and evening workouts that allowed little time for rest. During the early season, her Stanford teams spent nearly as much time on the track as they did on the basketball court. But those were twenty-year-olds, ardent owners of healthy knees and unjaded minds, ready to jump and sprint at the coach's command. And VanDerveer made no bones about the fact that she liked twenty-year-olds, even preferred them to the veterans. So why, reasoned Katrina, should she haul herself to Colorado Springs and kill herself to try out for a coach who would not only run her ragged but would fill her ears with a year's worth of strident opinions to boot?

Teresa and Katrina had been friends for so long, they couldn't remember the exact year in which they had met. They had been high school players competing in some sports festival, the location of which they'd forgotten, too. Teresa, says Katrina, was calm and self-possessed, radiating a determination that seemed to cow the other players, including Katrina. According to Teresa, Katrina was so shy, she hardly spoke a word the whole time. But she was kind and good-humored, and when Teresa threw the hardest and fastest no-look pass, Katrina was always there to catch it and lay it in. When several years later Katrina was recruited to the University of Georgia Bulldogs, where Teresa was already a sophomore starter, the two ended up as roommates. In time they were known almost solely by their nicknames, Tree and T, often uttered in the same uninterrupted breath. Like so many friendships born in a gym or on a playing field, theirs was a connection that was largely unspoken, an outgrowth of what happened on the court, an instinctive call and response, dependence answered by reliability.

Off the court, this translated into a quiet and comfortable unity. They had played together across the globe, had sat together in airports and hotel rooms and locker rooms all over creation, and found a way to laugh—Katrina with a wound-up, almost slapstick giggle; Teresa with a low, drawn-out chuckle—about nearly everything. Even when the reality of it stung, they had laughed about getting older and all the good old hard times and about the coaches who might not like their attitudes. But back in Georgia, after their seasons abroad this year, talking on the phone or getting together occasionally for a meal, when the subject turned to national team trials, Katrina tended to fall into silence and, following her lead, Teresa would too.

They had an inkling that VanDerveer had come away from the World Championships figuring them to be uncoachable, players whose games were competent but inflexible after so many years of doing their own thing, playing with minimal coaching abroad. But while Katrina had delicately laid aside the six-page agreement USA Basketball had sent regarding the national team trials, saying vaguely that she'd make up her mind later, Teresa had filled it out and faxed it in without a second thought. She was going. VanDerveer or no VanDerveer, this was important.

Teresa was not given to keeping her opinions to herself, but when it came to her best friend, she knew better than to push it. What, really, was there to say anyway? She could hardly step in as a friend and recommend that Katrina forgo $300,000 for what amounted to a USA Basketball gamble. Any athlete knew that a career lasted only as long as a body did, and as far as anybody knew, this could well be McClain's last chance to make that kind of money playing basketball. She'd heard her friend say many times that she wanted to fatten her bank account so she could retire and get married, have kids, have a normal quiet life in Georgia. Teresa couldn't argue with that, nor could she come close to guaranteeing that either of them would make the national team anyway. Thus she held her tongue, saying nothing, figuring that if Katrina wanted her advice, she'd ask for it. When she didn't, Teresa took a deep breath and resolved to go to trials alone.

The Antlers Doubletree Hotel sits about a mile from the training center, a thirteen-story three-star hotel whose west-side rooms look out onto the Rockies and whose east side faces and even seems to dwarf the low, unremarkable buildings and bosky thoroughfares of downtown Colorado Springs. The most upscale hotel in town, the Antlers is a hive of constant activity, with conventions rotating in and out weekly—firefighters associations and cosmetic sales and various Christian causes—along with the usual traffic of tourists, wedding receptions, and visiting businesspeople. In late May 1995, a collection of real estate agents had invaded the Antlers and so, too, in a far less conspicuous way, had the off-court cognoscenti of women's basketball.

While it was relatively easy to identify the basketball players trying out for the national team by their bags of ice, aching joints, and beleaguered expressions, the people who came to watch trials were far less recognizable, particularly in the lobby of a place like the Antlers, where nearly everybody was well-dressed, white, and given to crossing the plush green carpet with quick, purposeful strides. Armed with a keen eye and a passing familiarity with NCAA basketball, however, one might begin to pick out the notables as they came through. There was the strikingly confident Pat Summit, head coach at Tennessee, coach of the gold-medal-winning '88 Olympic team. There was Connecticut's Geno Auriemma, blue-eyed, with a helmet of immaculately blow-dried spun-gold hair and a dimly victorious air about him, having vanquished Summit's Tennessee Vols at last month's Final Four. There was Sylvia Hatchell, a small woman with a no-nonsense expression, whose North Carolina team had decimated both Summit's and Auriemma's the year before.

Next came Sue Levin, the thirty-two-year-old manager of women's sports marketing at Nike, then Beth Bass, who bore a similar title at Converse, and behind her a few folks from Reebok. Then, one by one, the sportswriters piled in, from *USA Today* and the Associated Press and *Sports Illustrated;* and eventually more coaches—some volunteering to help as floor coaches, several of them part of the thirteen-member selection committee that would chose the team, still others there simply to see the players they had trained and molded go head-to-head against the players trained and molded by the other coaches.

Andy Landers, the jocular coach of the University of Georgia Bulldogs, enjoyed the vein of competition that ran through the NCAA coaching community. Particularly among top-ranked schools like Tennessee, Stanford, Georgia, North Carolina, and Connecticut, rivalries could be fierce, particularly late in the season as the tournament approached, and in the mid-fall when recruiting battles heated up, but the summer months usually offered a friendly reprieve. Arriving at the training center, he waved amiably to several of the other coaches, somewhat surprised by the fact that so many of them had showed up.

He himself had no intention of coming until just a few days earlier. He had gone to Tennessee to visit family for the weekend, when, as he sat in his mother's living room at eleven P.M. on Friday night, four days before trials were to begin, the phone rang.

"Coach?" came a rasping familiar voice. "What are you doing?"

"Mac," he said, instantly recognizing Katrina McClain, a player he hadn't coached for eight years but with whom he'd remained close. Last he'd heard, she was making plans to play in Hungary. "I'm just knocking around. . . . What are you doing?"

"I'm going," she said. "I decided to go." Then, after a pause: "I'm just calling to see if you're going."

Surprised, Landers sat back in his chair and quickly rethought his plans, knowing his two old players would have to play their best in order to convince USA Basketball to take them. "Yeah, I'm going," he said. "I'll just see you there."

"Okay, good," said McClain. "Teresa wants to talk to you."

An audibly cheered Teresa Edwards came on the line. "You going out? Really?" she said. In the wake of Katrina's decision, she and Katrina had changed the airline tickets USA Basketball had sent so they could leave the next day, to join up with several other players to train together and adjust to the altitude before trials started.

"Absolutely," Landers replied, "wouldn't miss this for anything."

On Thursday evening, just as the sun began to drop behind the mountains, trials began. They gathered in the freshly cleaned, echoing Sports Center gym on the training center's west side: a chaotic cluster of players and evaluators, observers, trainers, USA Basketball employees, and there standing at the center of it all, arms folded, singular and serious, one Tara VanDerveer.

She wore blue nylon warm-up pants and a white USA Basketball golf shirt. A large silver whistle hung from her neck. At forty-two, she was relatively nondescript-looking, her coppery-brown hair cut so that it angled neatly away from her face, short enough to reveal the tips of her earlobes, in which she normally wore plain gold stud earrings. When she spoke, it was in a tone that was nasal and ringing, expertly whittled and honed over seventeen years of college coaching to cut through any kind of racket. When she watched, it was with piercing brown eyes beneath hooded eyelids, her lips parted almost imperceptibly. Even when she spoke, VanDerveer never stopped watching. Particularly on the basketball court but even in a place as unexceptional as an airport lounge or a busy restaurant, her eyes continually darted, her mind registering the surroundings as if to figure the odds and predict the results of whatever she saw, as if life itself were a grand-scale game.

It would go like this: two workouts a day; drills in the morning, scrimmages in the evenings, rest in the few hours between. VanDerveer would oversee every practice, regulating drills with bleats of her whistle, helped by her court coaches, whose job it was to be encouraging, who in their shorts, white golf shirts, and bright-hued sneakers looked not unlike camp counselors. The selection committee—made up of high school and college coaches—would watch it all. Sometimes they'd sit high in the bleachers, conferring; most of the time they'd sit at the long tables along the sidelines, scribbling silently on their clipboards. Either way, they were, in the manner of most good coaches, excellent observers: No turnover would be too small, no failed defensive assignment too minor to escape note. Late each night they would pull chairs around a low table in a room adjoining the gym and report to one another on what they'd seen.

The players were made to understand all of this in the customary speech that kicked off most trials, delivered by one USA Basketball official or another as the athletes, decked out in blue and white practice garb, twitched and fiddled in the bleachers. The speech covered the practicalities of the week ahead—meal tickets and laundry protocol—but it also always inevitably included a breathy riff on teamwork, on how the point was not to showcase yourself but rather to show that you could pass and play defense and make other players look good too, to be a team player.

Yet you couldn't go through a trials, even for a junior team, and miss the irony in this type of speech. Everyone in the room knew it: Trials were about exalting one's own high-flying self unabashedly over one's peers. If you made the others look good, then you got cut and they didn't. In the past, Olympic trials had been predictably high key, a trample-or-be-trampled rush to impress the selection committee. Any player invited to trials, a USA Basketball official once said, was talented enough to play in the Olympics. What trials determined was who wanted it most.

Some quiet banter aside, the players in the gym that night seemed wholly absorbed in their private preparations—lacing up their shoes meticulously, making final adjustments to the athletic tape that bound fingers and wrists and ankles, carefully removing the jewelry, earrings, and engagement rings that a number of them wore for luck until the last minute before play. Along the sidelines, several of the women bounced up and down on their toes as if that might unstopper some of the tension; others sat on a row of plastic chairs, elbows resting on knees, appearing to be lost in thought.

Sheryl Swoopes was fretting about her ankle, which still felt wobbly, and the details of her wedding, which was now just three weeks away. Ruthie Bolton was thinking about her family and her husband, Mark, of whom she'd seen too little recently. Sylvia Crawley was concerned with her finances, having left her season in Spain early in order to train for trials at home. Teresa Edwards thought about who would be judging her game that night. Rebecca Lobo thought about her college graduation, which she was missing in order to try out. Katrina McClain claims to have thought about nothing much at all, and Jennifer Azzi, a guard who'd played for VanDerveer at Stanford, was trying to think about anything but her failure to make the '92 Olympic team, which had rendered her a bawling, defeated mess.

Taking to the court finally, they ran and shot and scrambled after the ball as if kingdoms depended on it. Elbows flew, passes shot cross-court at bruising speeds, bodies ricocheted off each other with startling impact, often sending one or both players to the floor. They played fast and hard for nearly an hour, running drills and half-court offenses, paced by VanDerveer's whistle, before a scream went up and stopped them all dead. *My knee my knee my knee!* Dena Head, a five-foot-ten guard from Tennessee, had gone down under the basket, wilted over one leg.

As Head was loaded onto a stretcher and taken to the hospital—where she would learn that her anterior cruciate ligament had torn in several places, as busted as a knee could be—a moment of sweaty silence ensued among the remaining twenty-three players before the whistle sounded again and the howls of the fallen player got lost in the thunder of the game.

Arriving for the second practice on Friday morning, Andy Landers, the coach from Georgia, bypassed the gym itself, where most of the other coaches sat in chairs along the sidelines, and instead took up residence in the small, glassed-in boxing arena that overlooked the courts through a wide picture window. He watched the entire workout quietly from above, beginning at ten and going until noon, when Van-Derveer gathered the players at center court and dismissed them with a brief, upbeat comment or two and a see-you-tonight. The players lingered only long enough to throw on sweatshirts and change out of their shoes before dragging themselves to the trainers' room for ice or knee treatments or directly to the showers. Landers reached the court just in time to catch Edwards and McClain, who greeted him warmly.

"What did you think?" said McClain, grinning as she wiped her forehead with a white towel. "How're we doing?"

"Let's get lunch," said Landers, putting a hand on both players' shoulders. "Then we'll talk."

Thirty minutes later, sitting in a crowded Italian place with her best friend and their beloved old coach, McClain was riding high. So far trials hadn't been as tough as she'd thought they would be. In the end, it had been a conversation with her older brother, Troy, a machinist in South Carolina, that had resolved the trials issue for her. She had called him the day the agreements were due, and he had sat on the other end of the line, listening as she talked. She ran on and on about money and being tired and all the bogus things written in that agreement, like how they had to give up certain marketing rights and they had to wear a certain brand of sports bra or else they'd get fined, and Troy just listened. She wondered what the Olympics would be like in Atlanta. Troy would drive up for Atlanta, wouldn't he? She had talked about being old and out of favor, about the snappiness of VanDerveer's tone and the many miles that team would have to travel together. She talked, too, about the two past Olympics and how having a gold medal hung around your neck was the truest kind of triumph she'd known. From time to time Troy had asked a gentle question, prodded when a certain answer didn't make sense, but mostly he remained quiet, letting his baby sister ramble her way to a decision. The phone call went over an hour, at the end of which Katrina had signed her agreement and faxed it in.

At lunch she asked Landers again for his opinion of the trials.

"I'd cut you in a second," he said, then watched as a beat passed as they realized he wasn't joking, and their faces fell. "I'm sorry to tell you this, but that's how you look to me. You've gone soft, playing overseas. You're being lazy. You think the selection committee doesn't see you shortcutting on drills, throwing away your passes?" He was talking mostly to McClain now. "You're not impressing anyone out there, I hope you know that."

McClain was silent. Edwards studied her plate. The waitress came by with the check.

"So what are we supposed to do, coach?" said Katrina softly after a moment, looking into the face of the man who years before had taken a risk in recruiting her, a once-unaggressive and only mildly distinguished high school player, into his top-seeded program.

Landers inspected her face, noting the furrowed forehead and the impatience in her eyes. *"Try,"* he said.

Many of their workouts began with a prayer led by one of the floor coaches, a quick circle into which most of the players gathered, held hands, bowed heads, closed eyes: "We ask that you would just heal any hurts or strains or cramps or anything like that bothering us, and we ask that you protect us and keep us free from injury, Amen. Okay let's go, you guys."

For several days they scrimmaged past eight o'clock at night and then woke up in the morning to do it all over again. The routine of it started to feel regular. They marched from the dorms to the gym to the noisy cafeteria, then back to the dorms again. Between workouts they sprawled on their beds or in one of the cramped athlete lounges, listening to music or reading to pass the time. When they talked, it was mostly about basketball.

"You see that pass I blew today?" said Dawn Staley to Carla McGhee as they tromped through the chilled air to dinner one evening. Carla was a brawny forward with soulful brown eyes and a quick wit. Like Dawn, she was uncertain about her chances of making the team.

Hearing Dawn's question, though, Carla contorted her face into the openmouthed, exaggerated get-outta-town expression she often put on to amuse her peers: "Girl, I didn't see you blow *nothing* out there. . . . You see Tree knock me down in that scrimmage? *That,*" announced Carla, pulling a hand from her jacket pocket to pound her own chest, "was rough."

It was during these off hours that the fatigue manifested itself most. At night the dull ache in each of Dawn's knees worsened. Teresa spent extra time icing the minor calf injury she'd suffered early that winter in France. The workouts had shucked so much weight from Jennifer Azzi's already-thin frame that she made a special trip into town one afternoon to buy a powdered protein drink. Sheryl Swoopes could hardly keep her eyes open through a meal at McDonald's with Eric, who along with one of her older brothers had checked into a nearby hotel.

Tara VanDerveer, too, was beginning to look frayed. Her voice had gone froggy, her skin looked pillowed and pale, her expression seemed to grow more severe as the week wore on. Hunched over her knees on the bench during the nightly scrimmages, she knit and unknit her hands, watching fiercely the proceedings on the court. At night she lay sleepless in her hotel room. Much of her anxiety, one had to figure, came from her relative lack of power in choosing the team, the result of some small clause in the massive and elaborate USA Basketball constitution that says the Olympic coach cannot vote on player selection. VanDerveer would get to speak her mind at two of the selection committee's nightly meetings, but according to the rules, the committee was not particularly obligated to listen.

When she was appointed coach two months earlier, C. M. Newton, USA Basketball's president, had given her a stern introduction to her new job. "This isn't about silver," he'd said. "This is about winning the gold."

Later, VanDerveer was invited to lunch with NBA commissioner David Stern, whose organization was serving as the marketing agent for the women's team, drumming up sponsorship on the promise that this would be the most successful and talented women's team ever to play in the Olympics. During the meal Stern had turned to the coach and said, half seriously, "Well, there's only one thing that can go wrong: You could mess it up."

It was enough to keep anyone from sleeping at night. It was enough to make anyone crazy, being told in essence that you had to win the Kentucky Derby but that someone else would choose your horse.

As a college coach, VanDerveer was a methodical recruiter, assembling her Stanford team according to her own precise specifications: bringing in players who were more fast and lean than large and aggressive. Surveying the field at trials, though, recalling the size and strength of the international teams she'd competed against in the past, she wanted to fill the Olympic team with bangers—big, aggressive women who could take a charge from China's six-foot-eight, 253-pound center, who could tangle for a rebound with Russia's bullying forwards. Keeping an eye on the selection commitee, noting their various loyalties and prejudices, she sensed it coming: She wasn't going to get the mix of players she wanted.

One reason for this, she might have guessed, was the secondary agenda USA Basketball had laid out for the team, which had less to do with winning a gold medal and more to do with marketing. According to the player agreements the athletes had signed prior to trials, they would spend the year participating in public appearances, charity events, media events, photo events, organized autograph sessions, and more or less whatever was deemed necessary by USA Basketball or Stern's NBA Properties to promote the team, the sport, and most necessarily, the small cadre of corporate entities that had invested in the team's fate. The players on the team would be responsible for selling not just tickets, T-shirts, and posters but also television ad space, high-priced sneakers, and by the sponsors' bidding, everything from life insurance to tampons to Jell-O. Therefore, it needed pitchwomen with mediagenic looks and squeaky-clean personalities, quotable and cooperative, for if America was going to find a little room on its already-crowded athletic stage for a group of big, sweaty women, those women would have to squeeze themselves in politely and once there, they'd continually have to justify their presence not just with talent but with charm too.

The marketing efforts did not sit easily with VanDerveer. Players making public appearances took away from training time. Players who gave too many interviews could get distracted and, worse, egotistical. She was also a bit of a purist, holding true to the notion that athleticism sold sports, that the rest of it was relatively extraneous. At the very least, selling things was not part of her job description. What she needed was a team that could train and win together for over a year. She needed athletes, not media stars. There were some players who might fit both bills, she realized, like Sheryl Swoopes, whose striking looks and sunny public disposition were matched by explosive quickness and an unbeatable pull-up jump shot, and that was fine: She would make the team because she deserved to. More questionable and imminently troubling, though, was the current sweetheart of the sports-loving public, Rebecca

Lobo, who seemed clearly overwhelmed by the older players, looking distinctly intimidated each time she stepped on the floor.

By Monday, the selection committee had made its first five cuts, posting a list that said who stayed and who went, dismissing two guards and two centers, most of them older players who did not seem as sharp or conditioned as the others. Teresa Edwards, the oldest of them all, didn't need to look at the list to know that she was still in the running. In her estimation, she was playing well. But midway through the Monday-morning practice, her calf seized up suddenly, the muscle feeling like a thorn was being hammered into it, the flare of an old injury at exactly the wrong moment. She was examined by a trainer and told that trials for her were over, that her leg needed rest in order to heal.

For the next three days she watched two workouts a day from the sidelines, wearing sports sandals on her feet, an Ace bandage wrapped tightly around the hurt calf, shooting baskets by herself or simply just pacing the sidelines silently, her hands propped on her back, stealing glances at the selection committee as she wondered if what she'd done in four days was good enough to eclipse what others would do in seven.

Meanwhile, the competition had jumped up another notch as the trials moved into their end game. Katrina, who following Andy Landers's lecture had gotten far more aggressive, emerged from a rebounding melee with a bloody nose. Nikki McCray, a guard just graduated from Tennessee, was knocked to the floor on a lay-up and came up limping. When two inside players, Shanda Berry and Tari Phillips, grappled for the ball, Phillips let out a bloodcurdling scream and staggered to the sidelines holding her ear. Rebecca Lobo was missing shots left and right. Sheryl Swoopes was playing well, but could not let go of the old superstition, the legacy of injuries that had taken her out of so many trials in the past. Everybody, it seemed, was tense and starting to fall apart.

The calmest member of the group appeared to be Lisa Leslie, a serene-faced, skin-and-bones center from California, who as the others worried their way to and from practice, walked around the training center grounds with her nose sunk into her romance novel—a habit that eventually caused her to trip and fall down a dormitory stairwell. She banged up a knee and scraped both hands, missing a practice to get patched up, but when she sauntered back to the gym dressed in a bright red baseball jacket with the words SUPREME COURT printed on the back, her hair in two thick braids that hung down on either side of her neck, she made a cheery foil to Teresa's sideline anxiety. "Guess I learned my lesson," she told a group of bystanders, merrily dismissing her clumsiness with a goofy wave of the arm, "I'll never read and walk again!"

On Tuesday night, two more players were dropped—Sylvia Crawley, a center from North Carolina, and Niesa Johnson, a guard—leaving sixteen athletes still in the gym, including the ever-pacing Teresa. USA Basketball officials had said they intended to take between ten and twelve players for the national team, which would not technically be called the Olympic team, since the selection committee reserved the right to make cuts and additions to the national team any time prior to the June 1996 U.S. Olympic Committee deadline for naming an official team.

At the very least, four players still had to be cut. A Denver newspaper had already started making predictions: Four forwards—Shanda Berry, Tari Phillips, Carla McGhee, and Val Whiting—were at risk, and one additional cut would likely come from a group of four guards, Jennifer Azzi, Ruthie Bolton, Nikki McCray, or Teresa Edwards.

The last workout was brutal, not because it was any longer or more strenuous than the ones before it, but simply because it came at the end. Katy Steding felt so tired, she could hardly see the hoop, playing poorly through the final hours she had to demonstrate her worth. Val Whiting, one of Katy's former teammates at Stanford, felt relatively energetic through the last practice, but still, a bad feeling was hatching inside her, something she'd picked up almost unconsciously—an averted look from a committee member, a certain quietness on VanDerveer's part, something that told her even when she thought things were going her way, they really weren't.

"Last impressions count," said Carla McGhee, who went out and had a horrendous final practice, throwing the ball away, unable to muster the vigor required to post up. By the time the last whistle blew, the tears were brimming in her eyes as she berated herself silently. "I'm thinking, 'You start off great and you come to this,'" she'd say later. "I knew I had just blown it."

Lisa Leslie and Dawn Staley had tried to pep-talk Carla back to life. "C'mon, McGhee," said Lisa. "You had a great week. Don't think about it."

But Carla remained disconsolate, moping through a last dinner of green beans, pasta, and french fries at the cafeteria, where a number of them stared down at their plates dismally. After a week, training-center food got to be a drag.

"They just don't make it like Mama, do they?" said Dawn Staley to everyone and no one in particular as she heaped a baked potato with sour cream, her eye coming to rest on Katrina McClain's mammoth bowl of steamed broccoli. "Eat that up, Tree," she said, "come on now!"

At dinner they told one another how good they'd all been, knowing they could judge the week and their individual performances by whatever standards they chose, but it was the selection committee's assessment that mattered obviously, not theirs. USA Basketball's director of women's programs, a blond woman named Lynn Barry, had sent them off with a final set of instructions about the next morning. "At seven A.M. we'll come knock on your door in numerical order individually and we'll bring you up there and tell you yes or no and you're done. . . ." The ones who made it would stay for a press conference and photo shoot. The ones who didn't would be quietly whisked to the airport and put on the next plane home.

Nobody in the dormitory slept that night except Carla, who said that once she laid her 165-pound body down on the bed at night, there was no noise loud enough, no mattress thin enough, and no anxiety deep enough to prevent her from a luxurious night's sleep. Promptly at seven the next morning, the knocks began, rousing the players in order of the numbered jerseys they'd worn all week in practice, which roughly translated to alphabetical order, beginning with Jennifer Azzi.

She had walked down the very same hallway in 1992, on her way to receive the news that had crushed her, that she had made it all the way to the final cuts but would not be going to Barcelona, sorry. It seemed almost a cruel fate to have to walk the same hall again, after another week of trials, another two years of playing overseas, fostering another dream about another Olympics. Jennifer was feeling hopeful, but then again, she'd been hopeful in 1992 too, and thus she tempered the quickness of her heart with the somber memory of last time around. And then she was at the end of the hallway and she ran up the stairs to the third-floor lounge, where somebody opened a door for her and she was in the room with the table and three people—the selection committee chair and two USA Basketball staffers—and they were thanking her for her hard work and mentioning how tough the decision had been and just as her mind was going numb with disappointment, somebody cracked a smile and congratulated her. She was on the team.

From there it was a chaotic stew of emotions as player by player was led into the room and delivered the news one way or another. People making the team were instructed to exit through one door, where another staffer was waiting with a stack of blue warm-up suits for the players to wear to the press conference. The athletes who were cut were sent out another door, one that looped them back around to the rooms so they could get ready to leave.

They all ended up back in the hallway anyway though, giddy and crying and fuming and feeling great and sorry and devastated, depending on what had happened upstairs. "Praise the Lord," Ruthie Bolton had started shouting. "Praise the Lord!" Edna Campbell was cut. Shanda Berry was cut. When it came Teresa Edwards's turn in the room, the congratulations came and her whole face had begun quivering and she'd finally burst out sobbing, letting it all out like she hadn't in years. She was going. Linda Godby, a center, was cut. Lisa Leslie was not cut. Rebecca Lobo almost keeled over, hearing that she had made the team. Katrina McClain made it. Nikki McCray started hollering because she'd made it too. Carla McGhee showed up in the room looking dopey-eyed from sleep with a doo rag tied around her head. The officials ran through their spiel and ended on congratulations, at which point Carla looked at them, confused.

"What're you saying to me?" she said. "I made the team?" Then, seeing their nods, her voice escalated instantaneously to a shriek. "*I made the team?!*"

Tari Phillips didn't make the team, but coming after her, Katy Steding did, and so did Sheryl Swoopes after that. Next arrived Dawn Staley, who jumped up and down at her good news and then pushed through the door proudly to get her warm-up suit. There was one warm-up suit left on the table. She started to pick it up and then realized what it meant. Val Whiting had been standing behind her by the door to the lounge, waiting to go in and get her news. There was no warm-up suit for Val. The comprehension of this punctured her happiness. Val had wanted it so badly and Dawn, who'd had her hopes dashed in '92, knew exactly how that felt.

All that they could do, those who had made it, was to hug or high-five those who hadn't, to tell them again that they'd all had a great week and there was no accounting for the way decisions were made. Then those who hadn't made it picked up their bags and said good-bye to those who had. Left in the dormitory were the eleven women of the 1995–1996 U.S. national basketball team with one spot—the twelfth—left to fill sometime in the months before the Olympics: Dawn Staley, Sheryl Swoopes, Rebecca Lobo, Katrina McClain, Teresa Edwards, Nikki Mc-Cray, Katy Steding, Lisa Leslie, Carla McGhee, Jennifer Azzi, and Ruthie Bolton. The youngest, Rebecca, was twenty-one years old, while the oldest, Teresa, was almost thirty-one. Eight of them were black; three were white. Every last one had once been the star of her college team. All but Nikki and Rebecca had played professional basketball—if even briefly, as in the case of Sheryl—somewhere overseas. Most of them knew one another by now, if not from years past, then simply from the grind of the last week, but looking at one another then with the prospect of ten months of travel and training together ahead of them, they understood that the big grind was still to come. They were a team in name now, but still they were over 100,000 miles and sixty basketball games away from the thing they had been chosen for, to become the most influential women's team ever to step on a basketball court.

2
chapter

Seeing the Future

When the sun came up over West Texas on Sheryl Swoopes's wedding day, Lubbock couldn't have looked more beautiful. In the Southwest, June is the month when the land finally loses the brown husk of winter, the plains bloom with chamiso, and the sky brightens into a rich empyrean blue. Sheryl and Eric were married at seven in the evening at a Baptist church before four hundred friends and family members, she dressed in a long-sleeved white dress with a sequined bodice and a diaphanous veil, he in a white tuxedo. During the vows Sheryl had cried a little, and afterward, at the reception, they'd had their first dance, Eric's chin level with Sheryl's shoulder, spinning slowly to the Luther Vandross / Mariah Carey remake of "Endless Love," the song they'd chosen as especially theirs.

Among the wedding guests, it seems likely there was some discussion of basketball, a passing conversation about Sheryl's path to the Olympics, say, or the fact that Eric had decided to leave college in order to spend more time with Sheryl as she toured with the national team over the next year. There might have been chatter, too, about how bright the future looked for them, with Nike putting the final flourishes on the newly designed Air Swoopes, with Sheryl's agent calling in weekly with new endorsement or media possibilities. They were movers, Sheryl and Eric, haloed by good fortune and still humble about it. For their honeymoon, they were going to Disney World.

Sheryl did not think about basketball at her wedding. She brushed off comments about the shoe, the lighthearted questions about the Olympics or their impending move to Colorado Springs, and was happy for the thought that basketball could be this powerfully eclipsed by love. She'd put Eric on hold for nearly a year, training to make that team, relied on his patience and good humor when she got grumpy and disliked everyone, including him, for appearing to have it easier than she did. And so here, finally, was a single afternoon of him and her dancing, their families polishing off the last of the beef brisket from their plates and looking on proudly, his face so earnest and even grateful, his palm supporting the hard muscles of her back as they rotated gently around the dance floor, suspended in the rare and fleeting moment when basketball was finally second to them.

Summer was to be a last breath of freedom for all the players, a chance to connect with families and friends, to recharge on home-cooked meals and tend to the shoe contracts that for the majority of the players had been inked just prior to or during team trials, and to stay in shape without a coach harping over their shoulders at every turn. Of course, freedom was a relative concept: VanDerveer would send weekly individualized workout orders and expect regular progress reports in return. Anyone who slacked off for even one day, she warned grimly, would pay for it when they reconvened in the fall. The truth of it was that their lives had become sublimated the moment they'd been named to the team in May. From that day forward, they were governed by a calendar, the thing that for fourteen months would tick inside them like a secret heart: They had begun living for the gold medal.

With a road tour that would take them back and forth across the country and to the far ends of the world looming ahead, summer had a certain sweetness to it. Katrina McClain and Teresa Edwards went home to Georgia, while Carla McGhee divided her time between her apartment outside Atlanta and her parents' home in southern Illinois. For Katy Steding it meant returning to the house she owned outside of Portland, Oregon, and running a series of summer basketball camps for girls. Dawn Staley moved into a spare bedroom at her former college trainer's house in Virginia and had arthroscopic surgery to repair damaged cartilage in one knee. Nikki McCray devoted two months to developing her three-point shot, at the behest of VanDerveer. Ruthie Bolton flew to Florida to be with her husband, a high school basketball coach, and Lisa Leslie went home to Los Angeles, where she started each day running in the foothills of the San Bernadino mountains with her fiancé, Lorenzo, a six-foot-seven basketball player she had known at USC, who had presented her with a diamond engagement ring just before team trials.

What they couldn't know as the summer stretched on was how drastically the next year would reconfigure their lives. Out there somewhere were the teams from Russia, China, Brazil, Cuba, Australia, Zaire, and elsewhere, teams of women who, like them, had devoted their lives to basketball whether it was in a Communist-run sports academy or on an outdoor court on the African veldt. It would be up to VanDerveer and her new squad to figure out how to vanquish the others, to put American women's basketball back on top, and this would involve more hours and more sweat than any of them could imagine. Inevitably along the way there would be injuries and crises of spirit and relationships that fractured and new ones that rose up in their place. In moments, their bodies would fail them, or they would fail one another. In the end, some of them would wind up famous, some of them would have more faith in the world and others would have less, but none of them—and this was the only given—would stay the same.

       Jennifer Azzi's summer started in northern California, where she was inducted into Stanford University's athletic Hall of Fame and where she'd have a conversation that would significantly alter the course of her future. Jennifer and Katy Steding had been among Tara VanDerveer's first recruits when she took over the Stanford program in 1985. At seventeen years old, the two had much resembled the players they were joining the national team ten years later: Katy, a blond-haired, blue-eyed sometimes laconic but dependably skilled three-point shooter, Jennifer a hyperdriven guard and natural leader on the floor. Their senior year at Stanford, they had helped put the crowning feather in VanDerveer's coaching cap, winning the coach her first NCAA championship. That year Jennifer had been named Most Outstanding Player of the NCAA tournament and Player of the Year.

Jennifer was the kind of athlete you didn't soon forget. A comparatively small player at five eight, she ran the court with an intensity that seemed to universally thrill crowds. On defense, she would get down low, her arms winged out as if to embrace the opponent, her lips forming a tight O, dark eyes riveted not to the ball or to the opponent's face, but to some fixed place just above the other player's belt line, a focal point by which she could read the tiniest movement, the earliest genesis of a pass or a drive, and react with astounding speed. As VanDerveer characterized her, Jennifer was "all go." A former high school track star, she loved the fast break, loved to press on defense, anything that kept the action on the floor fast and furious.

She had built her career on extra effort and methodical discipline—qualities that made her the quintessential VanDerveer player. At Stanford, she had put in an extra hour of shooting practice nearly every day of the season. When the other players were complaining of being overworked, Jennifer was often sneaking out for an evening run or a solitary session in the weight room. Her teammates nicknamed her "Calves," after the pronounced and perfectly triangulated muscles of her lower legs. In her free time she plowed through piles of self-improvement and motivational books, sometimes taking notes on what she learned.

The trip back to Stanford was always an emotional one for Jennifer. Thanks largely to VanDerveer and Azzi and a handful of others who'd made Stanford's program a success, women's basketball was extremely popular in Greater San Francisco. In the years since she'd graduated, Jennifer had played professionally in Italy, France, and Sweden, all to little fanfare. As she walked into her old home court at Maples Pavilion, which had been filled with round banquet tables for the black tie Hall of Fame dinner that June evening, a few people applauded, and the feeling broke over her like a wave: It was good to be remembered.

The meal was quick but celebratory, punctuated by various speeches from the six inductees. When it was Jennifer's turn, she stood up and thanked Stanford and VanDerveer and the community at large, saying that basketball had given her every opportunity in her life, including the most important one, a Stanford education, and then, accepting another burst of applause, she sat down again and went back to her meal. Throughout dinner she'd made small talk with an amiable man with blond-gray hair named Gary Cavalli, who was seated to her left. Cavalli was a former asistant sports information director at Stanford, who now, along with a partner, ran the small marketing firm that had organized the Hall of Fame dinner. He'd met Jennifer several times over the years, but each time it had been only briefly. Tonight, however, he planned to have a real conversation with her. In fact, he had practically tailored the whole event around talking to Jennifer, having rearranged the seating chart to place himself by her side.

He had come with an idea to spring on her, one that he and an acquaintance named Steve Hams, along with a small group of contacts in the Bay Area, had been drafting for the last several months. He knew enough about Azzi to recognize that she would make a model spokesperson. She was articulate and poised—a strikingly pretty woman, really, with long, dark hair and brown almond-shaped eyes—and beyond her basketball prowess, she was smart, someone who thought about the question before she answered it, who could be immediately impressive. Going into the dinner, Cavalli had sworn to himself that before the night was over, he would have enlisted Azzi's support for his idea. Sitting finally elbow to elbow, he talked with her about her season in Sweden and recalled a few great moments from her days at Stanford and then, as the caterer filled coffee cups around the table, he began his pitch.

"Jennifer, there's a group of us putting together a business plan for a women's professional league . . ." he said, trailing off as he noted her impassive face.

This was something she'd heard before. The last league to get any attention had been the Liberty League in 1991—boasting teams of spandex unitard–clad women—which in the end had made a seeming mockery of the women's game, possibly setting them all back ten years. Despite the fact that Jennifer believed that professional women's basketball was going to happen someday for real—and despite the hours she'd spent talking to Teresa Edwards at tournaments abroad about how that might happen—she was not going to get overly excited about another casual conversation concerning the thing that mattered to her more than she could say. She was not just going to jump in blindly.

After a moment, she mustered a polite smile but no excess of enthusiasm. "That's great. Just send me your business plan and I'll tell you what I think."

While the initial conversation between Jennifer Azzi and Gary Cavalli hadn't progressed much beyond her halfhearted offer to look at a business plan, Jennifer's interest was still piqued by all that was happening in women's basketball. That spring alone, on the heels of UConn's banner season, a group in Idaho had announced plans for a women's professional league, as had another group in Tennessee. There had been a regional league, the Women's Basketball Association, playing in high school gyms in several midwestern cities, but that had been sold and then resold, both times to groups who in the end never once tossed up a ball. It seemed that plenty of people made noise about starting a women's professional league, but for one reason or another, they usually got no further than talking about it. Part of this, Jennifer had reasoned to herself, was that the people who planned these leagues generally knew little about women's basketball. Instead, they looked at the women's game with unrealistic visions of turning a quick profit, namely by throwing together a few teams, playing a few games, and then unloading the start-up enterprise for a hefty sum to the NBA or Nike.

The strategy was a familiar one. In America, similar to Hollywood, sports had sex appeal. It was the American Dream—replete with Cinderella stories and overnight millionaires—beamed via satellite into the public's living rooms every week of the year. It seemed logical, then, that any entrepreneurial-minded fan might yearn for a piece of it. Yet the irony was that like the film industry, the sports market was largely oversaturated, fraught with competition and thwarted start-ups, governed by an elite group of kingmakers, like Nike's Phil Knight or NBA commissioner David Stern—men whose power was derived largely from their ability to protect their individual dominions with lawyerly acumen, generating impenetrable screens of paper to protect trademarks, licensing rights, television rights, merchandising rights, and so on until, it would seem, there was little left anyway for an outsider to have.

Maybe this was why women's sports was looking like the last morsel of uneaten pie. After all, it had been the women's market—namely the aerobics boom—that had given Reebok a significant boost in the late eighties, for example, and a casual indifference toward that very same boom that had forced Nike to redouble its efforts with women in the years that followed. In general, though, mixing women and sports in the same financial cocktail was a riskier venture than most. Despite the increasing numbers of women participating in competitive sports and the popularity of some women's college athletic programs, America had yet to demonstrate any viable interest in seeing women's sports jump to a professional level. Even with shoe sales booming, with health club memberships at an all-time high among women, and little girls joining teams in scads, it was still difficult to imagine that the public could be depended on—so much so that a league could be staked on it—to sit down on a Saturday afternoon and watch women play professional basketball.

Later that week, when Jennifer was home again in Oak Ridge, Tennessee, a thick envelope arrived from California. Inside was the business plan for Cavalli's proposed American Basketball League. Jennifer sat down and read it once quickly, then again, taking more time. It outlined plans for twelve teams to start in October 1996, just after the Olympics, and—something she felt essential for a league to succeed—they would play only in markets that had already demonstrated strong support for college teams. They had an advisory board, a list of potential sponsors, and a fat appendix of carefully compiled market research. She read the plan one more time, then picked up the phone to call Teresa in Atlanta to deliver the most hopeful message she could have: These league people were for real.

Perhaps what separated them from the others, what gave their proposal not just vision but also a practical plan, was the league's chief founder, a man named Steve Hams. A self-declared optimist and vice president of a small software company in the Silicon Valley, Hams had an undeniably nice life with his wife and three daughters and a four-bedroom house in the town of Mountain View with a swimming pool in the backyard. One day in the fall of 1994, though, sitting at lunch with an old friend, discussing just how nice everything was, Hams had made an offhanded comment: "Wouldn't it be great," he asked his friend, "if we could all work at something we really believed in?"

The friend had an offhanded reply: He laughed. Sure it would be great. But what would "it" be exactly?

Hams had known the answer without really thinking. "Women's basketball," he said.

His thirteen-year-old daughter Lauren played basketball on her middle-school team. Three years earlier, he'd started taking her to Palo Alto to see Tara VanDerveer's team play at Stanford. He'd been surprised at first: The action was faster than he'd expected, the women played an unselfish, strategy-oriented game; they scrambled for loose balls, played hard until the final buzzer, and the fans cheered the team on whether they were up by two points or 40. His daughter was one of many hundreds of girls who showed up regularly to watch the team play. With them came their parents, their school coaches, their brothers and friends, plus Stanford students, professors, senior citizens, young couples, kids of all sizes, all ethnicities—an average of 5,300 per game—a group of people that almost defied classification save for their enthusiasm for the Stanford Cardinal.

"I just fell in love with the women's game," Hams would recall. "It's so exciting, the way they play is so pure. And my daughter loved it so much. The more I became involved, the more it seemed to be a crime that we didn't have a professional league in this country, especially when you get to know about the athletes as people."

Hams backed up his heart with a pragmatist's mind. Many of the kids flitting through the stands at Cardinal games wore $85 sneakers on their feet; the parking lot was loaded with minivans and Ford Explorers; people came to games and bought cheese dogs, baseball caps, T-shirts. Around the country, women's basketball was beginning to make money for the top college programs. The Stanford women had been producing revenue since 1990, the year VanDerveer won her first national championship. The Connecticut Huskies were in the midst of a season whose ticket sales and television and radio contracts would generate just under $900,000 in revenue. While the sums were small compared to the amounts the men's NCAA teams pulled in (the men's Huskies grossed $3.3 million in ticket sales alone in 1995–1996), many women's programs were nonetheless able to turn a profit, and their growth in popularity showed no signs of letting up. Wasn't it plausible that the market could sustain a professional women's league?

In the winter of 1995, Hams embarked on a one-man campaign to find fellow believers in the San Francisco Bay area. Six months later, he had found a former Olympic swimmer and sports marketing exec named Anne Cribbs and her business partner, Gary Cavalli, who joined Hams in signing on as the principal founders of the American Basketball League.

But if history was anything to go by, the ABL organizers had their work cut out for them. The most successful women's league, the Women's Basketball League (WBL), which struggled through three seasons between 1978 and 1981, was also the most widely criticized. Interestingly, the WBL had been launched in response to a similar set of conditions—growth in the sport, an impending Olympics, tidings of an open-minded public—that sixteen years later inspired Steve Hams.

Women's basketball had boomed in the mid to late seventies, due to the athletic dynamism of players like Ann Meyers, Nancy Lieberman, and Carol Blazejowski. At the time, universities were pouring unprecedented amounts of money into their women's athletic programs, scrambling to meet the government-set 1978 deadline for complying with Title IX, the 1972 amendment to the Civil Rights Act that barred gender discrimination in education. For every high school girl who played basketball in 1972, the year Title IX was passed, there would be ten more playing in 1981. Meanwhile, both the civil rights and women's movements ushered in new hopes for the acceptance of a sport that featured women performing in a traditionally male arena and showcased black and white athletes working together on a team. (Though notably Meyers, Lieberman, and Blazejowski—the most celebrated college players of that era—were all white.) To top it off, women's basketball had been included in the Olympic Games for the first time in 1976, where the American women had lost the gold medal to the Soviet team. Now the 1980 Games, to be held in Moscow, were fast approaching, and given the fact that the cold war was in full swing, it was likely that the American fans would pay extra attention to any U.S.-Soviet rivalry. As a result of all this, it had seemed as promising a time as ever to test the waters with a women's basketball league.

In December 1978, the Women's Basketball League tossed its first ball up, and the Chicago Hustle played the Milwaukee Does in the Milwaukee Arena in front of an impressive crowd of 7,824. The league had eight teams from Minnesota to Texas to New York. They played a 36-game season, complete with a championship series, and at least initially earned a reasonable amount of fanfare. Walter Cronkite covered the league on the national news, a few players received endorsement offers. One Chicago television station broadcast ten of the Hustle's games and drew an average viewing audience of 140,000, ratings twice as high as had been expected. Feeling optimistic, the league expanded to include fourteen teams its second season.

But as the novelty of the league wore off, media coverage was increasingly sparse and therefore discouraged the growth of a loyal fan base. ("There hasn't been much coverage of [the WBL]," wrote one sympathetic *Chicago Tribune* reporter in 1979, "because news space is needed to report on the hangnails of male athletes.") When the women players did get written up in the newspapers, they found themselves victims of an insurmountable catch-22, dismissed by accusations of not playing with the athleticism that men did and simultaneously lambasted for appearing "unfeminine." Averaging annual losses of over a quarter million per team, the league officially shut down in 1981.

Central to the WBL's struggle was the enduring marketability question. How to sell big, leaping, sweating, competitive women playing what was widely considered to be a men's game? The answer, as WBL management seemed to view it, involved presenting women's basketball, and particularly its players, as unintimidating, attractive, and irrefutably heterosexual. In other words, classically feminine. The teams were given names that underscored the harmlessness of women playing basketball—California Dreams, Minnesota Fillies, Philadelphia Fox—while by contrast the names of certain current men's NBA teams—Milwaukee Bucks, Toronto Raptors, Minnesota Timberwolves—celebrate aggressiveness. To this effect, several WBL teams played exhibition games against teams of Playboy Bunnies. The management of the California Dreams sent its players to a compulsory five-week modeling course, which included lessons on how to sit, walk, talk, and eat. "I wish we had Farrah Fawcett," said one general manager, discussing the need to woo the public with sex appeal. "We'd just let her warm up."

In the end, the WBL would be remembered as little more than a cautionary tale about the pitfalls of launching women's basketball on a professional level. Between 1990 and 1995, this was reinforced as at least four different groups attempted to start leagues and one after the other failed, primarily for financial reasons, most of them never playing a single game.

In other words, it might have appeared that Steve Hams was crazy, chasing down strangers and inviting them to get together with his small "advisory council" of friends and supporters to talk about creating a basketball league that actually worked.

For Anne Cribbs, a blond-haired, sporty woman with a busy career and eight daughters from two marriages, inspiration had struck several years earlier, when she'd gone to a sporting goods store in Palo Alto to buy sweat socks for one of her girls. Behind the counter, ringing up the purchase, was Molly Goodenbour, the just-graduated star point guard for the Stanford Cardinal who several months before had led the team to the 1992 national championship title.

"She was the MVP of the Final Four, and she was selling socks for minimum wage," said Cribbs, who herself had won a gold medal in swimming at the 1960 Olympics. "I was sick to my stomach." Three years later, a random phone call from Hams, inspired by a write-up of Cribbs in the local business journal, felt like a stroke of fate. "He started talking about his league idea and I almost didn't believe it. I don't think I was instantly enthusiastic, but I was convinced pretty quickly."

Next came Cribbs's business partner, Gary Cavalli, a garrulous forty-six-year-old with a broad, easy smile and a rangy John Wayne confidence. Cavalli, a self-described sports nut who'd grown up too cloddish and uncoordinated to excel as an athlete, took instead the available route for the cagey and uncoordinated—he became a sportswriter. Eventually, this gave way to a career in public relations and sports marketing, including a stint as assistant director of sports information at Stanford in the early eighties, just before Tara VanDerveer was hired. "You'd go to a women's basketball games and the audience would be two boyfriends, two parents, and the writer for the *Stanford Daily*," said Cavalli. "And I usually had to persuade the *Stanford Daily* person to come."

Over the next several months, Hams worked closely with Cribbs, Cavalli, and about a dozen unofficial advisers, refining his business plan to account for the failures of past leagues: ABL teams would play during the regular wintertime basketball season, in select regional markets, in mid-sized arenas, and on a reasonable budget that did not rely on enormous ticket sales the first season. In addition, the plan specified that the ABL would pay salaries averaging $70,000 (roughly what most American players made abroad), going as high as $125,000 for top-name players like the ones who would end up on the women's national team.

It was this business plan, a thin, spiral-bound sheath of paper, that Cavalli mailed to Jennifer Azzi in June after the Stanford Hall of Fame dinner. It was this plan that then prompted Jennifer to enlist the support of Teresa Edwards, who was doing her summer workouts in Atlanta. In the end, Teresa and Jennifer called the other members of the newly formed national team with the same request: If Hams calls you, take a minute and hear him out. One by one, Hams contacted each of the eleven players on the team. He sent business plans, answered their questions, and ultimately made his pitch, asking them to promote the league during their year with the national team—attending events, discussing it in interviews, wearing ABL paraphernalia, and generally making clear their intentions to play in the league when it got off the ground in the fall following the Olympics. The ABL would pay each player a nominal $5,000 for her endorsement.

"I think most of us were just grateful that there was somebody out there who was going to go about forming a league the right way," remembers Azzi. "It's hard to describe how hopeful we were, even if this thing was just a packet of paper and Steve was some guy we didn't know."

And so they signed on to the nebulous daydream of the American Basketball League: first Jennifer and Teresa, then Katy, Dawn, Lisa, Nikki, Ruthie, Carla, and Sheryl. By the time training camp began in October, the only players left unsigned were Rebecca Lobo and Katrina McClain. Katrina had given up a small fortune to play with the national team already; she was taking a look-before-you-leap approach to the ABL. Rebecca Lobo, too, felt there was no hurry. Her agent had advised her to hold off on promising away her professional future. So much had happened in the last six months, how could she predict what would happen next?

For the rest of them, the commitment was almost unconditional. Dawn Staley, cheered by the knowledge that she might not have to ship off to Europe again, promised to throw her heart and soul into promoting the ABL. Katy Steding was hoping the league would put a team in her hometown of Portland, Oregon. Sheryl Swoopes saw the ABL as her only chance to continue her career, since nothing would make her go abroad again. There were whispers, too, that the league was planning a team in Austin, which by Texas standards was Sheryl's backyard. For Teresa Edwards, helping professional ball get off the ground meant more even than winning a gold medal; it was the one thing that would make her athletic career complete.

All Rebecca Lobo wanted to do was lie out in the sun with some friends. She wanted to read a book or visit her boyfriend for the weekend or even mow the lawn at her parents' house in southwestern Massachusetts. She wanted, for one second, to feel like a normal kid who'd just graduated from college.

But even though she had graduated, and not just graduated but done so with a 3.65 GPA, she hardly would have known it the way life seemed to be trampling right over her, the way she hadn't had one second to look back. When she complained, it was quietly and even gratefully. She had a voice that was soft and low, like an oboe. Anything she said that might have been construed as grouchy was quickly amended by a phrase like "in the best possible of ways" or, "but I know I'm lucky." As the summer months passed, however, she smiled less and less as she said these things.

As Rebecca Lobo was discovering, being lucky in excess can take its toll. When the reporters asked her to characterize her life, she said, "It's like one dream coming true after another." When they wanted to know what she dreamed of now, she answered with a modest smile, "Maybe just having a little more time to myself."

She had left college abruptly and unceremoniously, missing her graduation to be at national team trials and so busy beforehand that her mom had to drive down and pack up her dorm room and drive her belongings in boxes to the apartment near campus she had sublet for the summer. While her mother was doing that, Rebecca was making appearances and giving speeches to kids, shooting TV commercials, and accepting awards at dress-up banquets all across the country. In July she jogged with the President. She was home maybe one night a week, often nodding off mid-conversation with her boyfriend on the twenty-minute ride back to Storrs from the Hartford airport. In her apartment two enormous boxes of unanswered fan mail sat in the corner.

If she had more time, she might have wondered how all of this—the autographs and mail and TV appearances—had come to pass. Her last season as a Husky had the obvious qualities of a dream: She and her teammates loved each other, they had beaten every single top team in the country, and loads of people had paid attention when they did. What was harder for Rebecca to figure was why the focus had so quickly shifted from the team to *her*, why four months after the buzzer sounded to end their championship game against Tennessee, people still wanted to talk to her about it. Celebrity, particularly her celebrity, confounded her. What value, she wondered aloud to her family, did people find in an autograph? "The only time my signature is worth anything is when it's on a check," she told people. She sometimes followed this up with a crack about how little money she had anyway, since anything she'd made had gone directly to a financial planner.

In truth, Rebecca Lobo had become a commodity. In the weeks following the end of the college basketball season and her simultaneous release from the NCAA's stringent eligibility rules, she had acquired an agent and a pile of endorsement contracts, including one from Reebok rumored to be in excess of $200,000. Conversely, her popularity sprung from the very reason she said she didn't deserve all the attention: She was just an ordinary kid.

She also had the most well-rounded basketball game the college field had seen in years. "She is not the best rebounder we've had, nor is she the best inside shooter or blocker," said her coach, Geno Auriemma, "But if you put together the sum of Rebecca's parts, what you get is unreal."

A March 1995 *New York Times* story on Lobo bore the subtitle "Complete Player, Complete Person." At Connecticut, she spent hours sitting on the couch in her dorm lounge, responding individually to the mail that arrived for her in weekly sacks. Finally, midway through her senior season, she had to ask a *Hartford Courant* sportswriter to print a message in his column from her: "I try to answer every letter I get," she wrote to her fans. "I kept up with it for a while, but I'm so backed up, it'll take months to catch up. I hope everyone understands."

And people did understand. How could they not? There was nothing Hollywood about Rebecca Lobo. She was just so unspectacularly *nice*. She adored her family, she looked after her teammates, went to church on Sundays, got good grades, knew a whole bunch of jokes, and in general viewed the world with an unspoiled optimism. She had a long sweep of shiny brown hair, a peachy blush in her cheeks, and clear hazel eyes. Her body was big and thick like a tree trunk, her laugh a deep and easy chortle. You might think of her the same way you once thought about your favorite baby-sitter—the neatest, funnest big sister you could imagine. And she had grown into a national sports personality unaided by the usual battallion of PR spinmeisters, untarnished by rumors of gambling problems, drug problems, or promiscuity that plagued other, mostly male, sports icons. Rebecca Lobo was simply herself, and America just soaked it up.

Lobo made an ideal figurehead for her sport in that her presence—the blend of shyness, modesty, and eagerness to please—fit the image the public had been conditioned to accept in female athletes, in the popular gymnasts, figure skaters, and tennis stars, the "sports cuties" of the past. Only Lobo was six foot four and 185 pounds and could probably bench-press two gymnasts at once. In some respects this combination of sweetness and strength gave Rebecca a unique power to advance women's basketball.

There were cultural factors that undeniably contributed to her popularity as well. Lobo was white, educated, and middle-class, a product of American suburbia, and beyond that a regional hero in a metropolitan area that housed the home offices of ESPN, *Sports Illustrated*, *The New York Times*, and any number of other major media outlets. These were things that made Rebecca Lobo more accessible to the masses and less vulnerable to the prejudices that too often hampered the way the public perceived its heroes.

True, Lobo's celebrity still hardly registered on the Richter scale when compared to that of Jordan, Barkley, Rodman, and some of the other mainstream luminaries of the NBA. Yet what made her relatively modest fame significant was not how many people loved her, but rather why she was loved at all. Her very presence in the media was working to loosen the deeply embedded notion that sports for girls, particularly aggressive team sports like basketball, were somehow unfeminine. In the span of only a few months she had become an unwitting idol, a poster child for women's basketball, a big-boned and smiling reminder that despite what we had been socialized to believe, sweat was genderless.

Yet in July 1995 what the icon wanted more than anything was a good night's sleep and maybe a day off from being Rebecca Lobo. Going to a Connecticut mall with her mother earlier in the year, looking for a dress to wear to the next banquet, she was so besieged by autograph requests and well-wishers that they'd had to go home after two hours of indulging the crowds—before she'd had a chance to try on one dress. Particularly in Connecticut it was hard to go anywhere unrecognized.

As summer bled into early fall and the fanfare ceased to die down, Lobo struggled to keep up with the workouts VanDerveer was sending, regular as clockwork. She'd had arthroscopy on one knee earlier in the summer, and it felt as if her recovery had been extra slow, probably because she'd had so little time to work out. She did what she could, though, following the coach's instructions to develop her conditioning and her outside shooting, working out at the UConn sports center, sometimes under the direction of her old coaches. She filled out the forms she had to send back to VanDerveer every two weeks, knowing already how short of the coach's expectations she was falling. Meanwhile, as she lifted weights or jogged on the track, students would often stop and stare. When at the end of a day she and her boyfriend Dave DeArmas, a kicker on the Connecticut football team, went out for pizza, people stared there too.

It was mid-September, though the air was still balmy and summerlike. Dave's football practices ran long each day, preseason basketball was about to begin, the campus buzzed with students. Paramount in Rebecca's mind was the fact that she would have to report to Colorado

Springs in another week and that she didn't feel at all prepared. Rather than think about it, she pressed on with her schedule, flying to Los Angeles to shoot an ad for Reebok, then posing for a photo spread in New York, then filming a commercial for a Chevy dealership in Connecticut, then smiling her way through a full-day appearance in Boston. She spent one night at home in Storrs, then drove up to her parents' house to give a joint interview with her mother. On the way she allowed herself to think about leaving and about how awfully tired she was, and the thinking led to crying, and by the time she got into her parents' living room, it was pouring out of her, the months of hype and stress and letdown.

When the day came to leave for Colorado, her mother brought her to the airport and her father met them there. In the last several days, she'd had emotional good-byes with her old coaches and teammates as well as Dave. Facing her parents now, she felt hollow and worn out. Her mother, a middle-school guidance counselor, had spent much of the summer dealing with her fan mail. Both of her parents had come to every home game of hers last season, even as her mother had undergone treatment for breast cancer. The tears started to sting at Rebecca's eyes again, but she fought them down. They made small talk for a minute, and suddenly she was crying for real, her head bowed so that her hair covered her face. She felt a tap on the shoulder and, turning around, saw a man with a pen and a quizzical look on his face, an autograph seeker suddenly made sheepish by the tears on her cheeks.

As she checked in at the ticket counter, an employee from another airline had come over with a note for her. It was from her Connecticut coaches, a message she would keep in her pocket throughout the months ahead, but one too that seemed to suggest the very thing that stood to cause her the most trouble. It said, "Smile. You'll always be a Husky."

In the fall of 1995, even with the endorsement of a full nine-elevenths of the future Olympic team, the American Basketball League was still an engine without oil. In other words, the business had no money when it needed millions. Hams, for his part, had taken out a second mortgage on his house and drained his savings. Cavalli and Cribbs had kicked in what they could, and they'd found several other small-time investors along the way, but they needed one big break, a hefty corporate sponsorship deal or a patron millionaire to waltz into the picture. They needed, it would seem, a small miracle.

What they'd found, however, knocking on various doors for money was that the path to respectability was littered with corpses of the old leagues, the failures of the past. In essence, nobody believed they could do it. In the eyes of a number of college coaches, television executives, and advertisers, the last great hope for the women's game was the dim prospect of the NBA starting a league for women. In the last several years, the NBA had lent increasing amounts of support to women's basketball, sponsoring events at the women's Final Four and participating actively in the formation of the women's national team. The organization, however, had thus far drawn the line at starting a women's pro league, supporting the belief among the inner circles of the basketball world that the time was still not right.

But there was a man in Atlanta named Bobby Johnson, a self-made millionaire who'd built his fortune on buying nursing homes—"doing business with my heart," he called it—who knew nothing about the leagues of the past. He knew nothing about women's basketball at all until one day early in the summer of 1995 he'd watched his thirteen-year-old daughter play an Amateur Athletic Union game. "I was sitting there in my suit," recalled Johnson, a thin black man with a pencil mustache and warm, puppylike eyes, "thinking about all the other things I was supposed to be doing at that moment instead of watching a bunch of girls run around a basketball court.

"Then I started paying attention, not just to the girls but to all the parents there watching. Everybody was so enthusiastic, and I started thinking, why not? Why can't girls' basketball be entertaining too?"

In addition to doing business with his heart, Johnson prided himself on following up on his ideas. ("Just think about the last four initials in the word *American*," he said often, smiling as he spelled it out, "I-C-A-N. I can.") Shortly after watching his daughter's game, he was making phone calls around Atlanta, asking for an expert on women's basketball. In August, somebody had put him in touch with Teresa Edwards, who had steered him in the direction of the ABL group in California. Suddenly Steve Hams had his miracle.

At the end of September, the day before they were required to report to training camp in Colorado Springs, eight of the national team players had gathered with the league founders in San Jose, California, for the press conference that would formally introduce the American Basketball League to the public. Anne Cribbs and Gary Cavalli had faxed media advisories to every major news organization in the country and arranged for a costly satellite uplink. Bobby Johnson, who after meeting several times with Hams and the others had agreed to invest $3.5 million and serve as the league's chief financial officer, had flown in from Atlanta.

The ABL now had a logo—a female silhouette dribbling the ball against a red, white, and blue background, something that closely resembled the NBA logo, only with a ponytail—and a slogan: "It's a Whole New Ballgame." Steve Hams had quit his vice-president position to work full-time on the league. And now they had nine of the best basketball players in the world lending their names to what still felt like a pipe dream.

The four officers—Hams, Cavalli, Cribbs, and Johnson—carried ABL business cards, though essentially they were nobodies, with little to recommend them beyond being the parents of fourteen daughters altogether. Sometimes they joked among themselves that they were drawing the response that Butch Cassidy and the Sundance Kid had in the eponymous movie: "Who are these guys?" Only it wasn't really funny. They could be broke within a matter of months. They'd insisted that the ABL would be a "players' league," one that made no compromises when it came to image—no modeling school or unitards or lowered rims—and that granted the players ten percent ownership of the league, but could they hold true to this if it meant their life savings were going to go swirling down the drain? They'd been cut down and ridiculed already, and they hadn't even gone public yet.

On September 26, 1995, Hams declared his intentions to make the American Basketball League happen. No matter that he'd spent his life nosing around computers and had no experience with sports management, that he needed $11 million and only had four, that his teams needed owners, that he had no television contract and not a single corporate sponsor. No matter that everyone else before him had failed. Hams, dressed in a suit and tie, lifted his chin and did his best to defy the skeptics. He was no fiery preacher. He looked like a man who knew computers, thin and unimposing behind the microphone that was hardly necessary for the sparse gathering of local reporters, but he believed, and he did not need to raise his voice or gesticulate wildly to make this understood. The sponsors were coming, he explained, maybe a little optimistically. They were working on television deals. Look at the players he had—the best in the world, the ones who were on their way to the Olympics, who themselves wanted a league more than anything. Look at the attendance figures, the soaring numbers of young girls taking up basketball. It was going to happen. He had rearranged his whole life in order to do this, risks and all. "I have no doubt," Hams told the reporters evenly, "that we will be a success."

The players sat behind a long table on either side of Hams: Dawn Staley, Katy Steding, Carla McGhee, Nikki McCray, Lisa Leslie, Ruthie Bolton, Jennifer Azzi, and Teresa Edwards, dressed in ABL T-shirts and ready to comment on why they, too, had joined the gamble. Sheryl Swoopes, who was in Chicago promoting her new Nike shoe, the Air Swoopes, flickered on a big-screen television via satellite to voice her support.

"It was all for one and one for all," Jennifer Azzi said later of the conference. "None of us knew what was ahead of us, but we were all in it together. It was a pretty special feeling."

Anne Cribbs remembers looking out at the slim media turnout and realizing just how hard they would have to work in order to be taken seriously. It was true, nobody seemed to think they could do it. Cavalli would get overeager and tell the press that they were "close to a deal" with Nike and "negotiating closely" with ESPN on a television contract. Sue Levin, the women's sports manager at Nike, would immediately refute this, saying carefully, "We're not close to a deal, but that's not any reflection of my feelings about the ABL."

The conference would get coverage in the local papers, plus a blurb in the New York and L.A. papers, but little more. *Sports Illustrated* would give them a short column in its "Scoreboard" section, though it all but dismissed Hams, describing him as possessing a "brazenness . . . [that] seems kind of ditsy"; the piece would run beneath a headline that suggested the failures of the past: "Another Try for Women's Hoops."

The truest of the believers that day appeared to be Teresa Edwards, who commandeered the microphone and sent out the only message that would be consistently quoted in the papers, the one that addressed the persistent charge that they would be giving up high salaries and good careers playing abroad.

"We're not making sacrifices by playing at home," Teresa told the assembled group. "Personally, I've spent years overseas and I wouldn't wish it on any one of these girls. What are we giving up? Lower phone bills? No English on TV? We'll get to play in front of our families." She had paused a moment, swallowing hard. "We're ready for this," she said, shaking her head slightly as if people out there would never understand, "we've been waiting for this."

3

chapter

Fall Training Camp

One way to wake them up was to do what she did, which was to assemble them in the gray light of morning on the track at Colorado College, the brittle wind biting at their faces, cold enough to cut through the sponsor-supplied layers of warm-ups and neon-bright shells and leave them raw, nauseated by the early hour, joints stiff and unwilling. She stood before them like a field general, herself swaddled in extra clothing, her voice gobbled up by the wind but unnecessary anyway because the eleven of them, there in a ragged line next to the track, understood well enough what this was about. It was a first assertion of Tara VanDerveer's rule as coach.

Work ethic and unselfishness, she liked to say, were the keys to having a successful team. Like most coaches, VanDerveer was a purveyor of aphorisms and catch phrases relevant to the game of basketball and therefore to life. She spoke often and extemporaneously about winning, losing, overcoming, focusing and so forth with a matter-of-fact earnesty that suggested she believed it all fervently. One of her favorite things to talk about was "mental toughness," the intangible factor she felt separated great basketball players from the merely good. Mental toughness was a relatively straightforward concept: It involved overachieving, competing against oneself as opposed to against one's opponents and never ever losing. It involved running and lifting weights and scrimmaging until it hurt, since pain—and this was something else she liked to say, borrowing from Nietzsche—made you stronger.

There were coaches out there, and players too, who would say she was tougher than she needed to be. The Angry Woman, some of the male college coaches called her. If her players had nicknames for her, she didn't care to know them. Being popular was not part of the game for VanDerveer. It seemed to be something she couldn't understand, why people worked so hard, gave up so much, in order to be liked. This was not to say that she was unpopular. To the fans in Palo Alto, who regularly packed the house to see her team play at Maples Pavillion, VanDerveer was a hero, the coach who had turned it all around for women's basketball at Stanford. Within the insular and highly political coaching community, she was both admired and resented for her distinctly impolitical tendency to speak her mind. She was known to hold grudges, cherish rivalries, and stand up fiercely for what she believed in.

For VanDerveer, the game was everything. She had been practically born a coach, with a mind programmed for the strategies and statistics inherent to the game of basketball. As a ten-year-old in Schenectady, New York, she'd watched the Boston Celtics on television, a pad of paper propped in her lap so that she could diagram their plays. In the afternoons she'd dribble around her neighborhood, shooting baskets in the next door neighbor's driveway. When they didn't want her to play, she remembers, they parked the car under the hoop. When her father, a doctoral student at the time, shouted to her from inside, "That's not going to get you anywhere. Come inside and do your homework," the young VanDerveer, a chunky kid with long red-gold hair and a fresh mouth, did not miss a beat in her dribbling, firing back, "Algebra will never take me anywhere!"

These were the mid-1960s, a time when boys played sports, and girls, for the most part, either cheered them on or busied themselves with other, more girlish things. Tara herself had been named after Scarlett O'Hara's pillared plantation home in *Gone With the Wind*, the essence of southern extravagance and tradition pinned on a girl from the north country who just wanted to shoot hoops. And the odds were her father was right: Hardly anybody, let alone his stubborn daughter, had a future in basketball. There were no teams for her to play on, no boys willing to let her join in. What he'd underestimated, however, was just how stubborn a stubborn girl could be. When her parents wouldn't drive her to boys' basketball games, young Tara forced their hand, signing up to take the undignified and very much available position of middle-school mascot, which required her attendance at every game. Reporting for duty in a moth-eaten and shaggy bear suit, VanDerveer quickly distinguished herself as the most uncharismatic mascot the school had ever known, slouching in a chair on the sideline, often removing the cumbersome bear's head and setting it on her lap so that she could better see the action on the floor.

Eventually, she played as a guard for Indiana University, though she is quick to point out that she paid her own way since there were no scholarships in those days. The best thing Indiana had going for it at the time was not its women's basketball team; it was rather the men's team, and more specifically the team's leader, arguably the most famous college basketball coach of all time, Bobby Knight. He was stormy, histrionic—characterized by violent outbursts and a tendency to throw chairs. He was not a nice man, but he was a good coach. His teams won more than they lost. Sneaking into his practices, as she often did, hiding herself high in the stands, Tara VanDerveer noticed that when he wasn't yelling, Bobby Knight spoke with unusual clarity about what he wanted his players to do. His players played a solid, purposeful game, and most important, they played as a team.

Finishing with a sociology degree at Indiana in 1976—a year in which Knight's team won its first national championship—Tara VanDerveer returned home to Schenectady and contemplated applying to law school. Instead, she spent a lot of time sitting around. Finally, her father ordered her to help coach her younger sister's high school basketball team, which was having an abysmal season.

"I was like, 'Aw, Dad, anything but that!' " VanDerveer remembers. But she had gone down to the school and signed on to help coach. By the end of the season the team was starting to win, and VanDerveer knew for sure what she wanted to do with her life. She went on to get a coaching degree, a volunteer assistant coach position at Ohio State, and then head coaching jobs at University of Idaho and Ohio State before joining Stanford in 1985. In less than ten years at Stanford, she was, at forty-one, one of the preeminent women's coaches in the country, a future neither she nor her father could have predicted.

She was what her colleagues called a "coach's coach," approaching the game with unusual scholarliness, poring over statistics and relentlessly studying videotapes of her own teams and their competition alike. She took notes on nearly everything she saw, often running practices with a crumpled piece of yellow legal paper—last night's notes—squeezed in one hand. A basketball game was an analytical challenge; a full season, with its ups and downs and long parade of incalculable opponents, was in itself a game of titanic proportions. In her mind it was all tied to discipline. She was an obsessive Scrabble player, a strict vegetarian. Her favorite book was *Atlas Shrugged* by Ayn Rand, a testament to reason over emotion. If she hadn't gone the basketball route, it was not impossible to imagine Tara VanDerveer drafting word problems for standardized tests.

She was also not one to muck up her coaching with too much emotion. Coaching, as she seemed to view it, was a high and lonely outpost. She didn't coddle her players, didn't ask about their love lives or dispense advice about agents or endorsements or have them over for dinner on holidays the way some of the other coaches did. Even if she'd wanted to get involved in their lives, there was something about her—an awkwardness, a hardness in her character—that seemed to send them elsewhere for counsel. When they did call sometimes, as Katy Steding had done after she'd blown out first one knee and then the other, playing abroad after college, she liked to think that she could help. What she had said to Katy was something like this: "Don't let an injury be the reason you retire. If you want to quit—if you're tired or fed up—then quit, but don't put it on an injury. If you want to come back, you can." Steding had come back as strong as before, and she and VanDerveer were proud together about this.

Now VanDerveer was coaching the most naturally gifted group of players she'd ever had—a joy that carried with it great amounts of pressure and a tangle of new issues, one of the most immediate being earning the loyalty of her players. Jennifer and Katy aside, each woman on the team was the product of a different coach, a different college program, and in some instances years of relative independence competing abroad. For many of them, old coaches were like family, they sat like angels on their players' shoulders: Andy Landers was a jovial friend to Teresa and Katrina, Pat Summit advised Nikki on everything; Geno Auriemma was a third parent for Rebecca.

She could never fill those kinds of roles or replace these people in their lives, and she had said it to them too, acknowledged it right up front several days earlier at the start of training camp: She was who she was, take her or leave her, though really they had no choice but to take her. "I'm not Pat Summit," she had said emphatically. "I'm not Andy Landers." Most of the players were staring at their feet. "I'm not Geno . . . I'm just, you know, me."

And thus they had gathered on the track on this blustery October morning for a small exercise in mental toughness, a part of VanDerveer being herself. All summer, as they had trained individually, the players filled out the charts she sent them, organized into neat columns with blank spaces in which they detailed the things that measured their growing strength: pounds of weights lifted, times and distances of runs, free throws made and free throws missed, minutes spent scrimmaging. Today they would add another set of numbers to VanDerveer's library, the results of an eight-lap, two-mile charge around the track. Anybody whose running fell short of her expectations would be out there the next day, same time, same place, with VanDerveer and her stopwatch.

Another coach might have limited the running to the gym or at the very least checked the weather and postponed the outdoor workout, but not VanDerveer. Months later, she would even look back fondly on that morning, visibly delighted by the memory of the frigid air and punishing Old Testament winds, the team clumped together in misery on the still-frosted grass. She was sending a message. This was real, it was business, and it was going to be conducted on her terms. For better or worse, they were VanDerveer players now. Maybe to let this sink in, she seemed almost to dawdle, preparing her clipboard and timer, conferring with her two assistants as the players bounced up and down on toes that had gone numb in their sneakers, waiting for her to wave them onto the track and make them run.

They would spend three weeks at training camp in Colorado Springs and then, starting in early November, the lights would go up on the national stage, the audiences would ramble in with their pretzels and their hot dogs, the TV cameras would start rolling, and for the women on the team—or girls, as they often referred to themselves—it would be time to perform. They were going on tour, the same way rock stars and circus performers did, flying into a city, setting up, playing, breaking down, and flying out again. They would do it for nearly ten months, sometimes getting a few days to do their own thing and sometimes going back to Colorado Springs together to regroup. They would play twenty of the best college teams in the country, making homecoming stops in many of the towns where they had gone to school. They would hold clinics for girls and visit children's hospitals and sign a whole lot of autographs. They would stay in hotels and get a $35 daily allowance for food. After they'd played the college teams, they would tour internationally.

Before they went anywhere, though, they got a few lessons on who they were supposed to be. This was America, after all. Image counted. Not only that, but putting a professional women's basketball team before the public, planting even the hint of a suggestion that it was a sport worth buying into, was basically a novel idea. People had seen men and women's college ball. They had seen the NBA, with its pyrotechnics and bad-as-you-wanna-be characters. But professional-level women's play was still uncharted territory. It was hard to know how exactly to package this kind of team.

The image question seemed to stymie USA Basketball, which had made itself one of the most rich and famous of athletic national governing bodies through its creation and marketing of the 1992 men's Dream Team. The confusion surrounding the women was perhaps best illustrated by the embarrassing raft of nicknames that USAB officials (most of them female) had rehearsed in the days prior to training camp: Dreamettes, Dream Team Too, Fab Femmes, Liberty Belles, the Hoop Troupe, the '96ers, the Golden Girls, and Chicks Who Set Picks. The names pointed to a question that has been around for as long as women have played sports: Should women athletes be marketed primarily as women or primarily as athletes?

In 1960, an Olympic year, *The New York Times Magazine* published a story entitled "Venus Wasn't a Shot-Putter," with the subtitle, "Do men make passes at athletic lasses?" In it, author William Barry Furlong mused on whether athleticism and beauty could ever mix, praising women who "frolic athletically in swim suits or brief tennis skirts" as upholding an acceptable feminine ideal, one he referred to as "the Image." At the same time, he attacked those women participating in what he called unattractive, "muscle-bunching" sports such as field hockey, softball, sprinting, and discus throwing. ("I for one have never met a lovable lady shot-putter. . . .") If America felt any pride in having "the best-muscled girls in the world," Furlong was worried: "Next thing you know, we'll be bragging about having the best-looking automobile wrecks in the world."

Over thirty years later, American culture continued to struggle to equate strength and competitiveness with femininity, holding tight to the age-old notion that women had a particular responsibility to be "lovable." The "Image" Furlong described still haunted every female athlete who stepped into the spotlight, subjecting herself to the enduring stereotypes that dismiss women athletes as freakish trespassers in a male arena. In an ideal world, the question of how to sell a basketball team to the mainstream public would not have merited significant debate. But in the United States in 1995, in a climate where female athletes had long stood their best chance with the public if they were dressed in a leotard or a skirt, how USA Basketball and its corporate sponsors chose to market the national team would perhaps affect the future of the women's game.

In the end, the nickname idea was abandoned altogether. The team would be known simply as the USA Basketball women's national team. The players would wear a standard uniform, jerseys and shorts that were as long and loose as the men's. The jerseys and shorts were not to be the traditional navy blue of past USA teams, however; they were instead a deep crimson red with blue stripes up the sides and white stars on the blue stripes. There was a white "USA" on the chest of jerseys and the left thigh of the shorts, and above each of the USAs was a red, white, and blue "C," which stood for Champion, which was the name of the team's official outfitter. The shorts had a broad elastic waistband, at the center of which, right at the player's belly button, was a white star the size of a cookie.

The uniform was neither particularly masculine nor feminine; rather, in the words of one USA Basketball official, it was "classy." Classy would become the operative word used to describe the image of the USA Basketball women's national team. When the players went through a compulsory day of media training at the start of training camp, they were instructed on how to be classy athletes by a media specialist who flew in from Virginia for the occasion.

Classy meant several things. It meant that in talking to the media, you used complete sentences. It meant you smiled even if you felt put upon or tired or sick of getting asked the same silly questions. You smiled if you won, and you especially smiled if you lost, since pouting did not qualify as classy. You never trashed your teammates or your coach or anyone else for that matter, but most important, since the reporters would be fishing for it, you never trashed your opponents. If you imagined your opponents would beat you, you spoke highly of them. If you knew they were nothing more than meat for your grinder, you spoke extra highly of them so as not to appear cocky, which, like pouting, was not classy.

In the media consultant's day-long seminar, the players were videotaped in various interview situations in which they practiced making eye contact with the camera, using complete sentences, and dealing with potential trouble spots. Lisa Leslie, for example, was asked to envision doing an interview with Cheryl Miller, the former USC star who was now a sportscaster. Miller was unpopular with a number of college coaches and players due to the fact that in 1993 when USC coach Marian Stanley had filed a gender discrimination suit against the university, suing to get a salary commensurate with that of the men's basketball coach, Miller had accepted the job to replace her, thereby undermining what many saw as a political effort in women's basketball to level the playing field. Lisa Leslie, who counted Marian Stanley as a second mother, was not especially fond of Miller.

"But here she is and she's working for one of the networks and she wants to talk to you," said the media consultant, putting Lisa on the spot. "What do you do?"

Lisa folded her hands in her lap. "I refuse," she said.

She was quickly corrected. "No, you don't. It reflects poorly on you, not her," said the consultant. She pointed to a cartooned drawing on one of her handouts that showed an athlete in the foreground and a bunch of fans in the background with the word "opportunity!" written beneath them. In between the athlete and the opportunity was a reporter holding a microphone. If this was to be a year of opportunity for the players and for the women's game, they were reminded, there was no room for being negative.

Lisa was someone who was just beginning to understand opportunity. She was twenty-three years old and skilled beyond her years in basketball. At six five, she was too tall for forwards to guard, and too quick for most centers, and was versatile enough to shoot three-pointers. Yet curiously, while other players would readily say that they had been born to play basketball, Lisa would insist that she was not. When she was not being entirely serious, she would suggest that she was born to wear lipstick and shimmery silk outfits or that maybe she had a gene that made her go after the wrong men. When Lisa cracked herself up, she slapped one knee and let out a big, horsey laugh. Then she composed herself again, her face dropping into an elegant and carefully moderated smile.

No really, her point was that she was born to be feminine.

What did feminine really mean anymore? Lisa had thought about this enough to first clarify that she had an answer that pertained only to herself. "For me, being feminine is having fun with looking good—doing my toes, my lipstick, wearing my earrings, my perfume, and dressing up in nice clothes, enjoying the part of me that's soft and gentle." Sometimes, said Lisa, she looked at the teenage girls, many of whom dress in trendy hip-hop clothing—big baggy jeans and shapeless, untucked shirts—and felt the urge to take them out shopping and dress them in things that flattered their bodies.

"I don't get it," Lisa mused. "I mean, I guess it's a fad, but it's an ugly one."

She prided herself on knowing what looked good on people and what didn't. She was fully capable of doing fashion makeovers at a glance. The next day, after the media training session, when the national team went shopping all together in Denver for dresses to wear to the Women's Sports Foundation banquet later that month, Lisa, who picked out her own outfit—a form-fitting black acetate dress—on the fourth or fifth try, stationed herself outside the dressing rooms and offered yes-yes, no-no commentary on everyone who came out to look in the mirror.

It was seldom that Lisa, who besides being tall was rather dramatic-looking, walked into a room and went unnoticed. Her face was all angles and planes, her cheekbones sharp and high, eyebrows arched cloyingly above a pair of fawn-like brown eyes. Her skin was smooth and iron brown. Her body was perhaps easiest described by what it was not, which was all the things people usually said about tall, skinny women: Lisa Leslie was not a stick figure, a twig. Rather, she was spindly but powerful, her legs, which were banded with long, flat muscles, had a heft to them that was all vertical. Her posture was flawless. The stretch of her arms and the bony fronds of her fingers allowed her to reach over eight feet in the air. Sauntering through a hotel lobby, Lisa gave the distinct impression that she could, at any moment, leap up and knock the lights out of the chandelier.

Lisa's mother had taught her how to be a lady. Lisa's mother was six feet three and drove an eighteen-wheeler for a living. She saw her daughter growing up and understood that there was no opportunity to hide: When you are six feet tall at the age of twelve, slouching your shoulders and trying to blend into the background simply doesn't work. Lisa's mother, Christine, passed on three bits of advice: "She said don't slouch. Keep your head up high," remembered Lisa. "She said being tall is a really positive thing to be."

Still, there were taunts to shrug off, indignities to suffer as the tallest girl ever to pass through her elementary school in Compton, a neighborhood of Los Angeles.

"They called me Olive Oyl, they called me all sorts of things," said Leslie. "The grown-ups mostly thought my height was beautiful, but the kids gave me a hard time."

There were moments, too, when Lisa's mother wasn't around to remind her about the beauty of being tall. Christine Leslie, whose face had the same sleepy-lidded integrity as Lisa's, started trucking when Lisa was nine years old. Prior to that, she had been a welder. "She was a single mom with three girls," said Lisa. "We had no money and we could've gone on welfare, but my mom wanted to do something she was proud of. She sat us down and said, 'This is what I've got to do. I'm going to buy a truck and learn how to drive it. It's going to take time for me to pay it off and get a local route. I need you kids to give me five years. You're gonna have to be patient with me, but in five years I'll be able to give you a better life than what we have.' "

Christine Leslie left her daughters with a set of rules—homework was done first thing, when the streetlights came on you had to come inside at night—and a housekeeper to watch over them. She traveled for weeks at a time, taking loads all over the country—hauling everthing from canned tomatoes to trade-show exhibits, driving the Interstates from L.A. to New York to Detriot, always keeping an eye out for a load that would take her back to the wide, run-down avenues of Compton, where her daughters were growing up without her. "She'd come back for maybe three days, and I'd have this love/hate thing, you know, like, I loved her so much but I knew she was going to leave again soon," Lisa would remember. "It was hard for her too; she was just trying to give us a good life."

On the playground, Lisa fought the teasing by being nice to everyone. She smiled, laughed at people's jokes, and perhaps possessing some innate understanding that size was equated with strength, and strength in a young girl was intimidating, she went out of her way to be disarmingly sweet, even to the boys who scoffed at her coltish awkwardness. Niceness was a way of telling everyone not to be afraid of her. She worked at being pretty too, because it was one thing to be tall and another thing to be tall and pretty in the city of L.A., no matter what neighborhood you lived in. Some nights she sat up late with beauty magazines. Other nights she had her hair elaborately coiffed by the hairdresser who came around to her aunt's house once a week.

Of all the comments she got about being tall, the one she found most offensive was perhaps the most innocent "Hey, do you play basketball?" The question sent Lisa into a preadolescent huff. It was as if a big body was good for only one thing, and a boy's thing at that. Didn't they see that she was pretty and gentle? Didn't they see that she had supermodel potential? She made sure to answer their question nicely, though, with a delicate but unwavering *no*.

Starting junior high, she felt lonely and out of place. Her mother was gone all the time now, coming home and trying to squeeze all her parenting into just a few days. Her older sister was in high school and dealing with, as Lisa saw it, "teenage issues," while her younger sister was still too young to be a confidante. In the first weeks of school, she watched as the seventh-grade class quickly divided and subdivided into cliques, leaving her standing alone like the unmatched gamete in a biology lab experiment, towering over the chattering kids in the cafeteria.

Her mother would phone in from truckstop pay phones in Kentucky, Florida, Toronto. "Don't worry," she'd say. "Some people grow on the inside and some grow on the outside. You're lucky, Li, because you're growing both ways."

And then one day the most popular girl in the school materialized before her, standing two heads below with a hopeful expression on her face. "I play basketball," she told Lisa. "And you gotta come join us. We *need* you, girl."

She showed up at tryouts only to be nice. She didn't want the most popular girl to think poorly of her, but she had no intention of playing basketball either. She cooperated only halfheartedly. "They just lined me up near the basket and said, okay, this is a lay-up; when we pass you the ball, you just bounce it once and throw it in the hoop." And this is what Lisa Leslie did. Pass, bounce, basket. No sweat. She did it once, then twice, and another time, and again, and soon all the other girls on the team were clustered around her, she like redwood among rhododendrons, and soon she was on the basketball team and her lay-ups were winning games. "I was so tall, they'd just throw the ball at me and I'd make the basket," she'd say later, blinking her eyes demurely. "All I did was do what I was told." That season, the team went 7–0.

The following year she moved in with her aunt in Carson, a neighborhood to the south, and started at a small Catholic school. This time the transition was easier because Lisa Leslie had found a different way to fit in. She had advanced beyond the lay-up and was now, with the help of an older male cousin, spending each night at a local gym, working on her spin move and jumpshots, playing on her school's team in the afternoons. "My cousin made me do push-ups and sit-ups and then we'd work on my shots. I think it was at that point I learned how hard you had to work to get from one level to the next," she says. "I would choose one thing and work on it until I got it."

He also pushed her to play with kids her own size, which meant playing with boys. "Boys would come into the gym and my cousin would set me up in three-on-three with them. Then he'd stand on the sidelines and say things like, 'Come on, just keep playing. Remember what I taught you. Rebound. You can always rebound.' " Next thing she knew, she was the least-appreciated player in a summer league that was otherwise all boys. "When I first started, the boys on my team wouldn't pass me the ball," she says. "They'd just pretend like I wasn't there, so I had to start stealing the ball from them, just to get a chance to go down and take a shot. When I made my shot, they'd all be like, 'Hey, she's a girl and she can score!' "

She was also learning that basketball messed up her hair—something that had bothered her at first—but now she was just skipping the hairdressing, keeping her hair up in a smooth topknot instead. She still cared about looking nice, about being nice, but being ferocious and disheveled on the basketball court was cool too.

Her mother had loved seeing what basketball did for her. Eventually she did get a local trucking route, moving Lisa and her sisters to Inglewood in time for Lisa to start at Morningside High School on the city's southeast side, in the shadow of the Forum, the L.A. Lakers' home court. After a time, Lisa was getting so many recruiting letters, she could hardly keep up, piling them in a big box in her bedroom. The tradition at Morningside was that in the final game of the regular season, the players would feed one senior the ball to see how much she could score. The year before Lisa tried it, the senior had scored 68 points, the year before that it had been 61.

Lisa scored 101 points in two eight-minute quarters before the opposing coach got angry and forfeited the rest of the game, the score 102–24. Lisa's 101 points were four short of the national high school scoring record for girls (ironically, held by Cheryl Miller), and she'd done it in just a half. The television trucks were waiting on her front lawn by the she got home that night. Lisa had been nervous first and delighted second, having never fully let go of her old longing to become a famous model, to become famous, period. She had squared her shoulders, patted at her hair, and smiled deeply at the cameras.

In Colorado Springs, Tara VanDerveer lived by herself in an upscale carpeted condominium with a living room that had wide picture windows and one of the best mountain views in town. The mountains of the Front Range, with their Byzantine grandeur and the intricate way they caught the sun, were the best part about Colorado Springs for her. An avid skier, she often looked up at them and wondered how long it would be before she could see snow up there.

Coaching basketball was the kind of job that kept you indoors, logging your time in a hermetic environment of conditioned air and manufactured light, with no sound but the beat of bouncing balls and squealing sneakers, whistles and clanging rims. After a few hours on a basketball court, it was easy to forget the weather or time of day, and sometimes even the season. If you thought about it too hard, you started to feel cooped up and restless. If you didn't think about it, you began to feel impervious to or even uncomfortable with the outdoor world, overlooking the leaves on the trees or ignoring the early autumn rain as you marched from place to place between practices.

VanDerveer was at heart an outdoorsperson. She'd spent the summers of her youth on a long and narrow lake in the far southwestern corner of New York state, about halfway between Buffalo and Erie, Pennsylvania. Lake Chautauqua was like something out of a summer camp movie, a deep clear pool with hilly pine forests that ran right down to its shores, a woodsy playground where mosquitos ruled and fishing was a good way to begin and end each day. As a girl, she went out on her brother's Hobie Cat and sailed for hours at a time, the sun warm on her back, the boat cutting swiftly through the dark water. In the winters she found a similar brand of freedom on the iced-over and windy ski slopes of Vermont and northern New York.

Basketball had largely taken her away from all this. Between recruiting and preseason practice and then the college season, which ran, at least in

VanDerveer's case, through the Final Four in late March, there was little time to go back home. In northern California she'd skied when she could, driving up to Lake Tahoe on the occasional free day, but the truth of it was—something she'd realized, looking up at the Front Range of the Rockies through her window recently—her life had been consolidated and distilled over the years until its most generous and cruel moments and the emotions that came with them had the same genesis, in basketball, the elaborate theater of ten female bodies over ninety-four feet of hardwood. This year the basketball would have an obvious heightened quality, which meant inevitably that she would stay on one side of the window and the mountains would stay on the other. The closest she'd get to Chautauqua, her one grasp of the peace that lay beyond basketball, would come in the mornings, in the solitary hour she'd find to run laps around a shallow, concrete-bottomed lake built into a grassy park near the training center.

At practice she wandered among her players as they stretched on the floor, appearing almost a little lost as she made an effort to check in with each one. She wore a red USA Basketball shirt tucked into blue nylon warm-up pants that ballooned out from her midsection, giving her an almost dowdy, pear-shaped appearance. In one hand she held a cup of water, priming her voice for the work ahead.

"Teresa, you hurt your knee this summer? The same one? . . . Do you feel like you're in good shape?"

"All right, you ready to go, old lady?" she said, moving on toward Katrina, who was bent over one knee. "Did you get that birthday card I sent you? How old are you? Thirty? Aw, that's a great age. I'd love to be thirty again. You did a great job on your summer workouts, you'll be glad you did them." With this, VanDerveer started to walk away, then, turning, she added, getting a shy smile from Katrina in return, "I don't know about those 'funk aerobics' though. I'll have to see what that really looks like."

To Lisa Leslie she said, "You ready to go?" To Katy, who was doing sit-ups on the floor, "All right, Kate, let's see what you got here."

It was impossible to walk past Sheryl Swoopes without noticing the shoe. "Is that it? Is that the shoe there?" said VanDerveer, halting herself in front of Sheryl, who in turn stopped stretching in order to lift one foot in the air for the coach to see. The shoe was a hightop made of white leather, with a flashy red band—a "stability strap," Nike called it—that

Velcroed over the shoelaces across the midsection of her foot. At the top of the tongue was the newly minted Air Swoopes logo, a basketball encircled by a large S.

This was not simply the Air Swoopes, the first signature shoe created for a woman, the first signature shoe Nike had created for *anyone* besides Michael Jordan: This was the Air Swoopes that was custom made for Sheryl Swoopes, hand-tooled to fit her narrow size ten foot and weak ankles perfectly, made in red and white as per the USA Basketball requirements on shoe colors. The Air Swoopes that would go on sale around the country later that month for $84.99 was a black shoe with a white stability strap. Nike would advertise an 800 number people could call to hear Sheryl talking about the shoe. Sheryl's husband had his own pair of Air Swoopes too, in a women's size fourteen, since they came only in women's sizes. The word Eric used to describe the way the shoe looked on his feet, even if it was not inherently a shoe for men, was classy.

At practice, VanDerveer leaned down to inspect Sheryl's foot. "That's cute," she said about the shoe. "That's cute," she said again, ". . . now we have to get it out there running around."

When stretching was finished and they gathered at the center of the gym, VanDerveer kept her remarks to a minimum. "This is a really special day," she said, scanning their faces, "and I'm excited to be here and I know that each and every one of you is excited too. It's fun and it's business. Let's start with some basketball business and have a good practice, everybody working hard." She put one hand forward and waited until they'd pulled in close around her, their palms piled loosely over her fist. "C'mon, USA one-two-three," said VanDerveer. They answered in unison, pumping their hands down and then up twice before they scattered across the floor, their voices echoing in a powerful, throaty chorus: "USA!"

"Four corner passing!" she yelled, sending them into position for a drill. "If you don't know what you're doing, get to the end of the line!" As they started to move, rotating in and out from under the hoop, VanDerveer watched with her hands on her hips. When she'd seen everyone go through the line twice, she blasted on her whistle and let it drop. "Here we go, we're going lay-ups, two balls on the right, two on the left," she called, her voice cutting the air like a bullhorn, pushing them back into action before they'd caught their breath ". . . two right, two left, two in the middle, that's it . . . Here we go . . . good job, good job, takin' it up, way to get it up, no dribble."

Her plan, in essence, was to deconstruct their game, to work on the fundamentals—ballhandling, man-to-man defense, three-point shooting—stripping them of some of the bad habits they'd picked up over the years, particularly given the inferior coaching most of them had received playing abroad, and with any luck, teaching them to see the game the way she saw it. She could pick out the wrong notes in a player's footwork or jump shot, and sometimes she knew how to correct them with the smallest adjustment. Like anyone with that kind of eye, she saw things in terms of negative space, what wasn't there. She recognized what she absolutely hated more often than what she liked. In her mind she carried a very particular vision—a perfect group of players, a flawless game, the purest kind basketball—and her life's work was to make it happen. It was not an easy way to live, and in order to get anywhere with her vision, she had to first get her players to buy into it.

She was going to work them harder than they'd ever been worked. When Lisa, Rebecca, and Carla had been the last three over the finish line during her timed run, VanDerveer had summoned the three of them to do it again the next morning and again the one after that, calling it "the breakfast club," which nobody seemed to find funny. She'd even made Rebecca come back a fourth time, standing there in the wind like some mad Ahab as Rebecca ran and ran—paced by Jennifer, who'd volunteered to help her—until finally Rebecca had broken sixteen minutes and VanDerveer released her. Nobody was exempt. Katy Steding was assigned eighteen hours of punitive "make-up cardio" because she hadn't fully recorded her summer workouts. Lisa and Nikki logged some extra time as well—an hour doled out for every mistake they'd made or short cut they'd taken in VanDerveer's summer training regime.

Looking at her new team that first week, she saw not a work-in-progress but a mess of raw material. Even if these were some of the world's best players, they were still unruly and disconnected from one another. There were weaknesses to help, problems to fix. Nikki McCray played the kind of basketball she'd played at Tennessee, a drive-it-inside game that rendered her almost useless on the perimeter, Sheryl Swoopes shied away from rebounding, Lisa Leslie let her opponents push her around, Ruthie Bolton sometimes made poor decisions with the ball, and almost all of them seemed to have forgotten about defense. This was par for the course with players who had competed abroad, given the European crowds' love for fast-paced, high-scoring games. The American players, usually the most talented members on their teams, faced added scoring pressure, which led to an even more pronounced lapse in defense. It wasn't the players' fault, VanDerveer knew, but defense had been the Achilles' heel of U.S. teams in the past, namely in their 1994 World Championships loss when they'd all but stood around and watched the Brazilians pepper the basket with unchallenged three-point shots.

With this in mind, she put them into pairs according to size—guards with guards, forwards with forwards—while an assistant coach set up a series of cones from one end of the court to the other. They were to zigzag through the cones, running side to side as they worked their way up the floor, one player dribbling, the other guarding as aggressively as possible. "Your palms are up," VanDerveer told them, "your pressure is on the ball. We're trying to get deflections."

They nodded. They fingered their mouth guards, fiddled with their shoes. They did not chat or joke with one another at all while VanDerveer was speaking. Sometimes, for emphasis, the coach snapped her fingers and simultaneously made a tomahawk chop as she talked. "When the shot goes up," she said, punctuating every other word with a snap and a chop, "you call *shot!* and box out."

With this they started to run, two by two, offense versus defense, down the court, through the cones, and toward the basket, where the offensive player would unleash the ball at the basket. Jennifer worked with Dawn, Katy worked with Nikki, Ruthie with Teresa, and Katrina alternated with Rebecca and Lisa. Sheryl and Carla, nursing ankle and quadricep injuries respectively, rode stationary bikes in one corner, lost in a fog beneath their Walkman headsets.

Watching the drill from the sidelines, VanDerveer kept up a steady torrent of high-volume commentary, interrupting herself only to toot her whistle periodically, stopping play to make a point: "Get low on your stance, get lower, Katy! Slide! Slide! Palms up, spring, sprint, recover! Stay low, Lisa, slide!" Whistle: "Hold up!" When they stopped, she said, "You guys, you got to work on good defensive habits. Pretend you have a ruler and put it right between your feet, that's as close as your feet should come together on defense. Work on good technique."

No matter how hard they ran, how loud the sound of their own breathing got, VanDerveer's voice was a continual buzz in their ears. "That's better, Lisa, drop and slide, stay low, stay low, keep her in front of you, work on good stance, good stance, good job, way to stay with them, *box*!" Whistle: "Hold up. Defense is looking better. Offense, you gotta go for the rebound. Okay, keep it going. Stay in your stance, Teresa, get low, get position, don't get overcommitted now. In your stance, Dawn, stay down, stay down, box! Come on, Dawn, get your hand on that ball. Get low, get low, keep your feet alive. Play 'em, *play 'em*!" Whistle: "Hold up." VanDerveer inspected her athletes, many of whom were bent over and heaving for air. "All right, if you want water, jog over and get a drink. Jog!"

After an hour of defense, VanDerveer sent them right into running and passing exercises, five players running at a full sprint down the court, passing the ball between them as they went, laying the ball in as they passed the basket.

Rebecca Lobo knew where this was heading. For her, practice had been a steep and slippery slope downward. Her legs had started to ache after ten minutes. The high-altitude air made her lungs feel as if they'd had a layer of skin peeled off them. When the coach had them run on the court, Rebecca had consistently been the last to finish, dragging herself heavily across the baseline, avoiding VanDerveer's eyes as she tried to recover. She was in the doghouse, and she knew it. She even sensed it from her new teammates, many of whom were huffing themselves but who at least had kept the pace. They patted one another on the back, shouted words of encouragement, but when it came to Rebecca, who turned twenty-two the first week of training camp, a number of them kept silent. She was out of shape. Some of it had to do with the slow recovery from arthroscopy on her knee, some of it came from the work-outs she'd missed in all those days of travel over the summer. The reality of what was ahead stung her. Here she was, the golden child of the sport, and she could hardly get through a two-hour practice. VanDerveer was not going to let up.

There were people who believed that Rebecca had made the team only because she was a personality, a hero to the little girls and the sponsors alike. The way she was playing, it seemed she was proving them right—a thought that washed her in a desperation she'd never felt before in basketball. She had never been a mediocre player. She couldn't say this to anyone on the team though, not even Jennifer with whom she was sharing an apartment because she worried the older player would think her spoiled or whiny. Instead, Rebecca hid her emotions away, saving them until long after she'd showered and left the gym, back home behind the closed doors of her bedroom on the phone with her older sister, Rachel, her parents, or Dave.

It felt like practice would never end. They divided into groups and sprinted at VanDerveer's whistle, their feet filling the gym with thunder. Jennifer and Nikki were several steps ahead, with Lisa and Ruthie staggered just behind, all of them holding themselves back to stay roughly in line with Lobo, whose gait seemed a shamble in comparison. "Move it, move it!" VanDerveer was shouting, "You gotta run, Rebecca!" The voice drilled into the back of Rebecca's head as she crossed the baseline and collapsed her body over her knees. Around her, Nikki was drenched in sweat; Dawn was bent over and wheezing slightly. Jennifer, for her part, looked unfazed by any of it, walking back and forth quietly, hands on her hips. Teresa, Katrina, Katy, and Lisa took their turn, and it seemed like a matter of seconds before they were back, retching for air, and Rebecca's group was up again. She leaned forward and readied herself for the whistle. When it came, she hurled herself forward again, determined not to be the slowest, but her legs and lungs wouldn't cooperate. The voice came again, this time slow and drawn out: "You got-ta ru-un, Rebecca!"

They scrimmaged for the last fifteen or so minutes. Rebecca's shots were sloppy, flat. Guarding the apparently tireless Katrina, she let herself get pushed around. "Take it up strong, Rebecca!" called VanDerveer. But Rebecca, who was feeling too wiped out to shoot, flipped the ball to Dawn on the perimeter. VanDerveer pounced, using Rebecca's nickname, "B, you need a better pass!" A minute later Katrina slipped past her and put the ball in, causing the coach to twirl her whistle angrily: "Come on, Rebecca, you gotta deny that!"

Finally, VanDerveer signaled it was time for free throws. Ten free throws and they were done with practice. Ten free throws was a breeze; the players instantly relaxed, taking a minute to kick the cramps out of their legs, towel off, or go for a cup of water. Sheryl and Carla, who had rejoined the group after an hour on the bike, shrieked and hooted to encourage the group. Rebecca's body seemed to slump with relief at the news that practice was ending. Her hair was matted with sweat, her eyes looking flat and defeated. She stopped for water and comforted herself with the thought of ten simple foul shots. But suddenly VanDerveer was upon her, singling her out. Five full-court sprints, the coach was saying, up and down, fast. Now.

And so while the others shot their free throws leisurely, Rebecca kept running, her body capable of no more than a slow lumber, with VanDerveer's voice riding her every step of the way, "On your toes, Rebecca, that's it, come on, high heels, high heels, bring 'em up!" She did one sprint and then two, listening as VanDerveer's focus finally turned to the others. "You get your ten, Teresa? Katy, your ten? Lisa, ten?" After another lap, Rebecca stopped listening altogether, knowing full well that the rest of them were done and that in a few minutes she would do her free throws alone, her body decimated by the workout, arms and legs weak, her face hot and red.

Homecomings

On a Tuesday in late October, Tara VanDerveer stared impassively out a hotel window at the Georgia Dome. In the drab autumn light, the building appeared almost menacingly impersonal—a white, oval-shaped structure made of mostly concrete and glittering glass with a white circus-tent top that rose to a girdered point in the middle—a grand-scale postmodern cupcake set down in the center of Atlanta. This was where, nine months from then, the final games of the Olympics would be played. For VanDerveer it was where the full pressure of her life as a coach would come to bear, where she and her team would distinguish themselves either as winners or losers.

After dominating the international game in the eighties, the American women, and their game—an exuberant run-and-gun brand of basketball—had been ransacked by the competition, chewed up by the Chinese and the Russians and even the Australians in the last few years. Losing to Brazil in the semifinals at the 1994 World Championships in Sydney hurt perhaps the worst. The next day, when Brazil beat China to win the gold medal, the Brazilian players had all but rioted on the bus back to the hotel, dancing and singing and hanging out the windows. Eventually the women had worked themselves into such a frenzy that when somebody produced a pair of scissors, taking turns, egged on by chants of *"Vivá Brasil!,"* they'd gleefully chopped off the hair of their male coach. Unfortunately, as it was common for teams to share transportation at international tournaments, the Americans had been on that same bus, having won the bronze medal game earlier that evening. VanDerveer remembered sitting up front, her back to her own team, all of them muted and glum in the twilight as the new world champions carried on boisterously behind them.

She did not want to lose again.

Though USA Basketball paid only for basic hotel rooms, the PR people at the Westin Hotel had put VanDerveer in the Presidential Suite for no charge, a two-story affair complete with spiral staircase, a baby grand piano, and a whirlpool. "I could have a party in there," she joked with the players, something that was funny only because they understood that VanDerveer was as equally ill at ease at parties as she was surrounded by opulence. In the suite she unpacked her things and kept them piled neatly in one corner, spreading only her paperwork out over the sleek coffee table in the living room. The whirlpool went unused.

For her, the highlight of the $1,450-a-night accommodations was the view from the 69th floor, looking out over Atlanta's downtown sprawl and toward the Georgia Dome, which from above looked flat and utterly conquerable. A lover of symbols and portents, VanDerveer was making a point to glance over at the Dome every chance she got during the team's stopover in Atlanta. On her morning runs with the team's administrative director, she jogged a slow circle around it, trying to view it from every angle, squinting at it front and back. In their several days there she would try to see the building in every light, gilded in the morning, milky and ominous against the nighttime streetlights, as if trying to establish herself in relation to it, as if to assert that whatever the Georgia Dome came to represent in her life, it would never catch her by surprise.

Training camp had ended a week earlier with a series of short scrimmages against teams from South Korea and Ukraine, which the U.S. Olympic Committee had imported to Colorado Springs for ten days. VanDerveer had given the players a few days off, then they'd kicked off the road tour with little fanfare, meeting up in Cincinnati to play Athletes in Action, a women's team fielded by a Christian organization. In a high school gym before a small but enthused crowd, the national team had won the game 83–57. Still, they played sloppy, lackluster basketball with too many turnovers and too many forced shots. It had been, to VanDerveer's mind, a terrible start, one that confirmed her worst insecurities. Her team seemed unsynchronized, too lax on defense, and more troubling, too weak in the middle. Lisa Leslie was getting pushed around. What VanDerveer needed was some heft underneath, a banger.

Now in Georgia, she wanted them to see the Dome. She wanted to plant a seed: It could happen here.

With the Georgia Tech football season in full swing, the floor of the stadium was padded with thick grass and striped with yellow and white yard lines. The smell of stale beer hung faintly in the air, and 36,000 empty seats rose up around them. As they filed onto the field, joking with each other, their voices seemed to float rather than echo as they would on a basketball court. The moment felt distinctly uninspired: They were a bunch of women standing around a football field.

VanDerveer gathered them together then and asked them to imagine a court and two nets and a game that unfolded flawlessly. Could they hear the crowd? How did the floor feel beneath their feet? Soon, transfixed, they were running the fast break seamlessly, hawking the ball on defense until their defense became an offense, wrenching down rebounds, looping full-court passes on the break. They imagined the red-lit numbers on the scoreboard ticking upward in their favor, the Brazilians or Russians or Chinese, *whoever*, frozen like pillars in their wake. The cheering of 30,000 fans rose up and crashed over them.

When they focused again, they saw only a short woman with a blunt haircut and a far-off expression, Tara VanDerveer on the 60-yard line. Marching them to some imagined midcourt line, she dug two objects out of her pocket—glinting and unfamiliar, discs too big to be a silver dollar and the wrong color too. She'd borrowed two gold medals from Teresa, from 1984 and 1988. The medals were heavier than most of the women had imagined, a quarter-inch of solid gold on a satin ribbon. As they took turns hanging the medals around their necks, VanDerveer had them pose individually for a photo—the athlete, the medal, and the Georgia Dome—a reminder for when they doubted themselves or each other or her at points along the way, about what this was all for.

They would carry these photos, plus another close-up of the medal alone, taped to a page in the notebooks they brought with them everywhere, simple black ring binders that would soon swell with flight schedules and hotel names and media obligations and page after page of VanDerveer's diagrammed plays.

It was going to be a long haul. This was something that VanDerveer seemed to understand more than anyone else. Less than a week into the tour, newspapers across the country were using phrases like "best in the world" and "women's Dream Team" to describe her players. The attention was good, but the optimism, the kind generated so glibly and so often by a national media quick to find heroes before actual battle, was dangerous; it could steamroll them if they weren't careful. The media would try to fit them into so many boxes, pumping out as-yet-unearned superlatives as the team jumped from city to city. They were beautiful (a new definition of American beauty!), they were all about togetherness (blacks and whites in a perfect microcosm of American racial harmony!), they had manners and humility and a deep-seated respect for the opportunity now afforded them (the antithesis of the NBA crybabies and buffoons!) and most significantly, they were going to win it all.

For her part, VanDerveer would discourage the hype as much as she could. It was one thing to appreciate the way her team played, what good people her players were, but it was quite another to predict victory nine months in advance. The reality was that China had a six-foot-eight center who hit eighty percent of her shots; that Russia had big, hungry players who were six nine and six seven; and the Brazilian team was full of fiery veterans who could pass the ball in their sleep. And all of them, she couldn't help reminding herself—no, obsessing on—had thumped the Americans at one time or another in the last five years.

Later, talking with an Atlanta reporter at the hotel, with the Dome looming again in the distance, she tried to be realistic. "There's a misconception out there that because we invented the game of basketball, it's a U.S. right to claim the medal," she said. When she gave interviews she rarely smiled, but she did give the most honest answers she could. She wanted the press to understand. "In order to win that gold medal in that building right over there, on August fourth at about two o'clock in the afternoon," she said, eyeing the Dome, drawing her breath in lightly, "we have a tremendous amount of work ahead."

While basketball is often and aptly called the greatest team game on earth, there are few people who would argue against the idea that every player on every team wants, badly, to be a starter. Starters fill each of the five positions on the floor: point guard, shooting guard, small forward, power forward, and center, or, in the shorthand used by most coaches, the one, two, three, four, and five positions, respectively. Players who are not starters sit on the bench, waiting to be substituted. Sometimes the wait can be long and frustrating.

The first time Teresa Edwards went to the Olympics, the 1984 Games in Los Angeles, she spent a lot of time on the bench. She had just turned twenty and was between her sophomore and junior years at Georgia. In the black and white team picture taken on the lawn at the training center, Teresa stands at one end of the line of players, cheeks shining, her hair curled and cheerfully poofed, looking relatively young and, considering that six of her teammates were six feet three or taller, relatively shrimpy. In Los Angeles, when the coach put her into games, Teresa turned in the worst performance of anyone on the team, making only one out of every four shots she took. In the end, she scored 15 points over six games while the team's high scorer, Cheryl Miller, who was Teresa's age and one of the best-known female players in the country, scored 99.

If her experience in Los Angeles suggested that Teresa Edwards had no place among the elite players of the world, the rest of her career would emphatically prove it wrong. "Show her something she can't do," says Andy Landers, who coached her for four years at Georgia, "and she'll throw it back in your face by proving you wrong." Returning to the University of Georgia, she played with an earnest intensity, holding herself and her teammates to impossibly high standards, playing, she liked to say, as if every day were her last. Two summers later, at the World Championships in Moscow, she matched Cheryl Miller nearly basket for basket. When Miller retired shortly after, Edwards kept going. At the 1988 Olympics she had the highest shooting average, the most assists, and the most steals of anyone on the team. In just a few years she had metamorphosed into one of the game's best players.

Yet in the fall of 1995, after three Olympics, three World Championships, and nine years of playing professionally overseas, Teresa seemed to be right back at the beginning. VanDerveer wanted Teresa to learn the point guard position, when she'd spent most of her career playing shooting guard. Beyond that, the coach seemed to have everything she needed, at least as far as starters went, with Dawn Staley at point guard and Ruthie Bolton at the two. She also had Jennifer Azzi as a backup point guard, so where was Teresa going to go? So far she'd spent more time on the bench than she had in years. She tried not to be desultory, but it was hard not to wonder if the coach had something personal against her.

Everybody was starting to wonder what the problem was between VanDerveer and Teresa. The coach gave her less playing time than the others, harangued her constantly during drills. "D it up, Teresa! You're not doing what I told you. Play position defense and pay attention! Come on, Teresa!" Teresa felt that she always did pay attention. She felt she was being treated like a child, but she swallowed it, not saying a word, knowing that she'd been dubbed uncooperative in the past, particularly on the fateful trip to the World Championships, when tension had been high all around, VanDerveer snapping at everyone, and Teresa being one of a few players to snap back. If she said anything now, Teresa figured, she'd just get labeled again.

Clearly, the coach's job was to be critical, but others would acknowledge that Teresa seemed to get it worse than the rest.

"I don't know why," Dawn would say months later, "but Tara came down pretty hard on T."

"She just didn't like me," Teresa would say later, "and I couldn't understand it because I'd never done anything to her, nor had I ever done anything to any coach I ever played for. I just went out and played. I felt she was taking things personally about the loss [at the World Championships in 1994] and it was all my fault.

"It made me have such awkward feelings about my career because I've watched great players go to the end of their careers and their countries celebrate them, and thank them, and reward them for all the years of giving, and here I was with the coach trying to make me feel like I wasn't needed."

Attempting to be lighthearted, Teresa joked with her teammates. "I'm right back where I started," she'd say, sitting next to Rebecca Lobo on the bench. "Twelve years of playing and I ain't gone anywhere."

In the meantime, Ruthie Bolton appeared to have become the coach's favorite, causing some of the players to joke about what seemed to be VanDerveer's mantra—"Good job Ruthie, good job Ruthie"—right through every practice.

Ruthie fit VanDerveer's notion of a solid defensive player almost perfectly. Short and stocky, her shoulders and arms knotted with muscle, Ruthie was an unshowy but intimidating presence on the floor, quick to dive for a loose ball or plant her body in front of a charging opponent. Unlike some of the others, she was even-tempered and did not seem to have the kind of good days and bad days that gave the rest of their performances an unpredictable quality. She did not shout or complain or even laugh loudly. At the first day of practice, as the other players straggled to the sidelines to pull their shoes off and heap bags of ice onto their aching joints, Ruthie had stood next to VanDerveer, hands on hips, surveying the court.

"That was a good first day," the coach had said, "but tomorrow we have to have a better one."

Ruthie had nodded vigorously. She liked a challenge. She did not question VanDerveer's authority, which seemed to reassure them both. Ruthie started most practices by leading the rest of the players in jogging a lap or two around the court, chanting military calls in a deep alto, to which they'd respond in a unified voice:

> *I could run to Tennessee, just like this!*
> I could run to Tennessee, just like this!
> *All the way to Knoxville, never quit!*
> All the way to Knoxville, never quit!
> *I could run to Texas, just like this . . .*

While Ruthie seemed to have a lock on the starting shooting guard position, Dawn seemed the logical choice to start at the point. The point guard is a basketball team's quarterback, its playmaker. Playing the far-thest away from the basket, the point guard's job is to bring the ball up the court at the start of a play or after a rebound, to choose an offensive strategy, signal it to her teammates, and then set it in motion. All this takes place quickly and on the go. A good point guard is able to see things before they happen, to anticipate the results of every possible action, the mastermind of a high-speed and unstructured game of chess.

Point players also act as extensions of the coach's mind, able to inter-pret, internalize, and execute a coach's vision on the floor. More than any other position, the point guard must also have the coach's trust, as she is continually called upon to make important split-second decisions without input from the bench. If something goes wrong, if the coach calls one offensive play and the point guard calls another, the hammer will fall on the point guard, particularly if the play goes awry.

The national team had three potential point guards, Teresa, Dawn, and Jennifer Azzi. Of the three, Teresa seemed like the least plausible choice as a starter. Jennifer had been VanDerveer's star shooting guard at Stanford and had done well playing point guard recently as well. Yet as methodical and exacting as Jennifer was in setting up an offense, Van-Derveer still appeared to prefer working with Dawn, a five-foot-six whirlwind who played with fiery abandon, improvising frequently and unapologetically, adding to the team a calculated wildness that seemed to set its opponents on edge, never knowing where Staley was going to whip her next pass.

Dawn had a weakness, however. She'd spent much of her life playing street basketball on an outdoor court in her childhood neighborhood in North Philadelphia. The pavement, coupled with her zealous style of play and a healthy dose of bad luck, had left her knees beaten up and strung with weak cartilage. In the last two years she'd had three rounds of arthroscopic surgery, the most recent taking place after team trials just several months earlier. She'd come to training camp fully recovered, though, with her knees buttressed by extra-strong leg muscles. Yet on a Thursday-night practice in Cincinnati before the team's first game as she zigzagged her way downcourt with the ball, she'd felt something give in her left knee, a painless twinge, something she had never felt before. And this was her good knee, the survivor of only two surgeries compared to the right knee's six. *Tendinitis*, she thought, downgrading the injury instantly, *has to be.*

When it came time for the Athletes and Action game, VanDerveer had put Dawn in the game, after being advised by the trainer that it was safe to do so. Dawn herself had been as upbeat as possible, cooperating with the trainer, icing her knee constantly, clinging to the idea that a tendon had simply flared up and swollen and that was all. Yet with each minute Dawn played in the Cincinnati game, it became more apparent that this was not true. She was running as quickly as ever, but passing the ball off early, shying away from driving to the hoop, avoiding putting herself in a full-contact situation with a defender, wincing slightly every time her weight came down on her right leg. Several baskets into the second half, VanDerveer pulled her out of the game, replacing her with Jennifer Azzi. Dawn had limped to the bench, shaking her head, her knee stiff and throbbing dully. It was time to face up to it: Something in there had torn.

"We're taking it cautiously with Dawn," VanDerveer had later reported to the press, "and will evaluate her daily."

This, of course, left a momentary opening for Teresa and Jennifer when it came to the point guard position. Neither player was selfish enough to actually be glad about Dawn's apparent injury. Indeed, they needed Dawn, as much off the court as on it. She served as the team's spark plug, her tiny body seemingly propelled by the force with which she chewed gum, the rapid-fire energy with which she ran her mouth.

If Dawn Staley was in a room, it was impossible not to know. At training camp she'd acted as a weight-room spotter for Jennifer, a job that for most of them meant simply standing by quietly to see if their partner required help lifting or setting down a barbell, but for Dawn entailed hovering directly over the weight bench, encouraging Jennifer at a full bellow, turning the head of the wrestlers, the cyclists, everyone in the busy but normally placid training center weight room: "C'mon Jen c'mon Jen c'mon Jen c'mon Jen C'MON C'MON C'MON!" When she shouted, her face contorted as if to mirror Jennifer's effort. When Jen, whose name Dawn pronounced "gin," made it through her last rep and accepted Dawn's help getting the barbell back on its stand, Dawn grinned as if she'd done the lifting herself. In the gym, Dawn goaded her teammates into one bet or another, speaking in the vernacular of North Philly. "How much says I can't hit this shot?" she'd call out to Teresa, dancing around a good twenty-five feet from the hoop, dribbling low to the ground, a devilish smile playing across her face. "C'mon, how much? Five dahlah? . . . One dahlah? Okay, you're on." When she missed a contested shot, she'd pay up quickly and without complaint; when she hit it, she'd march over to whichever teammate had been stupid enough to bet, snap her fingers impatiently a few times, then flip out a palm expectantly. Before the year was over, in her petty bets and higher-stakes card games, Dawn would relieve her teammates of hundreds of dollars.

If one were to take a thermal photograph of Dawn Staley playing basketball, the result would be a dynamic red blur, a fuzz of frenetic heat and sloughed-off energy, a daguerreotype of a kinetic, restless soul. In contrast, a similar photograph of Teresa Edwards would show sharply defined edges obscured by not so much as a single red blip, for Teresa was one of the most efficient players imaginable. As the others—namely Dawn, Carla, Lisa, and Sheryl—alternately cursed and high-fived their way through a game, allowing the court to serve as a theater for their passing emotions, Teresa channeled everything into her playing. When she ran the floor, it was with a silky, fluid motion, sidearming passes effortlessly but deliberately, her face reflecting an evenness that in a lesser player could be mistaken for indifference. But Teresa's careful conservation of energy paid off; she seldom lost control of the ball, seldom faltered in her playing, and often was at her best in the last five minutes of a game, just as the others began to flag.

Watching her in these moments, one understands why Coach Landers to this day calls Teresa Edwards "the greatest competitor ever to lace up a pair of shoes." He remembers having to drag Teresa to postgame press conferences after a loss at Georgia, less because she didn't want to face the media and more because to her mind there were no words when you lost. There was nothing to say, nothing to analyze; nobody could be more let down than you were.

Filling out the Athlete Personality Profile questionnaire for USA Basketball's media relations department over the summer, under "If I wasn't a basketball player I would be a . . ." Teresa had written in neat block letters, *Tennis player, because it's a very intense sport and you can only fail yourself.*

Under "The thing I would change about myself is . . ." she put down, *The mental pressure I put on myself.*

"What moment in history will you never forget?" *That moment in history,* Teresa wrote, *has not yet come.*

Over the years the girlish roundness had left her cheeks, uncovering a face that was square and contemplative. These days she kept her hair pulled back in tight cornrows, which seemed to enlarge her brown eyes and emphasize the proud expanse of her forehead. There were moments when she felt old, particularly watching her new teammates clown around or fuss about the way they looked or what they said in front of the film crew that the NBA had sent to training camp. Despite her differences with VanDerveer, this was one thing she shared with the coach: a blatant disinterest in fame, a love for basketball unfettered by vanity. ("What would you change about basketball?" *With the joy it brings me to play this game, I can't see changing anything.*)

If Teresa had been disappointed about not getting much playing time, she did not show it publicly. She was trying to be a leader, a veteran. If the coach wanted Ruthie and Dawn as her starting guards, she could do little to fight it. But the Georgia game was coming up, Nike had chartered buses to bring up her family and friends from Cairo, over 200 miles to the south; Katrina's family was coming in two buses from Charleston, South Carolina. They were going to play at home, before the people they cared about, for the first time in nearly a decade. The pride was beginning to kick in; Teresa wanted to have a great game. She was hoping VanDerveer would see fit to put her in as a starter, give her a chance to shine.

Driving across the University of Georgia campus between press appearances two days before the game, Teresa looked out the window of the team's rented van. "That's it right there, that's where we lived," she said, pointing excitedly toward a characterless brick dormitory called Oglethorpe. "Top floor of that building, on the left. I can't remember the room, though. . . . Was it 911 or 914, Tree?"

Katrina leaned forward, her face lit up by the sun. "I think 914," she said, smiling as she caught sight of the building. The memories had an indistinct quality; the campus seemed changed, the stories they told sounded as if they were almost about other people and not them. Still, they were unspeakably happy to be returning to Georgia. Playing overseas, it was easy to feel invisible, forgotten. Coming back, they suddenly had a voice. They'd joked with local reporters that Landers, famous for his disheveled appearance and frenzied coaching style, was the same guy they'd known ten years earlier, only a shade more patient and about six inches wider in the waist. Asked to characterize what made him such a special coach, Katrina said, "He treats you like a person and not just a player, which is rare."

On game day, VanDerveer assembled the players for a morning shootaround, a low-energy, game-day practice that involves mostly shooting the ball and running through plays. Dawn had missed part of their stint in Atlanta, having flown to Virginia to see her orthopedic surgeon, who had warned her that another arthroscopy was imminent. The newspaper had published a short blurb on Dawn's injury, which was still being called acute tendinitis, speculating—probably based on information from VanDerveer or from the team's media relations director—that Jennifer Azzi would replace Dawn in the starting lineup. In another hour Teresa's two busloads of supporters would leave Cairo, bound for Athens. She would not allow herself to think too hard about whether she'd start or not. It shouldn't matter, but it would feel like a blow. A homecoming after nine years and she'd be sitting on the bench? Katrina's starting spot appeared to be unchallenged, particularly since Rebecca was floundering and Carla, another post player, had done little to distinguish herself thus far. It didn't seem right, though, that Katrina would take the floor in front of the Georgia crowd without Teresa. The university had retired their numbers together, the fans who remembered them knew them almost as sisters. But VanDerveer, everyone knew, was not a sentimentalist.

The team practiced for just over an hour, when finally VanDerveer called everyone together for the customary game-day wrap-up. She consulted her clipboard as she spoke, her voice echoing through the empty Georgia Coliseum. "Sheryl, you're in tonight," she said. "Lisa, you're in . . . Katrina"—she nodded at Katrina—"Ruthie," she said, and then, as if it hadn't required any thought at all, "Teresa, you too."

If life were perfect, Teresa Edwards would have put on a show that night at the Georgia Coliseum, in front of 5,400 fans and her family, her esteemed old coach, and an opposing team full of kids who'd come to Georgia because of the legacy Teresa in part had built there. It would have been fitting if the stars had all lined up and Teresa had played a great game—the kind she'd played years back with Cheryl Miller—one that left no question that her talent was consummate with her experience and conclusively proved her worth to Tara VanDerveer, the keenest critic of all.

But the night did not pan out that way exactly. Teresa played a decent but far from transcendent game, making several assists and scoring three points. In the meantime, Sheryl Swoopes seemed to be floating, scoring 27 points, while Katrina sparked a chorus of ooohs from the crowd with a driving finger roll down the lane. The national team handed the Bulldogs the worst defeat in the team's history, 100–53, but somehow Teresa's moment never came. When it was all said and done, the only person who scored less than Teresa in the Georgia game was Rebecca, who mustered just one lay-up under the hoop.

The evening had a charged feeling to it nonetheless. The fans whooped and cheered every time Teresa or Katrina got the ball. Their families sat together in one section, wearing Nike T-shirts with ED-WARDS or MCCLAIN in bold red lettering on the back. At halftime, Coach Landers presented the two of them with University of Georgia rocking chairs, "so they'll have a place to rest their bones," he said, noting that the two were "no spring chickens." Both athletes beamed, Katrina plopping herself into the rocking chair and hiding her face as she laughed. When the game was finished, before they joined their families for a late dinner, they took questions from the hometown reporters, who did not seem to care one whit about Teresa's relatively unimpressive performance. The most significant thing, after all, was that with sixteen seasons in five different countries between them, Edwards and McClain were at long last playing at home.

Eight months had passed since Rebecca Lobo had played her last game for the University of Connecticut. Now she was coming home, and neither she nor the fans could have been more grateful. Never mind that she'd be back for all of three days; never mind that she would charge onto the floor at the Gampel Pavillion wearing colors that were *not* the Huskies' navy and white, that she was in fact expected to participate in the national team's likely chewing-up and spitting-out of the Huskies, a number of whom she counted among her best friends in the world. No, it was simply good enough that Lobo was coming back.

The women's championship game held in Minneapolis in late March had drawn higher television ratings in Connecticut than the Super Bowl had that year. In the fall of 1995 you'd have been hard pressed to find a resident of Connecticut who could not recount the game's final eleven minutes. The Huskies had been behind by six points, on the brink of letting a thirty-four-game winning streak go down in flames to the hard-driving team from Tennessee, when in stepped Rebecca Lobo, the French-braided, Victorian-skinned post player, who according to her coach had been suffering a crisis in confidence recently. Under perhaps the most pressure of her young life, Lobo had played brilliantly, sinking a lay-up, then a reverse lay-up, then a pull-up jumper from eighteen feet out, then shortly after, another jump shot. When the buzzer sounded, the Huskies had won 70–64, and Lobo catapulted herself downcourt, arms in the air, out of the thicket of teammates and dejected Tennessee players, past the refs and the coaches and TV cameras into an empty patch of hardwood, where she danced for a brief instant by herself before joining the team's center court pile-on, her index fingers pointing straight toward heaven.

A sports victory is one of life's few uncomplicated moments, a straightforward, high-voltage strike of joy that hits athletes and spectators simultaneously, a pure inclusive rush. It's the concept that fuels the multibillion-dollar sports broadcasting industry: Watching the right team win is like winning it all yourself, and the bigger the victory, the bigger the charge. Needless to say, UConn's win electrified Connecticut, a state that was still recovering from the devastation of economic recession in the late '80s, and was hungering for an uplift. When the Huskies flew back to Hartford after the game, some 2,000 fans awaited them at the airport, braving stinging late-winter winds to wave hand-lettered signs and banners. They shouted and cheered as the players loped off the plane, grinning resolutely at the crowd. Along the inter-state between Hartford and Storrs, hundreds of people had pulled their cars to the side to stand outside and wave at the team's bus as it passed by. The state's Department of Transportation had changed the comput-erized highway warning signs to blink UCONN WOMEN'S BASKETBALL and NATIONAL CHAMPIONS 1995. At the end of the road, another 8,000 sup-porters had piled into Connecticut's Gampel Pavillion along with the marching band and cheerleaders and the university's high officials for a rally. When the applause died down, the entire ensemble looked down at the women's team standing on a jerryrigged stage on the court and sang "We Are the Champions" in a single thundering voice.

Months later, after the mayor's parade in Hartford and the television talk shows, and Connecticut's long, humid summer, the newspapers be-gan to herald Rebecca Lobo's homecoming game, and the buzz reignited. The college basketball season had not yet started; the preseason game against the national team in early November would mark the Huskies' first postchampionship debut. And best of all, Re-becca Lobo would be home to play in it. Among other things, it was a happy excuse to get everyone together—players, coaching staff, and most important the hordes of Husky lovers—and get drunk on last sea-son's victory all over again.

Lobo herself was itching to feel the old feeling. Five weeks with the national team and she was beginning to revise some of her thoughts on the great sport of basketball. At the start of training camp she'd cheerily told an NBA film crew: "Basketball will never be a job for me, never. If it gets that way, it'll probably be time to get out of it."

For her, playing sports had always been a joy, an escape. She came from a family of robust, rangy athletes, the product of a six-foot-five father and a five-eleven mother. Her mother had played high school basketball in the late 50's, when "girls rules" restricted each player to a certain area of the court, thereby minimizing exertion as well as contact between players. A fifty-three-year-old middle-school counselor, Ruthann Lobo had the same hazel eyes as her daughter; her hair was wispy after the months of chemotherapy that had finally sent her breast cancer into remission; her smile was the same wide-lipped, slow-breaking gesture that endeared Rebecca to fans and photographers alike. Her posture exuded a confidence her daughter picked up early: "Just by the way she carried herself," says Rebecca, "I realized that being tall was really a great thing."

In the Lobos' small cape home in Southwick, Massachusetts, sports had always been a conduit for family communication, a way to compete, support, brawl, tease, and share. The driveway and backyard made up a kingdom to be conquered and reconquered in spirited games of touch football, whiffle ball, and basketball—the clothesline serving as both end zone and home run fence. Dennis Lobo, in teaching his three lanky kids to throw a baseball, did not distinguish between Jason, the eldest, and his two younger daughters, Rachel and Rebecca. Jason often refereed full-contact boxing matches between his two sisters, using a set of wind-chimes to signal the start of each round.

Theirs was a small egalitarian sanctuary, one that allowed young Rebecca to grow up hardy, unusually confident, and relatively naive to the societal dictates of what young girls were "supposed" to do. At the age of seven, Rebecca requested a football uniform for Christmas, which she got. At the age of eight, she proudly informed her parents that her long-range intention was to play with the New York Giants. Along the way, she shrugged off the seemingly well-meaning people who tried to push her in other directions. One elementary school teacher rebuked her for playing football with the boys; another told her she shouldn't wear jeans to school because it wasn't "ladylike." At ten, with lobbying help from her mother, Rebecca strong-armed her way onto the local boys' basketball team. Hearing that her grandmother was going to a Boston Celtics game, she dashed a letter off to Celtic president Red Auerbach in the hope that Granny Hardy would hand-deliver it. "I really like watching the Celtics play. You do a really good job," she wrote. "I want you to know that I am going to be the first girl to play for the Boston Celtics."

In the 1996 autobiography she wrote with her mother, Lobo recalls her first kiss in the sixth grade, taking place on a bench at the local rollerskating rink. Her boyfriend, the shortest boy in her class, insisted on a kiss, to which Lobo reluctantly obliged. She writes: "After we kissed, I said to myself, 'I don't want to do that again, that wasn't any big deal.' To him, I said, 'Let's go back out and *skate.*'"

She grew up to be six feet four inches with a thick, powerful body and a soft shooting touch with the basketball. In her first high school game, she breezed out and scored 32 points, upstaging every senior on her team—something she would do more or less continually throughout high school. During the off season she ran track and played softball. In the summers she picked tobacco in the fields outside Southwick. She went on to set the all-time high school scoring record for boys or girls in the state of Massachusetts. After one game during her senior year, she faced the coterie of regional reporters who'd shadowed her for four years and were now waiting with ball-point pens poised to hear how she was feeling, having just scored an unheard-of 62 points in a single game.

"Embarrassed," Lobo said, raising her eyebrows slightly as if having to explain it required some patience. "I mean, it's a team game."

Scouting reports ranked her as the number one high school center in the country; she received recruitment advances from over one hundred colleges, including a visit from Stanford's Tara VanDerveer her senior year. Lobo, an A student, would have been a logical pick for a coach like VanDerveer, who had the additional mandate of recruiting athletes who could not only play in a top-seeded Division I program but could keep up with Stanford's stringent academics as well. Whether Stanford or VanDerveer herself did not impress the Lobos—Rebecca's mother sat on the sofa and grilled each coach who came to call—it's difficult to know. Recalling VanDerveer's visit, Ruthann Lobo says firmly and without elaboration, "We knew pretty quickly that Stanford wasn't what Rebecca wanted."

What she chose instead was the University of Connecticut, which unlike Stanford and a number of other schools that had recruited her had never made it to the Final Four and had only a fair reputation academically. Still, it was ninety minutes from home for Rebecca and coached by the immediately personable and vaguely parental Geno Auriemma. Her official visit to the school had been relaxed; she'd struck up an easy camaraderie with several of the older players, laughed out loud at the jokes Auriemma cracked during practices, and had gone home nearly certain that she would end up in Storrs. Four years later, largely on the strength of Lobo's playing, UConn beat out Stanford in the quarterfinal round of the Final Four as VanDerveer grimaced on the sidelines.

———

Moving from one coach to another, one team to another, was like changing citizenship. After five weeks with the national team, Rebecca Lobo had found no entry point into her teammates' casual joking. On the bus to and from practices, she normally sat alone, staring out the window or at the pages of a book, feeling a bit more awkward with each passing day. Meanwhile, everyone else seemed increasingly at ease, even the bright-eyed Nikki McCray, who was as young and inexperienced as she was, but who bubbled over with energy, belting out Mariah Carey songs at the back of the bus and talking about her boyfriend and whatever had been on TV last night as if she'd known everyone her whole life.

Fitting in with her teammates might have been easier for Rebecca if the practices and games weren't so demoralizing. VanDerveer was clearly displeased with her playing: She was too slow, too out of shape, not aggressive enough. At practice, VanDerveer often had Rebecca do a defensive drill she'd cooked up purportedly to help her get quicker on her feet. The drill involved Rebecca guarding a chair dragged out from the sideline. With an assistant coach timing her, she was to scurry on command from the front of the chair to the back, to the side, to the other side, pretending the chair was an opponent looking to receive a pass. While Lobo did her work with the chair or the extra full-court sprints the coach regularly ordered, the other players mulled around, shooting free throws or icing their knees as practice wound down. At night in the hotel rooms she curled up on the bed and talked to Dave or her sister on the phone, half listening to the sounds of her teammates' raucous card games down the hall.

Basketball was definitely starting to feel like a job.

She had a sense that some of the others, particularly the older players, felt she didn't belong on the team, that she'd made it because she was a "name," and USA Basketball needed her to sell women's basketball to the masses, even if it was with her reputation—her clean-cut image, her white skin, and fan base—rather than the comparative level of her skills. She couldn't exactly blame them either. She often reasoned that if the fans turned up to see her play, they'd be even more titillated when they realized how much better someone like Katrina McClain was. It couldn't have been easy, coming back to the States after all these years only to find all the fans glommed onto one pretty unimpressive rookie. One *New York Times* writer had summed it up perfectly when he wrote: "The older players built the building; Lobo turned on the lights." Knowing this, Rebecca kept to herself, worrying that if she appeared too confident or too eager to fit in even, she'd confirm some suspicion that she was obnoxious or spoiled or ungrateful for the legacy those older players had indeed built.

"It's weird," she said one morning, mulling it over in front of a bowl of cornflakes. "You go from a college team, where you're talking to your friends about what may be people's first boyfriends, or whatever, to being on a team where people are talking about being married and having mortgages. I mean, going from talking about how am I going to get ten more dollars from Mom and Dad next time they visit to talking about this stuff . . . it's very different. It's weird though; now I've got a job. It's not what you do to pay your education anymore. It's different."

As the national team's chartered bus lumbered through northeast Connecticut on Interstate 84 on a Thursday night in early November, it passed the green highway sign erected the previous March that read UNIVERSITY OF CONNECTICUT, HOME OF THE 1995 WOMEN'S BASKET-BALL NATIONAL CHAMPIONS. The sign always gave Rebecca Lobo a little boost; this time she was downright grateful to see it.

The national team had left Atlanta early in the morning, flying to Chicago and then Hartford. From the airport they'd gone directly to the ESPN studios for a mandatory tour and from there to commentator Robin Roberts's home for an early but also mandatory dinner. Rebecca was aching to see her old teammates, her old coaches, her parents, who were driving down to see the game, and particularly her boyfriend, Dave. But by the time the team had loaded up and driven to Storrs, it was after 9 P.M. VanDerveer had called a team meeting for ten o'clock at the hotel. Rebecca rushed over to Dave's dorm and spent forty-five minutes with him before she ran back to the hotel, five minutes late for the team meeting, incurring a $10 fine from USA Basketball, which by her estimation was entirely worth it.

As luck would have it, the next day afforded even less time for visiting with Dave, due to Rebecca's morning practice and Dave's afternoon football practice and nighttime pregame meeting. Because the next day was a home football game, Dave's coach had moved the entire team to a hotel twenty minutes from Storrs to remove them from the "distractions" on campus, which, of course, among other things, meant girlfriends. By the time Rebecca got to his hotel, it was 10:30 P.M., a half hour before Dave's curfew. Beyond that, players were not allowed to have female guests in their rooms, which left the two of them with only a hotel lobby in which to sort out their feelings.

They'd started dating only in April, which unfortunately was precisely the point when Rebecca's life had ballooned and seemed to explode, the idylls of college life suddenly vaporized and replaced by the all-consuming fog of being a female sports personality. Dave, having just finished his junior year, had done his best to understand, shuttling Rebecca to and from the airport, listening to her talk about it all, responding patiently and often protectively, getting angry when she'd been slighted or when her agent had overfilled her appearance schedule, worrying when she began to look drawn and exhausted. He knew little about basketball—the fouls escaped him, the intricacies of an offense, he admitted, made his head spin—but this was something they were both glad for, actually, since it allowed their conversations to stray more easily from basketball. Lately, however, when they talked, it was often about Rebecca's struggle to fit in on the national team. The distance between them was further exacerbated by the fact that Rebecca was lonely much of the time, cast into an unfamiliar lifestyle, while he was still surrounded by a wide circle of friends, safely ensconced amid the ivy-covered buildings and bucolic pathways of the Storrs campus. Their phone calls recently had started to feel strained and anxious.

Finding the least crowded corner of the hotel lobby, Rebecca and Dave parked themselves on a windowsill and began to talk, their voices quiet, heads bowed. Within moments, though, there was the familiar eruption off to one side, the whispering that grew louder—*Is that? Is that her?*—and then the shuffling footsteps, the tap on the shoulder, the scrap of paper thrust in her face. As it usually happened, one autograph served to embolden an entire room; one request inspired another and another and soon a line had materialized—*Would you mind? My daughter's a big fan, this'll make her so happy*—and Rebecca Lobo's private time was over as quickly as it had begun, her first real boyfriend smiling weakly at the strangers who seemed always to get more time with her than he did. Curfew was five minutes away.

The next day, Saturday, Rebecca buried her head in her forearms on the long folding table at the national team's practice site at the University of Hartford and tried to catch a catnap before her homecoming press conference began. She could hear the journalists noisily taking their seats, the photographers fiddling with their equipment at the back of the room, someone testing the microphones nearby. So far that day, she'd led two basketball clinics for girls, sat through one autograph session, and made an appearance at a Sears store outside Hartford, where she'd smiled a lot and signed some more autographs. It was only two in the afternoon. After the press conference she still had practice, another autograph session, a weight workout, and a banquet with her old teammates ahead of her. After that she was hoping finally to get some real time with Dave, even if it was late at night again. Giving up on sleep finally, she lifted her head from the table and launched the press conference with a question of her own, "Does anyone here know the football score?"

Outside, it was a storybook fall day, leaves swirled up the streets of Storrs in small, colorful tornadoes, the sun hung cold and pallid above. In the football stadium, UConn beat Boston University by a score of 28–17; students rivered into the streets singing fight songs, a number of them with their faces painted in navy and white. At the Quality Inn, where the national team was staying, UConn alumni—presumably New Yorkers and Bostonians who'd escaped for the weekend, gray-haired men in varsity sweaters, women wrapped tightly in Connecticut scarves and wool coats—drifted into the lobby, rosy-cheeked and wound up after a morning of tailgating and an afternoon of football. "You guys better be ready for us!" a man shouted after Lisa Leslie and several of the other players, who were crossing the lobby on their way to the elevators, conspicuous in their red USA sweatsuits. "Connecticut's going to wallop you. We're going to beat you!"

Geno Auriemma once tried to characterize for a reporter the rabid insolence of Connecticut's fans: "They're schizophrenic," he said. "They want us to win so bad, to be a part of a winner so bad, they don't know how to be winners. But there is no one happier when they win, but they don't appreciate winning because they are afraid they are going to lose." For the same writer, men's basketball coach Jim Calhoun portrayed the relationship of Connecticut fans to Connecticut sports as "a passionate, passionate love affair that in a moment can turn to hatred— for a moment."

As far as Rebecca was concerned, the fans in Storrs were part of the extended jubilant family that had contributed to and shared in the spoils of a perfect season last spring. In her four years at Connecticut, she had been nothing but a beneficiary of the crowds' goodwill, the favored daughter, seldom subject to disapproval or criticism from the stands. Coming back, she'd hardly stopped to consider what it would feel like, stepping onto the floor as the opponent, which to fans and Huskies alike meant "enemy." The night before the game, however, the prospect of it socked her right in the face; a large handmade sign had been propped up on a road near the campus, calling up an old Husky threat: REBECCA AND THE NATIONAL TEAM, BEWARE OF THE DOG.

She realized it then for real; in the eyes of the public, she was a turncoat. The next afternoon she would suit up in the visitors' locker room, sit on the visitors' bench. When she scored, her points would register on the wrong side of the scoreboard. When the crowd cheered, it wouldn't necessarily be for her team, and if her team won, they wouldn't all skip their way into the locker room, laughing the way her old team used to. Instead, they would sign a few autographs, board another bus, catch another plane, and head off toward the next team to beat.

The sign brought on a secondary revelation as well: The Connecticut fans had no idea what was coming. Last they'd checked, the Huskies were the best team in the country and the much-decorated Rebecca Lobo was the best player among them. When they bragged that UConn would beat the national team—sure they'd heard of Sheryl Swoopes and maybe one or two of the others, but still, come *on*—they were serious about it. They had all been there together last spring, after all, they'd seen it happen, the giant, carefully constructed dream season, the happy-go-lucky team that coming into this weekend hadn't lost a game in over a year. What they didn't yet grasp was that Rebecca Lobo and her new teammates had come to Storrs to expertly and indecorously dismantle the whole thing.

The next afternoon, when the announcer called out Tara VanDerveer's name and she stepped forward to wave at the crowd, the boos avalanched down from the highest reaches of the Gampel Pavillion, catching everybody on the floor by surprise. The coach, dressed in a hand-knit American-flag sweater and blue slacks, bit her lip and looked straight ahead, trying to appear impervious.

Only twenty seconds earlier, Rebecca Lobo had taken her place with the Connecticut Huskies as a banner commemorating their NCAA championship was unfurled in Gampel's rafters. The crowd had seemed of an entirely different humor then, hooting and screaming for Lobo as if the Messiah herself had showed up to play. However good it had felt to be back at home—Lobo grinned widely and waved energetically at the fans—the feeling soured when she rejoined the national team's bench and the booing started, the Greek chorus of 8,000 unleashing its ire on VanDerveer.

The coach had proven herself to be a heretic, a nonbeliever, and the Connecticut faithful wouldn't stand for it. Speaking to Connecticut reporters in a teleconference from Georgia earlier in the week, VanDerveer had answered their questions patiently and frankly, offering a cautionary preview of what was to come. No, Rebecca Lobo would not be a starter. No, she was not the best player on the team. In fact, she was slow on defense, weak at the post, and needed to run the floor better. "This has been a big adjustment for Rebecca," VanDerveer told the press. "She's like a freshman and we can't wait for her to become a senior. She is definitely a role player, and I wouldn't expect her to have significant minutes [playing in the game against Connecticut]. She's not in our top seven or eight, but we hope everyone can play in every game." The coach's comments had been picked up and amplified in the newspapers across the state that week, triggering consequent editorials and letters to the editor, expressions of outrage that Lobo, the sacred cow of Connecticut athletics, was now lying at the altar of some unsmiling coach from California.

And yet, VanDerveer was right. The venerable Rebecca Lobo, the hands-down best in the nation just six months earlier, was now traveling in the company of players who could jump higher, run faster, shoot better, and generally make her look like a schoolchild in their midst. Among a lost generation of Rebecca Lobos—the Players of the Year from 1986, 1987, 1990, 1992, and 1993—who had spent years honing their games on the Europeans and Japanese, the real Rebecca was indeed slow-moving and unpolished, a rookie.

This was something Tara VanDerveer understood and Rebecca herself understood, but the fans did not. If anything, VanDerveer's comments were not just honest, but also a way of potentially relieving some of the pressure on Lobo. The coach had seen the autograph lines, the mobs who clamored just to get a glimpse of the young player. She knew they were going to be disappointed in the end, and talking to the media might have been the best way to prepare them for the hard truth that Lobo was actually fallible.

With ESPN cameras rolling, Husky banners draped on every over-hang, the game tipped off. VanDerveer started Katrina McClain, Lisa Leslie, and Sheryl Swoopes in the frontcourt. Ruthie Bolton went in at two-guard and Dawn Staley, her knee in a rubber brace, took the floor at the point. Rebecca Lobo watched from the bench, a few seats down from Teresa Edwards and next to Katy Steding, watching her old teammates Jamelle, Jennifer, Carla, and Nykeshia match up against her new ones, flanked on all sides by screaming fans. In four years the Huskies hadn't played a game without her there.

The noise got deafening quickly as Connecticut put in the first two baskets of the game. Rebecca watched Jennifer Rizzotti, the Huskies' point guard and a good friend, outmaneuver Dawn Staley with a stutter step, gunning the ball inside to Kara Wolters, the center, for an easy lay-up. After five minutes of play, Connecticut was ahead by four points and the crowd was all but hugging itself with a toldja-so sort of smugness. Rizzotti was playing as if her life depended on it. She spun out of Dawn's reach, passed the ball for a give-and-go; when the ball was back in her hands, she put up a long, arching three-pointer. Rebecca had to sit on her own hands to keep from clapping. Sheryl Swoopes, who had set Georgia on its ear with her shooting, tossed up an air ball. Meanwhile, as Rizzotti scored her eighth, tenth, and twelfth points in rapid succession, Rebecca turned to Katy, who was leaned forward on the bench, and asked, "Is it bad when I feel happy when UConn does good things?" Katy had only smiled.

After seven minutes the score was 10–8 in Connecticut's favor. When VanDerveer shouted down the bench for Katy to replace Sheryl, Rebecca gave her a little punch on the shoulder. "Go get 'em," she said.

If there was another outsider on the national team, it was Katy Steding, a forward who often kept to herself. She had made a point of chatting with Rebecca during practices, though, perhaps more able to intrepret the younger player as shy rather than standoffish, being somewhat shy herself.

Within two minutes of stepping into the game, Katy took a three-point shot from the right wing and tied the game at 14–14. Down the line, Jennifer Azzi went in for Dawn, Teresa substituted for Ruthie, and Rebecca watched as Katrina McClain and Lisa Leslie—the players she might be called upon to replace—slowly began to wreak havoc on her old friends, Katrina snaring every rebound on both ends of the court, Lisa sledgehammering her elbows left and right beneath the basket, clearing space to flush the ball overhead and into the net. The Huskies were starting to falter, a step behind now, running after Katrina, Lisa, and the others as if trying to catch an already-moving train.

It was about now that Rebecca happened to look up the bench and saw VanDerveer looking back down at her. The coach nodded, and Rebecca stood up and pulled off the T-shirt she'd worn over her uniform. Seeing her stand, the fans started to applaud as Rebecca jogged to the scorer's table, feeling glad to be back. There were nine minutes left in the half. Connecticut had cut the national team's lead to 27–21. Immediately, Rebecca grabbed a rebound and put the ball in.

For the first time in four years there was no cheering in the Gampel Pavillion when Rebecca's point dropped into the hoop. Despite the fact that she would play well that afternoon, making four of five shots, the only applause Rebecca would earn would come in the second half, when she went up for a jump shot and had it soundly rejected by her old teammate Kara Wolters, sending the fans to their feet, thrilled suddenly, it seemed, to see Lobo fail.

All told, Rebecca would play only thirteen of the game's forty minutes, seven less minutes than VanDerveer had given her at Georgia, a move that the public would interpret as an egregious show of the coach's ego, payback perhaps for the booing. When it was over, Rebecca would choke back tears, seeing her old friends exhausted on the other side of the floor, the fans pushing toward the exit without so much as a glance backward, the U.S. players coolly headed to the locker room for a shower after defeating the Huskies 83–47. Their bags were packed already. She would talk to the press ("A big piece of my heart is still with this team . . ."), eat a slice of pizza, give a kiss to Dave and a hug to her parents before she disappeared into the bus.

The evening news would narrate the story for all Connecticut that night—the coach who refused to recognize the legend, the legend who had changed sides, the college team whose undefeated dream had been succinctly laid to waste that afternoon. Indeed, a melancholy had taken root in Husky fans. It was something that Rebecca herself might have felt along with the rest of them that night in Connecticut, with the sun down and the first hard winds of winter blowing across New England, but she was far away by then, under the lonely dome of light above her airplane seat, paging absently through a magazine, the legend long gone.

5

chapter | **Sidelined**

Between November and February, they would play twenty different college teams in twenty different cities. In addition, they would spend ten days in Russia, five days in Colorado Springs, and travel to a handful of other cities to shoot commercials, lead basketball clinics, and on the rare occasion of a few days off, see their families and friends. In three months they would cover over 40,000 miles together.

Unlike their male counterparts in the NBA, the women did not particularly travel in style. They flew coach, stayed in Holiday Inns and Sheratons, hauled their own luggage from the carousel to bus, bus to hotel lobby, and so on. Each player traveled with a standard-issue red, white, and blue duffel bag the size and shape of a small trunk. In them, in addition to their streetclothes and personal gear, they carried two sets of red uniforms, two sets of practice gear (jerseys they could reverse to wear as either white or red to delineate teams during scrimmages, baggy red shorts), one set of workout gear (white USA Basketball T-shirts, blue mesh shorts), one set of warm-ups (bright red), and whichever model sneaker their respective sponsors (Converse, Reebok, Nike) had most recently supplied them with. Over the course of the year, they would each go through over a dozen pairs of basketball shoes.

When they traveled, it was with roughly one hundred pieces of luggage and a staff that consisted of one general director, one media director, one manager, one trainer, and one marketing liaison. The team director carried with her plane tickets and reservation numbers and schedules to be distributed. The media director lugged boxes of game programs that doubled as media guides, a laptop computer, a fat black appointment book, and a constantly tinkling cell phone. The manager brought with her a ball cart containing twelve balls, extra shoelaces, Super Glue to repair broken sneakers, and a pile of white handtowels, which she passed out along the bench at games. The marketing coordinator was responsible for the hundreds of Sharpie pens and cases of team photos they went through each week during autograph sessions. There was also a life-sized stand-up photo of the team in front of which girls and boys could have their picture taken, which when folded out was as long and high as a VW bug and weighed over one hundred pounds: It traveled by itself, freight class.

As they waited for their luggage to appear on the carousel, Dawn Staley liked to take bets—*one dablah? one dablah?*—on whose bag would be the first to come through.

Sheryl Swoopes not only kept her duffel stuffed to the gills, but usually carried three or four additional bags to hold, as she put it, the "spillover items," which included the booty from her frequent and prolifigate shopping expeditions and as many as ten pairs of shoes. Teresa Edwards, by contrast, was a minimalist; her duffel drooped at the corners, revealing plenty of empty space inside. As Sheryl pushed her luggage heavily across the floor of the airport arrival area on a trolley, Teresa would stroll out the door, duffel thrown casually over one shoulder.

Traveling like this, their lives would slowly twine together, compressed into the gyms and hotels and buses they shared, distilled to the point where the smallest joys—a good room-service pizza or a plane that arrived on time—could mean everything, while the annoyances—noisy hotels, cramped locker rooms, or a teammate who talked too long or too loud—were equally as acute. Slowly, though, a society grew up among them, a set of unspoken rules emerged. Nikki and Rebecca had rookie duties, cleaning up behind everyone else in the buses or locker rooms. At games, Teresa and Katrina always got lockers in the corner farthest from the door. Nobody tried to have a conversation with Carla before nine A.M.; nobody woke up Ruthie when she was napping. When Eric was traveling with Sheryl, they were given as much privacy as possible. Things like books, magazines, and CDs were lent freely, awarded to whoever yelled "I got next!" the loudest. When anybody on the team got a new hairstyle, it was mandatory that everybody else take a few minutes to fawn over it.

Their schedules were tightly built. They practiced six or seven days a week, lifted weights every Monday, Wednesday, and Friday, no matter where they were or how late their plane had arrived the night before. Several hours before each game there was the mandatory "pregame," soggy pasta, baked potatoes, white bread, and oversteamed broccoli served in the hotel restaurant at an otherwise curious meal hour, usually about 3 P.M. VanDerveer's rule was that everybody had to at least show their face at pregame, even if they chose not to partake. Lisa usually bowed over her food for a quick grace, "God is great, God is good, let us thank Him for our food. . . ." Carla often made it through two platefuls of pasta, while Sheryl went straight from pregame to McDonald's, where she protein-loaded with great gusto. On the way back to the hotel, she'd buy a Snickers bar to eat prior to tip-off.

After every practice and every game, they were required to hang around the gym and make themselves available to the media. Within the first week it was established who the media favorites were, namely Rebecca, Sheryl, and also Lisa, whose cachet with the reporters stemmed from the fact that she had a sideline career as a model and was as well versed in which purses matched which outfits as she was in the mechanics of basketball.

The reporters were taking a liking to Teresa too, not only because she'd been to three Olympics already and was the team's elder stateswoman, but because when she spoke it was honestly and with a good deal of conviction. Whereas she had avoided the media in years past, she now had a real reason to do interviews. Sitting on the sidelines with a tape recorder in front of her, she made a point of talking about the future of women's basketball, spreading the word about the budding American Basketball League and the fact that nine of the eleven of them had already committed to play in it. She was not alone in this: Another unofficial rule was that given the chance to pump the ABL in interviews, they would do it. Even Rebecca and Katrina, who had not yet decided to sign with the league, endorsed it every opportunity they got.

If they had been merely preparing for the Olympics for a year, their lives would have resembled the relatively uncluttered existences led by the swimmers and cyclists who stayed at the training center in Colorado Springs, the fixed points of their days being training and sleep, broken up by lazy communal afternoons in the TV room at the dorms. Instead, the basketball players lived like campaigning politicians; each stop on the tour was a chance to shake hands, sign autographs, and smile for the cameras; each ball they shot in front of the public became a promise they would be expected to deliver on in Atlanta. Once or twice a week, USA Basketball opened their practices to the public, usually drawing a crowd of five hundred or so. During these, Tara VanDerveer wore a microphone so that the audience could hear her comments to the team; after each one was over, the players signed autographs for twenty minutes.

The effect was wearing. Every few days, they received an updated schedule—three or four pages of travel information, appearance information, and practice plans—from Carol Callan, the team's director, which they dutifully stuck in their notebooks behind their photos of the gold medal, knowing that if they strayed from it by even five minutes, Callan would be back to issue a $10 fine.

Adaptability became key. For the taller players, namely the pencil-legged Lisa Leslie, folding one's already-sore body into an airplane seat every other day was taxing. When a large man in the airplane seat ahead of her abruptly threw his seat into full recline, she reacted with a startled "Jeezum crow!" but she didn't say more. In hotel beds she often had to sleep diagonally to fit on the mattress.

Each one of them found their private lifelines, the small things they could do in a day to stay balanced. Sheryl took baths or disappeared to get her hair done. If Ruthie was feeling low, she went running. Jennifer prowled the neighborhood for a good cup of coffee. A number of them found peace in reading the Bible. Katy wrote in a journal. Carla buried herself in a good romance novel, while Rebecca racked up her long distance phone bill. Nikki shimmied around under the headphones of her Walkman. Dawn and Lisa grabbed a deck of cards and went looking for two people to play them in spades, posturing and issuing challenges ("You can't beat us, but you can entertain us. . . .") until someone finally gave in.

Tara VanDerveer poured it all back into her coaching. Late at night she checked in with her assistant coach from Stanford, Amy Tucker, under whose care she'd left her old team, and when she was off the phone she often sat up watching scouting videotapes. She'd seen the fateful world championship game against Brazil so many times, she could recite each teams' plays before they happened; she'd scrutinized every move the Brazilian's star guard, a thirty-six-year-old former Playboy centerfold known, as most Brazilian players were, primarily by her first name, Hortência, and had diagrammed a notebook's worth of strategies to keep the ball away from her.

They would not meet Brazil until sometime in July or early August, but it was impossible not to worry about it. Ask Teresa who the best basketball player in the world was, and she would answer without pause, "Hortência." Everyone in women's basketball had heard of Hortência and the Brazilian point guard Maria Paula Silva, known as Magic Paula, who herself was thirty-four. Brazil was a moody, erratic team, one that had failed to even qualify for the 1988 Olympics and had eked out only a seventh-place finish in Barcelona, and then came back in an unexpected flash of élan two years later to slaughter the mighty Americans at the World Championships. "Given the national culture of Brazil, our athletes don't like to play defense," the Brazilian national coach once told a reporter. What this meant was that Brazil played free-spirited, carnival basketball: They could be brilliantly reckless, a concept so unusual that it intimidated the more programmatic coaches like VanDerveer.

The good news, however, was that Hortência was pregnant, due in April. Not only that, but she'd been in retirement since the World Championships. VanDerveer was probably not alone among Olympic coaches in hoping, possibly praying, that Hortência was fat and out of shape. Rumors went back and forth on whether she would come back for the Olympics or not, but given the fact that the Brazilians were as proud as they were flashy, it was likely Hortência would resurface in order to ensure the continuance of Brazil's reign over women's basketball.

Of course, the Russians felt they had their own claim on the world, having won the gold medal in 1992. VanDerveer worried about them even more than she worried about the Brazilians, since the Russians were a big team—loaded on the inside, exactly where the U.S. team was lacking. In general, her team was a fragile and still-developing entity, made up of players who next to the behemoth Russians and Chinese players would appear scrawny and unintimidating. She worried, too, that they already relied too much on Lisa Leslie and Katrina McClain to control the scoring and rebounding, even against the college teams. Katrina was the kind of athlete who readily threw herself into the fray, who *looked* for contact under the hoop. As a result, her thirty-year-old body had been beaten up over the years, her joints were worn down, her knees and hips showed the beginnings of arthritis. Lisa, while seven years younger, had a small frame and only two years of international experience, making her an easy target for bullying and susceptible to getting into foul trouble. She also suffered from chronic tendinitis in both knees. VanDerveer knew she could lose either or both of them to injuries at any point along the way. She would have to play them carefully, check in with them frequently, and in the meantime, turn her attentions to the weaker links in the chain.

Sitting on the sidelines before a shootaround at the University of Virginia, VanDerveer hovered over Dawn Staley, who had propped herself on the bottom row of the bleachers, a thick gob of bubble gum wedged in one cheek like chewing tobacco, and was lacing her shoes for practice.

"So what did we do today? Any treatments?" VanDerveer nodded down at Dawn's hurt knee, which, sheathed in a black rubber sleeve, was pulled up level with Dawn's chin.

Dawn blew a bubble, busied herself with her laces, then pushed herself off the bleachers. "Didn't have time," she told the coach, her eyes carefully averted, "but I'm gonna do it later, I will."

Tonight was Dawn's homecoming, the stop on the tour that meant the most to her, the one for which, the coaching staff suspected, she'd been denying the pain in her knee.

There was an element of fierceness to Staley. At five six and 125 pounds, she was a sprout, a twirp by basketball standards, swallowed up by her baggy uniform yet possessing the swagger of someone three times her size. When she walked, it was with a slightly pigeon-toed gait, her small body bouncing along on the balls of her feet. Perhaps as a result of her diminutive height, she kept her chin tilted slightly upward, suggesting a don't-you-pick-on-me defiance, the kind that long ago had bolstered her efforts as the only girl playing street ball in her inner-city neighborhood with guys with names like Funky Rod, Bub, and Big Herb.

When it came to pain, particularly in the knees, Dawn's tolerance was high. She loved to play enough so that she didn't care if her knee's cartilage was in tatters, but she also knew that if she didn't look after it, she'd pay for it later. When the rest of the team left Virginia the next day, Dawn would remain to have the knee she'd injured in Cincinnati dredged by the doctor who'd been treating her since college. The team's trainer had told VanDerveer that so long as Dawn didn't mind the pain, playing another game wouldn't do any more damage to the knee. "What pain?" she had said, wanting badly to hold out until the Virginia game before surgery. "There's no pain, not really. No pain."

On game days, warm-ups tended to be a casual, unregulated fifteen minutes of doing whatever it took to get the body ready to play. Today, Jennifer was running slow laps around the court, while Ruthie light-heartedly guarded an assistant coach. Sheryl, Lisa, and others were still strewn out along the bleachers, adjusting ankle braces and signing autographs for the several young kids who'd managed to find their way into the gym despite VanDerveer's rule that practices be free of all distractions.

Taking her leave of the coach, Dawn limped stubbornly onto the court and commanded the far hoop for herself, pausing to tug once on the knee band, then to adjust the purple scrunchie that pulled her hair into a shrublike ponytail high on her head. She chomped ferociously on her gum, bounced the ball in front of her several times, then popped it cleanly into the hoop.

She had been eighteen years old in 1989, arriving at the manicured and stately Virginia campus from her high-rise neighborhood in North Philly. It had been like the start of a giant, colorized dream for both Dawn and the then nearly invisible Virginia Cavaliers. Before Staley came to town, a women's basketball game at Virginia was lucky to get a thousand spectators. By the time she left, they were calling the continually sold-out 9,000-seat University Hall "Dawn's House." She became something of a cult figure around campus too, the can-do guard who turned it all around for the women's team. When it was discovered that a female student who was threatening to jump from the top of a Charlottesville parking garage happened to be an avid Cavaliers fan, Dawn Staley was called in and successfully talked her down.

Despite a harrowing freshman year academically—jumping from Philadelphia's blighted public school system to one of the country's most elite universities was no small trick—Dawn had persevered, working with a tutor and depending on the patience of her coach, Debbie Ryan, as she struggled to meet NCAA grade requirements. Soon she was pulling down solid grades, and the Virginia nobodies became somebody, having impertinently elbowed their way into the rarefied air of the Final Four, thanks mainly to Dawn's irrepressible verve as a high-scoring guard. Her junior year, Virginia suddenly found itself in the championship game, eye-to-eye with the notorious flesh-eating team from Tennessee. The score was tied with less than five seconds left to play; the Cavaliers had possession of the ball.

During the time-out, Coach Ryan had called her final play: "Get the ball in to Dawn and get out of the way."

The memory of what came next is forever burned in Staley's mind: She streaked down the court, dodged her opponent, caught the pass perfectly, flipped up a lay-up. The ball had pinballed inside the rim and bounced back out. Virginia lost the championship to Tennessee in overtime, 70–67.

The next year it would happen all over again, this time in the semifinals against Stanford, when Dawn's last-second shot missed its mark and her college career ended without its Holy Grail, the NCAA title. If there was something missing from her life, it was the Big Win, the kind of crowning moment she'd heard the others talking about. Sheryl had won a national championship, so had Rebecca, Carla, Katy, and Jennifer. Teresa and Katrina had their Olympic medals. Dawn had left Virginia with more career steals to her name than any other player in NCAA history, male or female. She'd been named Most Outstanding Player in two consecutive NCAA tournaments; she'd been *Sports Illustrated*'s Player of the Year; she'd had her number retired. But still, she had never done a victory lap on a national stage.

Nor did she have the opportunity to play professionally in the U.S. As Dawn swept most of the awards for top female player of the year, her equal on the men's side was a seven-foot-one, 305-pound Brobdingnagian out of Louisiana State named Shaquille O'Neal. In the months following their departure from college basketball, O'Neal landed a $40-million, seven-year contract with the Orlando Magic and a reported $20-million endorsement deal with Reebok, while Staley signed a contract for less than $50,000—a low offer even by women's professional standards—and moved to Spain.

She played abroad for three years, jumping from Spain to Brazil to Italy to France, more or less equally miserable in each place, the homesickness dulling her enthusiasm for basketball. Her first six months in Spain, she never completely unpacked her suitcase, certain that at some point things would get bad enough that she'd give in and move home. Once or twice she even packed up and caught a cab for the airport, but always there was one thing that made her turn around—the possibility of playing in the '96 Olympics, her last grasp at the Big Win. The selection committee had told her point-blank at the 1992 trials that she'd been scratched from the squad due to her lack of international experience, so here she was, getting a healthy dose of it. She got tougher as an athlete; she learned to take risks, wowing the foreign crowds with zinging, no-look and behind-the-back passes.

Off the court she fought off loneliness by digging into the trove of Oodles of Noodles and prepackaged macaroni and cheese she'd brought from the grocery stores back home. She begged friends to send care packages with videotaped movies and NBA games so she'd have something to do when she wasn't playing basketball. She spent thousands of dollars on transatlantic calls, talking to her boyfriend, Lance, in Philadelphia, her mother, her sister, and the host of old friends and teammates she liked to call her "peeps," for "people."

Dawn's peeps meant everything to her. Inexorably bored when she was alone, she sought out companions at every turn, if only to engage them in trash talk or a meaningless wager. Connecting with people was what she treasured most about the game of basketball, particularly about playing point guard, a position she'd moved into after college, playing for teams that didn't need her to score the way the Cavaliers had: You had to live a little bit inside your teammates' heads. One of Dawn's more exalted offensive moves was to drive to the hoop and, just as the opponent leapt to block, to casually heave the ball backward over her left shoulder in an act of blind faith that stunned opponents and crowds simultaneously as Dawn's small body continuing to hurtle forward, mouth open, face frozen in surprise as she waited for the explosion of applause that would confirm that her sixth sense was right, that the ball had landed in a teammate's hands.

The shootaround was brief that day, ending as most practices did, with the players dispersing into small clumps around the sidelines, uncuffing knee and ankle braces, liberating the feet from sweaty shoes and socks, slipping them into the sports sandals most of them wore between practices, and dissolving into idle chatter.

The next step was to corral everyone onto the bus to get back to the hotel, which always proved a harder task than one would imagine. The players spent too much time on buses as it was, and thus nobody wanted to sit on the bus for even five minutes more than she had to, waiting for the others to finish their media interviews or grab a soda from the vending machine or pull away from a group of fans. Whatever the delay, they'd rather be stuck in the gym than stuck on the bus, but loitering in the gym inevitably led to more distractions—by the time Jennifer was finally ready, Katrina was now not—and more waiting.

The half hour or so following practice, therefore, tended to devolve into an elaborate exercise in dillydallying, and tonight was no different. The Virginia team had arrived for its own shootaround, and immediately Dawn threw herself into their midst, exchanging high-fives and milling about as if at a cocktail party. Carla, a lover of anything social, jumped right in behind Dawn.

"Look at those muscles!" Carla said, grabbing the bicep of Tammi Reiss, a blond assistant coach and former teammate of Dawn's whose sleeveless shirt revealed a pair of deeply tanned and sinewy arms.

Reiss smiled brightly. "I'm trying to get like Ruthie over there," she said, jerking her chin in the direction of the iron-bodied Ruthie Bolton, who was at center court fiddling obliviously with the microphone for the arena's PA system.

"Aw, give up on that!" Dawn interjected, shaking her head at Reiss. "Ruthie's got muscles in her *face*."

This got a big laugh from Carla, who continually fed off Dawn's wise-assing. It was true too, Ruthie was cut like no other player on the team; her legs were short and steely, her biceps rode high on her arms, like polished apples, jumping upward anytime Ruthie made a fist. Her neck seemed to sink into a deep knoll between her powerful shoulders, and as Dawn had suggested, her face, set off by sunken brown eyes and prominent lips, was rounded and smooth and strong-looking too.

A native of Mississippi, she was the daughter of a Baptist preacher, on the younger end of a close and loving family of twenty children, all the product of the same marriage. She was deeply religious as well, her soft-spoken morality seeming to anchor the people around her. In a room with her teammates, Ruthie was sometimes the easiest person to overlook if only because she seemed to have no need to draw attention to herself. She attributed her mild manners to the lessons she'd learned growing up in a large family without much money, sharing a bedroom with four sisters. "In my family," said Ruthie, "there were times when there wasn't enough ice cream to go around and so you just learned to settle for a Popsicle instead. You were glad for whatever came your way." When somebody on the team had a problem, they often went to Ruthie, who offered counsel in a mellifluous voice.

She was also a singer. Having located all the proper switches and plugs for the University Hall PA system at that moment, Ruthie clicked on a microphone and drew in close with her duet partner, Nikki McCray. In the early days of the tour, they'd started singing primarily to pass the empty hours spent traveling, discovering quickly that Ruthie's powerful alto combined nicely with Nikki's soprano trill. Ruthie schooled Nikki in the soulful gospel songs she sang with her family back home; Nikki taught Ruthie the words to her favorite Celine Dion and Whitney Houston songs. Recently they had turned their attention to the national anthem, figuring that if the colleges they visited would allow it, they might perform together before some of the games. Holding the microphone between them, they traded lines back and forth, Ruthie singing one and Nikki singing the next.

"O-oh, say, can you see . . ." Ruthie boomed, her voice vibrating deeply through the arena.

Nikki's chimed in sweetly: "By the dawn's early light . . ."

Ruthie: "What so proudly we hail . . ."

Nikki: "At the twilight's last gleaming . . ."

And so forth.

As they finished, Ruthie blowing the lid off the "home of the brave" line with Mahalia Jackson–like force, everyone in the gym sputtered into applause. The Virginia players stopped their stretching. Sheryl and Rebecca clapped from the bleachers, Teresa had nudged the headphones of her disc player up in order to listen, Lisa let out a big hoot of approval. Both singers smiled broadly.

In an instant, Carla McGhee stood before them. Carla was something of the team mother, patting Dawn's unruly hair into place or straightening the collar on Jennifer's shirt.

"Nikki girl, you're screeching a little bit," she said now, tilting her head at both of them. "It's too high. 'And the rockets' red glare . . .' That line."

"Too high?" said Nikki, taking the mike out of Ruthie's hands.

"You're trying just a little too hard,"

"I should lower it a little bit?"

Carla held up her hand and pressed her index finger and thumb together. "Just a pinch."

Nikki flicked on the mike and tried the line again, her voice lifting through the gym: "And the rockets red glaaaare . . ." She stopped and looked at Carla, who had put her fingers in the air again, her face scrunched up in a pained expression.

"Another pinch, Nikki," she said. "Just a little lower."

Nikki sang the line one more time, evidently meeting with Carla's approval. But now Sheryl, the team's other mother, had come over from the bleachers. She was wearing a black Nike baseball jacket; her hair hung in short braids around her face. "Ruthie, you're sayin' your lines wrong. It's '*whose* broad stripes and bright stars,' not '*who* broad stripes and bright stars.' And it's '*bombs* bursting in air.' " She laid a hand affectionately on Ruthie's shoulder. "You keep singing 'bomb bursting in air.' It's bombs, a bunch of bombs, okay?"

"Bombs," Ruthie repeated. "Okay, I got it."

They'd started on a full run-through of the anthem, when their voices were preempted by VanDerveer's, which needed the help of no microphone—"*Move it out!*"—as the coach swept through the gym. Practice had been over for twenty minutes, and without a veritable earthquake from VanDerveer, who had finished her postpractice business and had her sights set on an afternoon of watching videos at the hotel, the players would have stayed in the gym all day.

The coach stood by the door and windmilled her arms impatiently, shouting like a harried girl-scout leader trying to get her minions out of the woods. "Kaaaaay! Round it up! If you get on the bus now, we'll have time for a nap! Come *on!*"

Dawn's peeps were coming from Philly, four busloads of them brought down by Nike. It was one of the perks shared by the six Nike players on the team: Dawn, Sheryl, Lisa, Teresa, Katrina, and Ruthie. While Converse (sponsoring Katy, Nikki, and Carla) and Reebok (Rebecca and Jennifer) treated their players well, paying for their apartments in Colorado Springs and furnishing rental cars for them when they were there, Nike outdid everyone with its lavish marketing budget. There was a certain status attached to being a Nike player. The company paid top dollar to hype its athletes in cutting-edge, stylishly directed television ads; its sponsorship deals were often hefty multiyear contracts; when under the company's care, the athletes were treated as royalty. Sheryl, Dawn, and Lisa had gone to New York to shoot a television ad directed by Spike Lee in October.

Nike players, in return, tended to bear a Mafia-like allegiance to the company. In the moments they were not mandated to wear their USA Basketball gear (manufactured by Nike's rival, Champion), they wore Nike hats, Nike jackets, Nike sweatshirts and socks, and, of course, shoes. Many of them wore a diamond-studded replica of the company's logo, the Swoosh—a gift a number of Nike's female endorsees had received at the Women's Sports Foundation banquet earlier in the fall—on gold chains around their necks.

It was less the diamonds and advertisements, however, that won their loyalties and more the fact that Nike acted like family, opening its coffers to fetch players' relatives and friends for homecoming games in as many buses as they could fill, that it bought every bussed-in supporter a ticket to the game and finished it up with an extravagant reception afterward. For someone like Dawn Staley, this was immeasurably appreciated.

As the national team warmed up an hour before the game at Virginia, Dawn paced in small circles, keyed up but—she insisted—not nervous. Outside, rain was coming down in torrents. Her family was due at any moment. All around her, her teammates shot balls and stretched on the floor, which was painted in the Cavaliers' orange and blue. The seats in University Hall were still mostly empty, spectators just beginning to drift in with their hot dogs and brimming sodas. Dawn found a ball and dribbled it around a few times, a pretense of a warm-up.

Lisa Leslie was stretching on the floor nearby, her legs splayed to either side. She was looking off into the stands. "Hey, Dawn, are we going to know who your peeps are because they got the same head as you?"

It was a running joke among them: Dawn liked to sit in airport lounges and spout off about who had the biggest head on the team. ("Definitely Katrina," she'd announce. "Katrina's got a meat head, but Rebecca's head is pretty big too, don't y'all think?") Katrina had bitten back, however, proposing that Dawn's preoccupation with the size of people's heads was easily explained by the size of Dawn's own head, which everyone had to agree was not small.

"Ha!" Dawn said to Lisa.

"Dawn, I'm not kidding. Do you see your head over there? It's huge! You can't see it?" Lisa pointed a finger toward the bleachers.

"Whah?" Dawn squinted to see.

"Do you see that thing? The Swoosh thing that says GO, DAWN?"

There, in the stands, was Dawn's head, a growing, bobbing sea of heads, in fact. Unbeknownst to Dawn and unaware of the team's joke, Nike had replicated a life-sized photo of Dawn's face and put it on hundreds of cardboard mountings for the fans to wave like signs. Figuring it out, Dawn threw her hands over her eyes and groaned. The others, Katrina in particular, started cackling. Jennifer trotted over to the stands and borrowed one of the heads from a fan. Dawn seized the head and inspected it up and down. It had been taken from a team photograph in which Dawn's face was lit by a mischievous half-smile, her hair in the trademark scruffy ponytail. After a few seconds of close scrutiny, she handed the head back to Jennifer, shaking her head dismissively, announcing to entire group, "That ain't me! That thing has no blemishes on it!"

The game began with Dawn's peeps filling an entire section of the arena, wearing Nike-furnished STALEY T-shirts and waving their cut-out heads in slow unison, a swaying gospel choir of happy-faced Dawn Staleys. Nikki and Ruthie sang the national anthem for the 6,000 fans, eliciting a tremendous wave of applause and a self-satisfied smile from Carla McGhee, particularly as Nikki floated gracefully through "the rocket's red glare." VanDerveer sent Dawn, Katrina, Nikki, Ruthie, and Lisa in as starters.

Shooting the ball that night, Dawn seemed to lose her poise, sending off wild, looping shots that didn't have a prayer of going in, but when it came to doing what a point guard is supposed to do best—make her teammates look good—she performed perfectly, running the floor with characteristic energy, the limp just barely discernible in her left knee. She made crisp passes, finding Nikki and Ruthie open for three-point shots. In other moments she forced the ball inside, through the tangle of her opponents' legs, to Lisa, who banged in to score again and again on the smaller, clearly weaker college players.

When it was all over, the national team had romped over the Cavaliers 96–68. Dawn, hearing at the press conference that she'd had 12 assists, cocked her head and looked at the room of reporters and shut one eye in mock disbelief. "Twelve assists—wow—I don't think I ever had twelve assists in University Hall. . . . Who was keeping stats tonight? Whoever he was, I'd like to take him on the road with me."

For Teresa, the statistics that night painted a gloomy portrait. It had been another evening spent as a second stringer for her, watching from the bench as Ruthie and Dawn controlled the backcourt, the prospect of ever proving herself to the coach growing more distant with each point the team scored without her. VanDerveer had used Jennifer as backup point guard, turning to Teresa, it seemed, only when the others clearly needed a rest. Jumping in and out of the game for spurts of only a few minutes made it nearly impossible for Teresa to get into the flow of the game, to find her own rhythm in the stampede of bodies up and down the court. Instead, in what was beginning to seem like a self-fulfilling prophecy, she played a solidly mediocre game, leaving the court with a disheartening sense of what the statistics would later confirm: VanDerveer had given her less playing time than any other person on the team.

One thing statistics couldn't do, however, was predict the future. As Dawn chatted merrily with reporters in the Cavaliers' press room, basking in the glow of her homecoming, her knee, red and wrinkled beneath a monstrous bag of ice, was beginning to ossify, the cartilage inflamed and stiff. The arthroscopic surgery would throw her off more than usual, and there was more bad luck beyond that. It would be a full three months before she played another basketball game.

6

Little Girls Need Big Girls

chapter

At Stanford, the bleachers teemed with girls. It was a Thursday night, and the national team had just flown across the country from Virginia. Down on the floor, the players spread out in a loose circle and followed Ruthie and Jennifer in stretching. The girls in the stands watched every move. When Sheryl at one point bent down to tie an errant shoelace on her gleaming white Air Swoopes, a heavyset black girl, a high-schooler decked out in chunky gold jewelry and a yellow and white basketball jersey, rose to her feet, cupped her hands around her mouth, and let out a long, plaintive howl, "Swoooooopes!"

This seemed to spark a movement among the others, who one by one joined in until the chanting crested at full volume, the name blurring to the point where a bystander might begin to understand that it signified not just the woman with the sneaker, not just the sneaker, but the whole wondrous notion of girls getting rowdy together in a gym: Swooooopes! *Swoooooooooopes!* They drummed their own sneakers on the bleachers, the sound of it mounting like a storm coming on. They were white girls and black girls and Latina girls. Most appeared to be in either junior high or high school, many wore their team jerseys and sat with teammates and coaches, others came with parents or friends. There were boys there too, but few enough that they almost got lost in the girls' steady rioting, which did not subside until finally Tara VanDerveer switched on her microphone to introduce the team.

The microphone was quickly becoming a sticking point for VanDerveer, who was expected to wear the wireless on her collar throughout the open practices, which were held roughly once a week. While she understood the importance of these events—one look at the group of 1,100 girls who had turned up in Palo Alto just to see the team practice confirmed it for her—VanDerveer felt the microphone detracted from her ability to coach as she normally would. She was not a screamer, she did not curse at her players, but she did want the ability to speak freely to them. If she wanted to chastise Nikki for not setting up her shot or Katrina for not boxing out, or whatever it was that day, she wanted to do it without having to think twice about everything before she opened her mouth, worrying that it would create a wrong impression. As her comments to the Connecticut press regarding Rebecca had proven, VanDerveer was not given to censoring herself. She had told USA Basketball officials that she would give speeches to the kids in the stands, she would give interviews until she was blue in the face, but coaching was sacred. The practice at Stanford would be the last time VanDerveer wore a microphone.

Each player, as presented to the audience by the coach, was an exemplar of something to strive for:

"This is Rebecca Lobo," said VanDerveer, causing the crowd to burst into applause as Rebecca stepped forward. When the noise died down, VanDerveer added, "Rebecca has been to visit the President. Rebecca was on David Letterman. Basketball has brought her all sorts of attention. She graduated Phi Beta Kappa . . . does anyone know what that is?"

She continued. "This is Ruthie Bolton. I always say that discipline and hard work are what it takes to play great basketball. Do you want to see some real discipline?" VanDerveer turned to the line of players to her left. "Ruthie, get out here and show them your push-ups."

Dutifully, Ruthie dropped to the floor and executed ten flawless, military-style pushups, her hands positioned close together, the muscles in her arms popping up and down with the effort. The girls counted along, "Eight! Nine! Ten!" and then burst into a fresh round of cheering.

Wherever they went, the eleven of them were offered as role models for the masses, and particularly for the increasing numbers of sports-minded girls who poured into games and practices to see the team play. It was not an entirely new situation for any of them, having come from popular college programs where signing autographs and attending community events were standard. But the scale of it—the size of the crowds and the almost desperate way people, kids and adults alike, waved posters and bits of paper in their faces for autographs, the clamor of hands that reached out and tried to snare a handful of their uniform or touch their shoulders as they walked to and from the locker room—was something nobody had ever witnessed before.

As Sue Levin, Nike's manager for women's sports marketing who had negotiated the company's sponsorship of Ruthie, Lisa, Katrina, Teresa, and Dawn, once said, "Little girls don't have sports heroes, but if you build them they will come."

Lisa considered the role-model business a responsibility. If the world was paying attention to them, if little girls were hoping to emulate the women on the team, well, then, they had some things to live up to. "We have to present ourselves well," she said. "We have to be tough on the court and polite when we're not playing, give the girls something to aspire to."

Teresa put it more succinctly, referring precisely to the hole she and her teammates had felt in their own young athletic lives: "Little girls," she said, "need big girls to look up to."

For the most part, presenting themselves well wasn't terribly taxing. They were an exceedingly well-behaved group off the court. (A hotel housekeeper had accosted several players gratefully in a hallway one day, remarking on the used towels hung tidily on their racks, the carefully stacked piles of clothing: "Y'all are *neat.*") Playing basketball, however, they bullied, thrashed, threw elbows and slammed into one another beneath the hoop. A number of them wore mouth guards that distorted their faces into permanent frowns; between plays they sometimes made gross sucking sounds as they cleared out the saliva. They wore baggy practice gear that made their bodies appear bigger than they already were. They passed the ball back and forth and hurled their shots; if an opponent's shot went up, they leapt up to bat it back down. They dripped so much sweat that a ball girl had to swab a puddle off the floor every time someone fell down. In short, they played basketball. When things went well, they shouted and slapped one another hard on the butt. What they did together on the court went against just about every traditional notion of what women were supposed to do.

And the little girls were coming in droves to watch them do it.

The practice at Stanford was swift and businesslike. VanDerveer, hyperaware of the microphone, kept her comments to a minimum, pushing the team through a number of drills. At one end of the court, the team's frontcourt players—Katy, Katrina, Sheryl, Rebecca, and Lisa—worked on offenses with one of the team's two assistant coaches; at the other, the guards—Teresa, Ruthie, Nikki, Jennifer—ran through in-bounds plays. Dawn had stayed back in Virginia and was scheduled to have arthroscopy on her knee the next morning. The doctors had predicted she would be out for three weeks. Carla had gotten news that her grandmother had died and had flown to Peoria for the funeral. She would miss two games.

On the polished floor of Stanford's Maples Pavilion, the rest of the world could well have disappeared before VanDerveer noticed. When she was coaching, it was with an out-of-sight out-of-mind philosophy. "The stands could fall down around me and I wouldn't know it," she acknowledged. If Dawn was gone, Dawn was gone. Same went for Carla. The players in her game were the players who stood in front of her; the only emotion was the emotion of the moment. She stood at midcourt in her blue pants and white tennis shirt, her shoulders slumped slightly forward after all the air travel and the decidedly unpleasant trip to Connecticut and directed traffic on both ends of the court, shouting alternately at one group, then the other. "More pressure on the ball, Nikki! Box out, Katy, box out!"

When the team transitioned into halfcourt four-on-four, Lisa Leslie drove the ball inside and made a dazzling spin move around Rebecca for a lay-in, prompting a girl sitting in the second row to make an elated and spontaneous pronouncement: "She is hoopin' her skinny butt!" The girl, pleased by the chorus of "uh-huhs" that went up around her, stood up on the bench and performed a quick, hip-wiggling victory dance, collected high-fives from her neighbors on either side, and plopped herself back down again.

Next came the autograph session, which involved the athletes toweling off, grabbing a drink, and then folding themselves down behind long tables in groups of two or three, while the girls and boys attempted to form a line at each table with their T-shirts and basketballs and team photographs and basketball shoes ready to be signed. The concept was that the players would sign for twenty minutes, during which time the kids would scuttle from one table to the next in an orderly fashion, presumably getting all nine signatures by the end. In actuality, the session took on a free-for-all aura that was part rock concert, part playground: 1,100 people, nine players, and twenty minutes equaled pure bedlam. There was pushing, there was shoving, toes got stepped on, team photos got crumpled and torn as the crowd heaved forward at the athletes' tables.

"Stand back! Stand back or she leaves!" a uniformed security guard screamed at the shoving mob of kids in front of Rebecca Lobo, who sat placidly holding her pen, an ice pack balanced on either knee. Sheryl Swoopes did her own kind of policing, primly directing line-cutters back to the outer reaches of the crowd.

"How long ago did you win?" a pigtailed girl asked Jennifer Azzi over the noise, referring to Azzi's NCAA title at Stanford.

"Five years," Jennifer told her.

"Five years ago?" the girl took a second to think it over "Oh, I was three."

In the far corner, a secondary explosion took place when Teresa Edwards took her shoes off and autographed them for a high-school girl who said she played Teresa's position. "I'm a guard too! I'm a guard too!" came the chorus. "Come on, I'm a guard!"

Teresa grinned at them all and shrugged her shoulders good-naturedly. "Sorry kids, I got only one pair."

While most of the fans' requests were harmless, the cumulative effect could be overwhelming. Personal time seemed to melt away when behind each girl there was another girl, or boy, wanting a smile or a handshake, and suddenly the hour between practice and dinner had passed before they could get out of the gym or the hotel lobby. Still, it was impossible to say no.

That female players worried actively about what people thought of them bore stark contrast to the prevailing indifference among male basketball players, even on the college level. After all, here was a culture that routinely lionized men for their athletic performances without holding them accountable for off-the-court behavior that sometimes included wife-beating, drug use, chronic gambling, and promiscuity. (Wilt Chamberlain, for example, once estimated that he'd slept with 20,000 different women over the course of his fourteen-year NBA career.) And while there were in fact many male role models, it was almost expected that male athletes who seemed larger than life on the court would conduct their personal lives excessively as well. Meanwhile women players were governed by a different set of standards.

Rebecca recalled being at an awards banquet where an older male guest spotted her at the bar and made a crack that she'd better not be drinking alcohol, despite the fact that she was above the legal drinking age. "It's like people expect us to be angels," she said. "Would the guy have said that to Charles Barkley? I don't think so."

If the women were sometimes treated as kid sisters to their male counterparts, it was something most of them were used to, having for the most part grown up as the lone girl on the court. Jennifer Azzi remembered showing up to play pick-up at a gym in her hometown in Tennessee—this being after winning a national championship, after a year playing abroad in Italy—standing on the sidelines in her shorts and basketball shoes, ball crooked under her arm, while some guy passed by and said, "Waiting for your boyfriend?"

The basketball court, particularly the rec center and playground courts open for pick-up, was a male preserve. Usually, Jennifer and some of the others on the team confirmed, the best way to deal with it was to jump in and shock one's detractors just by showing them what you could do. In general, a public court was where you could find scads of people who believed that women's basketball was slow and unexciting, and if it came down to a debate, they would often rest their case on one simple fact: Women, as a rule, do not dunk the ball.

And what is basketball without the dunk? The dunk, that hallelujah to male strength, the verb in basketball's sentence, the meat in its sandwich, the exalted moment in which a fellow unleashes himself on the hoop in a flourish that because an expression of ultimate power over the air, the net, and one's opponents, as he literally rises above them all to deliver the ball with one swift and punitive blow. *Slam!* Schoolboys aspire to it, spectators ogle it, and it alone reels in millions of dollars each year in corporate sponsorship and endorsement deals, not to mention inflated salaries for those able to articulate it most breathtakingly. Witness Michael Jordan, Inc. Witness the Shaq Attack. There is nothing subtle about the dunk. It is, in many ways, an extremely American gesture, an act of pure triumph.

Lisa Leslie was one of just a handful of American women, most of them six two or better and relatively lightweight, who could dunk the ball. Lisa had been dunking since the ninth grade. Given an alley-oop, she could suction the ball right out of the air with her right hand and usher it to the basket, over the basket, her fingers grazing the rim just as gravity started to pull her back to Earth. Throughout the national team's tour, when she dunked it was usually during warm-ups before practice or a game, and most often it took everyone by surprise. Touching down to an appreciative roar from the spectators, Lisa didn't smile, didn't take a bow. Instead, she just kept running. She was quickly becoming famous for her dunking, not because her dunks were particularly awe-inspiring—in earnest, they were quiet dunks, just-barely-above-the-rim dunks—but because she was pushing the envelope of what people expected women to do.

For this, people would chorus, "You go, girl!" and hope that she would do it again.

But dunking was becoming an oddly political issue in women's basketball. On the surface, yes, it was an undeniable crowd-pleaser, and with the ABL's future still tenuous, Lisa was dunking at a time when the sport perhaps most needed to enthrall its fans, to sway the critics who were so quick to point out the absence of above-the-rim play in the women's game. Yet introducing the dunk into the women's game carried with it a potentially dangerous backlash. The truth remained that dunking or no, women would never play the same kind of basketball that men did. Nor, many would argue, should they be expected to. To encourage and celebrate the dunk as a milestone in the women's game, some believed, put female players in distinctly unfair territory, throwing the door open to further comparisons between them and the men, which given the essential physiological differences between genders, doomed the women always to lose.

Tara VanDerveer believed that women did not need to be compared to men when it came to the way they played basketball. She found herself patiently explaining this over and over again to the media and to the fans, who seemed to cling to the idea that women were moving toward a point where they might play shoulder to sweaty shoulder with the men of the NBA. "Comparing them is not productive," she would say. "It's a whole different game. The women are not big enough to play basketball like men. They don't have the hormones, that's what I say."

Yet there was a curious power in dunking. If Lisa Leslie regularly dunked during national team games, it was likely the crowds would get bigger, and the buzz would grow. The more she was publicized for her dunking, the closer she came to being a sideshow, the more dunking would become the thing people came to see, expected to see, and the more Lisa stood to eclipse her teammates. Whether this was a good or bad thing for women's basketball remained entirely debatable.

The point was somewhat moot, however, as VanDerveer had asked Lisa not to dunk during national team games. The main reason for this was that she did not want Lisa to get injured if she were accidentally undercut—a large price to pay for being showy. Women were not used to being dunked on, and therefore might not know enough to get out of the way, she said. Maybe, just maybe, if Lisa found herself alone at the basket during a game, she might dunk then, but otherwise she was to limit the dunking to warm-ups when she had the hoop to herself.

Lisa liked to dunk for the girls at open practices, who unfailingly responded with a collective, delighted wail. "If those girls see me doing something that people think women can't do," said Lisa, "Well, then, maybe they won't listen the next time somebody tells them women can't do something."

Even without an audience, dunking was fun. Lisa's teammates loved it when she dunked. Nobody thought much about the politics aside from VanDerveer and others who saw the game more analytically. Caught up in the moment, when Lisa threw the ball down as she did several times a week during the college tour, it was a shared victory for all of them—part show, part exuberant release, a message to the world that said: Don't you forget me.

Tara VanDerveer was home, which was the perfect place to be less than a week after the Connecticut debacle. In northern California she was virtually a celebrity. The crowds didn't just accept her, they liked her, loved her even. For the three days the team was in Palo Alto, VanDerveer slept in her own bed in her house in Mendocino. She got her hair cut and visited the dentist. She dropped in on a Stanford practice, though because NCAA rules governed that she could not address the team or offer any overt coaching, she had to sit in the stands quietly, watching from a distance but ferociously taking notes on what she saw—all of which, one imagined, would get delivered back to the team through Amy Tucker, the Cardinal's interim coach.

On game day, VanDerveer was in high spirits, directing the national team through a weight workout at Stanford's facility for varsity athletes, an airy, open room packed with monstrous-looking Cybex machines, in addition to the more antiquated Nautilus and Universal equipment, and a broad turf-carpeted stretching area that looked out onto a rich green soccer field.

After six weeks under VanDerveer's daily command, the players' already-toned bodies were beginning to striate and warp with muscles added to muscle. The 140-pound Jennifer eased herself under a barbell and bench-pressed 120 pounds, not once but twelve times. Ruthie, who weighed 150, slid onto the bench next and punched out twelve reps at 145 pounds.

"Knock it out, Ruthie. Knock it out, knock it out," VanDerveer chattered. "Keep working hard . . ."

Lisa, her head swaddled in a red bandanna, strutted around with her Walkman thumping a heavy bass line. Spotting the coach hunched over Ruthie on the bench press, she halted her dancing and tapped up her headphones a half inch. "Hey, Tara," she said, calling across the room. "We got a game tonight, you know."

VanDerveer looked in Lisa's direction and gave a rare smile. "Oh, I know," she said dryly. "I'm excited."

She told them the same thing after every win, which was that beating college teams meant nothing. Each game was a learning opportunity, a chance to play hard every last second, even if the opposing team got tired and started to flounder after fifteen minutes, as most of them had thus far. So far they'd beaten Athletes in Action by 26, Georgia by 47, Connecticut by 36, and Virginia by 28. VanDerveer listed her expectations so often that any one player could have stood up and given the locker-room speech for her, smacking the back of her hand in her open palm or doing the snap-tomahawk chop gesture as she spoke: Playing college teams was an opportunity to work on good habits. They needed to spread out on the floor, concentrate on getting good shots, set their screens effectively, work together to run the ball hard and fast. She didn't want to see them get lazy, the way they had at Connecticut, taking the win without working hard for it, without playing at their very best. If they dropped to the level of their opponents, they would get eaten alive in Atlanta.

Thus she pushed them harder and harder, as if seeking the shadowy outer reaches of their athletic ability. They rode stationary bikes, churned their legs on Stairmasters, ran suicides on the court, all in addition to regulated weight sessions and an average of three hours of basketball practice daily. For the first time in VanDerveer's seventeen-year coaching career, a few short-term tournament teams aside, she was working with players who did not have to hurry off to classes or worry about grades. This team, these athletes, were all hers, and basketball was the only thing. For VanDerveer, who had spent a lifetime obsessed with the game, it felt like an unimaginable boon.

Lisa Leslie has been dunking the ball since she was in high school. Dunking is an undeniable crowd-pleaser, but many people believe it detracts from the women's game, inviting unnecessary comparisons with the way men play basketball. (Courtesy NBA Photos, Lou Capozzola)

Katrina McClain is widely considered one of the world's most formidable frontcourt players. (Courtesy Bob Breidenbach, *TV Guide*)

Teresa Edwards and Katrina—friends call them "T and Tree"—started playing together as teenagers at summer basketball tournaments. Between them, they have played eighteen years of professional basketball in four different countries and have won seven Olympic medals. (Courtesy AP/Worldwide Photos)

Coach Tara VanDerveer's exhausting, perfectionist practice regimen was unpopular with the players, but their superb conditioning made a difference. (Courtesy AP/Worldwide Photos)

The national team often scrimmaged against men's teams as part of their training. Here, Jennifer Azzi makes a move to the basket while Rebecca Lobo looks on. (Courtesy AP/*Lubbock Avalanche Journal/* Sharon M. Steinman)

It's a Whole
New Ballgame.

ABL
AMERICAN BASKETBALL LEA[GUE]

DAWN STALEY   CARLA McGHEE   NIKKI McCRAY   LISA LESLIE   SUSAN HAMMER

In September 1995, nine members of the national team endorsed the American Basketball League. What they couldn't have known was that although they'd worked to have one professional league for women in the United States, they would end up with two—something that would become a source of friction as the Olympics neared.
(Courtesy AP/Worldwide Photos)

Lisa dunked a few times during the U.S. team's games against NCAA opponents, but Coach VanDerveer ultimately asked her to stop, fearing she would get under-cut at the hoop and risk injury. The national team beat every top college team in the country on its pre-Olympic tour.
(Courtesy AP/Worldwide Photos)

Dawn Staley proudly tells people that she represents the inner city of Philadelphia. Here, she stands in front of the seven-story mural Nike erected in her honor. The U.S. players' endorsement deals signaled that women's basketball was finally beginning to get the attention it deserved. (Courtesy AP/Worldwide Photos)

In its ten-month tour, the women's team traveled 102,245 air miles, the equivalent of 5.4 trips around the Earth, and played basketball on four continents. Carla McGhee, Katrina, and Dawn (left to right) relax between destinations. (Courtesy NBA Photos/Andrew Bernstein)

Nikki McCray, shown here riding the team bus to a game, was the team's music queen, seldom without her headphones, quick to lead everyone in a song. (Courtesy NBA Photos/Andrew Bernstein)

Katrina goes up for a shot in the Olympic game versus Zaire, which set records for the most people to attend a women's basketball game in the United States (31,320) and for the biggest blowout in the history of Olympic women's basketball (107–47). (Courtesy AP/Worldwide Photos)

Tara VanDerveer was anxious that her team might be too small and too soft to stand up to the rougher, more physical opponents they would encounter in Atlanta. But along came the banger of her dreams, six-foot-four, 190-pound Venus Lacy, shown here battling with a Cuban forward. (Courtesy Bob Breidenbach, *TV Guide*)

When the last barbell had been lifted, she steered them toward the stretching area for an abdominal workout, led by Stanford's strength and conditioning coach, a burly middle-aged man with a camp counselor's enthusiasm. The man instructed but did not participate. Sprawled out across the floor, the women did pikes and leg lifts and five different kinds of sit-ups, groaning as they counted the eighteenth, nineteenth, and twentieth ones of each set. From here they would walk over to the gym for an hour-and-a-half shootaround.

"The man's trying to kill us," muttered Sheryl, spread-eagle between exercises, the muscles of her stomach smoldering painfully.

"We're gonna take this out on his players tonight," said Lisa, who was flopped out next to Sheryl. She raised her head and looked at the guy. "We're gonna take this out on your players tonight," she announced, then dropped her head again, waiting for the command to start the next set. She turned her head sideways to look at Sheryl. "Tara's trying to kill us," she said.

Eric Jackson paced the long hallway of the Holiday Inn in Palo Alto. He was dressed, as he often was, head to toe in Nike apparel, today's outfit being blue workout pants and a heavy gray sweatshirt. It was rest time for the team. The players had eaten their pregame meal in a private banquet room at the hotel and were now shuttered up in their rooms, watching television, reading, and resting their legs. The Stanford game, which began at seven-thirty, was just a few hours away.

"My stomach gets in knots before games," explained Eric, who was not allowed at pregames or any number of team functions. "I try to walk off some of the tension."

He was the lone man in an entourage of roughly seventeen women. There were two different male trainers who sometimes came along, but for the most part Eric Jackson was on his own. He insisted that he didn't mind. He liked women. He came from a family of them, growing up in a household that was overrun by sisters and aunts. Sheryl, he said, most resembled his grandmother, whom he called "Bigmomma." When Sheryl had a few hours off, the two of them sought out the nearest mall, where Sheryl shopped and Eric waited.

"Don't rush a woman shopping" was Eric's governing policy when it came to the mall. "She'll spend an hour in one store. She's got to have the shoes to match the purse, the hat to go with the dress," said Eric, who seemed always to be in a sunny mood. "I just sit there and watch."

Eric and Sheryl had been married five months nearly to the day. When someone asked how married life was treating him, his face lit up and he pumped his head up and down. "Real good," he'd say. "It's been a real good thing."

His long-term plan was to be a professional football player, a running back, but for the moment he'd put his career on hold to support his wife. His football career so far had consisted of a successful stint as a high-school player and one season of playing second string at Texas Tech. He was hoping someday to finish out his NCAA eligibility playing Division I football. Once the Olympics were over, he and Sheryl were hoping to move to Austin, hoping the ABL would put a team there, so he could get an education and play some real football. When people asked what he did for a living, as they often did, encountering him on the road with a bunch of women, he gave them an unflinchingly honest account of his football endeavors, including his failure to excel at Texas Tech, which he appended with a comment or two on his appreciable strengths as an athlete. "I can run," he would say, shaking his head as if he found his own speed somewhat unbelievable. "I can sprint faster than most any guy who plays football."

For the time being, however, he was supporting Sheryl emotionally, proud of the fact that he did not have an ego that got in the way of her career. In their apartment in Colorado, Eric took over most of the household duties while Sheryl worked at her game. "I run the kitchen and the living room," he once told a reporter cheerily. "I'm the chef. Just call me Mr. Belvedere."

Sheryl's basketball career, Eric explained, was almost a two-person job. "Sheryl is a small-town lady, so her being out here by herself is tough. She tends to get down on herself. Her game is great on the court, but then she'll do something to sidetrack herself. I tell her to be positive, to stay focused."

He could talk to her better than any coach could. He made sure to get to games early enough that Sheryl could pick him out in his seat, which was usually only several rows back from the court. During time-outs, she often looked over in his direction, awaiting an assuring thumbs-up or a mouthed opinion about what she should do differently. When the national team played Connecticut, Eric had surfaced on national television, chatting merrily with an ESPN commentator. He wore a natty blue suit and Air Swoopes on his feet. "What she needs to do," he told the nation, watching Sheryl miss two three-point shots in a row, "is settle down and let the game come to her instead of trying to jump into it like that."

Many of the team's players had significant others back at home, but Eric was the only one who pulled up anchor and signed on to follow the team's schedule, more or less. This had a lot to do with the fact that beyond the $50,000 salary USA Basketball paid each player, Sheryl, with her shoe royalties, endorsement fees, and basic sponsorship contract with Nike, earned far more than any other player on the team, save possibly Rebecca Lobo, whose deal with Reebok was rumored to be substantial as well. Aside from their trips to the mall, though, Eric and Sheryl lived relatively modestly. They had eyes on the Dallas real estate market, however, said Eric. "Soon," he said, "it's going to be time to settle in and have a family."

For the time being, though, he was merely an appendage to the team, the outsider who was barred from the meals and the bus and even the potluck suppers team members had held back in Colorado Springs during training camp. All the ladies, he liked to say, were plenty friendly. It was just that they needed to build the team on their own, to draw in tight and focus on the goal. At first there had been some resistance to Eric tagging along on the road, worries from VanDerveer and some of the other players that he would interfere in team business or upset the delicate equilibrium among the eleven women, or simply that his presence screwed up the hotel rooming assignments, but so far none of it had been a problem. Some of them seemed relieved, even, to have him there. He took good care of Sheryl, who could be moody and snappish in moments. He dragged her bags through the airport, ran out and got meals for her when she was tired. At practices he was quietly encouraging to each one of them. In general, he was unimposing, unselfish, and uniformly supportive.

At the Holiday Inn it was too early to get dressed for the game, too late to fit in a workout, as he often tried to do, keeping an eye on his football future. The game that night would be televised, which seemed to raise the stakes. It was another sellout crowd too, a homecoming for Jennifer and Katy and Tara VanDerveer. It was going to be a big deal. At moments like this he was aware of the fact that everyone else in the group had a job to do, like stagehands scrambling around, preparing for the curtain to go up. The trainer was beginning to tape ankles and ice hamstrings, the team manager was busy filling Gatorade bottles to distribute down the bench at time-outs, the media director was photocopying game notes for the press, the coaching staff was hunkered down in VanDerveer's suite, working through their strategy. The athletes were quiet in their rooms. Eric stood in the hallway, appearing somewhat hapless. Ahead of him was another night of basketball, another madhouse of fans screaming his wife's name.

"I always knew Sheryl was going to be a star," he said, tilting his head slightly to one side, "but I didn't think it'd blow up like this. She didn't have a female role model, growing up. She had Magic Johnson and Jordan and her older brothers. Now she's a role model to girls." He paused as a conflicted smile played across his face. "And I'm just glad to say I've been right there alongside."

For the first half of the Stanford game, it was as if the national team players were looking in the mirror. It was VanDerveer versus VanDerveer, two imprints of the same coach's mind, two teams horsewhipped by brutal conditioning routines of the same origin. Whereas the national team had trampled its other college opponents with a bruisingly quick transition offense, the Stanford players, most of whom had spent two or three years already under VanDerveer's command, were schooled in the same type of basketball. Jennifer Azzi, starting at point guard that night, was matched step for step by the spritely Jamila Wideman, who was one of VanDerveer's prize recruits, just as Azzi had been eight years earlier. When Jennifer outleted to Lisa, who passed it to Teresa for a fast break to score, Stanford immediately inbounded the ball and looked for a fast break of its own. After four minutes the U.S. led by one point, but then the Cardinal started sending up three-point shots with deadly accuracy. Soon Stanford had taken over, leading by two, then four, then six points.

With television cameras rolling and a capacity crowd of over 7,000, the noise was deafening. Eric Jackson felt his composure slipping away. He sat in his seat and yelled at the top of his lungs, his voice lost in the din: "Get down there on defense! Relax! Relax!" With five minutes left in the half, Sheryl broke free and took a pass from Teresa. Watching her in the split second she settled her feet and leveled her gaze at the hoop, Eric knew the ball was going in, a 17-foot jumper that put the national team ahead 32–31.

The players were beginning to distinguish themselves individually. Katrina McClain had formidable rebounding skills. Lisa had stunning inside moves, twisting her body in midair and hitting her shot, often drawing a foul. Sheryl appeared to float past defenders, her shots seeming measured and effortless every time. Teresa, too, was beginning to shine, helped along by the added playing time she'd had in Dawn's absence. She'd been scoring from the inside and the out and was particularly adept at finding Sheryl open at the wing or Lisa at the low post.

For the national team players, it had been hard to feel overly challenged by the weaker and less experienced college teams. But Stanford was running them hard. There would be no relaxing. For the Cardinal it was a thrill to pin down what was being billed as the best team in the world. The players' eyes drifted up to the scoreboard between plays; they were holding on to them, and they could hardly believe it. They hounded Katrina McClain at the perimeter and forced her to travel. They got their hands in the face of Teresa Edwards, who botched an easy shot from the top of the key. The national team could not pull away.

The person who was suffering the most in the final minutes of the first half was Rebecca Lobo, who had come in for Lisa Leslie. For as much as VanDerveer, Steding, and Azzi felt at home in the Maples Pavilion, Lobo felt like a stranger. Her lumbering gait and sluggish shooting was thrown into high relief against the backdrop of Stanford's phenomenal speed. She was getting pushed around at the post, unable to lose her defender. She was getting beat on the boards, and the harder she tried, the more ineffectual she seemed to become. At the very least, she was supposed to be last season's top college player, and now she was being intimidated by the very group of players she and the Huskies had soundly defeated in the semifinals of the NCAA tournament just months earlier.

At halftime, the U.S. team led by only six points. Walking off the court, VanDerveer was shaking her head. Rebecca trained her eyes on the floor and marched to the locker room. The audience was in a frenzy. It was hard to know what to be shocked by: Was the U.S. national team this bad, or was Stanford this startlingly talented, even with its head coach sitting on the opponent's bench? Either way, it did not reflect particularly well on VanDerveer, who stood before her team of older, stronger players in the visitors' locker room and after critiquing the team's defensive effort, its continually weak three-point shooting, she said evenly, "You went out there and let them give you a bloody nose. Now you gotta go back and start fighting."

The second half saw Stanford fall to pieces. Interim coach Amy Tucker would call it a "complete meltdown," full of turnovers and stupid fouls. Meanwhile, Katrina controlled the boards, while Ruthie pumped in threes one after the other, and Sheryl, in one swift move, made a key steal for a lay-up. Only Rebecca continued to founder, looking tired and weak in the post. After what seemed like forever, the game ended at 100–63.

In the locker room, the national players celebrated their first real challenge as a team. Rebecca stared glumly into her locker. She'd never felt so ill at ease on the basketball court, as she had in the last month. What had happened to her? Quitting was an option, but it would ruin her personally and professionally, and she'd never quit anything before. Her whole life had been built around the game of basketball. And now it seemed the game was built around her almost like a prison.

Across the way, Teresa Edwards was looking at her. "Hey, B," she said, jerking her chin into the air, "come on over here."

In the months they'd known each other, Teresa had alternately supported and criticized Rebecca, seeming to remember what it was like to be the baby on the team but still lacking sympathy for the white girl who got all the attention when she so clearly didn't deserve it. Rebecca was grateful when Teresa corrected her mistakes on the court and understood when the older player seemed standoffish. Teresa had been playing Olympic level basketball for fourteen years—an unbelievable career by anyone's estimation—and still nobody knew who she was. Teresa was also sitting on the bench nearly as much as Rebecca was, despite the fact that she played twice as well as Rebecca every time she stepped onto the court. It was difficult to understand VanDerveer's moods, but whatever they were, both Teresa and Rebecca were usually on the wrong side of them. The recognition of this had gone largely unspoken between them until Teresa beckoned her across the locker room following the Stanford game.

"Let me tell you somethin', Rebecca," she said. "She's going to make you feel like the team doesn't need you, she's going to make you feel bad about yourself when you shouldn't. You gotta keep your head up. You know you're good. Don't let her voice get too far inside your head, okay? Don't let anybody shake what you know about yourself."

Rebecca nodded. Katrina had drawn near to listen. She was playing well every game and had no overt problems with the coach, but she was also Teresa's best friend. She understood the struggle. Neither of them had tried particularly hard to be Rebecca's friend before now, and after tonight they wouldn't try that hard either. But for a brief moment they were all there together, Teresa talking, Katrina nodding, Rebecca listening. "Stay with it. Be strong," said Teresa, turning back to her locker. "That's how you survive."

7

chapter

Work It Out

From Stanford they went to Los Angeles and from Los Angeles to San Diego; from San Diego they went to Missouri and from there to North Carolina, staying just long enough in each place to practice once or twice, lift weights, play a game, meet the fans, and move on again. From North Carolina they went to Tennessee and from Tennessee to Washington state, then to Kansas, back to Tennessee, to Washington D.C., the cities beginning to blur into one another: Fayetteville, Indianapolis, Columbus, Auburn. They lost track of the season—snowstorm in Ohio, balmy in Tennessee—and sometimes of the day of the week, their exact location, and essentially everything else that did not directly stand in the way of their prearranged march from city to city, hotel to hotel, gym to gym.

"I couldn't tell you one major news event," said Katy Steding in San Diego. "We haven't gone to war or anything, right?"

In North Carolina, Katrina McClain called her brother, Troy, who was planning to drive up from Charleston to visit.

"Where are you?" he asked.

She thought for a moment. "Raleigh-Durham," she said, recalling the airport they'd just come from.

"Which one, Raleigh or Durham?" The two cities are twenty miles apart.

She thought again. "I'll have to call you back on that. I have no idea."

The more miles they covered, the more the rest of the world grew gauzy and disorienting. They traveled in a self-contained haze, their days governed by practice times and plane tickets and late-night movies on hotel Spectravision. They were together so much on the court, they tended to stay together off it too, less sometimes out of friendship and more out of habit. The thing was, nobody else could understand: Their bodies ached. VanDerveer's voice rang in their ears continually. They had no time for friends or family. Katy Steding tried to keep up with her business back in Portland, but ended up reluctantly turning much of it over to an assistant. Jennifer and Teresa tried to stay in touch with Bobby Johnson and Steve Hams of the ABL, but even that proved difficult, as each time they left a message, they had to leave three forwarding numbers along with it.

In Nashville, two weeks after her Raleigh-Durham episode, Katrina McClain dialed room service and ordered waffles. The meal never arrived. When she called to complain, she realized she'd sent the waffles to Room 708, which was not her room number, but the room she'd had in the last hotel in Kansas or maybe the one before that in Seattle. She didn't know.

The confusion was general; the travel, the practice, made their heads spin. "We're heading to the game and I say, 'Who're we playing tonight?'" said Teresa.

Yet those cities that they visited, the teams they beat up and the people who watched them do it, would not soon forget the U.S. national team.

"A monster basketball team is on the loose, shredding some of America's best college squads . . ." announced one *Christian Science Monitor* article. Across the country, newspapers told stories of the eleven athletes who played the women's game on a level nobody had really seen before. One by one, they slayed all the hallowed giants of NCAA basketball, first Georgia, then Connecticut, then Stanford, then Tennessee, departing almost as quickly as they had arrived, each time leaving in their wake another humbled team, another stunned audience. The newspapers registered the aftershock.

Purdue coach Linn Dunn gave the media her first impression of the team: "I saw them walk out onto the floor and I said, 'This looks like the Olympic track team coming out, not the Olympic basketball team. What event are they entered in, the four by four hundred?'" Her team lost 90–50.

"It happened so quick," said Arkansas coach Gary Blair, "I didn't have time to feel sorry for myself." His team went down 101–53.

"I thought I was out there with a bunch of men. They were really quick. . . . I've never seen any women play like that," said a player from North Carolina State, where the score was 98–52.

The coach at George Washington University, whose team had crumbled to the tune of 110–37, put it another way: "It's like watching a clinic," he said, "and you're the victim of the clinic."

There were a few teams that managed to hold on for the first half, the way Stanford had. Tennessee kept the score fairly even for the first fifteen minutes, thanks largely to a sensational freshman named Chamique Holdsclaw who, because it was still preseason, had yet to play an official college game. But then, as it always happened, the college team started to deteriorate—passes got sloppy, defenses broke down—a process that speeded up as it dawned on the college athletes that the national team was not going to let up, that the players simply did not get tired. Their bench was lined with superstars, which meant that when Lisa Leslie went out for a rest, Carla McGhee came in fresh, and the game only got uglier.

The audiences were always cheered by a good battle, particularly when it involved a shred of hope that the local team might bring down, or at the very least stay with, some of the best players in the world. What the public didn't understand, however, watching the two sets of players compete, was that while a college team would rest the day of and to a certain extent the day before a big game, the national team would arrive at a game ready to play on the heels of three full hours of weight lifting, conditioning and court practice earlier in the day. When the games got too easy, VanDerveer instituted several rules to keep them challenging and develop secondary skills for the U.S. team: The ball had to be passed five times before anyone could take a shot, and they would hold off on pressing the college teams, an act of chivalry that allowed their opponents to bring the ball down and set up their offense before the national team's defense attacked.

Even with the added rules, the U.S. team reliably crushed every college team it encountered, winning by an average of 40 points. "We don't want to embarrass anyone," Ruthie earnestly told a reporter midway through the tour, "but we do want to make a statement."

The statement seemed obvious. It was not about winning a gold medal in Atlanta, exactly; it was about playing at home, about getting the American public to take note. It was about coming back from exile to play in the ABL and securing their fans ahead of time. It was about catching the eye of potential sponsors for the new league, about proving that professional basketball could make good television, about convincing an indifferent America that college ball did not represent the outer limits of the women's game. All they wanted, really, was for people to understand how good women's basketball could be.

It was not an easy road. Several weeks into the tour, the lack of privacy had started to grate on players' nerves, and after some internal lobbying at USA Basketball, they were given their own hotel rooms instead of having to share. Sheryl got the flu around Thanksgiving and soon nearly everyone was cranky and sneezing. Carla dispensed tissues from the pilfered roll of toilet paper she carried nearly everywhere she went. Lisa was having relationship trouble. Rebecca still spent long hours hiding away, talking to her old friends and her family on the phone. Dawn had been out of commission for weeks rehabbing her knee, and despite the fact that Teresa had stepped up and played well in her absence, VanDerveer had given her little in the way of praise.

Sometimes on the buses to and from practice, Nikki or Dawn led the group in an old Southern church song called "Work It Out," modifying some of the words to suit their lives on the court.

" 'How you gonna pay your rent?' " sang Nikki, standing before them.

" 'Work it out,' " the others sang back.

" 'When your money's spent?' "

" 'Work it out.' "

" 'When practice goes too long?' "

" 'Work it out.' "

" 'When the ref calls a foul?' "

" 'Work it out,' " they sang, breaking into the chorus, " 'Jesus will work it out.' "

To make themselves feel better, they sometimes talked about the alternative to what they were doing, which was going overseas to play. Among the nine of them who'd been out of college for at least a year, they'd played thirty-three seasons in eight different countries. The memories were overwhelmingly bad. When they spoke of going abroad to the younger players, namely Nikki and Rebecca, the stories took on a cautionary bent, as if to say, most particularly to Rebecca, who had been fickle about signing with the ABL, we need your help, you don't know how bad it is over there.

Nobody, in fact, aside from the several hundred American women who played abroad each year in countries as disparate as Korea and Iceland, Israel and Brazil, knew what it was like. When their careers overseas came up in the media, it was usually only to illustrate the sacrifice they'd made to play on the national team, the oft-quoted fact that Katrina had turned down $300,000. What got mentioned less was that only a handful of players made six-figure salaries; the average was about $60,000 for backcourt players; $80,000 for frontcourt players.

Money aside, it was difficult to impress upon younger players the unhappiness that generally accompanied life on a foreign team. In parts of Italy, which along with Japan was one of the most popular places for Americans to go due to higher salaries, fans yelled and spat, sometimes using cigarette lighters to heat up coins and flick them at referees or players. The benches in Italy had to be protected by Plexiglas barriers. Many teams needed a police escort coming and going from games. "At the buzzer we had to run into the locker room," said Katrina, remembering her one season in Italy. "I just wanted to get out of there."

Jennifer Azzi had spent a season in Italy also, devoting as much energy to rejecting the amorous advances of her team's general manager as to playing basketball. "It was awful," she said. "He used to sit outside of my apartment to make sure I wasn't going out at night. If he passed by at two in the morning and saw my lights on, he'd call and ask what I was doing up. If I said anything about my personal life to my teammates, they'd run and tell him. They didn't let me have a life at all. They watched every single thing I did, they wanted to control every single thing I did. They feel like they've paid you to come over, so they own you."

In France the players smoked at practice, the coaches smoked at games. In Spain, one American complained, it was commonly accepted that a male coach would have affairs with several different players over the course of a season. Many European teams never delivered on promises they'd made to lure top players, such as providing a car or a plane ticket home. Paychecks were often diminished or withheld without explanation. In Japan coaches frequently struck their players. "I'm not talking about a slap on the arm," said Katrina, explaining. "They kick the women, they punch them in the stomach. Then the women run after the coach, apologizing. Women are really looked down upon in Japan."

In certain countries they were called "nigger." One American remembered being mobbed by kids in Japan, groping at her, trying to see if the black of her skin would rub off. Others received nicknames like "Chocolate Milk Shake."

To be fair, some players had positive experiences playing abroad, and nearly all of them would credit the experience for making them more mature, more patient and self-reliant—skills that seemed to prepare them emotionally for a challenge like the Olympics. Jennifer had enjoyed living in Sweden. Both Katrina and Teresa ranked Japan as "not so bad," given that the season was short, the food was good, and the people generally treated Americans with respect. Lisa Leslie had learned Italian and fallen in love with the food over there. Ruthie Bolton spoke longingly of her last season in Italy, playing outside Rome, where she moonlighted as a nightclub singer with three Italian men in a band called Antididum Tarantula. As if to qualify her happiness, however, Ruthie followed this up with a story about how her team's management had hassled her when she missed a few games to attend her mother's funeral the winter before, a memory that still caused her to well up with tears.

If anything, the ghosts of their careers abroad helped to keep things in perspective during the rougher moments of the college tour, on the days when practice had been lousy or the schedule too grueling. "If I'm having a bad day," said Jennifer, "here, at least, I have people to talk to."

For Rebecca Lobo, her older teammates' vigilance about not wanting to return overseas came back on her as pressure. "They're all mad at me because I won't sign," she sighed to a team staffer one day, referring to her decision to wait on committing to the ABL. Even though Katrina had held off from committing also, Katrina had, in three Olympics and nine years of playing abroad, already earned the respect of the others; she'd already paid her dues. McClain was also invisible with the public. Though it was impossible to quantify what it would mean for the ABL if Rebecca, the player with the highest visibility in the sport, endorsed the league, it was safe to say that it would have likely made a difference.

"I think we had the feeling she was trying to be a big shot," Teresa said in retrospect. "It appeared she was getting business advice, from her agent or her parents or whoever, to just sit still. It was like, here we were, laying the foundation for our sport, and she was being told she could just ride it out on top. The idea was, you don't owe anybody anything. There was no way of making her understand. Younger kids couldn't appreciate what we were trying to do, period. They couldn't know what it felt like to go away year after year and continue to give stuff up. The rest of us felt good about making our stance. We knew Rebecca could have an impact on the ABL, but we were prepared to do it without her."

Rebecca treated the subject delicately with her teammates. Maybe she couldn't understand the vexations of playing abroad, the extent of the older players' sacrifices, but they could never know what it felt like to be

Rebecca Lobo either, to be twenty-two years old and besieged by throngs of people who wanted to know you, who thought they knew you. She would commit when life had settled down a bit, she told them, her voice quiet, even apologetic. She really would. Publicly, she did what she could to support the league. "If there's an ABL next year," she often told the press, "I have no doubt that I'll be there to play in it."

       The operative word when it came to the ABL seemed to be "if." While the national team toured through the fall, Steve Hams had lit out on a tour of his own, researching potential cities for his teams, knocking on the doors of potential sponsors, potential television partners, potential general managers and coaches. What he learned quickly was that the battle was going to be more uphill than he'd anticipated. Nobody, it seemed, wanted to be the first to jump in. If you get a TV deal, then come back and we'll talk, said the sponsors. If you get a few sponsors, said the TV people, then we'll sit down and make a deal. He went to Seattle, Portland, Richmond, Long Beach, Columbus, Indianapolis, Nashville, Hartford, and Denver, in a number of cases introducing himself to the mayor of the city, touring available arenas, and making his pitch to everyone from IBM to Nike to department stores and automobile manufacturers. All he needed was a few key people to believe. All he got, at least initially, was a lot of naysaying.

After paying a visit to Kansas City in early December, Hams drove a rental car to nearby Lawrence to watch the U.S. team defeat the University of Kansas. The team played brilliantly that night. Sheryl Swoopes picked off six Kansas passes, Lisa Leslie scored 22 points and shot eight for ten, and overall the U.S. finished with 21 steals and a 101–46 victory. Watching it all from his seat, Hams quietly felt thankful for the one bit of stock the American Basketball League had, the nine players who'd signed on. It was essentially the only thing that separated him from all the other noisemakers out there.

There was another "if" that seemed to dog Hams's efforts with investors, a question so pervasive it almost seemed to defeat him before he could open his mouth with the corporate bigwigs: What if the NBA decided to start its own women's league?

Clearly, Hams and his cohorts had considered this question from the start. In the last several years, NBA commissioner David Stern had mentioned his support for the women's game in passing several times. In the sports business, a single note of interest from Stern was enough to send potential competitors scurrying. There plainly was no competing with the NBA anyway, at least when it came to men's basketball. In eleven years under Stern's aegis, the league had mushroomed into one of the most profitable and popular professional sports outfits in the world, with league revenues of over a billion dollars a year, merchandising sales of about $3 billion, and a $750 million television contract. NBA games were broadcast in 160 countries around the world. The price of an NBA franchise had increased tenfold between 1980 and 1995. When the NBA held its annual playoff games, some fifty-eight million people tuned in to watch.

It was commonly understood that David Stern was the wizard behind the curtain of professional basketball. When it came to the women's game, people paid attention to what he did or didn't do, trusting that if women's professional basketball was profitable, he would get involved. If in December 1995 Stern was not involved, then to the minds of the marketing and network executives on whose doors Steve Hams was knocking, women's basketball was, as it always had been, a losing proposition.

Stern's involvement was growing, however. In the months leading up to the women's national team's tour, NBA Properties, a division of his organization, had brokered deals with seven heavy-hitting corporate sponsors—from Sears and State Farm Insurance to Tambrands and Kraft—selling advertising time for games broadcast on ABC, ESPN, and ESPN2. It had conducted focus groups on everything from the women's uniforms and warm-up suits to the array of merchandising products— hats, T-shirts, and replica jerseys that would be hawked at national team games and at the Olympics in Atlanta—with a percentage of the profits going to the NBA, the rest to USA Basketball. Several NBA employees traveled regularly with the national team, overseeing the merchandise sales and halftime events that showcased the sponsors.

In essence, the NBA seemed to be monitoring the national team's image carefully: gauging how the public responded to the women's game and the players, studying the television ratings, tallying up attendance figures and merchandise sales with what appeared to be an eye to future profit. What Stern or his scions would not say but what was becoming obvious to those who paid attention, from the marketeers to the sponsors to the athletes themselves and particularly to Steve Hams and his partners in the ABL, was that through its agreement with USA Basketball, the NBA seemed to be test-marketing the potential for a women's league. If the national team experiment was a hit with the public, it stood to reason that Stern might throw his hat into the women's arena—an apparent death blow for the American Basketball League.

Sitting at the basketball game in Lawrence, Kansas, Hams had to prod himself to be optimistic. He had no money beyond what he and his partners had come up with, but only a few people had turned him down outright. At Nike, he felt that his proposal for a sponsorship had actually been well received. At ESPN, they'd at least acted interested. For the moment, too, David Stern was tucked away in his fifteenth-floor office in midtown Manhattan, wrapped up with the start of a new NBA season and recovering from a summer of epic labor disputes. When it came to the possibility of launching a women's NBA, Stern appeared to have no immediate comment, leaving the ABL as the self-declared pioneer, the sole boat floating on the horizon.

If you asked Carla McGhee what the best stop on the fall tour was, she would give you a wide smile and say in her voice, which was deep and gravelly: "Tennessee." This would not come as a surprise, because Tennessee is where Carla went to college, the Vols was the team she helped win two national titles, and Pat Summit was the coach who'd most affected her life. But this is not what made Carla's return to Knoxville so special. Asked to recall the visit, she would most likely skip over the more obvious details of the homecoming—the hollering fans, the decisive victory, the reunion dinner with Coach Summit—and skip to what, for her, was most significant, which was the romantic part.

Romance was important to Carla McGhee. She loved the idea of it, she kept tabs on every romance that went on around her. In her free time she read books with names like *Deception* and *Heartbreak*. By the time the team got to Tennessee, someone had bought the sound track to *Waiting to Exhale*, even though the movie hadn't yet come out. They'd all listened to it a million times: "Whitney and Toni Braxton can sing it, baby" was what Carla had to say. She had read the book *Waiting to Exhale* several times already, and if someone needed a quick thematic summary, Carla was there to give it: "It's about women tryin' to find good men and all the men bein' *dogs*," she said. When the movie finally was released several weeks after the game in Tennessee, Carla saw it three times in three days. She loved romance, she said, even when it went sour.

Carla had a romance of her own, with an NBA player named Willie Anderson, who at that time was playing for Toronto, though he would soon be part of a midseason trade to the New York Knicks. Willie was from Atlanta, which was where Carla had been living the last few years. Willie and Carla met at a gym called Run and Shoot in Atlanta. Willie had a handful of kids already and an ex-wife, and so Carla did not count on getting married, but it was a good romance, she said. Sometimes Carla would be standing there with Willie, and women would hand him the keys to their hotel rooms, just because he played in the NBA. A lot of women, said Carla, came on to Willie, but the two of them had a relationship that was based on trust. "He's a wonderful person," Carla said about Willie. Carla had one of Willie's credit cards, which she carried in her wallet. "I'm gonna call up Willie and get him to raise the limit on this thing!" she'd shout, waving the card around before a shopping trip. "That man ain't gonna *know* what hit him!"

What happened at Tennessee had nothing to do with Willie, though, or even, for that matter, Carla. Once the game was over, the announcer instructed everyone to stay in their seats for a special presentation. Then a Tennessee cheerleader dragged a chair to center court and Nikki Mc-Cray, who, like Carla, had gone to Tennessee, was called out to sit in the chair.

"Then out came Thomas," said Carla, giving her account. Thomas was Nikki's boyfriend of three years. Thomas had graduated ahead of Nikki at Tennessee and now worked as an engineer. "Everybody loves Thomas," she added as an aside. "All the girls on the team." When Carla talked about other people's affairs, particularly happy ones, her eyes grew wide and earnest, her voice became soft and vaguely maternal.

"So out came Thomas, and they gave him a microphone and he gave Nikki a plaque from the school and some roses, and we were all sittin' there on the bench, thinking, yeah, this is nice, but whatever, and then he said, 'Will you marry me?' And we were like, *what*? And Nikki was like, *what*? And she started gigglin' and all. And all the fans started clapping, and then he pulled out a ring and Nikki started flappin' her hand in his face, yellin' 'Put it on! Put it on!' and she grabbed the mike right out of his hands and screamed into it really loud, and all of us started screaming and crying and we kind of fell to the floor because it was like, we were so happy for Nikki. I mean, what a way to get asked, you know? I think I was more excited than anybody, maybe even more excited than Nikki even though she was completely surprised. It was just like, girl, you got yourself a good man!" Finishing the story, Carla paused for a minute, looking wistful. "That was definitely the best part of the fall."

When pressed to explain why, she grew slightly incredulous. "Because doesn't everyone love a happy ending?"

In moments, Carla could be moody and philosophical. She alternately fussed over the others on the team and withdrew completely. Her face was broad and slightly misshapen after a nearly fatal car accident years earlier, when she was a student at Tennessee. She had broken every bone in her face and lay in a coma for two days. Not a day passed now when she didn't think about the accident, she said. "I am a truly blessed person," she said, "but still, I just get down sometimes. My teammates know well enough to just let me be. I snap out of it, but only with some time."

The ability to intuit one another's moods was something they were developing slowly. "It's like someone can always tell when someone else is homesick," said Carla one day. "Or it's like, 'Ahh, I don't feel like practicing today,' and someone's always there to say, 'Come on, you can do this' or, 'I got your back.' That's our favorite phrase. I might say, 'T, I don't know if I can get through practice today,' and she'll say, 'I got your back.' We'll both go to practice but she might pick up some slack for me on the court. She's looking out for me. . . . We all do that for each other, and that keeps us motivated."

Carla's roommate on and off for much of the fall was Lisa Leslie. They passed romance novels back and forth between them and kvetched about men. On a rainy afternoon in Seattle, Lisa lay diagonally on one of the hotel room's two beds and watched TV. Carla sat in a chair by the window, when Jennifer drifted in carrying a cellular phone given to her by Reebok, her sponsor.

"You got that from Reebok?" said Lisa, eyeing the phone. "Let me see that. Wow, it's nice." She took the phone from Jennifer and tossed it to Carla. "Check this thing out," she said. "It's heavy."

"I've got to get my service connected before I can use it," said Jennifer, plopping herself on the bed next to Lisa's, picking up the room phone and dialing a number from the cell phone's brochure.

Lisa turned back to the television. "Okay, let's watch a talk show."

"We ain't gonna watch talk shows," said Carla, fiddling with the remote until she found a soap opera. She watched for a moment, then picked up a book, one of Lisa's, which was lying on the table next to her. It was called *Never Satisfied: Why Men Cheat.* Carla studied the cover for a moment, then laid it back down. "I still wanna know *that* answer," she said, shaking her head. "I'm tellin' you what."

She rested the remote against one cheek, idly watching the TV. "Monica can't stand him," she explained to Lisa, tuning into the show. "She's gonna have him try to kill her husband. . . . I say Monica should get over it."

Across the room Jennifer had connected with the phone company and was reviewing the brochure. "Okay, so when it says it's free on the weekends, does that mean it's really free?" She listened. "Oh," she said after a minute, sounding disappointed. "Only in area code 617?"

Their off hours tended to pass quietly and quickly and were mostly spent hanging around the hotels. When they went out, it was usually for one scheduled function or another. Some were exciting; some were not. In Washington, D.C, they began a day by jogging three miles with President Clinton. Afterward, he took them into the Oval Office and chatted casually with them for twenty minutes. Everybody deemed him a good guy. "He got a few votes today," said Tara VanDerveer afterward.

Later that day they lunched with the House of Representatives and got a tour of the Capitol. But it was not until Supreme Court Justice Sandra Day O'Connor led them into the courtroom that the significance of their visit to Washington began to sink in. Title IX had passed twenty-three years earlier, and, as O'Connor reminded, the eleven of them touring around, drawing fans from all over the country, was a part of its legacy.

"I wanted to meet you because what you're doing is important," the judge said to them. She looked over at Ruth Bader-Ginsburg, the Supreme Court's second female justice, and said, "I can't tell you how happy I was when she got to the court. It makes a night-and-day difference to have women on the bench."

VanDerveer, sitting among the players, felt her heart pounding. It was impossible to spend time in Washington like this and not feel the tug of patriotism, the appreciation for what they still had to do. "I was overwhelmed suddenly," the coach said afterward. "I was thinking, 'You're not just coaching a little college team now. You're coaching your *country*. You gotta start getting up earlier in the morning. These players have to work *harder*."

Finally, O'Connor took them to the Supreme Court gym, where she pushed the door open and announced, "Now, *this* is the highest court in the land." This prompted a burst of laughter from the players. The justice accepted high-fives all around, and then, picking up a nearby ball with what looked like great pride as well as some instruction from Lisa Leslie, she expertly banked a shot off the glass.

Arthroscopic surgery was no big deal to Dawn Staley. Each year she played basketball, her knees seemed to become less and less reliable, gunked up as they were with loose bits of cartilage that interfered with her motion the way a pencil caught in the hinges of a door might. She'd had arthroscopy for the first time when she was in college, when her body was young enough to recover in two weeks. In the years following, arthroscopy had become almost part of her routine. She'd befriended most of the staff at the University of Virginia Sports Medicine Clinic, surfacing at their door first once, then twice a year for surgery, saying cheerfully, "Fix me up, y'all!"

Dawn was twenty-five years old and her knees were a sorry wreck, riddled with discolored dots of scar tissue from all the scopes, sore and aching when it rained, a harbinger of early arthritis. But she needed her knees to play basketball, and the procedure was minor enough that she could sustain as many scopes as she needed to keep her knees cleaned out, recognizing in the back of her mind the fact that one day she would reach some unforetold limit, that a moment would come when her knees wouldn't hold up anymore on the basketball court. For now, however, her battered joints seemed to be on an extended warranty. While her team played against Stanford, Dawn sat in Charlottesville, cloaked in a hospital gown at the outpatient clinic, joking her way through another surgery.

She had been lucky, she knew, to get injured early in the fall, when the stakes were less high. If it happened again, closer to the Olympics, it was likely she would get cut from the team, her spot filled by someone whose body was not such a liability. For good measure she had the doctor scope both knees, suctioning out every last bit of loose cartilage in either joint—a secret she would purposely keep from VanDerveer and the national team training staff, fearing they would sentence her to a longer rehab.

As it was, she was supposed to spend two weeks in Virginia working with the UVA trainer on her rehab, missing five national team games, and rejoining the group after Thanksgiving in Seattle. But her strength was slow in returning and two weeks turned to three and then to four. Alone in the Virginia gym, she spent long hours shooting baskets, running feebly from one end of the court to the other on knees that seemed to refuse to heal up quickly. Occasionally, she'd get a call from Lisa Leslie from somewhere on the road.

"We ran all over Washington," she would say, or, "You shoulda heard Tara come down on us last night. Dawn, you be glad you're across the country, okay?"

But there was no way for Dawn to be glad. Each day, the team seemed to slip a little further away. Teresa was playing point guard for VanDerveer, and maybe that was nothing to worry about, but the fact was the team was moving on without her. She'd been on enough teams in her life to see it happen: A player goes down and disappears to get fixed, and the team chemistry quickly reconfigures itself to make do without her. The national team, she knew, was easily making do. Her teammates had come up with a remembrance, though, an honorary tribute to Dawn in the form of a child-sized baseball jacket they'd found somewhere and to its back had glued a number 5, her number. At every game Dawn missed, the little jacket hung draped over a chair on the bench in her honor, a reminder that in spirit she was still with them.

It was December 13, the tail end of the college tour, before Dawn Staley was released from her doctor's care in Virginia. Meeting up with the team in Indianapolis several days before its game against Purdue, she felt anxious and hyperactive, eager to prove that she hadn't missed a beat in her playing. While her teammates embraced her warmly, jumping right back into her card games and trash-talking in the hotel and at meals, she sensed the pressure mounting. Teresa clearly did not want to be unseated as the number-one point guard, and Jennifer was eager to hang on to her number-two spot. Teresa had acknowledged it briefly, diffusing some of the tension simply by owning up to it. "I gotta tell you,

Dawn, I'm worried she's going to send me back to the bench with you back, but we'll all work hard on our play, right? We'll all get our chance."

Her first practice with the team went well enough. VanDerveer was running them hard as ever, but the extra weeks of rehab had prepared Dawn. The team had worked on several new plays in her absence, but a natural strategist, Dawn picked them up quickly and within the hour was charging up and down the court, calling plays as if she'd never left. After practice she wrapped her knees in ice and quietly congratulated herself for having come back full strength.

The next day they scrimmaged against a men's intramural team from Purdue. Nearly everywhere they went, VanDerveer tried to recruit a men's amateur team to play them. These tended to be their best work-outs, the most physical basketball they'd play before meeting up with international women's teams over the winter. Playing against men sparked the competitive drive that sometimes got lost in their relatively easy games against the college teams. The men always wanted to win badly. They didn't want to get beaten up by a bunch of women, regardless of who the women were, and so they played hard and the women played hard back. In general, they tended to be fairly evenly matched against men's teams, though VanDerveer was careful not to keep her best players in for too long against the men. She did what she could to keep the score even, to keep her players alert and striving. Sometimes the women won, and sometimes the men won; it depended on where they were and what caliber team they were playing.

When they scrimmaged against a new men's team, it was common for the men to play a gentlemanly game for the first five minutes, avoiding contact under the net, and playing a soft defense. Inevitably, though, when they started to lose, or when Lisa started throwing her raptorlike elbows around, they forgot all about the gender of their opponents.

In Indianapolis the game got rough quickly, the score remaining close. For Dawn it felt like a slice of heaven. She was back in her game, tossing her no-look passes off to Sheryl at the wing, darting inside quickly enough to surprise the guys and sneak in a lay-up. Her defender was starting to slow down. She stole the ball from him once, then twice; then, as she flew back up court on a transition, the guy punched one arm out and knocked the ball away. Together they dove after it, ending up in a tangle on the floor. Getting to her feet, she felt a searing pain in her right hand. She shook it a few times and kept playing, figuring that whatever it was, it would eventually unjam itself.

The next day the pain was still there but the hand was not swollen. It looked oddly crooked though. The team's trainer poked and prodded at her wrist and fingers but had no answer. "It's no big thing," Dawn told her. "I'm good to go." She went through another practice, dribbling with only her left hand, grimacing a little when something knocked up against the injured hand. The morning of the Purdue game her hand was throbbing to the point it couldn't be ignored. The trainer took Dawn to the hospital for an X ray. She stared numbly at the flimsy celluloid etching. There it was: a broken bone, the fourth metacarpal, an impossibly rare injury.

She would be in a cast for six weeks, and she would be miserable. Whereas Dawn had once been the engine of the team, her quick wit and talkative nature keeping the rest of them light, in the weeks following her hand injury she seemed listless and sapped. This time there wasn't even rehab to focus on. She continued to travel with the team, riding a bike or running for exercise, sometimes taking the court before and after the team had practiced, flipping weak one-handed shots at the basket, one after the other. During games she wore a dress suit and sat silently on the end of the bench, chewing her gum and looking dejected as her teammates continued their undefeated run, glaring down from time to time at the hand that was itchy and withering, encased in its plaster prison.

They had won every game they'd played so far, but it was still not enough to make Tara VanDerveer happy. She couldn't have them go soft on her, couldn't let them lose their focus as the distractions seemed to balloon around them. Her players, at least some of them, were becoming small-time celebrities. Lisa, Sheryl, and Dawn were appearing on a national television ad for Nike, and this had seemed to up their stock with the public. Rebecca was flying all over creation between games to attend awards banquets for everything she'd won the season before. Jennifer had posed for an *Elle* magazine spread. Lisa seemed to be advertising herself as a runway model as much as a basketball player, and all of it, VanDerveer understood, would intensify as the year progressed and the country grew more and more swept up in seeking out its Olympic idols.

"Basketball," she told her team emphatically, "is not a popularity contest."

On a certain level, she understood why it was important to be in magazines and stand up at awards ceremonies. She had been around long enough to know that these were opportunities women athletes had rarely had in the past, that all of this was a positive omen of change. She had watched enough of her Stanford players wilt away in mediocre careers overseas. She was not so callous that she could look at Teresa Edwards and not understand how much having a professional league at home would mean.

But they weren't going to get anywhere without a gold medal. In America, nobody paid attention to a second-place finish. If they wanted to take the women's game to a new level, they would have to balance the politicking with the play. They would have to win. And yes, so far they were winning—big, easy wins—but while the rest of the country was looking at her team and seeing dizzyingly good basketball, VanDerveer was seeing a team full of holes. Their three-point shooting was uneven; their defense on the perimeter was spotty; when they came up against a team that could run the fast-break, the game suddenly became an even contest. What VanDerveer saw, looking at her players, was a team that was not yet good enough to defend against Brazil's guards, that could not match up against the post players from China or Russia.

She had to keep reminding everyone, players included, that the college games were like biddy ball compared to what they were about to encounter. In the international game, *everybody* could fast break. The teams were astonishingly well-rounded: They had a perimeter game, they had gigantic post players, and they could run the court for forty minutes without needing a break. The public didn't remember or didn't know about all the bronze medals in their closet: the '92 Olympics, the '94 World Championships, and the Pan Am Games. So even as the people clamored for them, even as the college teams bowed down to them, they had to recognize that it was all an illusion, that they were far from the best in the world. The coach kept herself up at night, worrying about it: they still had so far to go.

To this end, she added thirty-minute water-aerobic workouts to their routine three times a week when they had access to a pool. Her practices were bruising, her praise was sparing. Going into each college game, she instituted a set of goals, written up on the chalkboard in the locker room, which would serve as the true measuring stick for their progress. "Our goals relate to the things that will help us to be successful at the Olympics," she said. "We're developing good habits."

She reviewed the goals before every game:

"Let's come out ready to play. Get the first basket of the game, get the ball and go."

"I want us outrebounding the other team by twenty, every time. I want us to have twelve or fewer turnovers out there."

"Regardless of who you're playing, sprint back on defense."

"Regardless of who you're playing, you have to box out."

"Defensively, we really need to set the tone, closing on the ball, no transition baskets."

"Offensively, let's really look at spreading the floor and concentrating on getting good shots, let's work on our half-court offense, let's see a lot of good screens, everyone working together."

The players normally sat on benches in front of their lockers and listened silently, focusing on the blackboard when the coach diagrammed plays or wrote down goals.

There were nights when VanDerveer was pleased by what she saw— Kansas was "a good team effort," for instance, Ohio State was "one of our better ones," at Vanderbilt, Teresa made a move to the hoop that VanDerveer would talk about for months, but more often she came down hard on them for their weaknesses. At Old Dominion they played sloppily, ending with an unpardonable 24 turnovers. At Connecticut their three-point shooting had been abysmal. At Washington she did not see them sprinting back on defense.

When the team separated for a week at Christmas, VanDerveer boarded a plane to visit her parents, who had retired to Florida. Looking back on the fall, she knew she'd accomplished some of her goals, getting the players in top shape, for example, working on the fundamentals. They had played well enough to win, but not well enough to win in Atlanta. Her job was to anchor them, to keep the standards high, even if it meant picking apart every single win until it was nearly meaningless.

Satisfaction was something that losers felt before they lost. Winners did not get comfortable until the last game of the playoffs was finished. And besides, these had been college games.

"Swimming in a swimming pool," she had warned them after the college wins started to pile up, "does not prepare you for swimming in the ocean."

After Christmas they would head to Siberia and Ukraine to see the Soviet-inspired brand of basketball that had crushed the Americans in Barcelona. In the next months they would find themselves flailing in the final minutes of hair-raising games against the Russians, the Cubans, the Australians, and the Canadians, among others. They would fray at the edges and crumble at times under the media's glare. If VanDerveer or any of them had illusions about what they'd built so far, the waves had not yet broken over them. The ocean still lay ahead.

8

chapter

Swimming in the Ocean

In Siberia, public relations were something of a non-issue. The team was scheduled to play three games in five days against one of Russia's top women's club teams in the large industrial city of Ekaterinburg, set in the Ural Mountains about two hundred miles from the border of Kazhakstan—the heart of Siberia. It was January, twenty below zero. The sun, when it bothered to come out at all, hung blanched and ineffectual over the mountains, the sky remained leaden and cold. On the streets, people rushed about, braving the wind and almost continually drifting snow, burrowed in black wool coats and black wool scarves and fur hats, as in a page out of a Tolstoy novel. Nobody wanted an autograph. Nobody really spoke. There were no interviews to give or television crews to satisfy. To Coach VanDerveer's delight, there was only basketball.

The holidays had come and gone quickly, with team members scattered from L.A. to New England for ten days, recuperating and readying themselves for the months ahead. After Siberia they would play four games in Ukraine, then, returning to the States, they'd finish up the last two games of the college tour and have an extended training camp in Colorado Springs. From there it would be nothing but international competition, nothing but swimming in the ocean, as the coach would say. They'd go to China in March, to Australia in May, and in a series of exhibition games in the States between April and July they'd scrimmage the Olympic teams from China, Russia, Ukraine, Cuba, Canada, and Italy. Now that 1996, the Olympic year, had arrived, the countdown was on in earnest. July 19, the day the Olympics opened, was now six and a half months away.

They'd made New Year's resolutions too, written them down as a group for the team's media director, who would include them in the myriad press releases she churned out to keep the public back home involved. Jennifer Azzi simply wanted to eat more vegetables, though dining on boiled beef and overcooked potatoes beneath a cracked plaster ceiling at the hotel in Ekaterinburg, she'd quietly decided that February would be the month for salad. Sheryl Swoopes, having recently confronted a tide of credit card bills, wrote down: "Develop and live on a budget." Carla McGhee, whose spending sometimes got her in trouble with Willie, echoed with "Live on a budget." Lisa Leslie, who had delicately moved the diamond engagement ring she'd gotten from her boyfriend Lorenzo the previous spring from the left hand to the right hand, listed her resolution as "To find happiness, love, and a husband." For Ruthie Bolton the goal was "To be a better all-around person." For Rebecca Lobo: "Have a '96 that is as successful as '95." For Dawn Staley, who had stayed unhappily behind in her hometown of Philadelphia, her arm still in a cast: "Get healthy." For Katrina McClain, who along with Lisa was emerging as the team's most vital member, it was "Stay healthy."

They played in an icebox of a gym located on a gloomy, warehouse-lined street on the west side of Ekaterinburg. When they weren't at the gym, they holed up in the hotel and passed the time mostly by playing cards and reading. For many of them, the feeling was familiar. This was basketball overseas—wretched food, faulty, expensive phone lines, strangers gaping at them in the streets. At least this time, they told each other, they had American teammates to talk to. Katy Steding could remember going through entire days in Japan without having a conversation off the basketball court. Most foreign teams allowed only two non-native players per team, which tended to drive American players deep into their shells, isolated by language and cultural differences, the six-month season never feeling like enough time to fully assimilate.

Nothing, it was agreed, made an American athlete more patriotic than going abroad, even if it was only for a two-week tour like this one, and facing a paucity of creature comforts. Setting foot on alien soil, they suddenly craved all things American: diet Cokes, for example, Big Macs, network television, Popeye's Chicken. Sometimes they baited each other with the material charms that were suddenly 6,000 miles away.

"Who's got better fries, you think, Burger King or Mickey D's?"

"Dang, isn't today Thursday? We're missing Must-See TV."

Having sent teams all over the world for international tournaments, USA Basketball equipped its staff with a stockpile of survival items for trips abroad, a collection accumulated as the direct result of past horrors.

One favored war story involved the 1991 Pan Am games in Havana, when the accommodations in the athletes' village had been so sparse that USA Basketball had sent a staff person to Miami to send daily shipments of help items that included toilet seats and window screening to stave off insects in what was otherwise an open-air dormitory. Luckily if not ironically, the items could be hand-delivered by members of the men's team, since while the women sweltered in Havana, the men were commuting back and forth for games from their air-conditioned rooms at a plush hotel in Miami's Coconut Grove. (According to USA Basketball officials, the discrepancy in accommodations was the result of different game schedules: the men's games fell far enough apart to facilitate the commute, while the women had games nearly every day, making it necessary to stay in Havana.)

In any event, the women's national team had arrived in Siberia outfitted for Armageddon, hauling several heavy crates that included 72 packs of gum, 37 bags of assorted candy, 20 boxes of crackers, 20 rolls of toilet paper, 10 boxes of graham crackers, 10 boxes of granola bars, 19 jars of peanut butter, 15 boxes of cookies, seven packages of tortilla chips and canned cheese, nine boxes of Pop-Tarts, six jars of jelly, five air fresheners, four bottles of laundry detergent, and one box of powdered milk. They would use nearly all of it before two weeks were up.

On the court, too, the trip proved to be something of a survival exercise, one that separated the experienced players from the inexperienced. Switching from NCAA basketball to the international game entailed making several changes, the most significant of which was adjusting to a larger ball. While women's college teams played with a ball with a 29-inch circumference, the international women's teams used the same 30.7-inch basketball used by college men, the NBA, and international men's teams. Whether you were more accustomed to the "big ball" or the "little ball," as they were known, switching back and forth tended to throw off just about everyone's shot, particularly from the three-point range.

International basketball also differed from college basketball in that it was less position-specific; it required versatility. A center could not, for instance, simply float around at the low post, waiting to get the ball and use her height and size to muscle it in. Guards needed to be able to go inside; forwards had to know the perimeter. For players schooled in NCAA basketball, the international game often came as a shock. A perfectly honed three-point shot suddenly grew clunky with a heavier, wider ball. A brilliant post player would find herself defending another post player who could change directions as quickly as a wing. A six foot four forward who'd been treasured for her size would suddenly be staring at the Adam's apple of a woman who was six foot seven. Beyond that, many foreign players thought nothing of holding jerseys, elbowing wildly, pinching, and, according to Katrina, sometimes even biting. Where a college ref would call a foul, foreign refs hardly registered rough play.

In their first game against the Siberian team, it quickly became apparent who on the national team knew international basketball and who didn't. Katrina, for instance, seemed to step onto a higher plane, as if the exceptional performances she'd turned in at power forward all fall had all been done with one hand tied behind her back. Moving from manicured college campuses to the Siberian tundra, from neatly executed NCAA basketball to the more slovenly, riotous international game was like going from pet shop to zoo, and perhaps more than anyone else in the women's game, Katrina McClain loved the zoo.

One learned, watching Katrina match up against one imposing foreigner or another, why she was considered the best female power forward in the world. She was a study in aggression—a possessor of a balletic, prehensile brilliance. If the ball was spinning toward the hoop, then Katrina, if she was on offense, was going to shepherd it there, dancing under the net, holding off her defender with one hand, poised to leap for the rebound with the other. If a shot missed on either end of the court, Katrina, who might as well have had automobile springs for legs, snatched the rebound, braids flung in a wild spray around her, before her opponents had even thought to jump.

People were forever saying that Katrina was the owner of "great hands." This could mean any number of things, but in basketball, great hands are hands that never ever let go of the ball too early. Katrina's hands were like two power clamps. Once she had fastened herself to the ball, no amount of shoving, grabbing, or intimidation could get it away.

Another thing people sometimes said about Katrina was that she was the only female player capable of playing in the NBA. Whether or not this was true or even provable was hard to say, but the underlying point was there was no woman out there who played with the surefooted ferocity that Katrina did. Once, when asked what went through her mind when she went up for a rebound, Katrina, who off the court is surprisingly quiet and mirthful, thought about it for a second and then said, "I mean, I want the ball . . . Just like, I want the ball. I've got to have that ball."

The U.S. won its first two games against the Club Uralmash, a collection of pasty-skinned, long-armed, skyscraper-sized Russian women sponsored by a manufacturing company, and then, on the third night, the American team started to lose. In twenty games they had never trailed by more than eleven points, and no team had been ahead of them in the second half. But suddenly, before a crowd of several hundred crowing Siberian fans in a gym that seemed to refuse to warm up, the U.S. started to flounder. Rebecca, unaccustomed to the larger-sized ball, was not shooting well. Sheryl Swoopes appeared to be having a rare off night. On top of it all, the Russian refs seemed to be picking on the Americans. Tara VanDerveer was not the kind of coach to pace the sidelines or shake her fist at the referees; she was not given to showing her emotions outwardly. Rather, she seemed to compress on the bench, hunched forward with her elbows resting on her knees, her eyes never leaving the action on the court, mouth set in a grim line.

After Nikki had two consecutive turnovers, VanDerveer called a time-out. "Don't throw the ball to Nikki," she told the team. "She obviously doesn't know what to do with it."

When the game resumed and Nikki started to cry on the bench, Teresa, Jennifer, and Lisa made a human shield around her to protect her from the further indignity of having the coach see her weep.

Midway through the second half, the U.S. was behind by 11 points. Teresa Edwards watched the scoreboard anxiously. This was their test, she could feel it. The Olympics were still far enough away that one loss wouldn't kill them. Still, only two of the players on Club Uralmash were likely to go on to the Olympics. These were second-string players. Losing to them would not be that different from losing to a college team. And losing, for Teresa, was in large part psychological. If you refused to accept it, then you could overcome it. The game had nine minutes still to go.

What happened next had everything to do with experience. What experience taught you, Teresa often said, was to trust yourself no matter what the score was, no matter what country you were playing in, no matter who doubted that you could do it. She needed only to glance across the huddle between plays to sense that Katrina was thinking the old thought: got to have that ball. And so that became the plan, get the ball to Katrina. Between the two of them, they had been all over the world. They had been in nearly every kind of late-game situation, and they had won probably five times more than they had lost. All they had to do was trust. Ruthie and Jennifer understood the same thing, so did Lisa despite the fact she was a relative youngster. As the clock ticked down, they started to run the floor hard, pressing full court on the Russians which forced a few turnovers, giving the U.S. a blast of momentum and several transition baskets. Each of them did what they did best: Katrina exploded on the boards, Teresa kept the pace fast without letting the offense get sloppy, Lisa posted up hard against the taller Russians. Ruthie hit several critical three-point shots. In six and a half minutes the national team scored 28 points. Teresa remembers the appreciation washing over her as she ran downcourt in the final minute. This team had the flint that would carry them where they needed to go. They won the game 75–63.

Arriving back in the States late in January, they found that the mood at home was changing. Not changing exactly, but evolving. With the NBA and NCAA seasons in full swing, football season finally dispensed with, basketball dominated the sports pages and nightly television. On subways, in offices, on college campuses, people talked basketball. Beyond that, with 169 days to go, an Olympic fervor was beginning to percolate: Sponsors were starting to run preliminary advertisements, trials were taking place in other sports, forecasters were venturing early predictions of transportation problems, weather problems, crime problems, and general overcrowding in the relatively small city of Atlanta. The hype was beginning to build for real, and thanks largely to the vigilant public relations staff at USA Basketball, the women's basketball team was about to be swept into the maelstrom.

Dawn Staley had been waiting and waiting to get back into the action, and when the team met up in Ruston, Louisiana, for another college game, she got her chance. The cast had been off her hand for a week. While the team had traveled through Russia, Dawn had worked alone in the gym at Saint Joseph's University in West Philadelphia, shooting the ball over and over and over. She'd dribbled up and down the court for hours, getting her feel for the ball back, starting to delight in the prospect of what lay ahead.

Once again her teammates greeted her enthusiastically. "Y'all might get homesick on the road," she announced, sunk deep in a team huddle on her first day back, "but damn, I was *teamsick*!"

Louisiana Tech was then the second-ranked women's team in the country behind the Georgia Bulldogs. Unlike Georgia, which had played the national team during its preseason, Louisiana Tech was now at the height of its season, conditioned, practiced, and ready to play.

"Imagine Marcus Camby and the UMass Minutemen driving and dunking their way past Michael Jordan and the Chicago Bulls," wrote one local sportswriter the next day, conjuring the game for his readers. "Imagine the Nebraska Cornhuskers trading touchdowns with the Dallas Cowboys. Imagine the local Golden Gloves champ fighting Mike Tyson to a draw."

In other words, Louisiana Tech challenged the indomitable national team like no other college team had, competing hard for rebounds, with several quick-moving guards who refused to buckle when VanDerveer abandoned her rules and called for a pressure defense. The first half was played at a furious pace, with VanDerveer on the sidelines shouting unhappily, "Box out! BOX OUT!" as her team alternately trailed and led by only a handful of points. VanDerveer played Dawn sparingly, allowing her to get a feel for the game slowly. With just seconds left in the half, a crowd of over 8,000 roaring and the U.S. behind by three, Teresa Edwards—in a singular moment of self-possession—tossed a long, arching three-pointer from well behind the line to tie the game at 40–40.

In the opening minutes of the second half, fighting for a rebound, Katrina McClain twisted an ankle and was pulled from the game. While Rebecca and Carla rotated in and out to fill Katrina's spot, the Louisiana players continued their assault on the boards, limiting the national team to a single shot at the hoop each time it brought the ball down. With nine minutes to go in the game, Louisiana led by three, but then Lisa Leslie cut herself loose, pouring in 16 nearly consecutive points, leaping spectacularly to block several shots, and jumping in to pick up the slack on rebounding created by Katrina's absence. Almost entirely on her shoulders, the U.S. won the game by nine points.

At the postgame press conference, VanDerveer stared blankly at the assembled group of reporters, clearly disappointed in her team. She was forever telling them that they couldn't rely on three or four players on the team, namely Katrina, Lisa, Sheryl, and Ruthie, to do all the hard work. "You gotta step up," she would tell them. "This is like an orchestra, where on some nights one person is going to get a solo, but you gotta be ready to play, to do your part at any time." Tonight had been Lisa Leslie's solo. Without Lisa, and with Katrina down, they could've lost the game. When the reporters asked, she deemed what had just happened "a wake-up call" and "a reality check."

"If they would have had one more serious inside player," VanDerveer told the group, echoing what she'd said to her players moments earlier in the locker room, "we would've really been in trouble."

Throughout the college tour the coach had not stopped fretting about the national team's lack of a true center. Lisa Leslie weighed just 170 pounds—a featherweight compared to the players they were about to meet. China had their six-eight center who weighed 253 pounds and who was known internationally as "the Big Girl." Lisa was more suited to play power forward, a position that would better showcase her quickness and long-range shooting, but she was all VanDerveer had for a center at the moment. It was like playing a chess game without your queen. She had told the selection committee again and again during their monthly conference calls: They could be in tiptop shape, they could practice their skills until they could play with closed eyes, but as the Louisiana Tech game had most recently demonstrated, if they met one team that could seriously challenge them at the post—and, VanDerveer had assured the committee members, those teams were out there— the dream of a gold medal would surely go down in flames.

In return, the committee members liked to remind VanDerveer of two things: This was not the official Olympic team, i.e., if changes needed to be made, they would have an opportunity to make them, and, if they decided to keep the members of the current team, there was still one spot open for the twelfth player.

This was one note of solace. As far as VanDerveer was concerned, the open spot should go to the strongest and toughest bruiser of a basketball player they could find. The committee had assured her that she could hold a tryout for the twelfth spot, inviting a group of big post players to Colorado Springs sometime in March or April. Already she had a few hefty players in mind, but it was impossible to know which one would work, who the banger of her dreams would be until that player walked through the gym door in Colorado Springs and started bruising.

Rebecca Lobo was signing autographs again, the routine now so familiar—sign and smile, smile and sign—that she hardly had to think about it. Following the game at Texas Tech, she had flown to Atlanta for Supershow, the behemoth sporting goods trade show that invaded the city each February. Decked out from head to toe in Reebok apparel, Rebecca was to greet the salespeople and retailers who drifted through the warren of merchandising booths that packed the cavernous Georgia World Congress Center, signing and smiling all the way. This was all taking place a stone's throw from the Georgia Dome and nearly six months to the day from the gold medal game.

Standing there with her agent, Kenton Edelin, a tall black man in his early thirties who had played basketball for Virginia, and Dave, who had come down from Storrs for the weekend to see her, Rebecca felt comfortable, happy to be with friends. In the nine months he'd represented her, Kenton had become a buddy. He was an easygoing, upbeat presence in her life and had steered her toward sound business deals while approaching shakier-seeming ones more cautiously. Much like Rebecca, Kenton was careful to treat everyone he encountered with a friendly respect. Even as he had turned down countless offers and negotiated ferociously on Rebecca's behalf, Kenton never seemed to make an enemy, and this was something she valued.

The autograph seekers had formed a loose line in front of her. They were generally pleasant, making chitchat with her as she scrawled her name across the glossy black and white photographs the Reebok reps were handing out.

"Can you write 'To Bethany' on it?"

Rebecca smiled deliberately at each person who came through.

"My daughter watches all of your games—"

"I'm from Massachusetts too—"

"Hang in there, we're all pulling for you." It was a woman's voice. Rebecca lifted her eyes to look at the speaker, confused. *What?*

"They can't cut you," said the woman. "They just can't."

What?

"You don't know what I'm talking about? You haven't seen the paper today? *USA Today?*"

Rebecca shook her head no. It was early afternoon, and the paper had been out for hours, but unless she knew in advance there was going to be a story about the team, she seldom had a chance to read any newspaper.

"Oh, dear, I'm sorry," said the woman before ducking her eyes and awkwardly disappearing into the crowd.

Tara VanDerveer had gone public with her fretting, or at least she had slipped up and complained to the wrong person, a sportswriter named Steve Wieberg who often covered the team. The story was prominently displayed at the top of a page in the sports section with the headline "VanDerveer has concerns about team: Lopsided wins mask weaknesses."

In it, the coach seemed to steer the subject quickly away from the team's undefeated run to last month's trip to Russia. "The international competition . . ." she was quoted as saying, "exploited the inexperienced players."

Wieberg went on to discuss the fact that VanDerveer was shopping for a twelfth player for the team, and in doing so dropped a speculative bomb that Rebecca had not anticipated. "Any other new faces would have to be replacements: One potentially for the player most popular and by far most identifiable to the public, Rebecca Lobo."

Quoting VanDerveer again: "I think we have to really evaluate. I think experience is really important. International experience. And I just don't think some of our young players, particularly Nikki and Rebecca, have it, whereas there are other players out there who do." The writer made mention of Rebecca's low shooting percentage, 33 percent from the field, and low point average, 3.5 points per game, in the four-game tournament against the Ukrainians. McCray, it said, averaged 38 percent and two points a game. The article discussed the fact that VanDerveer had a "voice but no vote" in selecting the Olympic team, noting that selection committee guidelines allowed that a player could be cut only for "less than satisfactory performance of a continuing and substantial nature."

Rebecca bit her lip and tried to stay calm. She knew she had improvements to make, but she had never thought about being cut before. It had simply not crossed her mind, but now suddenly there was a big "if" to contend with. She'd had a sense before that the coach did not think she deserved to be on the team. But had her performance been "less than satisfactory"? Who was to judge? Rebecca didn't know anyone on the selection committee. She had no idea what to think. Her teammates were scattered across the country on break. After reading the article in a corner of the convention hall, Rebecca had had to continue signing autographs. When she got back to her hotel room later, there was a message from the team's media director, apologizing for not being able to inform her about the article sooner. "The article pissed me off more than anything," Rebecca would recall. "I was angry but there was nothing I could do. I couldn't control it . . . I tried to let it go, but it was hard."

The story had caught everyone by surprise. Back in the USA Basketball office in Colorado Springs, the committee members were calling incessantly, worried about what looked to be a public relations nightmare. Was VanDerveer trying to manipulate them by floating the post-player issue in the press? Why did the boom always seem to fall the hardest on Lobo?

VanDerveer had taken the day to go skiing and could not be reached. Almost anyone familiar with the national team, though, could recognize the voice and the sentiment in the article as classic Tara VanDerveer. She was not private in her griping. She'd made it clear from the start that she needed skilled post players. If she was unhappy with certain players' performance, she was not about to censor herself.

The *USA Today* article would send VanDerveer's detractors into conniptions over her apparent lack of sensitivity, but it was hard not to ask the question: Would anybody care if a men's coach commented on his players this way? She had been nothing but honest, the same way she had been when telling the Connecticut reporters not to expect Rebecca to play a lot. What was wrong with that? She had not attacked anyone's character. She had not attacked anyone at all. After nearly losing to a college team with just five and a half months to go till the Olympics, had she really been wrong to say "I think we really need to evaluate . . ."?

Certainly, there were men's and women's coaches alike who would insist that team business should not be discussed in the press. (VanDerveer would later claim that she thought she had an "understanding" with Wieberg that he would not use Nikki's or Rebecca's names. According to Wieberg, the issue of using names never came up.) Nonetheless, it was not uncommon to read about an NBA coach who basically advertised the fact that he needed a good forward or a strong three-point shooter when he didn't have one. Men's college coaches were forever discussing their recruiting needs.

Women's coaching unfortunately seemed far more political and open to scrutiny. It felt like everything had to be *earned*. At Stanford, VanDerveer had to win two national titles before her salary was raised to equal that of the men's coach. Across the country, other women's coaches had been forced to fight for pay that was commensurate with that for men's coaches. The most recent statistics available from the Women's Basketball Coaches' Association reveal that in 1993, the average Division I women's basketball coach's salary was 59 percent that of the average men's coach. In the wake of what would become known among USA Basketball athletes and staffers as "the *USA Today* thing," one wondered whether the final fight for women's coaches, particularly one as outspoken and successful as VanDerveer, would be for equal respect.

By the end of the day that the story ran in *USA Today*, word had spread to nearly every player on the national team, most of whom were at home. Teresa had just finished reading the story when Nikki called from her fiancé's home in Ohio. She was shaken and confused.

"Nikki's good about asking for a little help when she needs it," said Teresa later. "She just wanted to talk that day. I said, 'Nikki don't let this define you. You're not what you read about yourself in the paper, okay?' She was all right about the whole thing. It shook her up, but she was ready to fight back."

Rebecca called Geno Auriemma, her coach from UConn. By the time she called, Auriemma had seen the *USA Today* story already and was angry. He and VanDerveer had never been particularly friendly anyway. "There's no need to air that sort of thing in public," he said of the incident later. "If the coaching staff felt that way about Rebecca, that was fine, but there's no need to discuss it publicly. I was hurt for her because I knew how much time and effort she'd put into being on that team. I knew how badly she wanted to be on the Olympic team. I know I'm not coaching the team, and I don't know what the coaches are looking for, but I can't believe that having Rebecca Lobo on your team can hurt you, can keep you from winning a gold medal . . . no way, no how, could you convince me of that."

He shielded his anger from Rebecca though, knowing it wouldn't help her keep her spot on the team.

"What I told her," said Auriemma, "was 'It's not your job to worry about whether you're going to be on the team or not.' I just tried to get her to think about how she was playing, how she was performing, what her role on the team was and what she needed to do. The other things were out of her control, so she couldn't worry about them.'"

For the next several months the press would continually cross-examine Lobo for a response. She would adopt Auriemma's line of thinking, quietly avowing to work harder, and she would carefully avoid criticizing VanDerveer in public. "Everything that was in there was true," Rebecca would say when asked about the *USA Today* story. "I have no problem with the article or what Tara said in it. I only wish I hadn't found out about it the way I did, that's all. But that was out of everyone's control."

When Tara VanDerveer arrived at the USA Basketball office the following morning, she was promptly ushered into executive director Warren Brown's office for a meeting and asked to close the door behind her.

Lisa Leslie stood shivering in her bare feet on a nearly deserted Malibu beach. She wore a tight white tank top and white bikini bottoms that made her skin look richly brown. Her arms and legs had been coated with a thin patina of baby oil to give her muscles extra sheen. The Pacific rolled behind her, a lolling low tide. The breeze gave her goose bumps. There were several studio lights and reflectors set up on the sand before her, a photographer bent in front of a tripod, his lens aimed directly at her. "Pose like we discussed and look right into the camera," he said. "Move like you're playing basketball."

On cue, Lisa sank into a slight, catlike crouch, her arms bent at the elbows, her fingers splayed, her hip cocked toward the camera. Her hair had been slicked away from her face, plastered to her scalp with gel. She lowered her eyelids slightly, lifted her chin, set her lips in a thick, proud pout, and leveled her gaze on the camera lens. She looked beautiful and she knew it. Her mother used to say that their family descended from the Watusi people of Central Africa. Royalty, her mother said. Lisa loved this idea. In moments like these, she felt noble, her feet flat and long in the sand, her face as angular and exotic as her body was. It was mid-February and her dream was coming true. She was modeling for *Vogue*. The photographer in front of her was Herb Ritts, *the* Herb Ritts, who had photographed Kate Moss, Cindy Crawford, and Naomi Campbell. And now he was photographing her.

The national team was on a ten-day break, one that Tara VanDerveer had sanctioned in order to let her players rest before a two-week training camp at the end of the month and a tournament in China, scheduled for March. But rest was becoming something of a joke. The team had now won twenty-eight consecutive games, and the buzz was starting to grow. Being undefeated was a catchy and very American way to be. Factored into this was the ready-made comparison to the men's Dream Team, which, months away from its 1996 inception, was already getting a lot of advance press. As to the women, speculation ran rampant in the media. Was this the female Dream Team? Was such a thing possible? These questions inspired a visceral but more significant curiosity among the public: What does women's basketball look like anyway?

It seemed that people wanted to see the women's Dream Team, though they did not necessarily need to see them playing basketball. The words "dream" and "team" together meant more than basketball, really; they meant celebrity. Invitations poured in from around the country. As a group, the players had hit the NBA All-Star weekend in San Antonio early in the month, which included invitations to the "celebrity area" at the opening of a local Planet Hollywood restaurant, where they'd hob-nobbed with Bruce Willis, George Clooney, and Demi Moore. Late at night, Lisa Leslie and Dawn Staley, reunited after nearly a month of being apart, had loitered in the hotel lobby, waiting to see which NBA star, be it Shaq or Barkley, would pass through the door next.

Just days after VanDerveer had essentially told the nation Rebecca was not good enough to play in the Olympics, she was headed toward the Espy awards banquet, a televised black-tie event sponsored by ESPN and held in New York City. Once there, she was given the Women's College Basketball Player of the Year award, which came as little surprise to anybody there that night, but as the ceremony stretched on to its culminating set of awards, Male and Female Athletes of the Year, a murmur went up in the audience when Rebecca Lobo, a twenty-two-year-old at the very start of her career, won the women's award, beating out Monica Seles, Steffi Graf, and Picabo Street, rising from her table looking somewhat awkward in her ankle-length black dress to take her place at the podium with the men's winner, baseball ironman Cal Ripken, Jr.

Some of the players took to their celebrity better than others. Several of them actually worked at it, while a number of the others remained uninterested and for the most part, undiscovered. The running joke among them was that the public mistook every black player for Sheryl Swoopes and every white player for Rebecca Lobo. Sitting in a room before an appearance at the All-Star Weekend, Teresa encountered Kareem Abdul-Jabbar, the NBA legend of the seventies and eighties.

He looked at her once, then did a second take. "Hey," he said, "I know you. You're Sheryl Swoopes."

Teresa felt her face go hot. At seven-one, with broad shoulders and long arms, Jabbar seemed to fill up the whole room. She had grown up watching him play for the Lakers. He was a millionaire many times over, a Hall-of-Famer, a legend. She gave Jabbar her sweetest smile and fired back. "And you must be Magic *Johnson!*"

One way or another, February became glamour month. Lisa had her *Vogue* shoot. Jennifer was featured in an *Elle* magazine article and had taken to wearing a black *Elle* baseball cap when she traveled. Katrina had a walk-on part in the NBC sitcom *In the House*, which starred rapper LL Cool J. Sears, one of the team's seven corporate sponsors, flew all of them out to Los Angeles to film various parts of a television ad the company would run during the team's televised exhibition games and the Olympics. Representatives from Young & Rubican, the advertising agency hired by Sears, had met the team after a game in February and had walked away thrilled by the personalities of the players. Later in the month, assembling the players in Los Angeles, they filmed Nikki jogging in the rain, Nikki cooing at an infant, Sheryl posing in a skimpy black bikini set, Ruthie singing "Amazing Grace" on a bus and later talking to children on a playground, and Lisa in a cocktail dress and high heels, adjusting her stockings in the locker room. They filmed a little bit of basketball too, setting up the players to scrimmage in an airy rented gym.

Each player eventually would receive a residual based on how much she appeared in the ad, and how often the ad ran. The people from Young & Rubican wanted to keep things "spontaneous," to film the players behaving as they normally would, only dressed, of course, in clothing from Sears. As a result, the shooting, which was done over four days, was done somewhat impulsively, with a number of potential scenes more or less improvised in a hotel room. ("Sheryl likes to take baths?" an ad exec said enthusiastically. "Well, let's put Sheryl in the bath!") While most of the other players stayed at the filming only a day or two, Sheryl and Lisa remained for the entirety, cooperating eagerly. Lisa knew how to charm. She remembered everyone's name, made a point of smiling and saying hello to each member of the ad crew, and was entirely amenable as a small squadron of wardrobe, hair, and makeup people worked her over. Sheryl was duly cooperative, lounging in a bubble bath for the camera, complaining only a little when she had to wait hours for the director to set up a scene.

The two of them seemed to understand instinctively what it took to transcend the sports pages and become sports *personalities*. While athletes retired into obscurity, sports personalities went on to become actors or commentators or full-time celebrity endorsers. More than others on the national team, Sheryl and Lisa worked hard at becoming personalities. While Sheryl's Nike exposure had given her a solid head start in the fame department, Lisa, with her striking looks, her notoriety as a woman who could dunk the ball, and her blanket be-nice-to-everyone policy, was coming on strong.

The team reassembled in Colorado Springs during the third week of February for a two-week training camp before the trip to China. At the first practice, VanDerveer made a point of pulling aside Nikki and Rebecca individually to talk about the *USA Today* article. She told them that she hoped they hadn't been hurt by it. She told them she would help them work hard and improve. She did not apologize for what she'd done.

The *USA Today* incident was like a hand grenade thrown into the carefully laid camaraderie the players had built over the fall. They had been told from the start that the Olympic team would be officially named in June, but their understanding had been that disaster would have to strike before anyone got cut. Over time, they'd come to a point where they couldn't think about going to the Olympics without imagining themselves going as a group, as the eleven-member family that had gone through all the travel and adjustment and hard work together.

Yet, as the newspaper story had harshly reminded everyone, there were no assurances. If Nikki and Rebecca could get cut, then so could any of the others who often kept them company on the bench. Carla, Katy, and Jennifer were bench players too. VanDerveer might have favored Dawn in the early part of the fall, but it didn't quite seem that way anymore. Dawn would have to earn her minutes, just like the rest of the players. Teresa was still worried that Dawn's reentry into the team might eclipse all her own hard work in the coach's eyes. Suddenly nobody, really, was safe. The Olympic roster, which would list twelve players and six alternates, was due to the Olympic Committee on June 19. VanDerveer would start auditioning other players as potential additions or replacements on the team in less than a month. The upcoming trip to China was shaping up to be a sink-or-swim affair.

In the meantime, VanDerveer was moving her team to the second level of what she called their "training Pyramid." They'd spent the fall and winter getting in shape and building basic strategies; now they would use the next several months of international competition to develop strategy. She would introduce new plays regularly, while they would run through the existing repertoire over and over until they could do it flawlessly, effortlessly.

By now the players had kept up with roughly a ten-workout-per-week schedule for five months with little rest. Their bodies were rock-solid with muscle, their lungs no longer felt strained and overworked in the thin air of Colorado Springs. In the weight room, each player was lifting approximately a third more weight than she'd been lifting back in October. There were days when their own stamina surprised them. They had reached a point at which their improvement curve in strength and cardiovascular fitness was leveling off even if the workouts weren't.

The goal now was not to break down. Any Olympic-level athlete will tell you stories about reaching an athletic peak and then having one small injury topple the whole thing. Each member of the national team had an Achilles' heel, a tragic flaw in her bodily makeup that stood to demolish her shot at the Olympics, and possibly the team's. Things like this happened abruptly and without warning. Katrina had her arthritic hips, Sheryl had her weak ankles, Teresa had recurring calf and hamstring injuries, Katy and Dawn mistrusted their knees, Lisa wore tape around the area below her knees to take the pressure off her tendons. They nursed their weak points carefully, heaping their aching joints with mountains of bagged ice each week, seeking out the trainers at all hours of the day for ultrasound on their knees, massage for their shoulders, knowing deep down that beyond doing their best to maintain themselves physically, it was all a crap shoot. Statistically, it stood to reason that at least one of them would fall before July.

When it came to understanding the body's frailty, Carla McGhee stood somewhat apart from the rest of them. She had grown up a wisecracking kid in Peoria, in the central part of Illinois. As a child, she'd been passed back and forth from her mother to her grandmother and various aunts, and finally, at the age of fourteen, was adopted by family friends. Perhaps as a result of the instability in her home life, Carla's weapon—her way of reaching out to people—became her wit. She clowned her way through school, always seeking out attention. The one bit of unwanted notice she got came from being the tallest girl in the sixth grade.

"My classmates were like *ants* compared to me, I was so tall," she said of her childhood. "I was always in the back of the line, the last on picture day. It was terrible. I hated being tall! I was goofy, walking around all bent over, trying to be the same size as my girlfriends."

According to Carla, basketball appealed to her only insofar as it might be a chance to "grab a little spotlight," to catch people's eyes. Playing on her middle-school team, she discovered that her basketball game made people sit up and take notice, they clamored for her, and from then on, she says, she was hooked. She idolized Dr. J—"Oh, if I could glide like *him*"—and dreamed of going to the West Coast to play one-on-one with Cheryl Miller.

In high school she quickly became a star center, using her size to great advantage, developing a deft shooting touch that often won the team its games. Over time, she grew to be unapologetically arrogant. She surfaced at practice only when there was nothing better to do. During her rare appearances, she ignored the coach, teased her teammates, and refused to participate in routine drills.

All this and she was still talented enough to be recruited by the illustrious Pat Summit, who brought her to Tennessee on a scholarship in 1986. Subordinated to Summit's stringent work ethic, her scholarship in the balance, Carla mouthed off less and cooperated more, but she remained cocky and outspoken, never liking to be pushed too hard.

Then came the fall of 1987. On the night before basketball season was to begin, Carla folded herself into the passenger seat of a compact car belonging to a teammate, setting off for dinner at the home of one of Tennessee's boosters.

Next thing she remembered, she opened her eyes to an unfamiliar room. Someone was rubbing the palm of her hand urgently. "Who am I?" a voice asked.

The face shifted into focus, a round-faced woman with liquid brown eyes, and Carla knew the answer immediately—"You're my mother"— but she could not discipline her mouth to say it. She felt a searing pain in her abdomen, but could not lift her head to look at it. The walls around her were blindingly white. A hospital. She could tell by watching the emotion play across her adoptive mother's face that whatever had happened to her, it was bad. As it turned out, a truck had smashed into Carla's side of the car from a merging lane on the way to dinner that night. The ambulance crew had to cut through the car's frame to get to her. The accident had broken all but two bones in her face and shattered her right hip. She had a brain contusion. Her jaw was wired shut. Her body was in traction. She'd been in a coma for two days.

For a long time, her adoptive parents refused to let her see a mirror. Remembering, Carla twisted her face into a grimace. "My cheekbone was down here," she said, pointing to the line of her jaw, "my nose was over here." Her hand moved to her cheek. "My chin was up by my ear. I was one big, ugly freak."

Several weeks after the accident, she was moved from Tennessee to a hospital in Peoria. Her parents had the mirrors removed from the bathroom in her room. "I didn't have a lot of visitors at first either, because I guess my parents didn't want everybody seeing what I looked like," she says now. "Sometimes now I wonder, damn, what *did* I look like? But I guess I wouldn't want to know."

As her jaw healed, Carla was given a small chalkboard with which to communicate. *Hungry*, she would scribble to her mother, *thirsty. Bored.* Then, seeing her mother's face start to change again, she'd erase the word and replace it with, *I'm lucky.*

Several specialists flew in to evaluate her. She would need a series of plastic surgeries on her face; her hip was going to cause her real problems. Every doctor who saw her concurred on one major point: If Carla McGhee was ever able to walk again, it would be with a cane.

"I was like, okay, can't talk, can't walk, can't eat. . . . There has to be *something* good about this . . . and I was like, well, I'm alive."

In the next several months Carla McGhee defied every one of the doctors' predictions. By January, just ten weeks after the accident, she was back at Tennessee, walking to and from classes with crutches. By springtime she had moved to a cane. Slowly, she learned to walk unassisted. Then she tried to run a little. She tried pool workouts and riding a stationary bike. Over the summer, she was dribbling a basketball and mustering an occasional half-court sprint.

"There were days I was so sore I couldn't do anything," she said, looking back. "But I had realized, sitting all those weeks in the hospital, getting letters and visits from my teammates and my coach, that people loved me. I mean, I started to think my life would not be complete if I was not on the court with them"—she broke into a smile—"if I was not doing those *hell-ACIOUS* workouts with them.

"You don't understand," she continued, her voice going quiet again, "when you're with people like that, they're like your family. Those days I couldn't be with my team were the saddest days of my life."

When basketball season opened exactly a year following the accident, Carla showed up ready to play. She wore a giant pair of protective goggles and a thick hip pad for a while. ("I looked like a big old brute out there—*so* unattractive.") Nonetheless, her reentry into the game seemed, miraculously to take no time at all. With Carla as a starter, Tennessee went 35–2 that year, beating Rutie Bolton's Auburn team at the Final Four to win a national championship.

The accident was the end of what Carla has called "the era of the Almighty Me."

On the court she seemed to relax into her role; she was strong on defense, a solid rebounder, not someone who shone as a superstar. She doted on her friends, was famous for sticking her nose in everyone's business. At times she would withdraw, but when Carla was in a good mood, she launched into endless talking jags, laughing and telling stories in a voice cut with a curious urgency. "If me and you are talking," she once explained, "and I don't tell you how I feel, if I'm holding back . . . then what if I walk out the door and we never talk again?" The thought of this, even with a relative stranger, gets her agitated. "You'd never know what I was about!"

Physically, Carla's body seemed to have healed up well after the accident, though having sustained a major head injury, she would forever be at a higher risk for reinjury—a thought that hung at the periphery of her mind, and the minds of those who knew her history, each time she stepped on the court.

Training camp passed uneventfully. Colorado Springs would never feel like home to the players, even if it was the place they came back to when they weren't traveling and where they kept their belongings. Most of the team lived in corporate apartments high on a bluff outside the city's center, in two-bedroom suites that were not that much different from hotel rooms with their blond wood furniture, white linens, and thick carpeting. Teresa and Katrina lived in one apartment, with Sheryl and Eric across the hall and Carla downstairs. Lisa and Dawn, Katy and Nikki, lived in buildings nearby. Jennifer and Rebecca, the Reebok players, stayed in a downtown hotel, while Ruthie chose a Marriott close to the training center. The only real difference, it seemed, between being on the road and being in Colorado Springs was that their shoe sponsors also rented them cars (Nikki, Rebecca, and Lisa were still too young to rent and had to catch rides from teammates), and they had been in town enough to have favorite restaurants and to know the local mall inside and out.

In an attempt to get the women accustomed to bigger, tougher opponents VanDerveer had them scrimmage a local men's team every other evening in the week. They played the same guys every time they came to town, a select group of players, including a man named Eddie Johnson, a former Denver Nuggets player, who had once led the NBA in three-point shooting. The games were friendly but highly physical. One of the national team's assistant coaches would coach the men, while the other would referee. VanDerveer, of course, watched over her own team.

The two teams were evenly matched—if the women won one night, usually the men came back and won the next. The challenge put Dawn Staley in heaven. She was a busybody on the court—in all places at once, fiercely directing the play, jawing on a piece of gum all the while. "Our ball!" she'd shout each time the ball flew out of bounds, iregardless of who'd touched it last. "Our ball, our *ball!*" They quibbled over the scorekeeping and who should have been called on a foul. They talked trash and celebrated their shots with an exuberance that on the college tour would not have been polite. The scrimmages were fun enough to watch that they started drawing a small crowd of training center staff. Eric Jackson usually surfaced and watched from a plastic chair against a wall, calling out encouragement to the men. "You got her, Todd," he'd call. "Nice shot, Milt."

Then one night midway through their second week of February training camp, the two teams were locked in a close scrimmage, the players racing up and down the court in a fast transition game, when from deep in a cluster of bodies beneath the net, Carla McGhee went up for a shot and something went awry. Her body lurched and then fell. The sound of her head slamming onto the floor was like a cement block being dropped, emphatic enough that everyone in the gym felt it echo in their chests.

Normally, an athletic trainer will pause a moment at the sidelines to observe the immediate aftermath of a player's fall, using it to assess the nature of the injury and its gravity before going over to attend to it. Tonight, however, the trainer on duty, a man named Ed Ryan, who'd traveled with the team off and on throughout the fall, sprinted over without hesitation. This was Carla McGhee, and she'd gone down hard. Everybody in the gym knew it was serious.

The players gathered in a knot around Carla, whose body was laid flat out on the floor. Ryan charged into their midst and ordered them all to back off. He was perspiring slightly, his face somber, worried. He felt around at the base of Carla's neck, checking for a spinal injury. She was conscious. Her lips parted slightly, her voice made a high-pitched keening, as if she were trying to cry but the pain was too great.

"Cell phone!" called Ryan, keeping his voice even. When one was delivered from the sidelines, he called an ambulance. Carla's body was limp, her pupils dilated. As Ryan waved the players over to the sidelines, Katy Steding started to cry. Lisa and Jennifer draped their arms around Katy. Coach VanDerveer and her assistants hovered nervously nearby. The ambulance crew was there within minutes. They strapped Carla to a board, immobilizing her spine, loaded her onto a stretcher, and carried her away. The gym was silent, save for Katy's soft weeping.

At the hospital, after a skull X ray, a CT scan and an MRI, Carla was diagnosed with a second-degree concussion and a strained neck and released from the hospital after about six hours. She did not remember any part of the fall, what led up to it, what caused it, or anything before getting to the hospital. The doctors ordered that she be watched carefully for a few days. Her head throbbed, any form of light made her eyes burn, her stomach was a pit of nausea. Carol Callan, the team director, helped her back to her apartment, drew the curtains, made her comfortable and then, at Carla's request, departed. Lori Phelps, the team manager, called at two-hour intervals, as the doctor had suggested, to make certain Carla was okay.

The team practiced the next afternoon without incident. Carol Callan gave the group a report on Carla's health. She would not be going to China. They were looking to get a replacement for her, another post player, to come along on the trip. Back at the USA Basketball office, Callan had called Val Whiting, one of the last players cut from the team at trials last year, and tried to persuade her to come to China. Val had sounded reluctant. She had just returned from a season playing professionally in Brazil. She told Callan she'd think about it.

The last practice before the team left for China was held on a Thursday afternoon in the second-story gym they usually played in. The players were tired, edgy, worried more than ever about injuries. Rebecca had called Geno Auriemma for one last boost before she disappeared to China, her future with the team still uncertain. Sitting on the sidelines before practice, quietly lacing up shoes and straightening knee braces, they were a straggly, fatigued group. VanDerveer arrived, looking serious. Given that tomorrow was a travel day, they braced themselves for a grueling practice.

Then, at the far end of the gym, the door swung open. Carla McGhee entered the room, dressed in street clothes, her face hidden beneath a wide-brimmed hat and a pair of sunglasses, her neck wrapped in a thick brace. The lights of the gym made her wince, even behind the sunglasses. She moved like a decrepit old woman, shuffling gingerly across the hardwood, wobbling slightly as she made her way toward the bleachers. When her teammates approached, she waved them away, their motion heightening her nausea. Reaching the bleachers, she bent down slowly, moving as if her head were as heavy as a cannonball. Carefully, she stretched herself out, lying flat on her back, looking up at the ceiling.

Lisa Leslie walked over and said quietly. "Girl, what're you doing here?"

Beneath the sunglasses Carla mustered a pained smile. "I'm on this team, ain't I? . . . I came for practice."

9

chapter

Long Way from Home

Val Whiting said good-bye to her mother and father at the airport in Wilmington, Delaware, and boarded the plane that would take her to Denver and then to Colorado Springs, where she would join the national team players for a day before they all went to China. Six feet three inches tall and 205 pounds, Val never looked forward to being hunched up in an airplane seat. That morning, making her way down the aisle, she realized that her flight appeared to be full, the narrow plane teeming with arms and legs and people coughing and newspapers extended to maximum width, all of which made the prospect of the next four hours infinitely worse. Finding her seat, she settled in quietly, pulled out an Alice Walker novel, and tried to read.

She didn't want to go to Colorado Springs and beyond that, China. She had left team trials last May utterly dejected and had stayed that way for most of the summer. Getting cut had not been an easy thing to get over. She'd performed well at trials, she knew it. Everyone who'd seen her play that week in Colorado Springs had told her she was a shoo-in. She was the hefty post player of Tara VanDerveer's dreams. She'd played for VanDerveer during the heyday of the coach's career, a part of the '90 and '92 championship-winning teams. She had been in the best shape of her life, having worked with a personal trainer in San Francisco for three months before the trials. She felt she'd outplayed most of the post players, and still, USA Basketball had sent her home with a little pat on the shoulder and had given her spot instead to Rebecca Lobo.

Sitting on the plane ten months later, her body felt heavy and out of shape. She had spent the winter playing for a team in Brazil, living in a small city seventy miles north of São Paolo. She'd made friends, picked up a little Portuguese. She'd averaged a respectable 16 points and nine rebounds per game, and her team had gone to the semifinals of the regional tournament. Six months living among the Brazilians, whom she found to be passionate and good-humored, had done wonders for her mood. She'd taken three weeks in February to travel and had danced her way through Carnival—"Car-ni-*val*!" she said, describing it, wiggling her eyebrows at the debauchery the very word suggested—thoughts of her dashed hopes for the Olympic teams long banished.

The phone call, then, that she got from Carol Callan not three days following her return to the States carried a bitter irony. She had finally moved past the idea of not playing for the national team—who needed them anyway?—and now USA Basketball was on the phone, asking her to come back, if only to fill in for Carla McGhee for two weeks. She'd been on vacation, had hardly gone near a basketball for a straight month. She was in terrible shape, and they'd given her two days' notice. The enduring depression of last summer welled up inside her. She told Callan she'd think it over and call back.

With the team about to depart, however, there was little time to think. The next day, as Val was still considering whether to go, Tara VanDerveer had called. It sounded to Val like her old coach was almost begging. She'd said some things about how fun it would be—a three-day layover in Hawaii, a day in Hong Kong, and then on to China. She had friends on the team, VanDerveer had reminded her, her old teammates Katy and Jennifer. Not only would she be helping out her country, she'd get a leg up on the post-player trials being held in April. When Val told her how out of shape she was, she says that VanDerveer brushed it off as no big deal. "We'll understand," Val recalls the coach saying. "Don't worry."

And thus she had decided to go. Her father, who'd been her most ardent supporter through team trials and the miserable summer that followed, had urged her to give it a try. Who knew what would happen? There was at least one spot open for the Olympic team, possibly more. It could all work out for the best.

By the time her plane touched down in Colorado Springs, Val was all jitters. She'd been out of the country and thus had missed seeing the national team's televised games, though considering it again, she wasn't positive she would have watched them anyway. In any event, she knew nothing about how everyone had been playing, how the players got along, how her presence among them might be perceived. The team's undefeated record spoke for itself, but beating college teams and winning a few games in Russia did not guarantee much. Both Callan and VanDerveer had mentioned what was increasingly considered a dire need for a strong post player on the team. Val had a good twenty-five pounds and several years' experience on Rebecca Lobo, but then again, she told herself arriving in Colorado, she'd had those advantages at team trials too.

Seeing the players for the first time, Val relaxed somewhat. They hugged her and pounded her on the back, genuinely glad, it seemed, to see her there. The next morning the group of them boarded a plane and flew to Los Angeles, and then to Honolulu, for a few days' practice.

The air in Honolulu was humid, the city seemed to rise out of nothing, its white beachfront hotels glittering between sea and sky, the ribboned beaches of Waikiki stretching luxuriously around the curve of the island. USA Basketball had arranged for the team to practice in a small gym on a University of Hawaii campus. As the team ran through its regular paces of shooting practice and defensive drills, Val felt her lungs seize up. She huffed for air, her legs grew stiff and heavy like pieces of cast iron. VanDerveer's voice hawked in on her almost immediately: "Pick it up, Val! Come on now. You gotta run it!" Meanwhile, the others seemed to be gliding more or less effortlessly up and down the court, passing the ball between them. In Val's estimation, these players were three levels above what they'd been at trials.

After an hour and a half, every one of them was soaked with sweat, but joining the cluster at the Gatorade jug, Val was fairly certain she was the only one who felt ready to keel over. VanDerveer had been all over her case, commenting on every missed shot, every slow hustle on defense. "Sprint!" she'd been shouting at all of them. "Sprint back on defense!" But Val, the heaviest and slowest of them all, felt like she could do nothing to please. Already this trip seemed like a mistake.

The next morning's practice was not a lot better, but it was at least relatively short, and VanDerveer granted them the afternoon off. Jennifer Azzi had seen a brochure at the hotel advertising Jeep rentals and went about trying to recruit people for an exploratory outing. In the end, Rebecca was the only taker, the rest of the players begging off to nap at the hotel or go to the beach. Paying for a half-day rental, the two of them climbed into a Jeep and set off among the palm trees, along a winding dirt road that led from the outskirts of Waikiki up into the lush volcanic hills that overlooked the coast. The day was bright and balmy, classic Hawaii. They wore T-shirts and shorts and sunglasses. As Jennifer drove, Rebecca, who on a lark had her hair cornrowed the day before, tilted her face to catch the sun, her new braids fully back against her shoulders. It seemed like months since they'd spent any real time outdoors. Perhaps for this reason—for the stark contrast the cerulean sky and green bowl of ocean below bore to the relentless monochrome of the gyms, hotels, and airports of the last months—everything felt suddenly surreal.

They drove for hours, bumping along one road and then another, stopping the Jeep from time to time to take a photo or admire the view. As they drove, they talked, really talked, for what both of them would later acknowledge was the first time all year. As the two players on the team sponsored by Reebok, they stayed in the same hotel when in Colorado Springs and periodically had traveled to Reebok functions together. But for one reason or another they'd never shared much along the way. Rebecca would later blame herself. She'd been withdrawn from the start. "I was pretty quiet," she'd say. "I didn't think I could go to those guys with my problems or anything. I guess I wasn't sure if they'd understand."

In the Jeep, though, Rebecca slowly crept out of her shell. She cracked a joke about the coach getting on her all the time, and Jennifer laughed. Jennifer had known Tara VanDerveer for nearly ten years now. She'd seen her pick on players, sometimes fairly and sometimes not. For the most part, Jennifer tended to escape the coach's most stinging criticisms, though given the fact she was not a starter and spent plenty of time on the bench alongside Rebecca, it would be hard to argue that Jennifer received preferential treatment.

Soon, the words were pouring out of Rebecca—how alone she felt, how lousy it was to feel like she didn't deserve to be on the team, how strange it was to get the attention that she knew belonged more rightly to the older players. "It was the first time I'd actually really talked to a teammate," said Rebecca later. "And to have her understand was a bonus. It felt like I finally had a friend."

In return, Jennifer shared some of her own struggles. She felt that VanDerveer was keeping her on the bench just to prove that she didn't play favorites. The coach had told Jennifer in the past that she viewed her as a daughter, but Jennifer did not want to be seen as a daughter just then; she wanted to be seen as a potential starting guard. She told Rebecca, also, about how hard and isolating it had been to play basketball overseas—how loneliness was something most of them knew well. It was difficult, all of it had been difficult, but that was the thing, Jennifer pointed out to Rebecca, nobody was alone.

"You know," she said finally, looking across the seat at the younger player, "Most of us have been Players of the Year. Most of us have won championships and been celebrated. Maybe not to the extent that you have, but we know it's hard to move on to the next thing. We've all been where you are, one way or another. We do understand."

The final day in Hawaii, Sheryl Swoopes lost her footing during a scrimmage and fell to the floor, knocking her head against Katrina's shin on the way down. She was taken to a local emergency room, leaving the rest of the players in the gym to eye one another anxiously. All of them had played long enough to understand that basketball was a sport of inevitable violence. Hanging around basketball players, one starts to see that "minor injury" is a term used to describe anything from a sprained ankle to a broken nose or a ripped-up knee, or whatever it is that can be fixed by a surgery that requires less than two days in the hospital. In short, a minor injury is essentially defined as anything that doesn't threaten a career.

Sheryl spent several hours at the hospital under observation. She'd suffered a mild concussion and would be sent back to the mainland in another day. She would not be going to China.

Meeting in the hotel next morning to leave for the airport, the players' spirits seemed visibly dulled. The flight to Hong Kong via Tokyo was fourteen hours long. Once there, they'd have to wait another night before flying to a small island off the southwestern coast of China.

Finally, on March 9, the Olympics now four months away, the national team, minus two injured players and plus Val Whiting, landed in the city of Haikou, which sits at the northern tip of Hainan Island along a narrow saltwater strait that separates the Gulf of Tonkin from the South China Sea. According to a guidebook the team's doctor was carrying, Hainan was regarded as the "Chinese Hawaii," something that had provided some advance excitement among the team's entourage. Walking out of the Haikou airport, however, a one-room building housing a customs desk and a single ticket window, and boarding a van that took them through the city's muddy roads, they were suddenly hard pressed to understand the comparison. It was as if they'd touched down in a bizarre dreamscape, one crowded by stray dogs and loose chickens and noisy flocks of people pedaling three-speed bicycles along roads lined with mile upon mile of Communist-style tenements. They were in China, a very long way from home.

The tournament, called the "International Women's Basketball Challenge," sponsored by Basketball China, would take them to three cities in eight days, playing a round robin against the national teams from South Korea, Cuba, and, of course, China—all teams with the potential to win big games. In Haikou, the players from the four teams were housed in a high-rise hotel within walking distance of the basketball arena, an imposing, artless concrete structure set next to the bay. Meals were served buffet style in the hotel dining room, a smorgasbord of traditional Chinese foods—bean curd and bean pods, egg rolls, dumplings, broccoli in oyster sauce, dishes of stir-fried meat and vegetables— with great vats of rice set at the end of each table. The Americans regarded the dishes suspiciously.

"This look like chicken to you?" Dawn asked Teresa, hoisting a forkful of something covered in a reddish sauce into the air.

Briefly, the two players inspected the meat at the end of Dawn's fork before Teresa delivered her verdict: "That's either pork or something weird," she said, turning her attention back to her own plate, which was heaped with white rice and little else. "I can't help you there, Dawn."

The dislocation brought on by the strange food and jet lag and the way people stared at them on the street was not eased by the prospect of the competition ahead. They had twenty-eight victories behind them, but compared to facing down the Chinese, those games, even the ones they'd played in Russia and Ukraine, had been relative child's play. Not only did the Chinese have the home-court advantage, they had a degree of confidence, having finished ahead of highly touted and supposedly unbeatable American teams twice in the recent past. At both the Barcelona Olympics and the 1994 World Championships, the Chinese had taken two silver medals while the U.S. had settled for bronze.

To VanDerveer's way of thinking, playing China before the Olympics was nearly as important as playing China *in* the Olympics. They had to win now in order to know they could win later. As much as the Americans were sick of bronze, so too were the Chinese tired of silver. Under the Communist system, athletes were considered to be government employees and had been trained nearly full-time to play basketball. Most members of the Chinese team had played together for countless years.

If being in China felt like a strange dream, it felt like more of one when Zheng Haixia (pronounced Chung Hi-sha), "the Big Girl," showed up. She had a career as long and distinguished as Teresa Edwards's and a body so big that it forced opponents to restructure their offense to get around it. At the World Championships, Zheng had dominated, averaging 26 points and 13 rebounds a game. At the 1984 Olympics in Los Angeles, when Teresa was, at eighteen, the youngest member of the American team, Zheng (her last name) had been the baby of the Chinese team at fifteen. She'd gone on to compete in the '88 and '92 Games, too, and would no doubt be a premier player in Atlanta. Following the Barcelona Olympics, Zheng was rumored to have announced her retirement from Chinese basketball, citing plans to move abroad and make some money playing on a club team (the Chinese government paid its players a small salary for playing on the national team), but the government had intervened, allegedly barring her retirement until after Atlanta.

Over the years she had taken on a legendary status. According to various reports, she was six eight, six nine, or six eleven. Her weight remained a matter of vigorous debate. At the 1992 Olympics, one story went, Zheng good-naturedly draped an arm around Dream Teamer Karl Malone—who himself registered six nine and 256 pounds—and smiled *down* at him, dwarfing the guy outright. The Big Girl, Tara VanDerveer liked to point out, could shoot eighty-five percent from the field. Posting up against her, said the players who had tried it, was an impossibility. Her arms, others whispered, were as big as an average person's thigh. Whatever her actual measurements were, one thing was agreed upon: Not only was the Big Girl very very big, she was also extremely talented.

The first order of business for the Americans, however, was a game against Cuba, a team of big-boned, athletic players, six of whom were over six feet tall. In the first fifteen minutes the lead changed hands eight times, with no team managing to pull more than four points ahead. In the second half Cuba fell prey to the U.S. team's conditioning, unable to control the ball as the Americans kept the pace high, beating Cuba by a final score of 88–75. The win was hardly definitive and perhaps a bit troubling, considering the Americans hadn't counted on a real threat from Cuba.

Looking ahead to the next night's game against China, Tara VanDerveer knew that the Big Girl could exploit the glaring size deficit on her team, could set them down a path where all they began to see were their inadequacies, from Lisa Leslie's lack of muscle to the backcourt's inability to penetrate against China's Zheng-anchored defense. Having watched from the bleachers that afternoon as Zheng scored 30 points against South Korea to secure a four-point win, VanDerveer figured that if things got bad, she could use a zone defense to keep the Chinese from pounding the ball inside to Zheng. In general, the Americans would have to look to their outside shooters for scoring and hope that the post players could hang tough against Zheng.

At the shootaround before their game against China, perspiring in the muggy air of the gym, VanDerveer tried to ready her team offensively. Finding a discarded, moth-eaten broom in one corner of the gym, she picked it up and carried it over to the court, positioning herself in front of the net with the broom held high over her head.

"Okay now," she told her team. "If I'm the Big Girl, you've got to shoot over me. Now let's see you do it."

They worked for a while on quick, weaving offenses that would give the ball-handler several options for passing the ball inside, depending on who Zheng was defending. Zheng's size impeded her ability to maneuver quickly and thus, VanDerveer assumed, the more they moved the ball around, the more they cut and screened, the more likely they were to find an open shot without the Big Girl in the way. Running through the plays at slow speed, VanDerveer brandished the broom above her, stepping solidly in front of any player who came near the low post, forcing the ball back out to the wing. There was something comical in it, the coach waving her broom in their faces like that, but she was right: there was no way to prepare for the Big Girl but to play her.

As dusk fell on Haikou that night, the temperature cooled off somewhat, a light wind carried with it the tangy scent of saltwater. The last of the day's business finished, the street in front of the hotel fell into a relative hush. A quarter of a mile away, inside the gym, the Chinese fans filled only about half of the arena. A Chinese employee of Nike who traveled with the Chinese team explained that tickets were selling for the equivalent of $35, about half the average person's monthly salary. Basketball games, as it appeared, were for the elite.

Dulled by their jet lag, the American players had spent a restless afternoon, most of them trying unsuccessfully to sleep. Taking the floor to warm up, they looked slightly on edge. VanDerveer had decided on her starters—Teresa at point, Dawn at two-guard, Ruthie at three, Katrina at four, and Rebecca at center. It would be Rebecca's job to focus on the Big Girl, leaving Katrina open to do the scoring.

The Big Girl had shoulder-length dark hair she kept in a ponytail, a wide, expressive face, and lips that seemed curled in perpetual amusement. Rather than join her team in warming up, she remained on the sidelines and bounced up and down. Several times she jogged the length of the bench in a slow, labored gait and then stopped again.

She was so big, she almost defied imagination. Unlike Lisa, whose height made her look like a skinny, elongated version of an average-sized person, Zheng looked like an average person *doubled*. Everything about her was extra large and proportionally even with the rest of her. Her ears looked to be the size of a smaller woman's hands, her face broad and turgid, her hands hung at the end of her arms like two baseball mitts, the trunk of her body was thicker and stronger-looking than most men's. Laughing at a coach's joke, her voice rang out in a deep baritone.

If the Americans were nervous, they tried not to show it. Being undefeated naturally brought with it an extra pressure, a heightening of what was at stake, as losing a game suddenly meant more than simply losing a game. Losing would mean letting go of the thing that made them noteworthy in the public's eye. Each time the national team won, the hype surrounding them climbed up a notch. They'd been 10 and 0 and then 20 and 0, and most of the time they'd not doubted that they could win a game. Now, however, they were on the other side of the globe, fenced in by fans shouting at them in an inscrutable tongue, sleep-deprived after a night on hard mattresses in a hotel with paper-thin walls, fueled by food they couldn't discern, and about to face off against a woman who was arguably the largest player in the history of women's basketball.

When the game started, China took an immediate 4–0 lead. Backed up against the Big Girl, angling for position under the net on offense, Rebecca felt as if she were pushing against a deeply rooted tree. At the other end of the court, defense proved to be similarly fruitless. A lay-up for Zheng essentially involved her simply standing on tiptoe and effortlessly nudging the ball into the net.

Midway through the first half, the score was tied at 20–20. Val Whiting had come in for Rebecca and had little luck against Zheng, and later Lisa Leslie had tried to take over. Lisa's infamous elbows, which she extended like wings and used to clear out a space in which to negotiate her next move with the ball, were ineffectual against the Big Girl, however, and soon the two of them were engaged in a hopeless push-and-shove match at the post. It soon became clear who was winning the battle. Zheng scored once, then twice, and before long China had built a seven-point lead. Before the half, back-to-back jump shots from Katrina helped the U.S. to cut China's lead to three.

If VanDerveer wanted her test, she had it now. Sensing a possible victory, the Chinese fans started to chant. The air had grown hot and stale with cigarette smoke. The chorus of shouted Chinese words swirled thickly around the American players as they resumed their positions on the floor. VanDerveer took her seat at the edge of the bench and fell into her customary pose, elbows propped on knees, head thrust forward toward the court, as if it were all she could do to keep from running out and playing the game herself.

The Chinese hung on to their lead. At the point where teams before them had rolled over, victimized by the American team's pressure defense, the Chinese team seemed unfazed and energetic. The Big Girl's mischievous smile appeared to get bigger with each point she scored. Lisa, who'd been knocked flat on her back by Zheng twice without a whistle, was now glaring. Dawn shook her head in frustration.

On the bench, VanDerveer's jaw tensed visibly. How many times had she given her orchestra speech? Her team's usual soloists, namely Lisa and Katrina, were doing their best against Zheng, but for once it was not good enough. So where were the others? Hadn't she told them time and again that each one of them had to be ready to step up? Where *was* everybody?

Just then, off an assist from Dawn and a screen from Katy, Ruthie sank a jump shot from inside the perimeter. Amid the taller players, Ruthie almost seemed to get lost, her stubby body drawing little attention even from her opponents. She used her size as a means of subterfuge, rolling away from defenders, flitting almost unnoticed at the perimeter until the ball found her. She was a hot-and-cold shooter, capable of being either an embarrassment or a terror with the ball. As the game lurched into its final ten minutes, something seemed to kick to life inside her. When China missed its shot on the other end, Dawn put the ball back into

Ruthie's hands and she scored again. In the next minute, Ruthie dropped two free throws and knocked down a three-pointer, tying the game.

There was no looking back. With Lisa and Katy catching fire, the national team went on a scoring run as Zheng, who had played the entire forty minutes, seemed finally to tire. In the end, as the hissing of the fans died down, the Americans, exhausted but elated, walked out of the stadium and into the warm Chinese night with their record preserved at 29 and 0, the game won 80–66.

Somebody had told Tara VanDerveer not to fly on Russian-made airplanes. Russian-made airplanes, VanDerveer explained, were the kind that crashed most often, and China was supposed to be full of them. Having dispensed this bit of knowledge, she ducked her head to peer out the glass that made up one wall of the Haikou airport. Three planes were parked out on the runway, barely visible beneath the morning fog.

"Do you know airplanes?" She directed the question to the translator who had been assigned to the team. The translator, a trim, pretty Chinese woman in her mid-twenties, was named Gan Lu, but had insisted that the Americans call her Angela. When Angela looked confused by the airplane question and nodded her head no, VanDerveer elevated her voice and tried again with the group at large. "Does anyone here know airplanes?"

It was early in the morning and the airport smelled like a swamp. The American players were too busy dragging luggage to the ticket window to register the coach's question, even if her voice was not one they normally ignored. Next to the Cubans, the South Koreans, and the Chinese teams, all of whom carried small amounts of baggage, mostly shoulder bags and backpacks, the Americans—with their body-sized duffels, crates of extra food, a training table, and small arsenal of medical supplies—appeared grossly extravagant.

The planes from Haikou flew only to two places—Hong Kong, an hour by air to the east, and Guangzho on the mainland, ninety minutes to the north. The basketball players and their coaches and staff people were headed to Guangzho, where they would transfer to a bus to go to their final destination, an outback city called Zengcheng. As it turned out, the plane that would take them to Guangzho was a small Fokker. Fokkers, according to VanDerveer, were okay because they were Dutch.

The flight was short and uneventful, with a snack of cold noodles and a porous white ball lying in brown sauce (identified by Angela as "cake"). Zengcheng, when they finally got there, looked like a cold drizzly city on the edge of nowhere, but the hotel was modern and comfortable, and the athletes settled in quickly.

Later that night, the national team was introduced to several thousand Chinese fans before its second game against Cuba.

"*Rur-nie Bolton!*" said the announcer. "*Rikka Loco!* . . . *Nietszche McRah!*"

As it had been in Siberia, Rebecca Lobo received the same polite smattering of applause that the rest of them did instead of the usual hearty ovation. Ironically, in a country where people stopped dead in their tracks to gape at her white face, her six-foot-four frame, and western clothes, Rebecca felt the freest she'd felt in a long while. Even if the persistent staring made her feel as if she belonged on the moon, she was still anonymous and the feeling was glorious. VanDerveer had started her in the last two games, and while she hadn't exactly knocked the Big Girl over or shut down the Cubans on defense, Rebecca felt she'd done all right. If anything, she measured her progress by VanDerveer's increasingly longer silences at practice. Even several weeks ago, it had felt as if she couldn't turn around without the coach getting down on her for it. Now it seemed that VanDerveer had found a new project in Val Whiting, and finally Rebecca had been left somewhat on her own.

The national team defeated Cuba that evening by a score of 96–75, paced by 27 points from Lisa and 14 from Katrina. Next in line was South Korea, a team of players who could pass the ball with phenomenal speed and had twice challenged China with their quick and accurate outside shooting.

That night, to draw on VanDerveer's orchestral analogy, Rebecca had her first solo of the year. In the midst of the South Koreans' frenetic defense, she remained unruffled, moving slowly but purposefully with her back to the hoop, waiting for the pass to come. When the ball did arrive, there was no need to eye the net over her shoulder. She'd made the calculations already, understood the angles and alignments involved. It was simply a matter of seizing the ball, bouncing it once, then in what felt like one splendidly fluid motion, her body arched and pivoted, her right arm extending as her hand released the ball with just the right amount of spin.

A turnaround jumper, perfectly executed, was a work of art.

The more Rebecca scored that night, the better she played. She'd lost track of her points, but she knew there had been a lot. She'd even put in a couple of three-pointers, shots she normally had shied away from taking. But tonight she was playing like the old Rebecca, the award winner, the daunting center from Connecticut. She'd called Geno Auriemma for one last booster talk before leaving for China, and the coach's parting words now rang in her ears. "You didn't make that team because you're a nice kid," he'd said. "You made it because you're an excellent basketball player, and that's what you have to show them."

When it was over, she practically floated out of the gym. The U.S. had won its thirtieth game 94–69, on the strength of 24 points from Rebecca. She had played, finally, like she belonged.

Something was happening to Rebecca. Perhaps it had to do with the conversation with Jennifer in the Jeep back in Hawaii. Maybe it had to do with the fact that she was cut off from Dave and her sister and parents and old friends at home. ("I called everyone once to tell them I couldn't call them," she explained, having arrived in China and divined that her precious phonecalls home would cost seven dollars a minute.) Maybe it was because in China they were all on equal footing. Nobody was handing her any awards, nobody was screaming for her autograph. Whatever the case, all things seemed to conspire toward Rebecca's finding her place on the team, six months and eight thousand miles from where they'd started. She started joining in on the nightly games of spades. At meals she began to wisecrack about the food with the rest of them, her former shyness seeming to vanish.

As things got better for Rebecca, they'd decidedly grown worse for Val Whiting. Midway through the China trip, Val could not fathom why she'd agreed to come along. Wanting to play in the Olympics, obviously, had been the reason, but as she fumbled and sweated her way through the daily shootarounds, and as VanDerveer hardly used her off the bench in games, she was feeling those hopes slipping away. She alternately berated herself for taking such a long and unvigorous vacation in Brazil and wished she'd had the good sense to turn down the invitation to take Carla's place. She could have said she had an injury, an illness, a wedding to go to, anything that would have saved her the humiliation of showing up unprepared.

The memory of her performance at team trials, those afternoons she'd shined on the court, had grown depressingly dim, and probably for VanDerveer and Carol Callan, both of whom would have a say in the twelfth-player decision, entirely forgettable. What was real was who she was now, a clumsier, weaker version of her better self, defeated before she'd even lifted herself off the bench.

Sitting at meals with the nine players who'd traveled every mile of it, Val felt acutely like an outsider. There were jokes she didn't understand, bonds between people she couldn't interpret, old aggravations that flared and subsided as quickly as they'd come. These players had been on a journey together, and Val, lowering her eyes as she smiled weakly at their jokes, knew she could never hope to get inside. In the interstices between games and meals and sleep, she sat quietly in her room and read her book or searched the television for an English-language program, waiting for another day to pass.

The U.S. national team played China a second time on a rainy Tuesday night in Zengcheng. Several thousand fans packed into the arena, which was more modern than the one in Haikou had been, marshalled by a small army of green-uniformed policemen who looked to be no older than eighteen. The police, roughly seventy in all, clustered at every entrance to the building, smoking hand-rolled cigarettes and doing nothing more than managing to look authoritative and slightly menacing as the crowd tumbled in.

Everybody in China smoked, it seemed. Rather, every man in China smoked, and because the Chinese women for the most part remained shadowy presences behind the men, the prevailing impression was that China was a nation of maniacal smokers. At games, the lights over the court often illuminated a hazy cloud of blue smoke suspended above the athletes. (When members of the U.S. group commented on the smoke, it was as if a long-stopped dam broke within Angela, the normally reserved translator. "I know," she said. "I hate the smoke myself! Every man in my office smokes and all the women go crazy because of it, but we could never say anything because the men are our—how do you say it?—our higher-ups!")

The predilection for smoking seemed matched by the Chinese people's enthusiastic and uninhibited use of the cellular phone, particularly during basketball games. Waiting for a game between Cuba and South Korea to end, listening to the relentless ringing of cell phones in the audience above her, Lisa Leslie, her head swaddled in a purple bandanna, finally turned to look into the stands, exasperated: "Jesus, you think they're calling each other up there or what?"

Perhaps more than any other place their athletic lives had taken them, China was alien and disorienting, a country so vast and crowded that Zengcheng, a remote city that appeared to have a population equivalent to that of, say, Palo Alto, quite literally could not be found on a map. It was easy to feel lost and insignificant here. They were entirely dependent on the translator, who in turn was an employee of the government-run Basketball China. In Haikou, the television had picked up the *CBS Evening News* each morning from Hong Kong, and they'd learned that on precisely the day of their arrival, the Chinese government had started firing test missiles into the Strait of Taiwan, a military muscle flex that ignited an age-old conflict regarding Taiwan's self-declared independence from the People's Republic of China, causing a diplomatic uproar and a not inconsiderable amount of anxiety among the American party.

The U.S. team tipped off against the Chinese promptly at eight P.M. VanDerveer had thought long and hard about how best to attack China, deciding to put her biggest and most powerful players on the court and to keep them there as long as she needed them. Katy Steding, who at six feet was both a strong rebounder and a solid perimeter shooter, went in at the three, while Katrina, the lover of physical contact, took her usual spot at power forward. Lisa went up against the Big Girl at center. Teresa remained at point guard with Ruthie at the two.

As the Chinese strategy was to get the ball to Zheng on every play so that she could score, VanDerveer's ploy became simply to keep the ball away from Zheng. Midway through the first half, with the scored tied at 26–26, VanDerveer put Rebecca in at the post and moved Lisa to the perimeter, relieving Katy, who was shooting unreliably. As Rebecca shared the court with Lisa, Katrina, Teresa, and Ruthie, her confidence again soared. Against the Big Girl, it was a matter of staying calm and keeping herself in position.

The Big Girl leaned into her, bearing down with her weight, trying to force Rebecca out of position on defense. Up in the stands she could hear the Chinese fans laughing—laughing!—at her struggle. Earlier in the tournament, she'd seen the South Koreans trying to defend Zheng, practically bouncing off her giant body as they tried to beat her to a rebound. The fans had chortled then too, waves of laughter sweeping through the stands, which, Angela would explain, was a cultural trait, a standard reaction to embarrassment or discomfort. In other words, something to be forgiven. As a spectator, she'd almost caught the fever, stifling a laugh as the Big Girl almost unwittingly knocked over another South Korean player.

VanDerveer's voice brought her back to earth, drilling through the noise of the crowd: "Stance, Rebecca! Stance, Rebecca! Stance!"

When the second half began, Rebecca was back in her old spot between Jennifer and Nikki on the bench while the starters again took the floor. The U.S. had closed out the half with a 15-point lead. Within minutes, though, they'd fizzled, suddenly bricking easy shots, playing listless defense while the Big Girl capitalized with 10 easy points. With her big players flagging, worn out after a highly physical first half, Van-Derveer was in spot. She could send in her backup squad, but their smaller size would put them at an immediate disadvantage. Her options were limited. She needed to spark the players on the floor.

Rebecca heard the coach's voice float down the bench, calling her name. She was going in again for Katy. They needed her out there.

With Rebecca's help, China quickly lost its lead. VanDerveer shifted her team into a zone defense, pitting Rebecca and Katrina against the Big Girl, while Lisa and Ruthie worked to score and Teresa controlled the pace. For most of the second half they worked in perfect concert, each player filling her prescribed role masterfully—Rebecca wedged in tight against Zheng, Katrina going after rebounds, Ruthie and Lisa attacking from the perimeter, while Teresa swooped the ball downcourt on transition. For one short stretch the vision in VanDerveer's head was playing itself out on the floor before her. Ten minutes passed without the Big Girl mustering a single point. Meanwhile, Ruthie's shooting caught fire again, this time with a glorious long-range three-pointer, and the national team's lead crept up again, securing another victory, 73–67.

Back at the hotel, Rebecca put in a victory call to Geno Auriemma in Connecticut.

The next day the euphoria had not subsided. Lingering at lunch, a deep-fried chicken claw (which, according to Angela, is the Chinese version of the onion ring) languishing on a plate in front of her, she recalled the night before with a wide-eyed vigor. "The Big Girl, she's just so huge . . . I mean, they list her on the roster as 187, but she's at least 287 . . . oh, absolutely! I weigh 185 and she's out of my league."

As she spoke, Zheng Haixia was making her way through the buffet line, filling her plate, chicken claws and all. Rebecca dropped her voice.

"First of all, trying to guard her is impossible. It's, like . . . trying to get around an American player, it takes a step or two . . . with her it's like three or four! And when she gets the ball"—Rebecca's eyebrows rose—"you're like helpless, you're like an *ant*. You can't body her because she's just not going to move, and when you go in the lane to take a shot, you see her and it's intimidating. I don't think people could ever appreciate her size, even on television. Unless you see her in person, you really really wouldn't believe her."

Rebecca was happy, relaxed, looking forward to the next game, even. She hadn't signed an autograph in a straight week. "I love having fans," she said at lunch, "but it's nice to get a break from them, too."

Later that day, as the teams shuttled through the airport in Guangzho on their way to the tournament's final destination, a man's voice froze Rebecca from behind.

"Rebecca *Lobo*!" She'd been recognized. It turned out to be a Chinese-American man who lived in Ridgefield, Connecticut, and did business in China. Rebecca shook his hand and politely chatted for a moment before leaving to get on the plane, her streak of anonymity broken.

A basketball game advances itself spasmodically, the action hopelessly subdivided by starts and stops, whistles and substitutions, free throws, time-outs, halftimes, and the inevitable delay when someone gets knocked over and, due to one howling body part or another or simply because the bashee would like the basher as well as the officials to think twice about what just happened, has trouble getting up again. Basketball, in short, is not conducive to rhythm, and yet it is a sport in which rhythm is everything, where a game can turn entirely on one team finding its tempo, where everything reverses itself and suddenly the dark horse and the hero trade places—the losers have won and the winners have lost, and nobody could have predicted it.

As the four teams arrived in Ningbo, a largish industrial city southeast

of Shanghai and
be entrenched
could beat th
the South K
Americans

And the
pyramid,
Chinese
played
looki
and

a
b
players' in
living conditions
blue jerseys and standa
looked almost threadbare. Som
jerseys looked ready to fall off; a few w
made with strips of athletic tape. It look as
basketball shoes until the soles were scuffed to noth
through holes in the leather. At meals, as the American playe
ued to pick at the Chinese food, returning to their rooms to attack u
vast store of granola and Wheat Thins stashed in the team manager's
room, the Cubans lingered for hours, going back for seconds, thirds, and
even fourths of whatever it was the Chinese hosts dished up.

The Cuban coach was a white man who wore a baby-blue polyester suit and put his face close to the faces of his players when he screamed at them, as he often did, when they came in off the court. But after they beat the Chinese team in Ningbo, the coach waved his arms until he had all the players gathered in, and he hugged them tightly. Bound together in their thick scrum, the Cubans bounced up and down with excitement. There is nothing like an upset to get a team going. They had tempo now, they had momentum, and tomorrow they would have their last shot at the Americans.

Tara VanDerveer was not worried about the Cubans. She was happy for their sake that they'd beaten China. Otherwise, it didn't concern her. At practice the next day, she introduced a new offense called "the ned, was the antidote to a struc-

uld rely on aggressive screen-setting

t unlike other plays, they would not

oved where and at what cue. The double

yantly. It would be up to the players to

oor and react to it more or less spontane-

one another as they went.

VanDerveer told them. "The less I structure it,

out there and play it."

nutes against the Cubans that night, Dawn, at point

the double on several plays, and each time, the U.S.

o dissolve instantly, with whoever had the ball lobbing it

e net. Katrina missed. Ruthie missed. Teresa missed. The

, revved up and shooting well, built a two-, then a four-point

Dawn, nimble and quick-handed, stole the ball. Quickly, she

it out to Teresa, who bounced it to Katrina, who for one of the

times all year fumbled the ball and turned it back over to the

ubans, who ran away with it and scored.

Next time the ball was in her hands, Katrina went up for a lay-up and missed. As she paused under the net for a heartbeat, the frustration showed on her face. She had played most of every game for the last five nights. She was tired, starting to ache. The Cubans were leading 11–8.

On the ensuing possession, Dawn grabbed the ball and passed it to Teresa with a mandate: "C'mon, baby, *hit that!*"

Teresa's jumpshot clanked off the rim.

This was the opposite of tempo. It was outright deterioration, in which one misstep led to the next, each missed shot making the next one somehow harder to hit. VanDerveer began substituting wildly. She put Rebecca into the game, and she made one shot and then missed two others. Katy came in and did the same.

Finally, VanDerveer summoned Val Whiting from the end of the bench. Val, Nikki McCray, and Jennifer Azzi had played only minimally through most of the tournament. To Val, it had seemed that the coach had practically forgotten she was there, though here perhaps was her chance to make a statement.

She stepped on the court and immediately found the ball in her hands. Without hesitating, she surveyed the court, saw the net, and started to drive. *Wheeet!* She looked up to see the official's hands doing a slow orbit around each other; she'd been called for traveling, a stupid mistake, and Cuba would get the ball.

On the next possession, before the heat of the last embarrassment had drained from her cheeks, the ball zoomed back to Val. She froze for a second, clutching it almost in fear. She had not been expecting it. Didn't they know she felt useless? She looked to make a pass, saw nothing but the blue of the Cubans' uniforms. Worried about traveling, she began to dribble the ball slowly, buying herself time.

On the sidelines, her teammates had risen to their feet. The shot clock had only seven seconds left, and Val, in her ponderous dribbling, seemed oblivious. Six seconds, five seconds, four.

Dawn and Teresa cupped their hands around their mouths and screamed, "Shoot the ball! Shoot it, Val! Shoot!"

Jolted from her reverie, Val looked first at her teammates and then spotted the clock and, her face frozen in horror, she hurled the ball into the air, resetting the shot clock but putting the ball directly into the Cuban center's hands. Passing the bench on her way downcourt, Val didn't bother to look up, knowing she'd blown it once and for all.

With less than five minutes to play in the half, the Cubans were now ahead by seven. The fans were hooting and screaming. They did not need to speak English to make it clear they were backing the underdogs tonight. VanDerveer substituted Katrina for Val, who wouldn't get any more playing time tonight. Thanks to three-point baskets from Ruthie and Katy and two free throws from Katrina in the final minutes, the U.S. drew up to Cuba and closed out the half with a one-point lead, the score standing at 38–37.

In the second half, the double was abandoned, but somehow the damage was already done. The national team was scattered and unfocused, and for several minutes the Cubans recaptured, then lost, then recaptured their lead.

During a time-out, Dawn Staley chomped on her gum and cocked her chin jauntily at the scoreboard. This was her favorite kind of game. The jacked-up stakes, their undefeated record on the line, fifteen minutes to play. "Let's concentrate on getting good shots," VanDerveer was telling them, mortified by all the useless attempts at scoring. Katrina and Teresa were going back out to play. Among the three of them, Dawn knew, they could put up a good fight.

After the next in-bounds, she whizzed down the court, scored on a give-and-go from Teresa, hassled her woman on defense, zoomed back downcourt with the ball, launched a shot from behind the three-point line, and watched it fall. In four minutes she scored 11 points. When Dawn wasn't scoring, Katrina was. Miraculously, the national team had jumped ahead by 16.

For the first time in their thirty-four games, however, the Americans were up against a team that knew how to come back. In the next minutes, with their coach shouting wildly on the sidelines, the Cubans hacked the lead to five, then to two. With just over a minute to play, the U.S. was ahead by just one point, the score 77–76.

It had been a game so marred by American mistakes that it was theirs to lose now. It would be an inglorious way to go down. If anybody understood this, it was Teresa. She'd been asked the question a thousand times now: "What will you do if you lose at some point here? What happens if you go all the way to Atlanta and then you lose?"

To these questions, she only shook her head. "Life is ten percent what happens to you and ninety percent how you react to it," she liked to say. She would not think about losing until it actually happened. In the meantime, she was going to focus solely on winning.

When a Cuban player lost the ball on the next possession, Teresa grabbed it, dribbled the length of the court in what seemed like two steps, and dumped in a lay-up. The national team now had a three-point advantage with fifty seconds on the clock.

On Cuba's next possession, Lisa got called for a holding foul, stopping the clock at twenty-three seconds. VanDerveer called a time-out and drew her team in close. Hunkered over a clipboard, the coach mapped what would be their last shot at the hoop. If the Cubans hit the free throws, they'd be back to a one-point game. Each team would likely have one more opportunity to score. If the national team could score, the Cubans would have to shoot for three to tie the game. If the national team didn't score, the Cubans would need only one basket to win. On the next possession, they absolutely had to score.

The ball, said VanDerveer, should go to Teresa.

As predicted, the Cuban player drained two free throws, bringing the score to 79–78. Dawn brought the ball down slowly, deliberately running down the clock. The goal was to put the ball in the shooter's hands at exactly the right second, so she could shoot with enough time left for a rebound if necessary, but still with too little time for the other team to get back to the other end and score if they lost the ball. Dawn dribbled the ball with one hand, then the other—10, 9, 8, 7, 6 seconds—then sidearmed the ball to Ruthie, who sent it across to Teresa, who'd lined herself up at the left wing, receiving the pass and lofting the ball in the instant before a Cuban player descended on her.

Never had a shot been more perfect. The net shivered on its strings.

Panicking, the Cubans inbounded the ball and ran downcourt, but the time was too short to set up a shot. Dawn, knowing she had calculated it flawlessly, punched the air happily. The Cubans' final shot missed its mark and the buzzer blared; the national team had overcome his toughest and most surprising challenge, 81–78. Leaping off the bench, Lisa, Rebecca, Katy, Jennifer, Nikki, and Val charged the court to hurl themselves into the arms of the others. VanDerveer was on her feet.

An hour or so after the game, freshly scrubbed from the shower and buoyed by the victory, Dawn Staley left her hotel room and skipped up the stairway to the dining room for the customary late-night postgame meal. The dining room was low-ceilinged and dimly lit, crowded with long tables and rickety, high-backed chairs. Katrina, Teresa, and Rebecca sat eating at one table, while six or seven players from the Cuban team sat nearby. The room was largely silent, each one of the women exhausted from the game.

Along one wall, the hotel staff had laid out an elaborate buffet, with fifteen or twenty serving dishes wafting the salty scent of dumplings, rice, and a number of vegetable and chicken concoctions. At the far end of the serving table lay an enormous spread of fresh pineapple, banana, and papaya. Still another table held the drink options: bottled water, beer, or tea. As a concession to the Americans—one that was received like manna from heaven—there was a tray of hand-cut french fries.

Tonight, however, Dawn had brought her own meal, a box of Velveeta macaroni and cheese and a packet of red Kool-Aid mix. Grabbing a bottle of water from the bar, she made her way to one of the servers, a thin man who immediately snapped to attention when she approached.

The request took several tries to get across, with Dawn shaking and then opening her box of dry macaroni, pantomiming the boiling of water, and then twisting her hands in an exaggerated imitation of opening the small metal cylinder packed with processed, gooey cheese.

After a minute, the server began to nod and smile.

"Can you do that for me?" said Dawn, delight breaking across her face. "You know what I'm sayin' to you? You do?"

Pleased with herself, she plopped down at the table with the others and proceeded to mix herself a glass of red Kool-Aid. Behind her, the server appeared to be conferring with his coworkers, three of them studying the Velveeta box intently. Dawn looked first at her teammates, each one working quietly through a mountain of french fries, and then over at the Cubans, who were looking drawn and defeated at the next table.

Without taking her eyes from them, she took a long pull on her Kool-Aid and set the glass down. "Y'all did good tonight," she said in the direction of the Cubans, her voice raised slightly as it had been when talking to the Chinese server. She slowed down the words and tried again. "Y'all did real good out there. . . ."

The Cuban players smiled politely but clearly couldn't understand. Dawn turned to Katrina. "Tree, you know Spanish. Tell 'em they all did good tonight, okay?"

Katrina had learned Spanish years before, playing two seasons in Valencia. She faltered with the words, *"Ustedes jugaron bien."* One by one, comprehending Dawn's message, the Cuban players' faces lit up. For a moment everyone grinned at everyone, citizens of the same world. One of the Cubans, a tall forward with soft brown eyes, offered a response, which Katrina translated with a soft smile: "She says we did pretty good too."

Back on the team's hallway, the atmosphere was celebratory. Following the post-game meal, Jennifer pulled out the coffee drip filter she brought with her everywhere and a bag of ground vanilla macadamia-nut coffee she'd picked up in Hawaii. Using steaming water from a thermos furnished by the hotel, she started brewing a cup for herself. On a whim, she scrawled a sign and hung it outside the door to the room she was sharing with Rebecca: *Jen Chu's Coffee and Espresso Bar.*

Before long, her teammates started to drift in—first Rebecca, then Teresa and Katrina who had volunteered to work on Rebecca's braids, which had grown loose and frizzy with all the travel. Lisa came in with Nikki's portable CD player and speakers and got the music going. Soon Nikki herself surfaced at the door, asking if someone would help take out her braids—a project to which Ruthie, showing up behind Nikki, readily volunteered. Hearing the noise, Dawn surfaced and soon Katy stopped by for a cup of coffee, too. And for a while, they were all there, everybody talking and laughing, a Sri Lankan cricket match on the television and Monica on the CD. Lisa danced, Dawn told jokes, Ruthie worked on Nikki's hair and Katrina and Teresa hovered over Rebecca who was sitting smiling in a chair, stepping back finally to reveal a curiously flat-headed creature with a scalp so pale it almost glowed between the braids, a white girl with a black girl's hairdo, the shy rookie finally transformed.

They were more than ready to go home. It seemed like years since they'd seen the sun. Ningbo, by virtue of being north and near the coast, was permanently shrouded in clouds. It had rained each night, permeating the air with a damp, bone-chilling cold. At night they slept under several layers of coarse wool blankets, the hotel radiators clanking and moaning but generating little warmth. With the trip coming to an end, they ventured out one afternoon on a shopping excursion led by Angela that yielded a gold necklace for Jennifer, a brass gong for assistant coach Reneé Brown, and a set of porcelain worry balls for Tara VanDerveer. Dawn and Lisa had commandeered a rickshaw briefly, with Lisa perched on the bicycle seat, pedaling as Dawn lounged behind on the canopied seat. On the streets, people had crowded around them, poking at them, staring up at their faces.

"*Qiao Dan,*" someone said, triggering a chorus of shouts in the sea of bystanders. "*Qiao Dan.* Michael Jordan!"

The connection was purely associative; tall black Americans suggested basketball. Beamed in by satellite, the NBA Game of the Week was now one of the China's most-watched television programs. Jordan, Angela explained, was known in China as the Red Oxen or more commonly, the Flying Man.

One got the feeling that just as the gurus of the financial market had pinpointed the People's Republic, with its 1.1 billion people and rising tide of capitalism, as the next great moneymaking frontier, so, too, had the gurus who made sports their business. But China needed to be cultivated before it could be sown, particularly when it came to persuading people to unload what little money they had on something as leisurely and foreign as professional sports. The NBA was working to bring live basketball into China with a men's Asian league, but with mixed results. Nike was finding the women's market in particular to be impenetrable. (As one Nike China employee explained, Chinese women were just catching the aerobics fever that had swept the western world fifteen years earlier. "Let's put it this way," he said. "If we manufactured leg warmers, we'd be making money here.")

As the American players made their way through the noontime crowd in downtown Ningbo, the red of their sweatsuits contrasting sharply with the predominantly gray and black coats of the Chinese, they appeared as American sports heroes were supposed to—rich, exotic, otherworldly. They smiled at the people, and when the staring and the embarrassed laughter became too overwhelming, they began to look uneasy and retreated into the van that would carry them back to the hotel where, cloistered in their rooms, they could again be themselves.

On the final night of competition, the U.S. beat China by a score of 84–77. The Cuban team put away South Korea by 20 points, its largest margin of victory yet. The tournament was declared complete; each team was given a large gold-plated trophy and released to go home.

As Jennifer packed up her bags after the China game, the voices of her teammates coming back from dinner filled the hallway. Soon, Rebecca had arrived in the room and started packing. Having taken a liking to Rebecca's braids, Jennifer asked Teresa to do her hair that night. When Teresa showed up, Katrina tagged along. And behind them was Dawn, providing a running commentary on the hairdressing, dancing around, and refusing to take a seat on the bed or the floor, where the rest of them lay sprawled.

Katrina had joined Teresa as she worked on Jen's hair, and they both sat on either side of her, cupping thin strands of hair and weaving them tightly without having to look. They'd been braiding people's hair for years—cousins', friends', sisters'.

They joked and talked for a long while, reviewing the games they'd had, reliving Teresa's beauteous shot against Cuba several times. When Nikki suggested that the hour was growing late, she was dismissed summarily: They had to reset their internal clocks anyway. They could sleep on the plane. Slowly, though, one by one the players began to nod off on the floor. Even Dawn finally succumbed, clearing herself a space on the bed. For a while only Jennifer, Teresa, and Katrina remained fully awake, until the moment when Dawn's voice roused them all.

"Hey, everybody! Everybody! Look at Whitebread." Dawn had raised herself on one elbow and was pointing at Jennifer, whom she liked to call Whitebread for the white-girl things she did—like drinking diet Coke, for instance, when the black girls had iced tea. Jennifer's braids ran in tidy lines back from her brow and then flopped over her ears. Slowly, everybody woke up to see. The braids were slightly more flattering on Jennifer than they were on Rebecca, but still, seeing them, Lisa stifled a giggle, then Dawn laughed out loud. Soon all of them, including Jennifer, were howling with laughter.

Dawn raised her voice over the laughter. "You guys see her? Whitebread ain't whitebread anymore . . . ," She slapped her hand on her thigh, summoning a Southern accent, "She cornbread!"

10

chapter

Positivity

Just over three months before the torch was to be lit in the Olympic stadium, the city of Atlanta was a veritable dirt heap, a hard-hat heaven. From the earliest light of morning to the dying strains of sunset, jackhammers pounded, backhoes beeped, bulldozers bulldozed, and great yellow clouds of dust rose from the construction sites all over the city, part of a $500 million effort to rebuild, reconfigure, and reinforce Atlanta before two million visitors came to rumpus in July. In essence, every spot of unoccupied downtown land had been exhumed to accommodate new buildings, new parking lots, theme parks, temporary nightclubs and sound stages, as well as the twenty-one-acre Centennial Park, designed to be the social center of the Atlanta Games. As the Games' organizers envisioned it, the city would, before July 19, metamorphose from a crime-ridden and basically average midsize American city to a spit-polished and salubrious Olympic paradise.

When the national team rolled into town in early April, Atlanta was a disastrously behind-schedule work-in-progress.

Squeezed into a small corner lot on the city's southwestern side, however, there sat one completed venue, the gleaming 5,700-seat basketball arena at Morehouse College, where the preliminary rounds of both men's and women's Olympic basketball would take place. The building, a sleek and windowless brick box, was lauded as an architect's masterpiece, its front wall described in the *Atlanta Journal-Constitution* thus: "A curving pediment with a jaunty wafer-thin triangle jutting out of the top like a cockscomb crowns the entrance facade on Fair Street. . . ."

Jaunty triangles aside, this was where the first Olympic blood would be shed. To the delight and surprise of Tara VanDerveer, the drawings to establish the two pools for women's basketball had put their toughest competitors—namely China, Brazil and Russia—all together to drub and exhaust one another while the U.S. would face down a somewhat less intimidating group, including South Korea, Cuba, Ukraine, and Zaire. The most worrisome member of Pool B, the Americans' group, was the feisty and well-seasoned Australian national team, which had come within five points of stealing the bronze medal from VanDerveer's team at the World Championships in 1994. The Aussies, everybody knew, would fight to the death. The Cubans, as they had learned in China, were capable of upsetting them as well.

In the meantime, they had come to Atlanta to christen the Morehouse arena, to play two scrimmages and an official game—the scrimmages against Ukraine and China, the game against the women's College All-Stars. For the superstitious VanDerveer, playing at Morehouse would have to be a necessarily positive experience for her team. The scrimmages would be no big deal, the game against college players, most of whom they'd beaten playing their individual teams, most likely wouldn't test them too hard. The point of being in Atlanta at the best time of year, when the dogwoods were blooming and the air was pleasantly tepid, was to keep things upbeat and relaxing, to plant the idea that the Games themselves would go that way.

Taking a seat three rows up and behind the bench for the scrimmage against Ukraine, Eric Jackson settled in to wait for tip-off. The scrimmage was not open to the public and thus the stands were largely empty save for people connected one way or another with the team and a handful of Morehouse students who'd drifted in. Eric was dressed in a gray T-shirt, baggy denim shorts, and a crisp white baseball cap from the NBA All-Star game. On his feet he wore a pair of Nike Air Flights, white with green trim. Around his neck hung a chain with a gold Nike Swoosh pendant. Fresh from several uninterrupted weeks in Brownfield with Sheryl, who had recovered from her concussion quickly, Eric was in high spirits. Sheryl, on the court below, looked well rested and radiant. The two of them had been talking about their future, he explained as he watched his wife shoot free throws to warm up. It was time for them to get serious, he said, time for him to finish his education and for the two of them to find a house and a place to settle down. Early in January, the ABL had announced the cities where it would field its teams, and disappointingly, there was not a Texas city on the list. So they'd gone through the others carefully, dismissing them one by one: Portland, Hartford-Springfield, Seattle, San Jose, and Columbus were out ("too northern"), as were Richmond ("not much of a city") and Denver ("no way"). The only place for them, said Eric, was the eighth city on the ABL list: Atlanta.

They both liked Atlanta's southern friendliness, its large black population and good churches. In particular, it would be a good place for Eric to go to school. He had three years of athletic eligibility left and the city was loaded with colleges. In fact, he'd already spoken with the football coach at Georgia Tech. The conversation had gone well, but Eric knew he'd have to work harder on his training if he wanted a tryout with a top team like that.

This said, a quiver of frustration passed over his face. He'd been working out in hotel gyms and at the track at Colorado College in Colorado Springs. He was not allowed access to the training center facilities or the weight rooms the national team used when they were on the road. He hadn't found anyone to play football with in Colorado, and when they went home to Texas, his only training partner was Sheryl's eleven-year-old brother, Brandon.

"Imagine an eleven-year-old's arms trying to hook you," he said, smiling faintly. "It's just not the same sensation as playing against an adult."

It was utterly impossible not to like Eric Jackson. He appeared to be unswervingly cheerful, and not only did he seem to have something nice, truly, to say about everyone, he said these things frequently and with great earnestness. Over the course of the fall, as a nearly continual presence in the stands, wearing his admiration like a badge, Eric had become part of the national team's mojo—a single fixed object in the blurred backdrop of their lives as a traveling show.

He confessed that there was an obvious catch in his and Sheryl's plan to come to Atlanta, and that was the fact that the ABL had announced that each of the eight teams would feature two and only two marquee players. Katrina and Teresa, as long-term Georgians, had dibs on Atlanta. According to the rules, there was no room for Sheryl. The rumors they'd heard were that she would get sent to Denver, the closest team to Texas and a place they emphatically did not want to go. The ABL was getting ready to send out its player contracts, but, said Eric, he and Sheryl wanted to nail down where they were going before they signed anything.

"We don't want to hurt anybody," he said, his hands knitting and unknitting, sounding sincerely worried. "There's an ABL guy here we got to talk to, Bobby Johnson. He's supposed to drop by the scrimmage. I don't know exactly who he is, but I know he's the guy who'll get us here."

The scrimmage started with Lisa, Ruthie, Katrina, Teresa, and Dawn on the floor against the Ukrainians, a team of tall, thin white women in blue and gold uniforms. Dawn scored twice within the first minute, then stole the ball on the other end and brought it down for her third lay-up. Several seats behind Eric Jackson sat a row of male students. "U-V-A!" one of them began chanting in reference to Dawn's college background. "U-V-A!"

The Americans took an early and significant lead. In the sparsely populated stands, Dawn's small fan club seemed to grow more enlivened with each passing moment. When midway through the half, she leapt and caught a pass from Jennifer in midair, then darted inside to put in a shot, the entire group of male Morehouse students, about six in all, jumped up and started to yell with excitement. "She is real!" shouted one. "She is *real!*"

Eric Jackson bore witness to all of this with a soft smile on his face. He loved the team, loved, for the most part, being with the team. He took pride in what the players did, cheering throughout the game, calling down to the bench, about ten feet in front of him, at the start of each time-out.

"Nice pass, T. Nice pass!"

"You're looking good, Katy!"

"Yeah, Lis!"

With Sheryl he was politely restrained, clapping calmly when she brought down a shot and elegantly pivoted away from her defender to nail a three-pointer. Several minutes later, when a Ukrainian player swiped the ball right out of Sheryl's hands, Eric chewed his gum and said nothing.

When VanDerveer called a time-out, Eric shouted to the back of Sheryl's head on the bench. "Don't fall away on your jumpshot! Straight up, straight up."

This got no response from Sheryl, but Eric sat back in his seat anyway, appearing confident that she'd heard. This was how they communicated while Sheryl was playing ball. Even as he gabbed his way through a game, he seemed always to be absorbing and processing his wife's work on the floor. One could usually locate Eric's seat by simply following

Sheryl's eyes during time-outs. Usually, he sat as close to the bench as possible. Fingering her mouth guard, she would look up at him, then nod her head slightly, as if accepting a bit of advice. Sometimes she'd offer an assessment of her play by rolling her eyes. He could be five rows away or twenty-five: the information was quick and telegraphed each way.

Several minutes into the scrimmage's second half, a thin man wearing a gray pinstriped suit, walked toward Eric across the bleachers. It was Bobby Johnson. Eric, seeming to intuit, duly leapt to his feet.

"Mr. Johnson? How you doing? I'm Eric Jackson." He shot out a hand to pump Johnson's. Johnson, who had a narrow mustache above his lip, smiled broadly and took a seat next to Eric, who immediately began his pitch. He explained how much he loved Atlanta, how much Sheryl did too.

"Sheryl's ready to sign on the dotted line," he said. "Just say the word."

Johnson grinned at Eric. "We have to let things settle down," he said. "We can't make decisions just yet."

Sensing that Johnson was avoiding addressing the two-marquee-player rule, Eric pressed forward. "We'd go anywhere, actually. We're not trying to make trouble for you, or T and Tree. We just need a stable church, good people, a school for me to finish my education." He paused to watch Sheryl bring the ball downcourt and pass it off to Carla, then continued. "I just don't know about San Jose. It would be a lot easier for us to stay in the South. We're family-oriented . . . you know, like in four or five years, if Sheryl wants to have a baby, I want to be able to support the family."

"We'll make sure everybody's happy," said Johnson evasively, the smile not leaving his face.

Eric continued, his voice loaded with ardor. "I said to Sheryl, 'You've given your life to basketball, this is your chance to get something back.' . . . Obviously we don't want to upset Teresa or Katrina or you."

Johnson cut him off. "That's for us to worry about," he said, standing up. "It's all going to be fine," he said, shaking Eric's hand again. Eric stood up with him, hoping for just another minute to make an impression. "Hey, Bob"—he was calling him Bob now—"what you got going on after this? Sheryl really wants to say hello."

Johnson smiled again, kindly. "I gotta run back to the office. I'm sorry." For a second he looked like he might say something else, but then another man in a suit approached, a business acquaintance, it seemed. Johnson spoke for a minute with the man, then seemed to notice Eric still standing there. "Hey, I want to introduce you to someone." He nodded toward Eric. "This is Eric, Eric Swoopes. You know, as in Sheryl Swoopes." Eric shook the second man's hand without correcting the error, then watched as the two of them turned and walked away, back across the bleachers headed toward the exit ramp.

He took his seat again and watched the scrimmage's final minutes quietly. The U.S. won 82–74. Following the game, the Morehouse students got to their feet, shouldered their backpacks, and mulled around for a moment, debriefing the game. "I don't know about Swoopes though," one student happened to say, not particularly loudly. "She seemed kind of slow."

The comment snagged itself on Eric Jackson's radar. He turned around in his seat to look at the guy. "She just had a concussion," he said, his words friendly but firm. "She was in Hawaii and she got slammed in the head. She's just getting back. You come see her at the Olympics, okay?"

The uncertainty was starting to get to everyone. It was one thing to pass beneath the digital clock that hung over the freeway in Atlanta and see what everyone in the city seemed to be obsessing on, the big neon 100—as in one hundred days left before Opening Ceremonies—and it was quite another not to know whether, after nearly a year of preparing for the Games, you'd even be there to see them.

Driving back to the hotel with the team's media director after practice, Rebecca was fretting. The official word from USA Basketball was that the Olympic team would be announced on June fifteenth, two agonizing months, a trip to Australia for another tournament, and several exhibition games away.

"When are they going to tell us, really?" Rebecca asked the media director, Amy Early. "Are we going to know anything before June fifteenth? I mean, it's not like we're going to work any less hard if we know. . . ."

Rebecca looked for a minute out the window in silence, as if trying to let the impatience pass. They passed a deli, a bar, a men's shop, all of which had small PROUD SPONSOR signs hanging in the window. They passed Olympic billboards and taxis with Olympic advertising on them. The Olympics were everywhere. Rebecca knew that Early had no answer for her. It was useless to ask questions like that. Her fate and that of her teammates was entirely in the hands of the selection committee, a bunch of people they didn't know, and in the hands of VanDerveer, who could be so distant and unemotive that it quite often felt like they didn't know her either.

"They say that hotel rooms here are five thousand dollars," Rebecca continued after a moment, not complaining so much as commenting. "Can you believe it? . . . That's way too much. If we don't know anything till June, my parents'll never get a place to stay, they'll never get tickets to anything. . . ."

When she looked over at Early, she saw her shaking her head helplessly. "I don't know any more than you do, B," she said. "I'm sorry."

Even if they all made the Olympic team, not one of them knew for sure where their lives would take them after August fourth. They had notions, of course, but things were far from guaranteed. Katrina and Teresa were assuming, for instance, that the ABL would put them in Atlanta, Jennifer figured she'd end up in San Jose, in front of the fans who would remember her from Stanford, and Katy would likely end up playing in her hometown of Portland. But really, there were no assurances at all that the ABL would even get off the ground. Despite the relentless campaigning of Steve Hams and his partners, despite the fact that Hams and Cavalli had traveled to the women's Final Four and made their case before a group of several hundred college coaches, the ABL remained a dark horse in the basketball community. The league still did not have a television deal, nor did it have a shoe company backing it or even one major national sponsor. All it seemed to have was the cluster of believers within the national team and a small group of outside players who had been recruited for early signing.

Continuing to follow her agent's advice to wait on signing with the ABL, Rebecca remained the lone holdout on the team, as Katrina Mc-Clain had committed finally. China had helped her to feel more at ease with her teammates regarding the decision, which she knew did not make them happy, but at least they were starting to know her better as a person. All along, she'd insisted to everyone that she wasn't trying to hold out for more money. She just hoped that now they knew her well enough to believe her when she said it.

China, in general, had been a good experience for everyone on the team. Joining up with the rest of them after recovering from her concussion, Carla, the resident busybody, had been startled to realize just how many jokes and war stories and great games she'd missed out on. "They gelled without me!" she practically shouted one day after one of her first practices back. Not only that, but after nearly a month of training on her own, Carla was feeling that her playing had grown lopsided; she was fine on defense, but she seemed to have lost her offensive touch. Worse, VanDerveer had worked up several new plays that she and Sheryl now had to learn quickly. The worry seemed to dampen her penchant for chatter.

"I'm four or five steps behind everyone," she said with a sigh that day. "I don't know. I just can't wait to get back to where I was."

Sheryl, who concerned herself less with off-the-court chemistry, seemed unruffled about missing out on China. "I heard the food stories," she remarked in Atlanta, "and I'll tell you, I was happy to be at home, eating what I wanted."

The real difference between Carla's and Sheryl's attitudes about their absences had much to do with their status with VanDerveer. Sheryl was the kind of player who played during a game's most important minutes. The coach relied on her for her scoring and her quickness on the court. Carla, on the other hand, was a role player. In essence, she was a stand-in for Katrina, part of the relief squad whose job it was to come in and not mess up whatever lead the others had established. If Sheryl was vital, Carla was not. If Sheryl could safely assume that she would make the team, Carla was far less certain. If Sheryl missed the China trip, so be it, but if Carla missed the trip, it simply meant she had less time to prove herself.

For Katy Steding, who like Carla was a benchsitter, it seemed that the China tournament had hurt rather than helped. Blond-haired and serious, Katy was a three-point specialist, a player who could come in and make up a point deficit quickly and reliably. She'd done it for VanDerveer for four years at Stanford, and throughout the national team's tour, she'd turned in dependably solid performances, averaging about eight points per game. But arriving in China, it was as if the earth beneath Katy had shifted slightly.

There was really no accounting for it; something had shaken loose or some tiny imbalance had set in, and suddenly her shot was gone. She couldn't find her touch during one game and then another and then another. Over the eight games in China, she'd taken twenty-five three-point shots and made just three of them, which amounted to a dismal .120 on the stat sheet. As time progressed, the ball began to feel heavy and foreign in her hands, the basket seemed to taunt her each time she stepped behind the three-point line. Each time VanDerveer sent her in to play, she told herself that this would be the night when she redeemed herself, when she reconquered the three-point shot. When things didn't work out, her doubts grew, her playing worsened. How can you fix something when you don't know what broke? Katy had sunk into a basketball player's worst nightmare, the damnable shooting slump.

Coming back to the States, Katy had tried to talk herself out it, but slumps had a twisted logic all their own. VanDerveer, who had seen plenty of slumps come and go over the years, suggested that she try simply to banish the doubts, to purposely not dwell on her failures. This worked about half the time. It was hard not to think about one's performance when a spot on the Olympic team hung in the balance. "When you get in a slump," said Katy, her voice plaintive but matter-of-fact, "it's the worst thing that can happen to you, especially if you're like— not to say this in an egotistical-type way—if you're a finesse player, like if you do one thing really well. Shooting the three is a finesse thing. It's been trained into my brain a million times, so if I start thinking about it, it throws me off." She paused a minute, appearing lost in thought. "I try not to think about it so much," she said finally, smiling. "I'm not even thinking about it all."

Like Rebecca and Carla, Katy could only guess at where she stood with the coach. The *USA Today* fiasco had demonstrated that to all of them. It felt like years since they'd stood on that track in Colorado Springs in the wind with VanDerveer busting on them to run faster, and yet too many days felt like a repetition of that one. This was being done her way. They would be a team first and individuals second, and so they had subordinated themselves every day, even on the occasions when they just wanted to yell back, to challenge the coach: Why am I riding the bench? Why isn't anything good enough for you? What have I done?

Yet perhaps VanDerveer's genius lay in those deep-guarded silences where she made up her mind, where there was an A list and a B list, the starters, the subs, and the benchwarmers, and where her deeper philosophies about the game took root, in those secret moments when she chalk-talked herself to sleep and woke up with one plan or another—a way to adjust the defense, a play that needed to be abandoned, a new rotation of players on the court—and then set off to practice to make it all real.

At a practice in Atlanta, she divided them into Reds and Whites and let them loose on one another in a scrimmage—four-on-four, eight minute games. It was their favorite way to pass a practice, the heat of competition seemed to break them open, to release them from all the politeness and strict governance that ruled their normal routine. Following their scrimmage against Ukraine, they'd gone on to beat China the following day. Tomorrow they would take on the College All-Stars and beat them as well.

The truest challenge often came in trying to beat one another during their private scrimmages, where they did not worry how they appeared or what they said or which emotions flared at what moment. They were enough like family now to spat and brawl and lay bare the thing that drove them to play basketball—the fierce love of winning—without apology.

Jennifer promptly slammed into Dawn, knocking her flat on her back. When Jen leaned down and offered to help her up, Dawn pointedly refused her hand and boosted herself to her feet, her face in a snarl. This was how it went in scrimmages—eat or be eaten. Jennifer and Dawn often opposed each other as point guards, and in the last months they'd baited and bruised each other on the court so many times that it almost seemed habit. They were two of a kind, really, ferocious in their play, unafraid to argue or, when they could get away with it, play a little dirty.

They loved each other for it too. Each of them had grown up with an older sister, and perhaps consequently, they seemed to have reached an unspoken understanding that the territory between them was borderless, there was no line to cross that they couldn't come back from. Thus when VanDerveer pitted them against each other on opposing teams, they fought bitterly, snapped at each other, declared themselves enemies. Sometimes they would not calm down until they were showered and fed long after practice, but whatever it was they'd done to each other on the court, they were always finally able to leave it there.

The first blow delivered, the intensity of play escalated. White scored on Red, Red scored on White, each player celebrating her points and those of her teammates brashly, the way they never would in an official game. The team manager kept the score—one point for one basket—lit up on the Morehouse scoreboard. After six minutes, the scoreboard read 8–7 in White's favor, when Carla snatched the ball and halted the game.

"Seven!" she shouted at the coaches lined up on one side, her voice slipping into a whine. "They got seven and the board says eight!"

Instantly, Dawn materialized next to Carla, hands planted on hips. "Eight," she said. "We got eight points, all right? Fair and square, Carla, fair and square."

Ignoring Dawn, Carla directed her plea to the assistant coaches. As was the custom, the losers would have to do sprints up and down the court while the other team hung out at the Gatorade cooler.

"Seven . . . I swear it, it was seven," she said, abandoning the shout. "Lisa, back me up here."

"I think it was seven . . ." offered Lisa.

The bicker was on. A few of the others drew in closer and began to review the last six minutes. "You scored, then I scored, then Nikki scored."

"Nikki scored twice."

"No she didn't."

"Yeah she did."

Dawn, in the vortex of the storm, stomped her foot, looking petulant. "It's eight, y'all. The score says eight. Now come on, come on, *come on* . . . let's play."

VanDerveer, as if to back Dawn up, blew her whistle impatiently. She seldom got in the middle of arguments during scrimmages, seeming to view the friction as necessary, but she was not tolerant of delays that lasted long enough to let their sweat dry. The game resumed with the score unchanged. Lisa scored once to tie, then again to put the Reds ahead. Dawn responded by bringing the ball down and plunging inside, dodging Jennifer to put in a lay-up, burying an elbow deep in Jen's side as she went by.

She might as well have won the lottery. As Jennifer tried to catch her breath, the fury mounting on her face, Dawn danced a few steps and then strutted a slow circle around her foe. "Yes, yes, yes!" she shouted, crowing her victory for all to hear, knowing there was no need to apologize since it would all double back on her—the sweet would go sour, the jousting would continue—the next time Jen had the ball.

Athletes are generally people who like to keep score, to tally and measure things just to keep track of where they are in relation to others. Competition is an organic part of every day, a means of self-expression, even. This is not always an unfriendly thing. For the eleven women on the national team, it meant nightly card games and debts that had to be paid up quick. It meant that if something could become a contest, it did, whether it was guessing whose luggage got dumped on the carousel first or batting a stray balloon around on the bus to see who dropped it first. On the road, they raced hotel elevator cars and took turns playing solitaire on Amy Early's laptop. They were gracious losers, each one of them, but programmed as they were, every synapse wired toward victory, they much preferred to win.

Shortly after the team returned from China, a videotape arrived from Sears—the final cut of the television spot they'd shot in Los Angeles back in February. Gathering in a hotel room one night, a video machine having been procured, they sat down to watch the ad. Lisa was dressed in sweat pants and a T-shirt with a doo rag on her head and sat on the bed next to Carla, who was dressed identically. Most of the rest of the team was there too. They waited five minutes for Sheryl, who was out somewhere with Eric and had said she'd be back, and finally gave up. Once everyone had settled in, someone flipped off the lights and pressed play.

On the screen, Ruthie came up, sitting on a bus, singing "Amazing Grace." Everybody in the room started to scream. From there, the ad was a pastiche of quick scenes meant to represent the team's gypsy life, intermixed with several basketball shots and striking, artful images of their muscled bodies. There was Sheryl dallying before a white screen in a matching bikini set, close-ups of Jennifer in a sports bra, Ruthie in a sports bra. Nikki running in the rain, Nikki holding an infant. Other scenes showed Lisa, Dawn and Carla dancing, Lisa dunking the ball, Lisa tangled in the sheets of a hotel bed, Lisa injured on the court, and Lisa in a cocktail dress in the locker room, looking serene and elegant. The ad ended with a close-up on Lisa's face as she let out one of her great horsey laughs.

When it was over, a beat passed before there was a reaction. While several of them clapped a little, agreeing that it was well done, Carla sat gaping at the blank TV screen. "Is that it?" she said. "Lisa, you're the only one on there!"

This was not quite true—in fact, USA Basketball's rules stated that each player needed to appear at least once in any sponsor's ad, something that was taken care of with a quick group shot—but Lisa was inarguably the star. Lisa could hardly contain herself. It was a beautiful ad. She looked beautiful. She leapt to her feet and did a victory lap around the room, squealing and laughing—half joking and half not—while her teammates looked on, half smiling and half not. From that night forward, the ad was referred to as "Lisa's show."

When Sheryl and Eric showed up to see a replay, Lisa celebrated all over again. A number of Sheryl's scenes, including her bathtub shot, had been cut. Mostly, Sheryl said nothing. Eric, for his part, loved Sheryl's bikini shots. For the next several weeks, people asked him on numerous occasions if he minded his wife's half-naked body showing up on television like that and he would laugh. "Everybody keeps expecting me to jump up and down and rant and rave," he said at one point. "I enjoy that commercial. My wife and a lot of the ladies have great figures. They have great personalities too, they have their own personal styles and that's what the commercial shows. They're proud of what they're trying to accomplish. I think the message is, 'We are out here showing people that we are extremely talented on the basketball court . . . but off the court we're as soft as a baby's bottom.' And," he added with a let's-not-kid-ourselves grin, "the males out there would like to picture themselves alongside as the companion in that kind of situation."

Lisa's uninhibited rejoicing over the Sears ad was met by her teammates with basically good-natured eye-rolling. All of this was part of the game. When it came to media exposure, there was no competing with Lisa anyway.

"She works too hard at it for us to even think about keeping up," Teresa, who rarely sought out attention, joked.

Lisa's agent had even gone about setting up some interviews with major modeling agencies in New York for her. She was intent on building a career for herself. She liked modeling, she said, "because you just have to stand there and look nice."

Yet there were moments when Lisa's exuberance crossed a line. Early in the winter, when one of Jennifer's sneakers ripped during a practice, Lisa had inspected the hole in Jennifer's Reebok and, referring to her own endorsement deal with Nike, had said, "Hey, our motto is Just Do It . . . Yours should be just *glue* it."

Rarely did the players discuss their shoe contracts with one another, understanding implicitly that there were likely to be vast differences between what they made. As much as they were a team, and as much as they looked to consider one another as equals, they were valued in varying amounts by the world outside their tight circle. Lisa was getting called for photo shoots. During the break following the China trip, Rebecca had spent a day in Los Angeles filming a cameo with Tom Cruise for the movie *Jerry Maguire*, in which he starred as a sports agent. (Her scene was later cut.)

Rebecca's value as a public figure became an issue within the team only when it came to the ABL, where everybody knew Rebecca's endorsement could boost the league in the eyes of potential investors. As it was, the ABL could make the claim that it had commitments from ten of the national team's eleven players, but it was still not the same as having the entire team, and to have the most famous player in the country as the one abstaining didn't help either.

"She's getting business advice," said Lisa at one point. "I think she'll come around, but I think there are people telling her to wait."

Geno Auriemma, Rebecca's tried and true adviser, had revealed his feelings about the ABL somewhat backhandedly at a postgame press conference following the national team's game in Atlanta, where Auriemma and Tennessee's Pat Summit had shared coaching responsibilities for the College All-Stars. When a question regarding a professional league was directed at both coaches, Summit had immediately passed the microphone to Auriemma, who himself looked momentarily reluctant to answer.

"I think we all want a league to start in the States," he said, choosing his words carefully. "I don't know if everyone agrees on who the right group to be at the forefront of that league is."

When another reporter remarked that Auriemma didn't seem excited about the prospect of a league, the coach grew edgy. "If someone called me tomorrow and said that CBS or NBC is committed to televising forty-two games next season, if anyone says that twelve owners have committed ten million dollars each to their teams, I'd be excited." He leveled his gaze at the reporter. "Have you heard that? No? Well, we're in the same position then."

It was beginning to feel like a strange time in women's basketball. For years, the women's game had flourished within the carefully protected fiefdoms of the NCAA, USA Basketball, and to a much lesser extent, the Amateur Athletic Union. The community of coaches and administrators who had invested their lives in women's basketball was a relatively insular and infamously political one, made up of old cronies and old rivals, most of them holding deep convictions about how the women's game should grow. With the women's game reaching unprecedented heights of popularity, with the approaching Atlanta Olympics—sure to be the largest platform women's basketball had ever had—the professional future of the sport had been abruptly hijacked by a bunch of nobodies calling themselves the ABL and, perhaps more vexing, the country's top players had jumped right in behind them. Though many NCAA coaches were trying, as Auriemma had, to remain diplomatic in their public comments on the ABL, the prevailing sense seemed to be that there was something mutinous and out of control about the whole thing.

In the meantime, Tara VanDerveer had more immediate concerns than worrying about the ABL. In mid-April, six of the country's largest women basketball players arrived in Colorado Springs to strut their stuff for her, giving the coach, at long last, her chance to look at new players to bring onto the team. They were a hand-picked collection of bangers, the shortest among them six-feet-three inches, the tallest six eight. Somewhat surprisingly, Val Whiting, having been invited, decided to give it another try. She'd had several weeks to work out on her own, she was in better shape now, the memory of her Brazilian vacation long faded, the memories of China still disconcerting and slightly bitter, but they were at least, she reasoned, a part of the past too. She was ready to make everyone forget what she'd looked like in China, particularly Van-Derveer, who she blamed for wrecking her confidence in China with her continual haranguing and unfair expectations. In coming to Colorado Springs, Val wanted to show she was ready to wipe the slate clean and play hard. Here was her last shot at making the Olympic team.

For five days the coach put them through their paces. The first day they practiced on their own, shooting and running through drills, and then the second day she threw them to the lions, dumping them in to practice with the national team, which was back in town for several days between games. After eleven months on VanDerveer's workout regimen, the national team players seemed almost bionic. Venus Lacy, a burly, 190-pound center who had taken a break from her season in Greece to audition for the coach, had difficulty keeping up with them as they ran the court. Sylvia Crawley, a willowy six feet six, was quick enough on the run, but so thin that even the narrow-framed Lisa Leslie could knock her over. Kara Wolters, a six-seven center and former teammate of Rebecca's from UConn, had the size VanDerveer was looking for, but she was young, just having finished her last college season, and was likely to get steamrolled by the rough international play. Val Whiting thought she was playing pretty well, finally. She was relaxed on the court, tough during the scrimmages, and shooting the ball well. But, she would later lament, it seemed that VanDerveer hardly gave her a second glance.

In general, there was no guessing exactly what the coach was looking for. Only VanDerveer, with her full grasp of the puzzle, could recognize the missing piece when she saw it. After just a day or two, however, VanDerveer's predilections became more clear as she seemed to hone in on two of the six players, Sylvia Crawley and Venus Lacy, playing them more and more during scrimmages, watching them carefully, her eyebrows knit, as if she were trying to work out a complex mathematical equation.

The plan was that USA Basketball would invite one of the six players along on its Australian tour in May, purportedly laying the groundwork to offer that player a spot on the Olympic team the following month. After nearly a week in Colorado Springs, the players were sent home with a promise that they would be contacted within the next ten days. Meanwhile, the national team to flew to Philadelphia to play the first of its pre-Olympic exhibition games against other national teams, this one against the Chinese.

If you met Lisa Leslie, it would likely take a while to divine where she came from, though her brightly colored clothing and fondness for short shorts and her easy, laconic charm might help you to guess at southern California. You might catch a trace of Tennessee in Nikki McCray's bubbly voice, or a bit of the Carolinas in Katrina McClain's husky laugh. Meeting Tara VanDerveer, you might sense the hard weather and bleak landscape of upstate New York.

When it came to Dawn Staley, however, you would know within seconds that she hailed from the great city of Philadelphia, because, with a politician's flourish, she would tell you just that.

Philadelphia was Dawn's town, as much as Colorado Springs, with its suburban sleepiness and overwhelmingly white population, was not. Spending time in Colorado Springs, said Dawn, was like spending time in another country. Throughout the national team's journey, coming and going from Colorado and dropping in and out of nearly every major city in the country, seldom did a day pass without a little bit of Philly creeping into Dawn's conversation. "I represent the inner city of Philadelphia" was how she began her speeches to the groups they met along the way. In the warm-up sessions prior to televised games, Dawn would often dribble past the commentators' table and instruct ESPN's Robin Roberts to "Give a shout out to my peeps in Philly, okay?"

With Dawn, there always seemed to be energy in need of shedding. If she was standing, she liked to dance in place. If she was sitting, she fidgeted with everything she could get her hands on. If there was someone to hear her, she would start talking. If someone was posing for a snapshot, Dawn would find a way to sneak into the background and strike an obnoxious pose. Anything to keep herself amused. She relieved boredom by starting some lighthearted squabble or suckering someone into an inane bet. Early in the year, a producer from NBA Entertainment had asked each of the team's players in individual interviews what they would be doing if they didn't have basketball. Rebecca had said that she'd still be involved in sports some way. Katy mentioned business school, Katrina talked about law school, Lisa predicted that she'd be attending community college and working part-time if she had never played basketball. And while Teresa and several others said they couldn't possibly imagine life without basketball, Dawn had stared unblinkingly into the camera and announced that if she didn't have basketball, she'd either be a high-roller in Atlantic City or stuck in Gamblers Anonymous.

On the team's media relations questionnaire, next to "What is your philosophy on basketball?" Dawn wrote, *Whatever it takes.*

"Your philosophy on life?" *Live it up.*

Arriving in Philadelphia for the game against China, it was all Dawn could do to sit still. She had not played an organized game in Philly since her Virginia team had matched up against Temple five years earlier. But Philly, as far as Dawn was concerned, was not about organized ball anyway. She was itching to go back to her old neighborhood in the city's north end, where she'd grown up in a small brick row house with her four siblings, a father who was on disability, and a mother who had worked to keep them all together. Their house was a part of the Raymond Rosen projects, a densely populated grid of tenement high-rises with several streets of row houses with low, angled roofs built in their shadows. Like so many of the public housing developments that proliferated in cities across the country in the seventies, isolating low-income, mostly black families in out-of-the-way neighborhoods by essentially stacking them one on top of the other, Ray Rosen had become a dangerous cliché, an ideal petri dish for the drugs and violence afflicting America's inner cities.

Though the Moylan Recreation Center, a squat brick building on the corner of 25th and Diamond, offered no real physical refuge—the outdoor court sat behind a chain-link fence on an exposed lot across the street from a row of condemned buildings, the indoor court was open to everyone who walked through the door—for the boys in Dawn's neighborhood, playing ball at Moylan was a good way to form loyalties without joining the gangs, to pass the time without being lured into one kind of trouble or another. For Dawn, following her older brothers to the court and elbowing her way into their games was a good way to be a pest, to expend the energy that seemed to keep her continually keyed up and jumpy, even as a kid.

She had always been a squirt, small for a girl, even, and given that playground basketball was ruled by a strict meritocracy—play until you lose, lose and go home—Dawn had been forced to learn a creative game of basketball in order to earn her time on the court. Playing had become an addictive thrill. "Being so short, I wasn't able to get my shot off all the time, so I had to perfect different parts of my game. I had to learn how to dribble, I had to learn how to pass, and I had to learn how to be just tough," she said, looking back. "I mean, the guys have molded me into the player that I am today. Some players are sort of finesse-type players, but growing up in the inner city, that's nonexistent. We all go out and we play as aggressive as they come."

She played with a style designed to unsettle her larger opponents. She dribbled with dizzying speed, pattering around her back, through her legs, and so low to the ground that stealing from her was nearly impossible. Passing the ball was something she did slyly, an abrupt no-look or her trademark over-the-shoulder all delivered with astonishing certitude. When she slipped past the boys and scored on them, they told her to go back to the kitchen, to go jump rope with the other girls. But that was the thing about Dawn Staley, even at the age of twelve: Telling her to go was the best way to make her stay.

"You had to be good to play," she said, recalling the hot summer nights when crowds of thirty and forty people would gather in the small Moylan gym. "I mean, of course there were times when they didn't let me on the court. I had to wait and wait until I had winners and I could pick my team. . . . To be one of the first ten picked is a privilege, and I don't think I could say I was one of the first ten for maybe a couple of years."

When the Moylan was locked for the night, sometime around eleven, someone would hunt down a milk crate, pop out the bottom, and mount it on a telephone pole so that the game could go on. Dawn was always there for it. "She came home only to eat and sleep," remembered her mother, Estelle. "We couldn't get her home for anything."

Estelle Staley had moved to Philadelphia from South Carolina in 1957 and had lived in the Ray Rosen projects since 1965 with her husband, who was on disability. She had two daughters and three sons, and though she worried equally about her children, Dawn, the youngest, was at times the hardest for her to understand, disappearing for hours on end with the neighborhood boys, coming home at three in the morning on summer nights.

When Estelle asked where she'd been, her answer was the same every time: "Just playin' hoops, Ma."

Late one night, motivated as much by curiosity as by suspicion, Estelle Staley went out looking for her baby girl on the streets. She found her just where she'd said she'd be, under the streetlights, the lone girl among a bunch of sweaty boys, just playing her game. Whatever skepticism she'd felt previously about Dawn's obsessive ballplaying evaporated after that. Basketball, Estelle came to understand, was a blessing for a daughter. When years later an offer came from the University of Virginia for a four-year athletic scholarship for Dawn, Estelle bowed her head and thanked God for taking her youngest girl's restless soul out of the inner city. One blessing would come from another. Dawn would graduate from college, have opportunities to travel, meet a nice boyfriend, a Temple football player named Lance, and always care enough to come home every chance she got. When Estelle separated from her husband in 1993, she moved out of Ray Rosen to North Philadelphia's Logan section.

Though she had followed her daughter's career closely over the years, Estelle Staley could have no way of knowing the extent of her fame until the day in April when she boarded the No. 33 bus going east on Market Street, headed toward the heart of the city, where people were gathering to celebrate Dawn's homecoming with the national team. Nike, Dawn had told her, had commissioned some sort of mural that would be dedicated in a ceremony. It was noontime on a Friday, the streets rivered with businesspeople in suits on their way to lunch. They were in the heart of the city now, on a bustling downtown block of department stores and sandwich shops and beauty salons, nothing like the broken-down streets of North Philly, where every other building was boarded up, everything looking frayed and ready to crumble. Estelle wore a black sweater and skirt, her hair was brushed back smoothly from her face. Dawn had said there might be television cameras, though she knew her daughter well enough to predict that she'd surface in a sweatsuit herself. Just then the bus lurched around a corner at Philadelphia City Hall, and Estelle happened to glance out the window. Normally she was soft-spoken in public, but what she saw caused her to shout before she could think about it. "Oh, my God!" Then came the tears, pearling down her face, while a sob seized up her throat.

The woman in the seat in front of her turned around, looking surprised but kindly. "What's wrong?" she said.

Estelle Staley drew herself up slightly and pointed a finger out the window. There on the corner of Eighth and Market, so high she had to crane her neck to look up at it, so big and lifelike she could hardly believe it, was a painting of Dawn dribbling the ball, her jersey billowing, her mouth open, eyebrows arched, just playing her game. Estelle's lips trembled as she answered the woman, "That's my baby up there."

The mural, seven stories high and sixty-seven feet wide, had shocked Dawn when she'd come down to look at it the night before. "I thought this was going to be *little*," she said, shaking her head at her own image looming above. "Seeing myself up there, it seems like it's not even me. It's someone else." Nike had eight other murals of its athletes around the country. Charles Oakley hung over a New York block, Michael Jordan and Scottie Pippen soared over Chicago, Barry Sanders was in Detroit, Jerry Rice in San Francisco, Cal Ripken in Baltimore, Mike

Piazza in Los Angeles, and Mookie Blaylock in Atlanta. And now, the girl among the boys, Dawn Staley in her great city of Philly.

"I'd like to thank [Philadelphia '76ers rookie sensation] Jerry Stackhouse for signing with Fila," she quipped for the hundred or so people who'd gathered in an unpaved parking lot across the street from the mural for the dedication. Her teammates, along with Carol Callan, Tara VanDerveer and her assistants, had gathered in the sun, next to a collection of Dawn's aunts and buddies from Moylan. Later, they would all head to an aunt's house and eat home-cooked soul food to celebrate. The event was, as Nike events often were, Swoosh-happy. Nike had put up a hoop with a Swoosh on the backboard, representatives were passing out Nike posters and Swoosh paraphernalia, but in the end these were just window dressing on a moment that belonged purely to Dawn Staley, her family and friends, and her supporters in Philly. For the women on the team, during the half hour or so they stood beneath Dawn's likeness in the city that meant the world to her, everything that could ever divide them was banished. It didn't matter who wore Nikes and who wore Reeboks. It didn't matter who played the game and who sat on the bench, who showed up in the magazines or for whom the fans screamed the loudest. For a minute, even the gold medal didn't matter. This was about Dawn and her peeps.

Lisa Leslie stood alongside Estelle Staley and wept proudly. From there, she and Dawn's family would go back to Moylan, which was now called the Hank Gathers Recreation Center, to give a clinic for the neighborhood kids. The Ray Rosen towers had been razed a year earlier, but the rest of it—the gangs and violence, the tight-knit community and the basketball—still thrived. To the children in the neighborhood, Dawn Staley was a hero, and more important a hero who always came back to the neighborhood to play ball with them.

Standing behind a podium, Dawn told the assembled crowd what she would tell later the kids. "When I see the mural, I see positivity and hope," she said, squinting out at the crowd. Despite her showiness on the court, she was not a public speaker at heart, but today the words seemed to come easily. As she spoke, she tried not to look at her mother's new flood of tears. Her teammates had never seen her cry, and she wanted to keep it that way. She continued, "I see hope for people like me who grew up in the inner city and thought that was all there was. Life is out there for you. You have to take it."

In 1988, after a car wreck that put her in a coma for two days and broke nearly every bone in her face, Carla was told she would be lucky to walk again without a cane. Her return to basketball defied all odds. Stepping onto the court to play, she says, she must fight back fears of suffering another head injury. Here, Carla gets roughed up by an Australian player. (Courtesy AP/Worldwide Photos)

Jennifer, who was the MVP of Tara VanDerveer's first championship-winning team at Stanford, was famed for her hyper, driven style of play at point guard. (Courtesy NBA Photos, Andrew Bernstein)

Lisa reads up on the national team's routing of Italy in a pre-Olympic game in Indianapolis. (Courtesy NBA Photos, Andrew Bernstein)

Dawn's razzle-dazzle passing frequently brought fans to their feet. When a reporter at the Olympics blurted out his admiration, Dawn said, "I've been doing these same things for the last few years overseas. It's a shame you guys didn't get to see that." (Courtesy NBA Photos, R. Eckert)

Ruthie Bolton scores on the inside against Brazil's most famous player, Hortência. Her trademark, however, was the long-range three-point shot. (Courtesy NBA Photos, Scott Cunningham)

Sheryl Swoopes is known as one of the quickest and most versatile basketball players in the world. (Courtesy NBA Photos, R. Eckert)

Coach VanDerveer advises Ruthie during an Olympic game. (Courtesy NBA Photos, Andrew Bernstein)

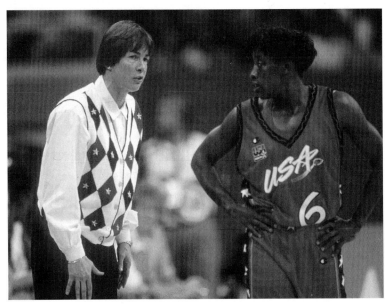

Ruthie and Sheryl shed tears of joy as the gold-medal game winds down. (Courtesy AP/Worldwide Photos)

Jennifer and Dawn do cartwheels to celebrate the team's final victory. (Courtesy AP/Worldwide Photos, John Gap III)

At last, the gold medal. Left to right, Jennifer, Lisa, Carla, Katy Steding, and Katrina wave to fans at the Georgia Dome. (Courtesy AP/Worldwide Photos, Susan Ragan)

Teresa, who was in many ways the soul of the U.S. team, has now been to four Olympics. The medal she won with her teammates in Atlanta after a year of grueling preparation is the one she says means the most. (Courtesy NBA Photos, Andrew Bernstein)

Rebecca and Sheryl show off their WNBA jerseys several months after the Olympics. (Courtesy AP/Worldwide Photos)

The next day, as Zheng Haixia warmed up with her team-mates at the Philadelphia Palestra, a number of American fans tittered in the stands. Zheng was as big a person, male or female, as most anybody had seen, and not just the children but the adults seemed struck by the cruelest form of discomfort, their shocked giggling drifting downward to the court, where Zheng practiced free throws, appearing oblivious.

The Chinese had been in the country for two weeks, and as their Nike interpreter, a native of China himself, explained it, America was like a Technicolor Disney World to them, as curious and disorienting as China had been to the American players just a month earlier. The Chinese team had played a number of scrimmages during their stay and had spent a few days at Nike's headquarters in Beaverton, Oregon, on the Nike "campus," a collection of corporate buildings constructed around a shimmering, human-made duck pond and ringed by a jogging path.

Today, Zheng was limping slightly, wearing a brace on her left knee, and appearing slightly worn out, jogging a slow circle around the court. By contrast, Dawn flitted between her teammates, half dancing, half dribbling, too worked up to go through the motions of warming up.

In the stands that day sat the eleven members of USA Basketball's player selection committee, who would meet after the game to discuss what was becoming known as the "twelfth player issue," making a decision about who would join the team for the Australia trip. They would also likely talk about whether or not to cut any of the existing members of the team, which meant they would be watching the game that day carefully.

For Dawn Staley, there was no audience but the one that sat several rows up at midcourt, the group of family that had come—her mother, her several aunts, her sister Tracey, two of her brothers, and her boyfriend. Playing in front of her family and particularly her mother made her anxious. "I don't know why. Every time she sees me play, I get nervous. I think my family is my worst critics," said Dawn. "Every little thing that I do, they're going to tell me about it afterward. But they're my biggest supporters too. I know that."

Dawn lived her life at a slow boil anyway, and thus when something got her antsy, she tended to fulminate and sometimes explode. There were moments when she played the game too loose or too fast, when her flash bit back at her with a pass thrown too quickly or an overambitious dribble that went awry. She played a baroque, ad-libbed game, one that kept her teammates charged up but, at times, put Coach VanDerveer's stomach in a knot. Dawn did, on occasion, lose her head. Following her NBA hero Maurice Cheeks, she wore a rubber band around her right wrist which, when she caused a turnover, she would snap against her skin as a reminder to stay in line.

At the wrong moment, in the wrong game, her spontaneity could cost them everything. When Dawn successfully executed one stunning move or another, the coach was as impressed as the next person. When Dawn overdid it, VanDerveer, who espoused a straight-up, almost contemplative game of basketball, often pulled her out of the game without a word. Dawn knew the rap. She'd shake her head when she messed up, chalking it up to her natural style, one she characterized a bit sheepishly as "too much mustard on the hot dog."

When the national team took the floor against the Chinese team in Philly, Dawn's pistons were firing at full steam. Seeing her fly through the first few plays was like watching someone start a marathon at a full sprint. She chased down the ball, tried to snatch it out of one of the Chinese players' hands, and was immediately called for holding. This, she knew, meant trouble. Fouling early in the game was on VanDerveer's list of cardinal sins: Letting one's game get too sloppy or too physical before the score even mattered was simply a waste. Dawn cursed herself silently as the Chinese player scored on both free throws. She focused her mind on playing better, on controlling herself, but as it often did with Dawn, that kind of thinking had an adverse effect. Two minutes later, she fouled again—this time on a charge—and she knew she'd gone too far. VanDerveer's antidote to sinning was a set of ironclad rules, one of them being if you foul twice in the first ten minutes, you're out for the half. Out of the corner of her eye, Dawn could see the coach motioning for Teresa to jump in for her. Just five minutes into her big hometown game, Dawn was back on the bench, seething at herself quietly.

The Chinese team seemed to have lost its luster since the Americans had seen them in China. Their defense was lax, allowing Lisa Leslie to slip inside and score at will. The Chinese coach, clearly concerned about Zheng's knee, had kept her out of the game for the first five minutes. When he finally did send her in, she played listlessly, missing even routine shots and allowing Lisa to get in her face on defense. Meanwhile, the refs were calling fouls on the Chinese what felt like every twenty seconds. Midway through the half, with the Americans ahead 20–8, the Chinese coach stopped the game altogether and shouted at the refs through the Nike interpreter. "Unfair!" he screamed in Chinese. "Unfair!" When the refs threatened to call a technical foul on him, the coach motioned his players back onto the court and grimly took his seat. By halftime, his team was down by fifteen points.

The Chinese team was playing uncharacteristically poorly, and for a while it was difficult to tell why. Prior to the start of the second half, however, the coach drew in his team and spoke animatedly, poking a finger at his clipboard, which was marked up with Xs and Os. Meanwhile, Hugo, the mascot for the NBA's Charlotte Hornets, had roadtripped to Philly to do the halftime show. Hugo was himself supposed to be a hornet. He wore an enormous bee head and teal tights, and part of his routine involved doing a flying leap off a trampoline at the freethrow line, flipping in the air and dumping himself into the basket so that his head got caught in the net. As the Chinese coach plotted his strategy for the second half, Hugo was just finishing up his trampoline act on the floor and, one noticed, he had the rapt attention of every last player on the Chinese team. The game's second half passed much the same as the first half had, only Dawn came back and redeemed herself by playing a measured but energetic rest of the game. Lisa demolished Zheng, scoring 23 points altogether while limiting Zheng to just four. In general, the Chinese faltered and fumbled throughout the game's final minutes while Hugo did acrobatic splits and leaps along the sidelines, taking the opportunity during time-outs to storm the court and slingshot mini basketballs into the roaring crowd. While it would be hard to blame a hornet for what eventually became a 85–52 victory for the U.S., the loss seemed indicative of what the general problem seemed to be—one that did not bode well for the Chinese team's hopes for Atlanta—something the team's interpreter summed up unhappily after the game. "They cannot deal," he said, "with this Disney World."

11

chapter

Changing Fortunes

Sue Levin, Nike's thirty-two-year-old manager for women's sports marketing, bore the standard characteristics of Nike staffers, who as a rule were young, smart, and athletic. Nike was the kind of place where employees stormed the soccer fields behind the office buildings at lunchtime. In winter, they cross-country-skied around the berm that enclosed the corporate campus, or played a vigorous game of basketball on the Bo Jackson Center Court, part of the state-of-the-art Bo Jackson Sports and Fitness Center. A former freelance magazine writer and world-class ultimate Frisbee player, Levin, a shortish woman with a long frizz of dark hair, had been brought into Nike's public relations department in 1994 and, on the basis of her industriousness and depth of knowledge about women's sports, had then been promoted to the more powerful marketing department and put in charge of women's sports after just three months.

In her new position, Levin controlled a basketball budget of several million dollars a year, which was parcelled out to college teams, youth programs, and individual sponsorship deals with female athletes. In essence, she acted as a talent scout, traveling frequently, keeping tabs on various athletes and sports programs around the country, deciding if and to what extent they merited Nike's support. It had been Levin who in the months leading up to national team trials had gambled on which women's basketball players would likely make the team, and beyond that, which ones would bring Nike the kind of exposure it desired.

As testament to Levin's acumen, all five of the players she'd chosen to sponsor that year had made the national team. As it was, Levin's players—Lisa, Ruthie, Teresa, Dawn, and Katrina, in addition to Sheryl, who had signed with Nike prior to Levin's arrival—turned out to be VanDerveer's starters, with the exception of Dawn, who was now playing backup point guard. Interestingly, Tara VanDerveer was a beneficiary of Nike's deep pockets as well. As was common with top-tier college coaches for both men's and women's basketball, VanDerveer had a shoe deal of her own, inked in 1990, just as her first crop of Stanford recruits was coming of age. Catching sight of a Nike vice president at the women's Final Four in March, VanDerveer had joked that based on who her emerging national team starters were, people were going to start thinking her loyalty to Nike influenced her coaching, though in truth the preponderance of Nike footwear on the court had far more to do with Levin's savvy decision-making.

From the start, Gary Cavalli had wanted more than anything to sell Sue Levin on sponsoring the ABL. What he and Hams had found when they'd first met with her back in May 1995, however, was that she'd heard a lot of pitches in her short time at the helm of women's sports marketing, and as a result was naturally skeptical. It was as if everyone who thought they had a good idea about sports figured they needed only to bring it to Nike to foot the bill, an unfortunate byproduct, it seemed, of the company's almighty "Just Do It" image. In the months prior to Cavalli and Hams showing up at her door, Levin had heard from people wanting to start women's sports Web sites, television shows, magazines, in addition to professional leagues for women's volleyball, soccer, and softball. When it came to women's basketball leagues, Levin had informed them at their initial meeting, the ABL was the seventh group she'd heard from. She had seven leagues on paper and not much that distinguished one group from the next, aside from the fact that they were decidedly premature in asking for her help. Politely, she had instructed Cavalli and Hams much as she had the people who'd come before them: Keep working on it and stay in touch.

Cavalli and Hams had been scouting out their potential competitors, however, and, aside from the possibility of the NBA getting involved, Cavalli was brashly certain that the others would self-destruct. By April 1996, Cavalli declared himself ninety percent certain that the ABL was going to happen as planned. As the national team got more and more press attention in the Olympic buildup, so, too, did the ABL. Cavalli, who had the most experience with media relations, handled most of the press and with the buzz about the league snowballing, his phone was ringing continually. Meanwhile, Bobby Johnson was handling finances and hammering out the details of player contracts. Over the course of the winter, they had received hundreds of résumés, interviewed a number of candidates for coaching and general manager jobs. In anticipation of filling the team rosters, they had planned player tryouts and a territorial draft, both scheduled for June.

Meanwhile, Cavalli was almost positive that they had Nike in the bag. The ABL had wooed Sue Levin carefully over the months, disclosing the details of their ongoing talks with ESPN, Prime Network, and other potential sponsors, and relying on the Nike players, namely Teresa and Dawn, to keep her abreast of the players' continued enthusiasm for the league.

Meeting with the ABL organizers over the women's Final Four weekend held in Charlotte, North Carolina, in March, Levin had sat down and finally agreed to talk specifics with Cavalli and the others. Together they had mapped out what amounted to a $750,000 deal in which Nike would sponsor three ABL teams—most likely Atlanta, Richmond, and Portland—providing each team with $100,000 cash and $150,000 in Nike products. It seemed like an equitable arrangement; Levin had said she was optimistic that the deal would work out.

Later that night, Cavalli, Hams, Cribbs, and Johnson had gone out for a celebratory dinner in Charlotte, choosing an Italian restaurant crowded with people in town for the tournament. As Hams would remember it later, the four of them were in as high spirits as they'd been in a year. In the span of one weekend, they had interviewed several potential coaches, they'd finally gotten an audience with the college coaches, and last but most important, Nike had finally climbed on board. As it happened, they bumped into Sue Levin and several associates at the restaurant, and Levin had sent a bottle of wine over to their table. Raising their glasses, the ABL's principal founders toasted their good fortune, courtesy of Nike.

In the weeks after Charlotte, Cavalli spoke several times with Sue Levin. She informed him that she had received the approval she needed from her superiors and later, that Nike's attorneys had drafted an agreement for the sponsorship of three ABL teams. Cavalli and the others were ecstatic. Levin, however, would later say that she was harboring some doubts about the ABL's lack of a television contract. Anne Cribbs had been negotiating with ESPN, but as of yet, nothing had been formalized.

Encouraged, the ABL was moving ahead with its plans, securing arenas and hiring staff in its eight charter cities. One day at the end of April,

Cavalli and Hams flew to Hartford, Connecticut, where they were working to set up the team they hoped would feature Rebecca Lobo.

That afternoon, at a New York press conference following the semiannual NBA Board of Governors meeting, David Stern had pronounced women's basketball "ready to bloom." The NBA, he'd said, would be launching a women's league in the summer of 1997, eight teams in eight existing NBA cities, playing during the men's off season, June through August. Few other details were provided. Rather, Stern and vice president of business affairs Val Ackerman had promised that they would elaborate on their plans following the Olympics.

Hearing the news from a sudden barrage of people, Cavalli felt his heart sink. "This is probably a terrible analogy," he would say later, "but it's like when you have a relative who's dying and you prepare for it, and you know it's going to happen, but when it happens it's still quite a shock." Hams had gone back to his hotel room to get a group of similar messages. *USA Today,* the *Los Angeles Times,* and others were calling the California office frantically, wanting to know the ABL's response. Was this the end? How did they feel? What were they going to do?

Months earlier, anticipating a moment like this, Hams had suggested that they should respond with as much optimism as possible. After all, who said the NBA couldn't play in the summer while the ABL played during the traditional basketball season of October through March? As the media geared up to see the shark swallow the guppie, Hams vowed to stay positive. "This just validates what we're doing," he would tell people. "This is all good for women's basketball."

Cavalli, however, was cut from a different cloth, preferring to acknowledge the fight. Getting on the phone with a writer from the *L.A. Times,* his voice brimmed with confidence as he began by referring to the NBA as a "900-pound gorilla," explaining that the ABL had the key thing, the national team players. "We're going ahead with the league," Cavalli told the reporter. "We'll see what happens."

While Cavalli worked damage control with the press, Bobby Johnson, sitting alone in his office in Atlanta, was losing his cool. He had sunk three and a half million dollars into the ABL and let go of the business he'd run for fifteen years, and in truth, they had no players to speak of.

"I'm settin' there and I said, 'Well, it wasn't a surprise,'" Johnson would say later. "The only thing that surprised me was that we hadn't heard from the players and we didn't have the contracts. I thought, what does this mean?"

Knowingly or not, Stern had timed it perfectly, announcing the league at precisely the moment before the national team members signed binding contracts. He'd caught the ABL at its most vulnerable moment. Who knew what kind of money the NBA would offer? Who knew if they'd been talking to certain players secretly? Johnson and the others had suspected all along that somebody—most likely an agent or several agents, many of whom were unhappy about the ABL's strict salary structure—had been leaking the ABL contracts and business plans to the NBA. Now, as he sat dumbstruck behind his desk, Johnson was certain that was the case.

The *Los Angeles Times* article that ran the next morning claimed that Stern had informed a group of NBA owners in a private meeting that they would choose teams based on the regional draw of certain players. The article hinted that three players had been mentioned in conjunction with this idea: Sheryl Swoopes, Lisa Leslie, and Rebecca Lobo.

Meanwhile, the national team players were on a two-week break, spread out all across the country, incommunicado.

"Have you heard from anyone?" Johnson asked Cavalli and Hams each of the several times he spoke to them that first night.

"No, have you?"

Each time, Johnson heaved a sigh. "No."

The next day he got a call from Teresa Edwards, who was home in Atlanta. She had heard about the announcement the same way everyone else had, by word of mouth and through the newspapers.

"We're with you," she told Johnson. "Don't worry about it."

"Teresa," Johnson said back, "how do we know that if there are no contracts?"

That afternoon, Teresa tried to track down her teammates to get some reassurances for Johnson and the others, but had trouble finding most of them.

"You talk about a dark moment," said Johnson later. "The next day Teresa came to my office on her way to see a play. And we were just standing there talking. Teresa says, 'It's not what we want. We don't want the NBA because I'd rather go back overseas than play in the summer like that. I won't do that.' I said, 'Teresa, we need to think about this. The NBA has a lot to offer. You know they have a lot of resources. They've been at this a long time.' She says, 'Yeah, but we don't want to be a sideshow, playing in the summer. We don't want this.' She said, 'Don't worry, I've talked to players who are with us.' I said, 'We don't have any contracts, not one.'"

The NBA announcement had come on a Wednesday, and the weekend passed without a word from the players aside from Johnson's two conversations with Teresa. His "I can" tenet was leaving him quickly. He could hear the optimism ebbing in the voices of the others now back in California, even as they tried to remain confident. "You talk about gutcheck time," Cavalli would later say. Hams would remember it as a "miserable week." Anne Cribbs would recall the mood among the ABL founders as "very tense."

Back in his office on Monday, Johnson's thoughts were a jumble: "If the players want a league and they want the NBA's league, then I'm done, because our number-one goal is to establish a high-quality professional league here in this country for the women. So great, I'm done," he told himself. "Now I can go back and have a very easy life. I don't have to work six, seven days a week, fourteen hours a day, doing all this, when I'm not getting paid. I've invested all this money and time. Why am I doing it? Here I am doing this, I don't know why . . ."

Sometime in the midmorning, Teresa visited Johnson. She said, "Give me a few hours, Bobby, and I'll be back with my contract, okay?" True to her word, she returned in the early evening, signed contract in hand. "I'm with you," she said, offering a smile that seemed to say she understood that it was still not enough to set his mind at ease.

When Teresa left, Johnson picked up the phone and called Cavalli, Cribbs, and Hams, who had spent the day rehearsing all the "what-ifs." What if they lost all the players? What if they lost the "name" players like Swoopes and Leslie? Was Lobo now a lost cause?

"We got Teresa," Johnson told them. "I feel good."

A few hours later, Jennifer Azzi called to say that her contract was going into that day's FedEx. Then Katy Steding faxed hers in. Nikki McCray called Steve Hams with a question about the contract, which she was reviewing with Pat Summitt one last time that morning before getting it in. Slowly but surely, contracts arrived from Katrina McClain, Carla McGhee, and Dawn Staley. Despite nothing from Lisa Leslie,

Ruthie Bolton, or Sheryl Swoopes, and the continued silence from Re-becca Lobo—all four, marquee names that could be key in assuring the success of the ABL—it suddenly felt like the players were still with them.

"One by one, the contracts started coming in over the faxes, in the mail," Johnson said later. "I thought, 'We're back in business.'"

Several days later, the national team reconvened in Colorado Springs and started up with practice as usual. The blessing about this basketball team, Teresa Edwards would say later, was that practice could go on as usual, even if everywhere the players turned, people were demanding to know how they felt and what they were going to do now that they had two professional leagues to choose between. "Stepping onto the court," said Teresa, "we didn't think about anything that was going on outside of the team. Nothing could touch us when we were playing basketball."

Off the court, however, the league issues persisted. The press had glommed on to the prospect of warring women's basketball leagues with an almost rabid eagerness. As the Olympics drew closer, the media would try to mine as much emotion or conflict as it could from the national team players regarding their loyalties. Feeling that it was important to talk to one another, Jennifer and Teresa called an informal player meeting one night at the apartment Teresa shared with Katrina and Lori Phelps, the team's manager, whom they'd rescued from the largely unsavory training center dorms.

All the players were there. And as was often the case with player meetings, Teresa started the talking.

"Y'all, are we still in this thing together, or what?" she said. "Because if we're not, we have to tell Bobby so he'll quit losing money. We have to give Bobby that much, okay? So if you're going to do it, get those contracts in. If you're not going to do it, be straight up."

The response in the room, particularly from the players with delinquent contracts, was immediate. Lisa spoke up and said her agent had come up with a few questions regarding her ability to have a modeling career on the side, but as far as she knew, everything had been worked out. Sheryl said she had no problem with the ABL and that her agent, too, was tying up a few loose ends. Ruthie attributed the delay to the fact she'd recently signed with a new agent, who was just getting caught up with her business. Only Rebecca remained silent. The others chimed in with their feelings: The NBA was going to play in the summer, and who wanted to play basketball in the summer? The NBA had done nothing more than make an announcement, so who knew for sure if they'd ever get a league going?

"Y'all the power of women's basketball is in this room," said Dawn. "It's right here. It's us. If we stick together, we're going to make things happen. If we start splitting up, it's gonna get tough."

"You tell Bobby we're all with him," said Carla McGhee emphatically. "You tell him to put that ball in the air next October and we'll be there to jump for it."

Teresa and Jennifer came away from the meeting happy. Yet even as the team tried to maintain an even keel, things around them seemed in a continual state of flux. Three new assistant coaches had joined the team, while the two assistant coaches who'd been with them all year, Reneé Brown and Nell Fortner, had departed as planned, due to a clause in USA Basketball's constitution stipulating that assistant coaches for the Olympics had to be head coaches of college programs. The new faces on the sidelines, new voices directing them, belonged to Nancy Darsch of Ohio State, Ceal Barry of Colorado, and Marian Washington of Kansas, all coaches of top-ranked college programs.

Meanwhile, Sylvia Crawley, the lanky six-six center who'd auditioned for VanDerveer along with the other post players earlier in April, had been chosen to come to Australia. She had been VanDerveer's second choice behind the brawnier Venus Lacy, but Lacy had encountered trouble extracting herself from her contract playing in Greece and had reluctantly turned down the invitation for Australia in order to finish her season there. Crawley was given two weeks with the team and no guarantees. Showing up in Colorado Springs for two days of practice before leaving for Australia, she had found, like Val Whiting before her, that after all these months together and miles traveled, the team operated with a startling efficiency. The players moved through practices as if the routine had been programmed into them, they seemed almost to communicate without speaking, they knew their plays so automatically that Crawley, trying to catch on, felt like a stick thrust into the spokes of a wheel.

Meanwhile, the selection committee invited another crop of players—a group of top perimeter players this time—to try out for several days in

Colorado Springs. The new tryouts seemed to indicate that VanDerveer's needs did not stop with a big center, that she or the members of the committee were considering making changes at the other positions as well, which would mean cutting people.

If they thought about it, most of the existing players had reason to worry. Katy was still reeling from her shooting slump, Dawn's too-much-mustard-on-the-hot-dog syndrome would forever worry the coach, Nikki had remained largely undemonstrative, Jennifer was playing fewer and fewer minutes in each game, and Carla had not quite caught up to speed after missing the China trip. While Rebecca would look back at the China tournament as pivotal for her, VanDerveer had all but dismissed the performance. "Maybe it helped her confidence playing against Korea, but basically they're five foot eight. I mean, they're shrimps . . . and against China, all she had to do was sit in a zone," said VanDerveer. "It's like, I know people want to be positive about Rebecca, but I mean, we're looking for scraps here." She would add, a moment later, "It's just that much more competition at this level. Rebecca is struggling. . . . It's not like I'm out to get her."

Basketball is the kind of sport where the smallest flagellation of self-doubt can come as a club to the knees. Even with the new players arriving to try out just as the national team was leaving for Australia, most of the original eleven players tried desperately not to think about the prospect of getting cut. The confidence principle applied to the team as a whole too. If one player started to wobble, the delicate equation that held them together could be thrown off kilter. Now, under the microscope, they had to hold each other together, to make each other look good and, most of all, to keep winning, for they imagined it would be harder to tinker with the chemistry of a team that didn't lose.

They left for Australia early on a Wednesday and, on a series of flights that would take some twenty-six hours and carry them over the international dateline, they would not arrive until Friday morning. On the leg that took them from Denver to Los Angeles, Tara VanDerveer happened to be seated next to Teresa, who was dressed in her USA sweatsuit so she could sleep and armed with a Walkman to tune out for the long flight. The two of them seldom socialized off the court. For Teresa, it was all she could do to get over the bitterness she'd felt sitting on the bench all fall, listening to the coach carp on her in a way that seemed intentionally harsh and frequently unnecessary. As far as she was concerned, she'd fought harder than she'd really ever had to fight for anything to get what looked to be the permanent starting point guard spot on the team. To her mind, she'd had to prove VanDerveer, whom she was convinced had no faith in her, wrong.

"I wanted to have it in people's minds that you gotta be a fool to keep Katrina and Teresa sitting down," Teresa would say later. "I had to be so good that she had no choice but to play me."

By the time May rolled around, Teresa was playing most of every game. She'd rescued the team several times from imminent losses, and when it came to her troubled relationship with the coach, it seemed they'd finally found some balance. Part of the bargain, Teresa felt, was limiting their interaction to what happened on the basketball court, where they each had a job to do. They were different people on the court—perhaps more compatible in their desire to win above all else—than they were off it anyway. Out of her element, VanDerveer sometimes had the appearance of a girl who'd been thrust suddenly onto a stage, blinking into the glare of the lights, unsure of who was in the audience. When she was not coaching, she was often quiet, even shy with strangers. With her players she was less retiring but still somewhat ill at ease, as if there were no escaping the distance inherent between coach and athlete, as if whatever bridges they might build off the court had, by necessity, everything to do with what transpired on it.

Teresa, for her part, prided herself as able to separate basketball from everything beyond it. "Life is bigger than this little ball we're bouncing," she once said. Like Jennifer, Teresa could compete vociferously with Dawn during a scrimmage and still walk away knowing whatever feelings the game brought out were just that. It was liberating, she said, to be able to feel the full heat of competition without having it turn into something ugly, something personal. She called it a "comfort zone," the thing that allowed them to say anything to one another, to play rough with one another, to get angry or upset without apology. She'd been on enough teams to know that the comfort zone was a precious and distinctive thing. It would be, she hoped, what allowed them to overcome anything that got thrown at them in the next several months—the possible cuts, the potential losses, the inevitable pressures on the horizon—and do what they'd set out to do.

The comfort zone, at least as far as Teresa was concerned, did not include Coach VanDerveer. As VanDerveer viewed it, a coach's job was to stand slightly apart from her players anyway, though there were moments when they might have understood that she cared for them personally. When they left the court, the power dynamic seemed to swing mightily: There were eleven of them and one of her. VanDerveer was aware that they talked about her—how could they not?—and that surely they griped. But she did respect them, all of them, the same way she hoped they respected her back. As a coach, though, she was not into the ephemeral matters of how people got along, how people felt per se. This was basketball at its highest level: It was about winning and losing. "Team chemistry to me is something overrated," she said. "I mean it's something, yes, but team chemistry won't mean doodle if you don't win a gold medal."

Sitting elbow to elbow on the plane to Los Angeles, VanDerveer and Teresa worked at making small talk for a while. They both enjoyed reading, and when they talked, they often cautiously kept the subject on books: But this was a long flight, and somewhere over Nevada the topic turned to the thing that had been on both their minds anyway, the ABL and the NBA.

One did not need to know Teresa Edwards well to understand that she was deeply passionate about the ABL. Throughout the year, she and Jennifer had acted as the liaisons between the league organizers and the national team players. She spoke with Bobby Johnson at least once a week and often more. Johnson referred to her as "Madame President," and often told Teresa he expected her to work him out of a job. When she was ready to retire, he said, she would come in and run the league.

For whatever reason, VanDerveer decided to play devil's advocate that day on the plane. Like many of her peers in the college coaching community, she'd been slightly suspicious of the ABL from the start. After all, who were these guys and what could they possibly know about running a basketball league? Wasn't it natural for her to worry that her players were going to get hurt in the long run, particularly with the NBA now in the picture?

As the coach voiced her questions, Teresa's anger ignited.

"She kept saying, 'How do you know these guys are on the up-and-up? The NBA is established, you know. They know what they're doing.' She was on the NBA trip, big time, and I'm up there fighting nails and tooth with her, telling her why we believed in the ABL," Teresa would remember later.

"Hey, Tara, you got a job when this is all over," she told her coach. "What do we have to do? Where are we going to go? Why are we going to put our future in the hands of people who haven't even told us anything about what they're doing, who haven't even done anything concrete?"

When the team deplaned for a layover in L.A., Teresa was so upset she couldn't meet VanDerveer's eyes. She'd been under the coach's thumb for nearly a year now, eight months of which had been spent traveling. And now VanDerveer was wrapped up in the league stuff too, acting like she knew better than any of them, suggesting, it seemed, that they were being foolish and impulsive in sticking with the ABL.

"Is it so wrong for us to fight for something?" she'd asked the coach before they landed, the emotion rising in her throat. "Tell me what's so wrong with that."

May in Australia is the equivalent of November in the northern hemisphere, which meant that the players arrived in Melbourne to find themselves met by an autumn chill. For two days they stayed in a hotel on the south side of the city, strolling to and from practice through the Royal Botanic Gardens that covered a hillside next to the Yarra River. Walking through the damp, brusque air, surrounded by stately oak trees in their slow golden molt, was at moments like being cast backward in time to the endless days of the college tour, or perhaps telescoping ahead to a time when the Olympics would be long past, when one way or another everything would be settled safely in their memories. Either way, the effect was strangely relaxing.

For Ruthie Bolton, coming back to Australia brought no hard memories of losing the World Championships to the Brazilians and the Chinese a year and a half earlier. There was no need to dwell, she said. Lacing up her shoes before one of their first practices in Melbourne, Ruthie started talking about what she liked to call the PMA.

The PMA was something Ruthie considered a life tool, passed on from her father, the Reverend Linwood Bolton who at seventy-six was still preaching in four churches in Mississippi. "That's the Positive Mental Attitude," explained Ruthie, who had a throaty, mumbling way of speaking. "And it means to stay positive no matter how rough things get. It's helped me tremendously. I constantly repeat it in my mind, 'Keep the PMA, keep the PMA.' " Linwood and Leola Bolton had raised their twenty children—of which Ruthie was number sixteen—in a five-bedroom house in McClain, Mississippi. Linwood had no tolerance for internecine sibling battle, which meant that among the Bolton brood, keeping the PMA was a requirement. Ruthie's closest friend was her sister, Mae Ola, who had played basketball a year ahead of her at Auburn, where they were roommates. Both sisters had tried out for and been cut from the 1992 Olympic team. Shortly after, Mae Ola had been injured in a car crash and had to abandon her career. Ruthie had vowed that if she won a gold medal in Atlanta, she would give it to Mae Ola, who she credits, along with her mother and father, with teaching her the PMA. On the national team, Ruthie steered clear of arguments over the scores at scrimmages. When the others started to complain, she normally kept quiet. Either that or she offered another of her favorite aphorisms: "It takes more muscles to frown than to smile." On the side, she had gravitated toward network marketing and was using some of her PMA to sell her teammates a long-distance phone service called Excel.

In Melbourne, Ruthie led the team in a jog around the court to shake off the travel-induced charley horses, the haze of feeling it was 3 A.M. when it was really 3 P.M. She'd adapted several of her army reserve songs to suit the team, amusing everyone, even the coach, by replacing the word "sergeant" with the word "Tara." Today she chanted one of the group favorites, hollering out each line in a singsong rhythm and then waiting for her teammates to repeat it:

Up in the morning, all day!
   Up in the morning, all day!
I don't like it, no way!
   I don't like it, no way!
I went to Tara on my knees!
   I went to Tara on my knees!
I said, Tara, Tara, feed me please!
   I said, Tara, Tara, feed me please!

In thirteen days, the tournament would take them all over eastern Australia, playing against the national teams from Cuba, Ukraine, and

Australia. The Americans had played the Ukrainian team several times in the States, and the Cubans were now almost like old friends. Leaving China, in fact, Dawn had launched an informal clothing drive, collecting everything from sneakers to extra athletic tape and practice gear and passing it over to the miserably underfunded Cuban players, who accepted the gifts graciously. And so while they were happy for the added competition, the Americans had not come to Australia to play the Cubans or the Ukrainians again; they were there for the Aussies themselves.

At practice, they spent more and more time rehearsing the plays they'd amassed over the last months. VanDerveer had piled a new play onto the existing lot nearly each week, until their heads were like libraries full of a kinetic language that needed to be practiced and relearned until it became automatic, internalized, a collective heartbeat that could be triggered with one word.

"Georgia!" Dawn would call, dribbling the ball up, her eyes carefully measuring where her teammates were downcourt.

The plays were mostly named after places they'd been or teams they'd played against, or some old association of VanDerveer's. Together they formed a quixotic roadmap: Georgia, L.A., Arizona, Iowa, Texas, Connecticut, Kansas, Tennessee, San Fran, Ohio, Louisiana, Hawaii, Kentucky, Atlanta. They ran through the plays again and again, working through them the way Buddhist monks recited their koan over and over waiting for enlightenment to strike, the ball handler calling out a play and then five of them executing it, then calling the next, one after the other until they'd done the full rotation, which also included calls like Four Corners, Special, Double, Motion, and Wheel.

From time to time the plays would bleed into one another in their minds. "Excuse me," said Lisa, interrupting the action momentarily, "on this one do we want to be as low as possible?"

"Where does two go now?" asked Sheryl, poised at the three-point line. "Somebody remind me."

Basketball plays, like designated plays in many team sports, tend to be more art than science. They may begin as an exacting squiggle of Xs and Os and arrows across a coach's clipboard, but passing from coach to team, they become imperfect. Show a painting to five people and they will reproduce it for you five different ways. Tell them a story and they will retell it five different ways. Tell them the same story every day and over time their stories might more resemble one another, but like any good story, a basketball play will always remain open to interpretation.

At its best, an offensive play provides players with a starting point, a general plan for outwitting the defense, a sense of whether the wing is going to cut right or left, whether a post is going high or low, whether they should aim to put the ball in one player's hands or another's, but the beauty of the game is that there is no telling what might happen. No matter how calculated the strategy, what happens on the court most often resembles an extemporized square dance, a flitting, spinning gambol of action and reaction—one that either works flawlessly as planned or, more often, passes into the realm of the unscripted. It is from these latter situations that basketball's most surprising and captivating plays arise, the moments of pure improvisation, of opportunity seized—a quick-handed steal, say, or an intricate, twisting move to the hoop—the moments that elevate the game and raise spectators to their feet.

But these moments begin necessarily with the play, the carefully plotted notion of how things should go. VanDerveer built her plays on the hours of videotape she studied at night, trying to divine what it would take to get around Brazil or outscore Russia.

At practice in Melbourne, she called them in close and added another to their repertoire.

"It's kind of a fifteen-second, twelve-second play," she said. "It's called Sacramento."

VanDerveer set up five of them around the basket while the others stood at midcourt and watched.

"Post people are going to exchange. Carla's going to screen." Saying this, she gently relocated Carla two feet to the left as if moving a life-sized chess piece, motioning for Nikki to move in through the lane that opened up with Carla's pick. "Nikki drives in and looks for the lay-up. If the defense comes in, Carla's got to roll. If they post up, then Nikki's got to pitch it. Got it?"

She moved them through the play several times, allowing for questions, and then had them divide into two groups and work through it on their own at either end of the court, directing from her usual spot midway between, her eyes never leaving the action.

That night, playing in the tournament opener against Cuba, they gave Sacramento a whirl, the movements they had pantomimed earlier in the day suddenly sped up, with real-life, big-bodied defenders to negotiate around. Once or twice the play worked, and once or twice it didn't. When it didn't, they regrouped quickly and attacked the basket a different way. Cuba was missing one of its star players due to an injury, which seemed to unbalance the scales almost ridiculously, and the U.S. kept a steady, growing lead. In the game's final minutes, though, Katrina Mc-Clain went up for a defensive rebound and landed off balance on her right foot, her ankle wrenching and sending her to the floor.

In the confused instant following a player's fall, a similar chain of thought runs through most everyone's head, from the coaches to the trainers to the players who, hovering right there, usually have the best immediate vantage point: conscious? blood? knee? not knee? (relief) ankle? yes? (more relief). While for the bystanders, the fright of any injury is tempered by what worse might have happened, for the player it's hard to feel grateful or spared. One has, after all, been forced to swallow a spoonful of fate, leaping one moment for a rebound in the flush of competition, the next toppled and whimpering on the floor. As the pain shot through her ankle, as the Australian fans murmured above her and her teammates stood by, Katrina sat back on the floor under the net with her foot limp in front of her, her eyes closed and face lifted as if she were willing the pain away, slamming one hand repeatedly on the court.

For VanDerveer, Katrina's sprained ankle was actually a bit of providence. Not only would Katrina reluctantly get a rest, but it threw the ball to the others on the team, giving their presence a new urgency. Katrina had scored 22 points against the Cubans before she went down. Now the others would have to make up for her absence.

The following night Katrina watched from the bench as the U.S. played Australia before a packed house in Canberra, the country's capital. The Australian players looked as if they'd stepped right off the beach, a group of trim, ruddy-cheeked, mostly blond-headed players who wore the standard Australian basketball uniform for women—sleek, body-hugging unitards that covered them thigh to bicep. Warming up, the Australian athletes waved cheerily at the crowd and obtained a jubilant round of applause in response. The players on the team had been culled from the country's thriving professional league, one of whom, a forward named Fiona Robinson, played locally for the Canberra Capitals. Before the game had even started, a group of cheerleaders bounced along the sidelines to "Pump Up the Jam," while the fans rollicked in the stands, prepared, it seemed, for a good show. Australia, the Americans thought, felt a lot like home.

As the national team stood in a line and took turns doing lay-ups on their side of the court, Sylvia Crawley dunked the ball. Like Lisa Leslie, Sylvia had the perfect aerodynamic proportions for dunking—she was tall and needle thin with enough strength to propel herself high in the air. She had mastered dunking while playing in college for North Carolina, patterning it after the way she'd done the high jump in high school, launching into an explosive, curving run and then firing her body at the hoop. By contrast, Lisa, who also had high-jumped in high school, approached the basket straight on, her body appearing to lift off the floor before she'd even stopped running.

Sylvia's dunk sent the Aussie fans into paroxysms of cheering, eliciting a faint grin from Sylvia. Lisa quickly followed up with a dunk attempt of her own, only she missed, the ball hitting the rim and bouncing away. The fans seemed to love this too. When it was Sylvia's turn again, she tried for another dunk and missed. Next, Rebecca, who had never dunked in her life, took a stab at it, her fingers hitting the rim but her body not high enough to coax the ball in, trotting back to the end of the line with an amused smile. By now the Australian fans were screaming for more. Dunking made great entertainment at a women's game, if only for its novelty. Sylvia, dunking again, became the crowd's clear favorite, and smiled broadly when she made it now, while Lisa, with a determined expression, wound herself up for another try. This time she hit everything right, her body sailing forward, arm cocked like a tomahawk until she reached the apex of her jump and fired the ball squarely into the basket, the rim shuddering in her wake. So there.

There was nothing like a little competition to get Lisa going. That night she took every shot she could find, moving through the shorter Australians as if they were mere underbrush in her path to the basket. Still, the U.S. team suffered without Katrina, struggling for rebounds and letting the Aussies' tight, hands-in-the-face defense mess them up. The Australian point guard, a celebrated spritelike player named Michelle Timms nailed one three-point shot after another, as Lisa countered by scoring inside. At the half, the Americans had a 50–44 lead.

Led by a prancing, king-sized kangaroo mascot named Boomer, the fans rioted in the stands, shouting, "Ozzie ozzie ozzie!" and hurling insults at the refs, who were being unusually permissive with the rough play.

The uproar seemed to provoke Lisa to play harder, score more. The U.S. held a slight but precarious lead for much of the second half, with Timms matching Leslie's scoring almost point for point. Midway through the second half, the Australians had limited Lisa's shooting by setting two defenders on her, and the Americans were ahead by just four.

On the U.S. bench, concern was starting to show. Even as the team hung on to its lead, Carla waved her hands anxiously, following the action on the floor. Nikki watched the scoreboard, bouncing up and down in her seat. What the Americans saw in the Aussies went beyond the score—indeed the U.S. began to pull ahead in the last five minutes, increasing its lead to six and then nine—but rather revealed a team that after thirty-five minutes of go-go basketball was playing as if the game had just started. After a three-pointer from Ruthie, a steal and lay-up from Sheryl, and another lay-up from Ruthie, they knew Australia wouldn't challenge them tonight, but still the opposition had gotten under their skin, dogged them until the very end, and perhaps quaked their confidence just enough to leave them vulnerable. If a player like Michelle Timms were to get on a similar streak and her team were to hit a number of threes—like in Atlanta, for instance—the Americans realized now how easily their fortunes might change in the future.

To see Lisa Leslie glide into a Sydney restaurant at dinnertime on a breezy May evening, one got the sense she was headed toward stardom. By virtue of her height and the regal way she carried it, not to mention the added boost provided by her high-heeled sandals, she was simply impossible not to notice. She'd been stared at her whole life, and unlike some of her towering peers in basketball who still fought off the childhood habits of slouching to look smaller, Lisa seemed to love making heads turn, the happy inhabitant of a body that on a different person with a different attitude might have come off as gawky and uncomfortable. But Lisa had the composure of a princess. Her shoulders formed a perfect T-square with her elegant stretch of neck, her legs were so long they appeared stiltlike beneath her clothing. Tonight she wore a faded pair of jeans and a plain white shirt and still managed to look sophisticated and put together—the kind of woman other women envy instantly.

A small group of players and team staff had taken advantage of their one free night in Sydney and ventured out for dinner at a seafood restaurant that fringed the water, just outside of the city, looking back at the glittering harbor. Lisa ordered fish and then sat back to wait, listening to Jennifer and Katy talking at the other end of the table.

Intermittently, Lisa talked about what the food had been like in Italy, her dog at home, a chow named Simba, and her mother's recent marriage to a man who worked in the loading bay of the company her mother drove her truck for. The two of them had been friends for a long time, said Lisa, and then they were fishing on a day off and something "clicked" and they were in love.

"It was very storybook," said Lisa, speaking tenderly of both the wedding and her mother, who, according to Lisa, taught her everything about being proud.

These days, as the future seemed to shift in and out of focus for all of them, Lisa seemed to have the clearest vision of all. She was not going to get cut from the team, that much was certain. She had played consistently well throughout the year, and once they'd gotten into international competition in particular, she'd played a radiant inside game, one that clearly pleased the coach. With each successive game, she seemed to become more confident on the court. Unlike most of her teammates, she had not had to worry about getting enough playing time or not being a starter. Along with Katrina and Ruthie, Lisa had been a starter from the beginning. She rarely had a bad day playing basketball.

Beyond that, her Malibu beach spread was in the current issue of *Vogue*, the Sears commercial in which she figured prominently was airing regularly, and just prior to coming to Australia, she'd signed a contract with Wilhelmina, a prominent New York modeling agency. Meanwhile, her agent was working overtime to get her appearances and more modeling gigs. While the Olympics tended to give birth to a certain kind of hero—the spunky Mary Lou Rettons or strong-valued Bonnie Blairs who went on to build careers in commentating and motivational speaking—Lisa and her agent had in mind a different brand of celebrity for her, one that ideally would involve Hollywood parties and photo shoots in Paris. If anyone was going to make women's basketball fashionable and trendy, it was going to be Lisa Leslie.

Sitting at the restaurant, Lisa sipped on an iced tea and remained relatively quiet. When someone burst out laughing at the other end of the table, she craned her neck to catch the joke, saying with some degree of urgency, "What's funny? What's funny?"

After some time, a burly young man in a rugby shirt approached the players' table, swaying slightly, addressing the group but looking primarily at Lisa, asking where everyone was from.

"I'm from New Zealand," he offered. "Thirteen million sheep and no women . . ."

Lisa looked at him serenely. She was always nice to strangers, unless they were rude. "Too bad for you," she said, then, smiling to herself, went back to her meal. When the man had safely receded, she looked up at the others around the table and burst into giggles. "Daaaaang," she said. "Some *people!*"

She was not the kind of person whose public self had yet cleaved from her private self. People who met her remembered Lisa as exceedingly sweet and good-humored, quick to crack a joke but never loud enough to seem brash or inappropriate. Her teammates would characterize her much the same way, though several would note that Lisa was indeed changing. If there were people to get to know, Lisa made sure to know them. If there was a camera around, the others on the team liked to joke, then Lisa was around too.

Over time, she had become a pro with the media. At press conferences she always spoke in complete sentences. Her smile exuded a groundedness, a demure beauty. She knew which stories from her childhood would get the reporters scribbling. She was an exceedingly gracious winner. She could come up with jokes spontaneously, liked to laugh at herself. Following dinner that night, after Lisa had delicately laid her napkin over a mangled crab carcass belonging to someone else at the table so she wouldn't have to look at it, she went outside to give an interview to a television producer who'd set up several lights and chairs on a walkway outside, with Sydney harbor glittering in the distance.

"Who's got lipstick?" Lisa asked the others. "Anyone? Lipstick?"

Ruthie fussed in her purse a moment. "I got two," she said, pulling out two lipsticks. "Red and pink." She uncapped one, then the other, so Lisa could examine them. Then she extended the pink.

Lisa took a step back, as if Ruthie had made a move to slug her. "No way, honey, pass me the red."

To understand what a natural Lisa was with the media was to watch the way some of her teammates struggled with it. Early the next morning, Ruthie did an interview on Australia's version of *The Today Show* from the hotel lobby in Sydney, where she was lined up side by side with the thirty-six-year-old captain of the Australian team, a blond guard named Robyn Maher. Both players wore hidden earphones and smiled into the camera, listening for an unseen news anchor to begin his questioning.

The thing the Americans were quickly learning was that like their basketball team, the Australians in general were a brazenly confident lot. The Sydney newspaper reported almost gleefully on Atlanta's various problems—behind-schedule construction projects, predicted troubles with crime and traffic—all of it registered the way someone might comment on behavior considered appalling and undignified, laced with the implication that Sydney, the site of the 2000 Olympics, would put on a flawless, well-planned event four years down the line. When it came to the basketball players, it seemed not to matter that they'd lost to the Americans two nights earlier.

When the news show anchor questioned Maher first, she looked directly into the camera and said something to the effect that the Americans were not the Dream Team everyone made them out to be, and that the Australians were, if anything, an equal team. She delivered her words clearly but not particularly warmly. Listening to her, Ruthie shifted a bit in her seat, her smile beginning to fade. The anchor was trying to bait them and Maher, while composed, was rising to take it. "I'm confident we'll put on a good show," Maher was saying ". . . they're tough but they're beatable."

Suddenly, it was Ruthie's turn to talk. The anchor wanted to know what she thought of what Maher had just said. Ruthie darted her eyes to look at Maher, who was sitting with one leg draped over the other as if she had been born for television. She tried crossing her own legs, then uncrossed them again. She didn't like trash talking. She never did it, even privately. She paused a minute and summoned the PMA, remembering what the media trainer had taught them all those months before about not answering negative questions, about turning everything into something positive, all the good words a person could use. Lisa would have found some way to deflect the question with humor, she knew. Lisa would have looked the camera in the eye and won everyone over with what she said.

Ruthie drew in her breath, put the smile back on her face, and charged forward, her mind racing. The media trainer had told them to take control of a question, turn it into a platform to say what they wanted to say. "We've had lots of time to prepare," said Ruthie, smiling into the void where the anchor was supposed to be. "We been together a long while, but we look at every game like a challenge. . . ." She paused to glance at Maher, who was looking blankly at the camera. Ruthie would later look back on this as a minor victory. She was saying the right thing, just like the media person had said. She was killing them with her graciousness. "The Australian team is strong and tough," said Ruthie, the triumph creeping into her voice. "They are definitely a challenge."

Tara VanDerveer was worried about the business with the leagues. Perhaps it had something to do with the way Teresa had seemed to snap at her on the airplane, perhaps it had something to do with how she felt things might go for the ABL. Most immediately, she was concerned because an Australia-based NBA executive had invited the entire team out to dinner in Melbourne, and she worried that the players would be split on whether to go or not based on their various feelings about the ABL. The issue preyed enough on her mind that the afternoon of the NBA dinner she had summoned the players to her hotel room for a meeting. The players would later say that she seemed agitated and serious, as if some crisis had erupted.

Facing them, she had stated her concerns quickly and without much elaboration: With two leagues starting, she didn't want anybody's divided loyalties about the leagues to divide them as a team, particularly with only two months left before the Olympics.

"None of this means anything without a gold medal," she said. "Our job right now is to focus on winning the gold."

Her words seemed to touch a nerve among the players. Lisa spoke up immediately. "I don't understand what the big deal is," she said. "I don't think it's necessary to have this conversation, because it's not dividing us. We know where we stand. Our minds are at ease about this, but if you need us to put your mind at ease, we will. . . . We're more interested in beating Australia than we are in anything else right now. We're focused on this tournament and beyond that, the gold medal."

Carla offered her two bits. "You know, there's something unfair about us even sitting here having this meeting, talking about problems that we haven't had," she said. "How come we never had a meeting when the ABL started back in the fall? How come we have to talk about it now?"

The sentiment seemed to be largely unanimous. Several of the players would walk away from VanDerveer's meeting feeling as if it had been a waste of time, a way of pointing up a potential problem before it existed.

Still, there were hints that things might not go as the players had planned. A few days later, after about half the team attended the NBA dinner, the *Sydney Australian* had carried a story on the women's NBA that included a piece of information that surprised nearly everyone who saw it: "It is understood the base salary will be $US40,000, while one American player has already been offered $US225,000 to play in the league."

The Australian article, if it was accurate, offered a first glimpse of what kind of salaries the NBA expected to pay its stars, which predictably were far higher than the $125,000 the ABL was offering. In the meantime, Teresa had called Bobby Johnson in Atlanta and learned that Sue Levin was suddenly backing away from the proposed Nike deal and ESPN had turned the ABL down flat in light of David Stern's announcement.

To top it off, it appeared that someone among them was talking with the NBA already, which—unless it was Rebecca, who immediately and emphatically denied that the newspaper was referring to her—meant that someone who had initially signed with the ABL was now entertaining the counteroffer. Suspicion fell to Sheryl and Lisa, two of the three who had not returned their ABL contracts. (It seemed clear that Ruthie, the third contract delinquent, lacked the star power to become the new league's charter spokesperson.) Most bets seemed to be on Sheryl, who was one of the team's more fickle members and had participated less than the others in ABL business.

She was also Sheryl Swoopes, the woman with the shoe, the woman whose name people loved to howl, the woman who was one of the quickest and most gifted female players the country had ever seen. Beyond that, she had the requisite degree of beauty and articulateness to make a model ambassador. If you had money to offer and a league to start, wouldn't one of your first advances be in her direction? Likewise, if someone came along and nearly doubled the offer you'd initially accepted from the ABL, if someone wanted to make you the superstar of the women's NBA, wouldn't you at least sit down and think hard about accepting it?

Sheryl, sitting in the lobby of the Furama hotel at the end of the day, said she did not want to talk about the NBA or the ABL. She had stolen away for the afternoon to shop, which was something she did when she wanted to get away and think.

"I didn't get as much as I wanted to, 'cause I don't have any way to take it back," she said, her voice merry. "I brought only one big bag and it's already full." When the topic was right, Sheryl was an endearing person to talk to, leaning forward in her seat and speaking excitedly, her voice lilting and sweet. "But I'll tell you what I'm going to do when we get to the last city, I'm going to give a lot of the stuff I brought, like my Nike stuff, to the Cuban team, and then that way I can buy some stuff and take it back with me. I got presents for my family today," she explained. "The next shopping I do will be for myself."

Several days later, the worry was starting to show on Jennifer Azzi's face. She and Teresa had been talking continuously about the ABL and how it would compete with the NBA. Jennifer, who was never shy about broaching a subject, had spoken briefly with Sheryl about her plans one night, and while Sheryl would not say one way or another what she was going to do, nor did she confirm that she'd been approached by the NBA, she did confess to being uncertain about the ABL.

"You want to feel like everyone's together, but I mean, you start to sense that some of them aren't, especially one in particular is not," she said, avoiding mentioning Sheryl by name, sounding more frustrated than angry. "And I think it's more, well, they want the marketing, the glamour, and the money, which is nice, but it's all going to come anyway. . . . I don't understand how when you commit to something you can back out."

At the very least, Sheryl's sudden waffling made Rebecca look better for not having committed yet. Rebecca herself seemed to feel some empathy for those on the team who might be considering backing out on the ABL.

"You know," she said one day in Australia, considering it all, "whether it's right or not, professional sports is a business. If you go with your heart, you're signing with the ABL as soon as they come forward because they're the only people who come forward with a professional league, so obviously, you're going to sign with them. But you can't always think with your heart, and that's too bad, but it's the way it is, sort of." She went on to add, however, "I'm glad I waited, because I wouldn't have wanted to sign and then have had to face a lot of pressure, because I think if you make a commitment, you have to stick with your commitment. . . . That's the situation I didn't want to get into, making the commitment and then having to second guess it."

Realizing it or not, Rebecca was touching upon a problem that was endemic to women's sports. While male athletes worked for the most part within the comfortably established parameters of their professional sports, where players' unions had been established, where agents had decades of experience, where everybody seemed to have some idea of what they were worth, female athletes stood at the hazy edges of a new frontier.

Rebecca recalled her first phone call from Reebok in April 1995, which came essentially at the moment she was released from the NCAA rules that had previously disallowed her from even discussing endorsement deals, several days after the championship game. "It's funny, because they came forward with these numbers and I was like, hey, that sounds great to me, 'cause I'm going from nothing to something. They said they wanted to get the deal done fast so they could make a commercial. . . ." Within a span of three weeks, she had signed first with an agent and then a three-year contract with Reebok—all while trying to take final exams and enjoy her last days of college life.

"When I signed [with Reebok]," said Rebecca that day, "there was no prospect of professional basketball in the U.S. I hadn't tried out for this team yet, and I didn't really feel like I had a good chance in making it, and so a multiyear deal seemed like an intelligent thing to do, because you don't know what's going to happen. . . ." She added that a year later, she was still happy with her relationship with the company.

Because neither athlete nor sponsor can ever know exactly what a given season will hold—whether an athlete will get injured, sit on the bench, or star on a winning team—most shoe deals are freighted with bonuses, which reward everything from scoring a certain number of points to winning a championship or gold medal. According to the Atlanta lawyer who helped Teresa Edwards and Katrina McClain negotiate with Nike, a contract like Katrina's, which he said earned her $80,000 from the shoe company, would include another $20,000 in bonuses based on the team's performance at the Olympics. Teresa, he said, who hadn't really negotiated at all with Nike, made slightly less.

In general, nobody could say for certain what the precise marketing value of a female basketball player would be. Investing in women's basketball was like dealing in junk bonds—the risks were high, but so were the possible rewards. If the women's game was poised to take off for real, as the ABL and the NBA were betting, then for the shoe companies, the corporate sponsors and advertisers, and the agents trolling for new female clients, now was a good time to get involved.

Late one afternoon, Lisa Leslie sat on the balcony of the twelfth-floor hotel room she shared with Dawn, contemplating her worth. After several days in Sydney, during which time the Americans had beaten the Ukrainians and then the Australians, the tournament had moved north to more tropical climes and the seaside community of Townsville. Earlier in the day, playing against Cuba, Lisa had scored 16 points and pulled down 11 rebounds, contributing to what was a relatively easy victory. The hotel looked out over a stretch of sandy beach lined with drooping banyan trees. The air felt luxuriously warm. Beyond a small forested island in the bay lay the Great Barrier Reef. Dressed in a skimpy tie-dyed tank top and cutoff denim shorts, Lisa kicked her big, barefoot feet in front of her, slouched down in her chair, and idly watched the setting sun.

"It's hell being overseas," she said after a minute, referring not to the Australia trip, but to the memory of playing professionally abroad. "It's very hard. I mean, it's lonely," Lisa continued. "If the game today had been for an overseas team, you would come back and you would just sit here like this and wait for the next one. You're by yourself. You think, okay, I could handle this for maybe one day, one week, but when you go six months, eight months, it's like, whoa."

She had been in Italy during the fall of 1994 when she got phone calls from both Nike and Reebok representatives. "It was weird," she said, "because that was probably my first business proposition and then to be overseas to deal with it without having anyone to help." Lisa, like a number of the others, had no agent when the shoe companies started calling. "Basically they call and introduce themselves, say they are interested in signing you and would like to send you some gear," she said. "That's the first stage, then you get into contracts. I was just out of college. I didn't even know the type of wording that could be put in contracts, or even how to read contracts, it's so difficult.

"I think growing up, you see that the men get shoe contracts and you think, 'God, they must make so much money doing things like that.' And then this opportunity comes along for us. I think Reebok was offering ten or fifteen thousand dollars for a year, you know. And you think, 'Is that good?' I didn't know, and I've come to find out it really wasn't, but at the time you don't really know what's good and what's not good, and they're trying to sign you for three years. . . . And you don't know what you're capable of doing and most of us were just hoping at that time that we would make the national team."

Sitting in Australia as the national team's leading scorer, all this felt like ancient history for Lisa. With Dawn advising her from France, she had played Nike and Reebok off each other until she'd boosted the sponsorship offer substantially, eventually signing a three-year deal with Nike. Dawn had done the same. Now Lisa had a lawyer representing her interests, and a modeling agency too. Nike, she said, was a "first-class company."

The conflict between leagues seemed to raise a similar set of questions to the ones raised by the calls from shoe companies a year earlier regarding which way to go in a world where there were no precedents to follow.

"In my mind, I always thought the NBA was the only league that could really get women's basketball to the next level, but they kind of waited too late and we've done it ourselves." Saying this, Lisa studied the horizon, the tawny late-day light seeming to bronze her forehead and cheeks. She let out a small sigh. "It's going to be very interesting to see what happens."

Slowly but surely, VanDerveer's orchestra was coming together. Headed into their final two games of the Australia tournament, the coach was pleased by what she had seen in the last week, namely that her bench players were finally starting to shine.

Katrina's ankle had healed up well, but VanDerveer had decided to play it safe and keep her out for the entire tournament, forcing her to rest. She'd sent Carla McGhee in to start in Katrina's place, and Carla had not disappointed, rebounding strongly, playing a rough physical game against the other teams' top players without drawing unnecessary fouls. Meanwhile, Ceal Barry, one of the new assistant coaches, had been working with Katy Steding on her three-point shooting, helping her to make a microadjustment in the positioning of her feet that with a little bit of practice had put Katy back in business. Finally, young Nikki Mc-Cray had started to play with real pizzazz, smothering her opponents on defense, forcing the turnovers that often seemed to get the rest of the team rolling, providing the spark that could break open a close game.

As the tournament wound down, Sylvia Crawley was worrying constantly. VanDerveer was not giving her a lot of playing time, which was to be expected since she was a newcomer, and while Sylvia was in top shape and keeping up with the team better than Val Whiting had in China, she sensed that it was still not good enough. Sylvia was a thin-faced black woman who at twenty-three had played one season abroad.

"It's just that I want to score more," she said one afternoon, reviewing her own performance in a plaintive voice. "This would be the perfect time for me to start scoring, so Tara will say, 'Look, we had a crisis, Katrina sprained her ankle and Sylvia stepped up and showed she could score on the low block and help this team, and' "—Sylvia smiled weakly, imagining the words she wanted to hear the coach say the most—" 'I want to keep her.' "

In the meantime, her sister had called from the States to say that she'd seen a newspaper article saying that Venus Lacy would be joining the team for several exhibition games back in the States. "It's only fair, since Venus was their first choice for this trip," she said. "But it's frustrating because I know I can play a lot better than how I'm playing but it's just . . . they have so many plays and they've played so long together that I'm like, where do I fit into this picture? I cannot see anyone stepping into play with this team, because there's no way they can be prepared. It's hard, and it's going to take a really positive person, I think, to come in and be that twelfth player."

The connections between the original eleven players came through in the smallest ways, for example the things they said to one another in the heat of a game.

"Use me, Jen," Carla would call, planting her body, arms crossed over her chest, to set a pick.

"See ya, T," Sheryl would shout as Teresa handed the ball off to her.

"Get low, B! Get low! Get low!" Lisa would yell to Rebecca as a play developed.

And Dawn, the unofficial mayor of basketball city, rarely stopped talking, passing the ball on with one emphatic mandate or another, a "Pop it, baby!" or "Bring it in, baby!"

There was no louder player, however, than Nikki, who diving for a loose ball or lunging for a steal often opened her mouth and let out a high-pitched, unbridled shriek—*waaaaah!*—which was usually enough to set her opponent back for another beat, allowing Nikki to escape with the ball. Her yelping on the court also provided the others with a mid-game laugh or two. Once, playing a scrimmage with a men's team in Colorado Springs, Nikki threw herself under the hoop, elbowing past a male defender to sink an improbably difficult shot, her voice ringing in earnest through the gym as she sailed past: *"Excuse me!"*

But if VanDerveer was beginning to feel she had everything she needed with her existing team, those feelings evaporated when the U.S. played a disastrous game against Ukraine in the tournament's semifinals, held in the city of Adelaide on the fourteenth of May.

It was as if after all this time training together they were suddenly looking at one another like strangers. They shot the ball without looking first, they forgot to pass, they lapsed into sloppy defenses and rushed offenses. Ukraine was not playing particularly well either, which perhaps contributed to the American team's general deterioration as the standards seemed to lower as the game wore on. The Ukraine lurched to a four-point lead in the first five minutes, only to have the Americans suddenly get hot, scoring ten points without their opponents scoring once. Midway through the first half, the U.S. led 21–11. Five minutes later the U.S. still only had 21 points, while Ukraine had boosted their own score to 22. Lisa was shooting one for three from the field. Ruthie had yet to hit a single three-pointer. Teresa's passes were wild. The more VanDerveer substituted players, swapping them in and out, looking for one person who was having an on night, the worse it seemed to get. By the time the buzzer sounded for halftime, the U.S. had regained a one-point lead at 27–26, the lowest-scoring half the team had ever had.

Marching them into the locker room and sitting them down, VanDerveer flew into a fury. "You're giving them hope!" she yelled. "What are you doing, giving Ukraine hope that they can beat us? You're being lazy out there, you're wasting your shots, you are an embarrassment!" Several of them would later say they'd never heard VanDerveer get so angry. "I would've been crying if anybody ever got that mad at me," one team staffer said. "She was cursing at them and screaming, and they were all just sitting there, looking at the floor. It was bad. It was as bad as it could get."

Needless to say, the coach's ire seemed to have an effect—briefly. The Americans began the second half with a 15–0 run. Lisa Leslie alone scored ten points in just a few minutes, seeming suddenly to rediscover her confidence. The score, with five minutes to play, was 54–34 in the U.S. team's favor. For a moment it looked like it was going to be business as usual.

But Lisa's scoring run was like lighting a match to a damp newspaper. Ukraine scored once, then twice, then three times, while the Americans lost the ball each time it came to their end of the court. Even Sheryl wasn't hitting her shots. The numbers on the scoreboard ticked upward as Ukraine closed the lead from 20 to 18 to 15 to 13 to 11 to 10 to 8 and then finally to five measly points. VanDerveer had ceased all encouragement, her mood appearing to blacken more with each bungled play.

With 3:20 left on the clock, she called a time-out and drew the team in close. If there was one sure thing on the team, it was the switch that seemed to flip inside Teresa Edwards when a game was on a line.

"When nobody else wants the ball, that's when I want the ball," Teresa said once, trying to describe it. "It just happens. Something clicks on."

VanDerveer had seen it enough to know and thus called for plays that would put the ball in Teresa's hands. Accordingly, Teresa scored twice, effortlessly, as if she were having the greatest game of her life. The final score was 62–51. They'd won again, though nobody celebrated, knowing what was on the way.

Back in the locker room, as they'd guessed, VanDerveer was not ready to forgive them, not by a long shot. They had one more game in Australia and then they were supposed to go home for a week off. Supposed to. They had gotten lazy, cruising on their undefeated record, and the coach was going to reassert herself. Standing before them again, looking at the tops of their bowed heads, she told them that if she didn't see some major improvements, she was calling the travel agent and having every last ticket changed so that instead of going back to their homes and families, lovers and friends, they would stay with her, holed up in that gym in Colorado Springs, working harder, she assured them, than they'd ever worked in their damn lives.

The next morning the order came down through Carol Callan that VanDerveer wanted them to get taped for that day's shootaround. This meant she was still angry. Taping was what you did before a real practice, a hard practice, when ankles, wrists, and fingers needed to be fortified with yards of athletic tape, not before a shootaround, not after playing six games in the last eight days and hours before the tournament playoff.

If the move was meant to inspire dread, it succeeded. They were tired, and sorry for the night before too, but mostly they were just worn out. And now it seemed she was going to exact some repentance by making them sweat, pushing them at the moment they least wanted to be pushed. The thing was, a bad game never sat well with anyone, particularly players who were accustomed to winning, who knew they'd gotten lazy and almost lost it all. Maybe it had happened because they'd played Ukraine so many times now, each game prior to last night's being almost painfully easy to win. Maybe it was because they were so far away from home, hidden away in a small, rainy city on the south coast of Australia, playing to empty seats. It was hard to know. The mediocrity of their playing, though, had left them sour and deflated.

The gym was cool and silent, and arriving for practice, the players seemed to slip inside it and try to make themselves invisible, taking their places on the floor to stretch without a word, the jovial banter that had become part of the routine lost, the atmosphere distinctly funereal. Earlier that morning VanDerveer had been seen storming out of the hotel to go running, looking, it was reported, still angry. A staff member, also on her way out for a run, pointedly went in the opposite direction to avoid bumping into her.

She was the kind of coach who blew up only when things got very bad, making her anger, when it surfaced, extremely potent. She also did not forgive easily. As VanDerveer conferred quietly in the corner with her two assistants, the players took extra time stretching the parts of their bodies that ached—Sheryl's hamstrings, Lisa's hip flexors, Teresa's back—the time seeming to crawl as they waited for the coach to call them together and do what most of them assumed she would do, which was blow up again.

They finished stretching and stood up and lingered a moment, nobody looking exactly in the coach's direction, but sending a signal that they were ready. Jennifer, walking to get a cup of water, passed the section of bleachers where the team staff had gathered, and raised her eyebrows, a mischievous smile flashing across her face.

"We're not scared," she said almost inaudibly, and then continued on without looking back.

Still, the silence pervaded. They would play that night against Australia, the team whose members had been boasting in the newspapers that they would finally beat the Americans, but this time the U.S. team would play a nearly flawless, focused game. Australia would play them closely, keeping the score even until the game's final minutes, but again the Americans would prevail, each player on the team stepping up to do her part. The game would thrill them all, even the coach, who would like what she saw enough to release them from the threats she'd made earlier and let them go home.

That morning at the shootaround, however, none of this had been determined. Instead, the players grouped around VanDerveer at center court, looking wounded and sorry and mostly scared. They wanted their week off. They were tired. This would be their last chance to collect their breath before the final push to the Olympics. They held their breath and waited for the coach to start unloading.

"All right," said VanDerveer, her voice calm. "I just want to say that records are irrelevant. We have won a lot of times in a row but that isn't going to help us win the next one." She had stayed up late the night before, she said, replaying the game on video, taking notes on what she saw.

"What's the number-one thing they want to do?" she asked her team now. "Carla, what do they want to do?" She did not wait for Carla to answer. "They want to run you. . . . Half our problem is that we're not sprinting back. We are not turned around. . . ."

VanDerveer continued, making her trademark tomahawk chop with one arm. "You have to be really committed to sprinting back, not jog-ging, in transition so you can see the ball. Sprint back, see the ball. Everybody," she said, "has got to help."

Slowly they had begun to realize that she wasn't going to yell. It was another day, another practice. Like the rest of them, she was picking herself up and moving on.

12

chapter

The Twelfth Woman

"Lisa's very effective, but she's not big and bulky. Every once in a while it would be nice to have a big old banger in there who can root some people out. . . . I don't know if we can find that person. We need somebody to get in the rotation who can really get things going."

—Tara VanDerveer
quoted in *Basketball America*, May 15, 1996

Venus Lacy was not glamorous the way Lisa Leslie was glamorous. She was not fast like Katrina McClain nor famous like Rebecca Lobo, but Venus was big and Venus was enthusiastic, and Venus was, as she put it, planning to rock everyone's world.

"Tara said, 'Venus, we need your big body,' " the six-four, 190-pound center from Louisiana told a gathering of reporters after she'd been asked to join the national team for four games. "I said, 'Okay, if that's what you want. . . . I take that as a compliment, my wide body and all.' "

Few had heard of Venus Lacy before. She'd had a flash of renown playing for Louisiana Tech between 1988 and 1990, setting scoring records and bolstering the team in several Final Four appearances, then she'd gone the way of the big women before her, vanishing overseas, where it was easy to be forgotten by the folks back home.

Venus, however, tended to make an impression wherever she went. After two seasons in Japan, she had moved over to the notorious Italian leagues and quickly immortalized herself as one of the country's most preeminent bangers. And banging in Italy meant that not only did you jam up the passing lanes, battle for rebounds, and post up hard, not only did you use your body like a weapon, but you also had a fiery passion that sometimes showed itself in a little shoving and general rough-housing that from time to time inspired one player to land a punch on another's jaw. Venus Lacy was distinguished for her passion. Her playing drew large crowds in Italy. She was ejected from games with fair regularity, and once or twice had been temporarily suspended from the league.

"She is physical all over" was how Ruthie Bolton put it. Ruthie had played against Venus plenty of times in Italy. "Venus can get really mean. She gets on the court and she means business."

As far as Venus was concerned, she played basketball with her heart. Born with feet that were nearly turned backward, she'd worn braces on both legs from the age of two until the fourth grade. Growing up in Chattanooga, Tennessee, Venus was carried to school each day by an older brother. Since then, said Venus, she's appreciated what she's gotten.

"I just get so excited out there," she said shortly after joining the national team's road tour, her voice low and sugary. "I forget all about myself." To her credit, Venus's brawling seldom went beyond a bit of unnecessary shoulder-butting or an occasional hard push. When it did, Venus and whomever she was tangled up with were immediately ejected to a mixture of cheers and hissing from the boisterous Italian fans. As Ruthie would verify, the Italian players liked to provoke Venus. She was a force to be reckoned with, and this was precisely what the national team was looking for.

Off the court, Venus seemed to throw her heart open to the world. She had large brown eyes, spaced widely on her face in such a way that they seemed to take everything in at once. Her lips were flat and full, often accented with the gold-hued lipstick that Venus tended to favor. Her laugh was a rumble that seemed to start from deep inside her thick body and rise up until all of her was beaming, her eyes lit up, her cheeks drawn in a wide smile, the comprehensive force of Venus's happiness cast outward on the world. When she was in a mood for talking, the words tumbled out of her.

"*Gone With the Wind* is my favorite movie. It's my movie," she said one day. "They don't make movies like they used to. . . . When I first saw that movie, I just had to watch it again and again." Saying this, Venus let out a big sigh. "I don't care how many times you see it, you always pick up something new. Rhett Butler? Oh, man, if I could meet a guy like that . . ."

She followed up by saying that Butler was perhaps an odd object of desire, "being white and made-up an' all." Venus had a man she loved anyway, and she was quick to dismiss the subject of Rhett Butler in favor of the subject of Harry, her husband of eleven months, who owned a liquor store in Ruston, Louisiana. The story of how they met involved Venus and a bottle of Chivas Regal she was buying for a friend.

"I liked the way he looked," Venus said of Harry, whom she spotted behind the cash register. The smile rose on her face when she told the story. "Oh, did I like the way he looked."

Harry was a good husband, said Venus. He was forty-five and had been married once before and his last name was Levingston, which Venus sometimes went by and sometimes didn't, depending on her mood.

"I said to him, 'Why don't you go by Harry Lacy?' I told him early on that I wasn't going to change my name unless my husband went by my last name," said Venus, "and my husband was going to cook, clean, et cetera. Everything a woman does, he was going to do."

Did Harry measure up? "Well, at first he was terrible," said Venus. "He's not into the cleaning and stuff, but Harry, he can cook. I'll give him that credit." He did not, she added, use the last name Lacy, but he did give her strength. Harry believed in her, she said.

Venus, like Jennifer, Katy, Sheryl, Ruthie, Dawn, and Lisa, had been cut from the 1992 Olympic team. "It tore me up," she said, looking back. "It hurts you, you know. I got an ulcer after those trials. I wish I'd had Harry back then, because he gets me through." Unlike the other players, however, when USA Basketball invited her to come to the national team trials the next time around, Venus had declined.

"I thought to myself, do I need to go through that again?" Venus said. When she'd been called again in March, USA Basketball had found her in Greece and offered to buy her plane ticket home. This time, she said, she was ready to go through whatever it took to get herself on that Olympic team. "If I make it this time, it will be a dream," she said. "If I don't make it, it's going to hurt, but I will get over it. I will not let it break me."

Having just finished up the season in Greece (no ejections at all, she reported), Venus joined up with the national team with high hopes, her voice reflecting the same nervous optimism that both Val Whiting and Sylvia Crawley before her had held. "I just hope I can make it," she said one afternoon early on. "I hope they like what they see with me."

The team was fifty-two days away from the Olympics and just over two weeks from the day the Olympic team would be officially announced at a press conference in Chicago. There were five games to play before the announcement, six games to play before the Olympics started. Most of the time the players didn't bother counting, however, instead taking each day as it was handed to them on the computer-generated schedule Carol Callan distributed at team meetings or on the bus to practice. Besides, the numbers themselves were simply too wearying: When a staff member tallied it up, they'd spent 205 of the last 246 days away from home.

At the ABL headquarters in California, the league's short history had been chopped in two—the time before the NBA announcement and the time after. Before, there had been no questioning the loyalty of the various players. Then, less than a week after the NBA announcement, while the national team was touring Australia, ESPN's senior vice president for programming had turned down the ABL's proposed television deal, saying candidly that with the NBA now involved in women's basketball, the network felt it was important to wait and see how things developed.

Then came the call from Sue Levin at Nike, where word had spread that the ESPN deal had collapsed.

"There's a problem," Cavalli remembers Levin saying. "The TV deal matters."

Levin was wavering in her decision to sponsor the ABL. She had spent untold hours in the last year or so cultivating personal relationships with the six Nike players on the national team. She'd taken them out for countless dinners, flown back and forth across the country numerous times to see them play. At team trials a year earlier, when Lisa Leslie had dragged Levin into the Olympic Training Center dorms to point out the closet-sized rooms, with their thin walls and narrow beds, in which USA Basketball was planning to house the team during its stints in Colorado, Levin found money in her budget to rent upscale apartments for her players, causing the other shoe companies to follow suit. Within Nike, she'd campaigned to get her female basketball players as much marketing exposure as possible. Lisa was starring in one of Nike's six Olympic television ads. Teresa's face was going up on billboards all over Atlanta, and Dawn's image skyed over downtown Philly.

There was no questioning the fact that Levin had done a lot for the Nike basketball players, but less than two months before the Olympics were to begin, she was realizing that she couldn't do the one thing that some of them wanted most, which was to lend her support to the ABL. Anticipating catching up with the players again, she was not sure they'd understand.

After a week off following the Australia tour, the national team flew to Providence, Rhode Island, with Venus Lacy in tow. There, they spent three days practicing, promoting, and dealing with business before a game against the itinerant Cuban team. On the team's printed schedule was a first-of-its-kind item, a meeting with NBA vice president Val Ackerman regarding the NBA women's league, which had been dubbed the Women's National Basketball Association (WNBA).

Ackerman, thirty-six, a thin, five-foot-ten woman with blond hair and pale blue eyes, had been one of the first women ever offered a basketball scholarship at the University of Virginia, arriving in the late seventies to play small forward. From Virginia, she played briefly in Europe and then came back to the States to attend law school. In 1988, David Stern hired her on as a staff attorney at the NBA.

In November 1994, Ackerman had been a key participant, along with USA Basketball representatives and a handful of Nike people that included Sue Levin, in the initial conversations about putting together a women's national team to train for a year before the Olympics. When the plan became reality and a team was selected six months later, it seemed clear that in exchange for serving as the national team's marketing agent, the NBA would receive in return an invaluable bird's-eye view of how America responded to the women's game and its stars, as well as a trial run for marketing a women's team, aligning it with sponsors, merchandising its paraphernalia, and selling advertising space on its televised games—all food for thought as Stern and his advisers mulled over the idea of a women's league. In the meantime, he'd put Ackerman in charge of developing a model for the proposed league, which ultimately was the one he and the NBA board of governors had approved in April.

Taking a chair by the window in a small hotel room in Providence in late May, Ackerman addressed the twelve U.S. players, VanDerveer and her assistants, as well as several USA Basketball staff members. The time was finally right for the NBA to get involved in women's basketball at a professional level. The national team, obviously, had helped significantly to bring the NBA to this point. She praised the team's record, the players' success with the public, their commitment to the sport. "You have exceeded everyone's expectations," she told them.

From there, Ackerman outlined what she could about the plans for the WNBA: the ten-week summer schedule beginning in June 1997, the intention to put teams in established NBA cities, the league's allowance that its players could play for other leagues, either in the States or abroad, during the WNBA's off season. She seemed to carefully avoid mentioning the ABL by name.

For most of the players, this was the first time they'd had any communication with the NBA regarding the professional league. What they knew was mostly what they'd read in the papers. Jennifer would later say she had expected Ackerman to give them more information than what had been formally announced, but she didn't. Venus would dismiss Ackerman's meeting as a "whole lot of nothing." For the players who were deeply committed to the ABL already, the NBA meeting bore stark contrast to the meetings they'd had throughout the year with Cavalli, Hams, Johnson, and Cribbs, where the league organizers had asked for suggestions and feedback on everything from contracts to team names.

For those who were less involved with the ABL, talking with Ackerman was a good opportunity to ask some questions: Why play in the summer? (Because the winter season was too saturated with the men's NBA and men's and women's college games already, plus the NBA could use existing stadiums and staff people for the women's league in the summer.) Why didn't you do this any earlier? (The timing wasn't quite right.) Tara VanDerveer made a comment that basketball was a community sport, that they just couldn't import a team of outsiders into a city for the summer and expect people to show up and support them. Ackerman acknowledged this point, then mentioned that each franchise might hire one player per team to be a year-round, active member of her team's community, attending events, making appearances, and keeping the public engaged during the off season.

Finally, Lisa Leslie raised her hand politely. "Why can't you just merge with the ABL?" she said. "Can't you guys work together on this?"

Ackerman had been asked similar questions about the ABL by the media. She answered more or less the same way every time, saying, "We don't see this as a competitive situation" and "We don't know any specifics about the ABL." She told the team essentially the same thing, adding that she was not fully aware of which cities the ABL was sending its teams to.

According to several teammates, this answer did not sit well with Lisa, who, along with some of the others, believed that Ackerman was not being up front on this point. Just about everybody in the business of women's basketball could rattle off at least a few of the ABL's prospective cities at that point. Beyond that, most of the press attention the WNBA received included a mention of the ABL's plans—even if Ackerman didn't view the situation as competitive, the media certainly did—and with this, the articles frequently listed the eight ABL cities. It seemed unfathomable that Ackerman wasn't aware of which cities the ABL had targeted. Looking back on the conversation months later, Ackerman did not recall talking with the players about the ABL's cities. Of the meeting with the players, she said, "We weren't in a position to reveal our plans. In many respects, there wasn't anything to reveal at that point, since it really wasn't until Labor Day [of 1996] that we started to seriously focus on the details of the WNBA. . . . Whenever asked, our response to players and agents was always, 'Keep your options open. This is an exciting time for women's basketball. Don't put yourself in a position where you won't have choices.' "

Teresa would recall walking away from the meeting in Providence thinking that if Lisa had been confused about which league to sign with, Ackerman's comment had resolved the issue. "I thought we had Lisa at that point, I really did," she said. The day before, Teresa and some of the other ABL players had argued with Sue Levin about her ultimate decision not to support the league. "We said, 'Sue, you got the power. You can make the league work,' " remembered Teresa. "But I think with the WNBA happening, everything with Nike had suddenly changed. Everyone was telling us a different thing, when all we wanted was for people to be straight up with us."

————

Like Ruthie Bolton's PMA, Venus Lacy had her own set of things she told herself to stay upbeat and focused. The first thing was "I'm not out here to impress anybody but myself." The second was "If someone like Teresa sends me a nice little pass, then I have to say thank you by putting the ball in the basket." In Providence she had mentally blocked out the television cameras and the roaring crowd and, for the eleven minutes she was in, she played a game of please and thank-yous, graciously accepting her teammates' passes and promptly bucking all 190 pounds of herself into the air to score, punctuating the effort with a startling and wholly vigorous grunt.

Venus was like a volcano erupting on the basketball court, a full-on blast of heat, her intensity seeming simultaneously to intimidate her opponents and enliven her teammates.

"Yeah, La-deeee!" Carla shouted, rising to her feet from the bench when Venus laid the ball in. Along the bench, players high-fived one another in Venus's honor.

Venus herself celebrated a basket by thundering a few steps back downcourt and then unconsciously pausing to strike a quick adrenaline-inspired pose—teeth bared, elbows pulled in, fists clenched, eyes bulging—a look that suggested that whatever Venus was getting, she wanted more of it. If the clock permitted, Venus liked to share her happiness by greeting the first teammate she encountered with a big bear hug, boosting the player off her feet before letting her drop again. That was Venus. When things didn't go so well, when she missed a shot, or, as happened once or twice in Providence, did not see a pass coming, she stomped a foot mightily on the ground and turned her face downward, looking bitterly disappointed. Her emotions were so penetrating, it was difficult not to root, and root loudly, for her.

The national team beat Cuba in Providence, an easy, embarrassing 48-point game, interrupted only when Jennifer took a slam to the face toward the end of the first half and left the game with blood gushing from a shattered nose, which would later require minor surgery, two nights in the hospital, and six feet of gauze packed into each nostril to support the nose as it healed. Venus, for her part, had done relatively well against Cuba, flubbing a few passes, but scoring seven points and grabbing six rebounds in just eleven minutes on the floor. From Providence they flew to Colorado Springs for a few days, and from Colorado

Springs to Canada for a three-game tournament with the Canadian Olympic team.

It was June already, or June *finally*. The closer the Olympics got, the more time seemed to slow, the days stretching out until they felt interminably long. For Tara VanDerveer, the pressure was building by the day. The country seemed to be paying unprecedented attention to her team, to their hopes for a gold medal and the attendant plans for the professional leagues. Several players had been booked to appear on *Oprah; Sports Illustrated* wanted to put the team on the cover of its pre-Olympic issue; Annie Leibovitz had shot Teresa for *Vanity Fair;* the team had scrimmaged with Regis and Kathie Lee; Jay Leno had invited Lisa to be a guest on his show; Rosie O'Donnell had called, looking for Rebecca; *Time* wanted a photo shoot; so did *TV Guide*. The demands on the players' time were piling up quickly, all at precisely the moment when VanDerveer most wanted to yank them all out of the public eye so they could focus on the task at hand, the Olympics, now just over a month away.

There was no arguing with publicity, however, particularly when every new fan was like money in the bank for the future of the women's game, as well as for the players themselves. The attention helped to make their work feel worth it, to feel appreciated by a public that had been uninterested in the past. Still, even as the advance spin on the Atlanta games was that women athletes were going to steal the spotlight from the men, the media in moments seemed conflicted on how to portray the basketball players. While various magazines and newspapers published plenty of photographs of the players in action, these were counterbalanced by what seemed a prevailing interest, particularly within the mainstream media, in dressing the women in something other than the baggy, figure-hiding traditional basketball uniform.

In early June, Lisa and Sheryl appeared in a *Newsweek* cover story, entitled "Year of the Women: Why Female Athletes Are Our Best Hope for Olympic Gold." Curiously, the accompanying photo spread showed a swimmer swimming, members of the U.S. softball team posing in workout gear, a female mountain biker posed in race gear, a beach volleyball player in an action shot, the U.S. field hockey team wearing their practice gear, women fencers in their standard regalia, and then Lisa and Sheryl in separate photos—Lisa skipping along a beach in a black bikini, and Sheryl posed in a vacant lot, wearing pink lipstick and a thigh-hugging, midriff-exposing outfit of white lycra, holding her arms tightly to her chest, looking decidedly cold. Not a basketball or a drop of sweat in sight. Perhaps inadvertently, the photos seemed to underscore a point made in the text: "However much women are becoming part of the sports culture and becoming influenced by it, the vision of the athletic woman remains vague and inchoate." (The only other athlete photographed in what appeared to be fashion as opposed to athletic wear was the captain of the U.S. soccer team, Carla Overbeck, who was shown heading a soccer ball, dressed in a cleavage-revealing leopardskin-print lycra unitard.)

Later in the month, *The New York Times Magazine* would devote an issue to the female athlete, putting Sheryl Swoopes on the cover, standing before a brown West Texas landscape looking strong and slightly menacing in sunglasses with a basketball held overhead—a far cry from the vulnerable-looking image projected in the *Newsweek* photo. This time she wore her USA Basketball uniform, but now she had her shorts hiked up ridiculously high on her waist until the band sat just below her rib cage. According to Sheryl, the photographer had instructed her to pull the shorts up to uncover more thigh. In another photograph inside the magazine, Sheryl reappeared dressed in a red sports bra and matching tight-fitting compression shorts. (A third albeit smaller photograph showed a sweaty, mouth-guarded Lisa Leslie leaping to score during a game.)

In each of these instances, the point was to showcase the athletic female body, which considering the waifish figures who graced the covers of most fashion magazines and helped to sway a full two-thirds of girls between the ages of thirteen and eighteen to diet, was hardly a malicious aim. As style writer Holly Brubach wrote in *The New York Times Magazine*'s special issue, "In athletes, we recognize women who own their bodies, inhabiting every inch of them, and the sight of their vitality is exhilarating." The question raised by the bikini shots was whether to celebrate the women's bodies or the women themselves, at their most vital, participating in the sports that had shaped those bodies.

In any event, as VanDerveer would say, the hoopla wouldn't mean doodle until it was capped off by a gold medal, and as her players rushed around fulfilling various media obligations, she never once forgot how many days she had left. "Thirty-nine days," she said to the reporters who now swamped her at every opportunity, "but who's counting?"

As the media trumpeted the rise of women athletes in general and women's basketball in particular, shouldering the national team with the Dream Team moniker (though often in a dulcified version like "Dreamettes" or, in the case of *Time*, "Dream Girls"), VanDerveer sometimes appeared like a lone soldier, fighting to keep the players' focus on basketball and basketball alone. She seldom kept track of the media, seldom commented on one photo spread or another. Instead, she and her three assistants spent long hours huddled up in gym corners and airport lounges, or in VanDerveer's hotel suite, working on strategy. Each assistant had been assigned several teams to scout, and VanDerveer herself traveled with boxes of scouting tapes, which she watched until late each night on the VCR in her suite. By day she coached with an implacable sense that things were not yet right, that her team, if it was to win, would need to play flawlessly. She knew what the other teams looked like, inside and out. She could tell you that Russia had post players who could knock the Americans on their ears or that Brazil's guards could find a way through just about any defense.

"On a good day, any one of those teams could beat us," she told the team. "And that's what we have to remember."

In Canada, this point seemed to drive itself home. Playing in Calgary, the U.S. team turned in a sluggish, uncontrolled performance, allowing the Canadians to pull within four points with just two minutes remaining, but breaking away finally to win 82–68. From there the U.S. team went to Vancouver for a rematch with the Canadians. While VanDerveer hunkered down for more strategizing, a number of her players invaded the Pacific Harbor Mall, looking for outfits to wear on *Oprah*. Lisa, shopping with her on-again off-again fiancé-demoted-to-boyfriend, Lorenzo, found an elegant, peach-colored silk two-piece evening outfit on sale from a four-figure price to a three-figure price. Sheryl, shopping on her own, bought a crisp white pantsuit, though learning about Lisa's purchase, she started to second-guess.

"If Lisa's going to look that good," said Sheryl, smiling but giving the matter some serious consideration, "then I might have to rethink what I'm wearing."

Oprah, to everyone's great dismay, would cancel on them several days later.

Eveningwear aside, the team was beginning to resemble the walking wounded. Canada, a team that played with a rough, aggressive style similar to that of the Australians, had come into Calgary and capitalized on the Americans, who were battle-scarred and exhausted after months of nearly continuous international play. Jennifer's shattered nose in Providence proved to be the first of a string of injuries that set upon the team like bad weather. Practicing in Vancouver, Carla wrenched an elbow going up for a rebound and doubled over in pain. Katrina had one hand taped up and was limping slightly between drills, the result of minor bursitis in one hip. Sheryl, in addition to her two ankle braces, had added a knee brace. Rebecca had several sprained fingers and a forearm taped for support. In another two days, she, too, would don a knee brace. Lisa still wore rubber tubing taped around her shins to take the pressure off her tendons, Dawn was never without her knee brace, and even Venus, the newcomer, was having trouble with cramping shoulder muscles. Jennifer, who could not have any contact, practiced her shooting, a massive metal cup taped over her nose.

Gina Konin, the team trainer, ministered to their injuries carefully, dashing out from the sidelines frequently during practice to massage a hyperextended joint or deliver a bag of ice during a break. Konin carried with her a notebook three inches thick with the complete medical histories of each player. She spent an hour and a half before each practice wrapping their various weak joints with athletic tape.

"I could pick any player right now and say, 'Do you have pain?' " said Konin, "and she would say yes."

By contrast, the Canadian team seemed indefatigable. When the Vancouver game tipped off, the Canadians took an early lead and managed to hold on to it through the entire first half of the game, as the U.S. post players racked up personal fouls—three on Rebecca, three on Carla, two on Venus—giving Canada 13 points off free throws and leaving each of VanDerveer's big players, with the exception of Lisa, who had hardly played, under threat of fouling out. (International rules, like those of the NCAA, allow five personal fouls.) Katrina, plagued by the bursitis, was sitting out, as was Jennifer. The game proceeded at a bruising pace, with the U.S. team shooting a wretched twenty-nine percent from the field, leaving the court at halftime with the Canadians ahead by 12, the largest halftime point-deficit the Americans had ever faced.

Walking into the locker room, Ruthie Bolton was shaking her head.

She'd thrown up a bad pass, missed a host of three-pointers. "Dang, what happened to my shot?" she said to nobody in particular.

VanDerveer did not waste time getting emotional. Instead, as Ruthie would recount it after the game, the coach set to work keeping the team calm, mapping a plan for the second half. Canada was running back-door plays, slipping the ball out to a wing. They needed to step up the help-side defense. "Don't think about the score," she told them. "Don't worry. Stay with your man on defense. On offense, stay wide . . . keep going for the open shot."

To Ruthie she said, "Don't think about those seven shots you're going to miss. Go out there and think about what you can do. Think about the shots that are going to go in. We have to keep shooting."

Later, VanDerveer would say, "This team waits till it gets a bloody nose before it starts fighting . . . but this was not a bloody nose, it was a knockdown."

The knockdown continued well into the second half. Venus, pumped up and wanting to prove herself, took a pass from Dawn and made a jump shot, her voice—*yaaargh!*—ripping through the noisy arena. She then celebrated by hurtling herself into an exuberant frontal body slam with Carla. Next time the ball was in her hands, she was fouled on her approach to the basket, a boon she commemorated with a violent, two-handed high-five with Sheryl. Venus was charging the team with life, but Canada still led by 11. Not only that, but Venus's vigor got the best of her as she rushed headlong into a competitor, committing her third foul of the game. Moments later Dawn got called on a foul, her third, and looked over at VanDerveer, biting her lip.

The Canadian fans, over 5,000 in all, were chortling in the stands. With six minutes to play, the U.S. had cut Canada's lead to six. The game had become a battle of wills—Canada relentlessly driving at the hoop, the U.S. scrambling to get its transition game going, tempered somewhat by the climbing number of fouls. They needed every player now. Ruthie scored once on a jump shot, then again off two free throws. Canada was ahead by just two. Then Carla, leaping to defend at the post, fouled, sending Canada to the line again.

Four minutes to play and four points to make up. VanDerveer started calling plays to Ruthie, gambling that her star perimeter player would get hot. Teresa brought the ball up court, passed it to Ruthie, who fired it to Lisa inside, who sent it back to Teresa, who flipped it again to Ruthie, who without one second's hesitation shot the ball and landed it perfectly. The scoreboard read 68–66 in Canada's favor, and then Lisa scored on a jump shot, tying the game.

VanDerveer was on her feet, gesturing and shouting to the referee, waving a hand at the scoreboard. The scorekeeper had given Ruthie only two points for a shot worth three due to the fact that there were two three-point lines painted on the floor, one at the NBA marker (23.9 feet) and the other at the international marker (20.6 feet), and the ref had been looking at the wrong line.

"It's the inside line!" VanDerveer was yelling. "The inside line!" The entire U.S. bench was on its feet. After a moment of confusion, the score was corrected: The U.S. led by one point, 69–68.

Still, they could not shake the Canadians. Lisa scored again, but they scored right back. Lisa, drawing a foul, scored one point at the free-throw line. Carla, committing a foul, gave Canada another point, 72–71, the U.S. still ahead by one. Fouled again, Lisa drained two free throws and boosted the lead to three, but almost immediately the ref whistled Rebecca for blocking and the Canadians scored another two.

One minute to play and a one-point game. Substituting Katy for Rebecca, VanDerveer called another play to Ruthie. They needed a three-point shot here, badly, to put the game out of reach. Teresa came barreling downcourt, tossed the ball to Katy, who sent it to Nikki at the wing, who shot it to Ruthie, who put the ball in the air again, knowing the second it left her hands that it wasn't going in.

They were so damned tired, the cumulative effect not so much of the forty-nine games they'd played but of all the hours of practice, the interviews and autographs and the travel on top of the weight sessions, the pool sessions, the hours riding stationary bikes and running drills and eight months of biding their coach's every word. To fall prey to Canada, ranked seventh in the world, would be a disastrous way to lose.

After a Canadian turnover, the U.S. tried again for a three, setting up the play carefully but quickly, sending the ball around the clock until it found Katy Steding's hands. It had been a rough few months for Katy, battling her way back out of the uneven shooting that had plagued her through much of the winter. This time, though, there was no time for her confidence to get rattled, no cloud of uncertainty in her mind. She found her grip on the ball and then let it fly, scoring the three points they so desperately needed.

Canada would score only one more point on a free throw, while Lisa hit on a jump shot, ending the game at 81–74. Taking to the floor to shake the opponents' hands, the relief seemed to gush out of the U.S. players. A close game, provided it turned out right, left everyone joyful. They huddled briefly at center court, Venus Lacy's long arms binding them all together for a big, sweaty group bear hug and then releasing them to mingle on the court.

"Come back, Tree, come back soon, girl, 'cause we needja!" said Carla, pulling the injured Katrina into an embrace.

"I almost had a heart attack!" said Jennifer, swatting at Rebecca's shoulder. "It's harder to watch than it is to play."

Ruthie, named the game's MVP for her 13 points and three assists, accepted a bouquet of flowers and limped off the court, one knee beginning to swell a bit from an incident with a loose ball during the game. As the others slowly made their way to the locker room, Venus lingered a moment, savoring the thrill of the noisy crowd, the flush of a close game. She was playing well, she thought, but it was impossible to know whether it was well enough to earn her a spot on the team. She had one game left to play with the team, another matchup against Canada in Oakland, California, two nights away.

Just then, the coach's voice rose up behind her. Venus turned to see VanDerveer, standing next to the bench, grinning. "Good job, big girl," she said. "I'm proud of you."

Early the next morning, the team flew out of Vancouver. Venus, having stayed up late the night before eating room service club sandwiches with Ruthie, was beginning to feel like a member of the team, though she was quick to add she woke up every morning worried that she still needed to perform better.

Kicking her airplane seat into full recline, she settled back and pulled her headphones over her ears. "Have you heard of that new group, the Fugees?" she said, leaning over in her seat. "I'm going to get the CD when I get back home. . . . I rock a lot, you know. Even in the States, they're not used to a rocker. So I get in my own world with my headphones on my head and I rock and I rock. I could rock constantly, you know what I'm sayin'? People are like, is she crazy? But when I've got my headset on my head and I'm singing, nothing can worry me." She paused to smile up at a flight attendant passing by before continuing. "I know I have to play good to be on this team, you know, but I'm not worried, I'm not worried." This said, she flipped the switch on her Walkman, closed her eyes, and let herself go.

Ruthie's injury had happened undramatically, but it ended up being fairly serious. As she'd chased after a loose ball with a pack of Canadian players, the ball had gotten underfoot and Ruthie had stepped on it. She had fallen to the floor but so had everyone around her, all of them scrapping for the ball. If anybody had noticed the pain registering on Ruthie's face, the awkward way her leg had twisted, if there had been any concern at all, Ruthie had banished it by grabbing on to the ball and then passing it back into action, lifting herself to her feet and beginning to run again. Ruthie had made it through the year without so much as a minor injury, really.

But that night in Vancouver Ruthie's knee swelled and stiffened until, lying in bed, trying to sleep, she could not move without pain blazing up one side of her leg. The next day, the trainer wrapped her in a knee brace, consulted with VanDerveer, and scheduled an appointment with an orthopedic surgeon for her in San Francisco.

The word *surgeon* sent chills up Ruthie's spine. They were five weeks away from Opening Ceremonies, which left basically no time for recovery if anything serious was wrong. Arriving in Oakland, Ruthie went straight to the doctor, who X-rayed her knee and pronounced the injury a severe ligament strain but nothing that would require surgery. She would be out for a month.

"Usually I'd be upset about missing a month," said Ruthie shortly after, "but all I thought was 'A month means I'll be back for the Olympics.' "

Still, Ruthie's injury represented a significant weakening in the team's core. She had been averaging 13 points a game. VanDerveer was visibly agitated about the injuries plaguing her team. "You have to take care of yourselves!" she almost shouted at them one day before practice. "See the trainer, get taped, get your treatments or it's going to come back around on all of us."

When the national team landed in Chicago a week after the Vancouver game, the city was cast in a humid, early summer haze. It was now the height of June. All along the city's Lake Michigan shoreline, young professionals jogged in the sunlight that stretched into an early-evening pink. The neighborhood basketball courts were clogged with bodies. Chicago was a basketball town, particularly in June, when, more often than not in recent years, the Bulls were marching toward another NBA championship and, in the fleeting pause between winter's deep freeze and the furnace blast of summer, the entire city, it seemed, crawled out to play. As the national team players checked into their downtown hotel, the Bulls were in Seattle, up three to one against the Supersonics in the NBA finals, one win away from the title. An air of expectancy seemed to hang over the city.

Based on her nine points and six rebounds in Oakland, Venus had been invited to remain with the team for one last game, their last game as the national team, in fact, a Saturday afternoon matchup against Russia. Members of the selection committee had flown in from around the country to watch the game and make their final evaluation. The Olympic team would be announced on Sunday at a press conference. When asked who was nervous about possibly being cut from the team, the team's marketing director without hesitating named half the team: "Rebecca . . . Dawn . . . Katy . . . Carla . . . Nikki . . . Venus."

The team had followed up on the Vancouver game by beating Canada in Oakland in a no-contest, 12-point game, but it still hadn't been enough to please VanDerveer, who had offered her evaluation to the press afterward: "I'm not pleased with either our offensive or defensive rebounding. We were standing around a lot. . . . We weren't boxing out well, we weren't finishing on some shots that we should've. . . . We have lots of work to do yet."

It was here that the sentiments of coach and players most radically diverged. "What we need is a rest," said Lisa the day before the Russia game in Chicago. "She's been working us too hard. I mean, I got two knees that are going to give out on me, Ruthie's got one and so does Katrina. We need some rest."

In the final play of the Oakland game, Lisa had made a spectacular block and whisked the ball downcourt until she was all alone with the ball and the basket and a screaming audience of 9,000, not a defender in sight. Her teammates, too, had started to yell. If Lisa was going to dunk the ball during a game, on national television no less, here was her chance. She would make news across the country. She would grab a little piece of history as the first woman to dunk in international competition. It could be huge. But she'd settled for a lay-up instead. Her teammates had hounded her in the locker room afterward, razzing her about missing the prime moment of the year's highlight tape. Walking out for the postgame press conference, she got the same question: How could she pass up an opportunity like that?

"My mind was telling me to dunk," Lisa told the reporters, smiling gently and almost apologetically, "but my legs just wouldn't let me. This team is fatigued right now."

It was as close to a complaint as she would dare make publicly. No matter how tired they felt, no matter how loud the groaning got behind closed doors, there was no going to VanDerveer and asking for a break. "If I said something," said Lisa privately, "it'd come back around on me, like suddenly I wouldn't start or something. Maybe we could say something to Carol, but Tara, she don't get it. I mean, we're professional athletes and we don't want to be whiners, but we go hard all the time. We just need some easy time."

On Friday afternoon following practice in Chicago, Lisa sat behind a small table, wedged between two Sears "Dress Like the Best" stand-up posters of the national team, signing autographs at a store on the city's west side. The team sent one or two players to a Sears branch in nearly every city it played, part of USA Basketball's sponsorship deal with the company and something the players rarely complained about, particularly Lisa. The Sears television ad, which was running during the national team's games, was contributing to her fast-growing fame.

Following tomorrow's game, when the team got a five-day break, Lisa would fly to New York for a press conference announcing her one-year modeling contract with Wilhelmina. The event was to be held at the Fashion Cafe, the restaurant jointly owned by Cindy Crawford, Claudia Schiffer, Iman, and Elle Macpherson, the giants of Lisa's new industry. She'd heard rumors that *Inside Edition, Extra,* MTV, and VH1 Fashion would be there. She was going big time.

Her lawyer, Londell McMillan, who also represented Dawn, had basically attached himself to her side. As a crowd formed in front of Lisa's autograph table at Sears, McMillan loitered among racks of clothing. Watching over his protégé, McMillan, a well-dressed black man who boasted Spike Lee and the Artist Formerly Known as Prince among his clients, expressed a degree of worry about Lisa and Dawn. He had advised both of them to wait on signing their ABL contracts while he gathered information on the NBA's plans, and while Lisa had duly delayed, Dawn had paid no heed, sending hers in immediately during Bobby Johnson's moment of crisis back in early May.

"There's a tremendous loyalty among the players on this team to each other," said McMillan in Chicago. "The team's nucleus made a decision without seeking the counsel of others, so now the ABL has signed one of my players but not the other. You don't have any player on this team thinking as an individual right now . . . I want to give them as much information [about the two leagues] as I can, but I have to fight both of them to even put the information on the table. It's making the process tense," he said. "I'm telling Lisa to make a decision not just on her emotion and team loyalty but on what's best for her in the long run."

According to others in the team's entourage, Lisa and Dawn, the inseparable duo whom the media had formerly dubbed "Beauty and the Brash," were spending less and less time together—the product, some surmised, of Lisa's newfound fame and the missing paperwork at the ABL.

Lisa often discussed her friendship with Dawn warmly, recalling that she had been in eleventh grade the first time she encountered Dawn at a USA Basketball trials for a junior team. "We clicked more on the court first than off the court," said Lisa. "As I recall, we kind of had that one-two punch. She'd get the ball, fake, pass it on to me. I'd score, or I'd run long and she'd lob it. . . . I'd just look in her eyes and I could read what she wanted to do by instinct. She just made me so much better, and she's always going to do that. . . .

"And then off the court, we've come to find that we are just totally opposite, yet we complement each other in the sense of, I mean, I'll put on a miniskirt and pumps and lipstick in an instant, and Dawn, I can barely get her to put on lip gloss!"

This made Lisa laugh and then turn serious. "Dawn is a great person. She has a good heart and even though she shows a rough side like she's going to be mean or something, she's really sweet. She cares about people. I'm very sensitive and I'm a lovey person, where Dawn, she doesn't forgive easily, so that part of us is opposite . . . but we just enjoy each other and have a lot of fun . . . I mean, we have our times when we're not getting along and they'll probably last for five minutes. I'm like, 'Forget it,' and she says, 'Yeah, well, forget you too.' And then you talk about something else, kind of like you do with your sister. I mean, you don't stay upset forever. . . ."

If some felt Lisa's celebrity had gone to her head, it was difficult to see it as she greeted the public at Sears. She was dressed in a simple black corduroy shirt with a white tank top beneath it and a faded pair of jeans. Her Sharpie pen poised, she smiled genuinely at each face that surfaced before her, keeping up an ongoing stream of dialogue with the people who presented her with posters, basketballs, and team photos to sign.

"How long you been playing?" she asked one girl. "Since kindergarten? Boy, you're going to be really good."

"Sandy . . . is that with an 'i' or a 'y'?"

When an older woman approached and said, as Lisa signed, "They got a women's NBA coming up, huh?" Lisa smiled up at her. "I'll be playing with the ABL," she said. "The American Basketball League."

Another woman pushed her heavyset daughter in Lisa's direction. "She's only in the third grade," the woman told Lisa. "She's going to be really tall."

"Do you speak Spanish?" a man asked. "*Un poco*," Lisa answered. "I speak Italian, actually."

As the autograph session wound down, a stoop-shouldered girl of about twelve who was easily six feet tall shyly appeared at the head of the line. When Lisa asked if she played basketball, the girl shook her head no.

"How come you don't play?" Lisa asked. "Are you afraid?"

"Yeah," said the girl, her voice just audible in the din of the store.

Lisa's voice grew soft and private. "You think people will make fun of you? You won't be good enough?" When she saw the girl nodding, she continued. "Don't be afraid. When I first started, it was pretty scary, but it makes you feel good, I swear it. When I'm scared, I pray a lot. It's about yourself," Lisa said. "It might really make a difference in your life. You're tall, you're proud. Keep your head high. My mother used to always say to me, some people grow on the inside and some on the outside. You and I are lucky," she told the girl. "We did both."

Taking the team photo the girl had in her hands, Lisa covered one corner with her loopy scrawl, "Keisha," she wrote after learning the girl's name, "Best wishes and keep your head high, Lisa Leslie."

Leaving Sears, Lisa crossed the street to a small corner beauty shop to get a pedicure so she could wear open-toed, high-heeled pumps to the Fashion Cafe appearance. The last strains of sunlight had turned the sky purple. In anticipation of the Bulls winning the NBA title that night, police in riot gear had posted themselves in clumps up and down Irving Park Road.

Sauntering down the sidewalk, Lisa reflected briefly on the young girl at Sears, Keisha. "She's so much like I was," she said. "I was so afraid of everybody, and even when I didn't play basketball, everywhere I went, people asked me if I played. . . . I mean, everyone thought that because I was tall, I should play basketball. It makes starting to play kind of scary because you might screw up." She laughed, her voice sweet and melodic. "If you're tall, everybody thinks you're a basketball player. It's still the first thing people say to me. It's like, 'Are you a basketball player? Are you a basketball player?' Everyplace I go."

Ducking through the door of the beauty salon, Lisa started fretting over what to wear over the next few days, as the Olympic team got announced and she headed off to New York. "I got to remember to call my mom and tell her to send the red dress," she told McMillan. "I'm a beginner here. I don't know anything. I have to be ready. What if I wear my orange outfit tomorrow . . . is that too much?"

Lisa's entrance turned every head in the beauty shop, which on a Friday was mobbed. Her high-heeled sandals made her six feet seven, so tall that her head appeared dangerously close to the ceiling of the shop. WELCOME TO NAIL TOWN read a banner over the door. A TV mounted high in one corner was tuned to the pregame show for the Bulls-Sonics game. Lisa smiled shyly at the rows of women sitting at manicure tables and then made her way to the receptionist's desk. The receptionist, a Latina woman in her early twenties, stared up at Lisa through a mass of teased hair, the inevitable question starting to form on her lips.

"Are you . . ." the woman stammered, "a model?"

Lisa's face lit up with a startled delight. Here in basketball's big city, on one of the biggest basketball nights of the year, the woman saw Lisa the way she was just now hoping to be seen. She gazed down at the woman and blinked her large, doelike eyes, looking as if she wanted to bend down and hug her. "Why, yes," she said, "I am."

For most athletes, the cover of *Sports Illustrated* represents a eight-by-ten-and-a-half-inch patch of the promised land. To show up on the cover of the magazine—shipped out to some 3.1 million people each week, vaunted on newsstands across the country—is to truly arrive in the established beau monde of sports. Sponsors love it, agents love it, athletes and publicity directors love it. Not ironically, the cover of *Sports Illustrated* has traditionally not been a place where women athletes surface regularly, or even semiregularly, or hardly at all. Part of this can be explained by the fact that eighty-two percent of the magazine's readership is male, and that as a whole, demographic research shows that these readers prefer to pore over articles about men's sports.

Which is why when the staff at *Sports Illustrated* started talking about putting the women's Olympic basketball team on the cover of its pre-Olympic edition, a thick double issue that would sit on coffee tables and newsstands for a whole two weeks in July instead of one, USA Basketball was going to do whatever it took to accommodate the request. In this instance, it meant staging a photo shoot two days before there was even an official Olympic team to speak of. For scheduling reasons, the cover had to be shot prior to the selection committee announcing who would be on the Olympic team, which meant that the players who were shoo-ins, VanDerveer's starters, had been rounded up and posed early on Friday morning, a day before the game against Russia: Sheryl, Lisa, Teresa, Katrina, and Ruthie, along with the coach herself.

The rest of them, the seven players purportedly on the bubble, knew about the photo shoot, but were not included, their absence from the *Sports Illustrated* cover not a surprise, of course, but unsettling nonetheless. Everyone had figured the starters would make the team, but the rest of them boarded the bus for the Russia game the following day with more than the usual butterflies in their stomachs.

The afternoon game was being televised on ABC. Beyond that, the Bulls had lost to the Sonics the night before and now both teams were headed back to Chicago to play the sixth and potentially determining game of the series on Sunday night. This meant that the national sports media had descended on Chicago, and as the women players tromped into the University of Illinois–Chicago Pavilion with their gym bags, the media section was jammed full of writers who normally covered only men's basketball.

For all intents and purposes, the Russians counted as the defending Olympic gold medalists, though the team that had won in 1992 was officially the Unified team, having drawn players from provinces that had since become autonomous, notably Ukraine. Still, the Russians had several '92 veterans with them, a wiry blond point guard named Irina

Sounuiuiikova and two post players VanDerveer called the "twin tow-ers." Beyond that, they'd added a player who at the Goodwill Games in 1994 had stunned everyone with her long-range three-point shooting. Taken as a whole, the Russians were formidable competition, and the Americans were about to face them feeling dragged down and weary, with Ruthie, their own ace three-point shooter, grounded on the side-lines with a bum knee.

"If we see this team again," VanDerveer said before the game, her voice premonitory and promising at the same time, "it'll be in Atlanta, in the quarterfinals, the semifinals, or the gold-medal game. . . ."

The Russian team was made up of women with skin pale enough to suggest that the sun rarely shone in Russia and bulging muscles that seemed to say who cares about the sun when you have the weight room anyway? When the game started, the two teams paced each other basket for basket, foul for foul. Much as it had been in Vancouver, the American players seemed somewhat off their rhythm, weak on rebounding, unable to spark the fast break that had helped them romp over opponents in the past. Meanwhile, the Russians scored repeatedly on the inside, slipping through holes in the U.S. team's defense, maintaining a slight but con-tinual lead. Fifteen minutes into the game, Russia was ahead 33–29.

During a time-out, VanDerveer squatted before them on a bench. "We're not being aggressive enough!" she said, her voice raised to cut out the noise from the crowd. "You're just going through the mo-tions. . . . We need a little more energy defensively!"

This said, she sent Venus Lacy into the game to hold down the center. For the next several minutes Venus boxed out and grimaced and gener-ally womanhandled the Russian center, a thick-bodied, dark-haired woman named Elena Baranova, as if her life depended on it, effectively shutting down her inside scoring. But the Russians merely started firing their shots from the perimeter. With thirty seconds to play in the half, Russia was up 41–36. The Americans were beginning to look frenzied, searching for an open shot and finding Russian arms and bodies every-where they turned. On the final play in the half, the ball went from Teresa to Rebecca to Jennifer to Katy to Rebecca and back to Teresa, who finally faked at the top of the key and slalomed between several defenders to bank the ball in at the buzzer, ending the half at 41–38.

Suddenly the days of effortless wins, the parade of college teams they'd devastated in the fall, seemed like a bygone era. It was the second time in a week they'd been behind going into the locker room, something the players would chalk up to their growing fatigue, while VanDerveer would view it as an indication of the work they still had ahead of them. In any event, they were encountering competition that seemed increasingly revved up and focused, not to mention entirely capable of beating them. Even more troubling, VanDerveer and the team's two Olympic veterans would remind them, the foreign teams were going to arrive in Atlanta even more hyped. "When other teams get to the Olympics, they get better," Katrina once said. "The level just elevates immediately."

The dilemma of the moment, however, was the Russians huddled in the visitors' locker room in front of their coach, a heavyset man with a buzz cut who had spent most of the first half stalking the sidelines, hurling angry-sounding words at his players.

Standing before her own team, VanDerveer was still calling for defensive energy. If they could surprise the Russians with some good defense—getting deflections, stealing, rebounding—then they could wrest control of the game's tempo, swinging into the fast-paced transition game that usually wore out their opponents quickly.

Her words sank in. Before long, they were back on the fast break. Katrina seized control of the offensive boards, Lisa led a 12–5 scoring run. Sheryl stole the ball, Carla stole the ball, Katy stole the ball, all in rapid succession, while Nikki jumped on defensive rebounds, the entire team seeming to kick into a higher gear as the U.S. pulled slightly ahead, building a lead slowly as the half progressed. With under four minutes left to play, the score was 78–68 in the Americans' favor. Russia had scored only once in six minutes. If the coach had wanted defensive energy, they were giving it to her now.

A late-game lead can be a stunningly transitory thing, however, the contest's internal momentum subject to shifting without notice. In the next several minutes Russia picked up its own transition game, allowing the U.S. only one shot at the basket each time the team came downcourt before grabbing the rebound. The Russians scored once, then twice, picking up a few free throws along the way, blocking one of Katrina's shots under the hoop and playing a zone defense, forcing the Americans to take their shots from the outside, which without Ruthie, they were doing extremely poorly. And suddenly they had a two-point game on their hands, the scoreboard registering 78–76 with less than a minute to play.

It is in these kinds of situations that basketball becomes pure mathematics, each play carefully harnessed to the tick of the clock. With twenty-six seconds still to play, Russia intentionally fouled Dawn in order to stop the time, gambling that she would miss one or both of her free throws with enough time for them to hit a three-pointer to tie or win the game. The Russians had been shooting a phenomenal sixty percent from the three-point line thus far. The team's coach, perspiring wildly on the sidelines, wore the want on his face like a banner.

Sensing the exigency of the moment, the crowd, which had spent most of the second half chanting "U-S-A! U-S-A!" fell into a hush. Dawn marched to the foul line, the sweat beaded on her forehead, her ponytail puffed out like a little woolly creature behind her. Though too many years and too many games had passed for Dawn to think often of it, someone who knew her history might at a moment like this recall the two last-second shots she'd blown in play-off games at Virginia. One didn't need even to look back to know that Dawn could get overexcited in pressured situations.

But Dawn herself had pushed all of this out of her mind, settling her small body at the line. Fixing the basket with a mean stare, she licked her lip, took a breath, dribbled the ball once, twice, then dipped her knees and sprang, sending the ball gracefully into the net. The bravura rushed back, a coy pout overtaking her face as she flipped out either palm to accept congratulations from Lisa and Sheryl. Barring a miracle, the best Russia could do now was tie the game, sending them into overtime. Dawn quickly dispensed with this possibility, however, sending up her second shot without pause, right on the money, making it a four-point game. The Russians immediately snatched the ball and drove downcourt, putting up and making the three-pointer that seconds earlier, without Dawn's contribution at the foul line, might have won them the game. The buzzer sounded and the national team had just barely secured its fifty-first straight game, the final score 80–79.

Harry Levingston, Venus Lacy's husband, had driven twelve and a half hours from Louisiana to see his wife play in Chicago. Harry was six-feet-two with a thin beard and a smile that resembled Venus's in that it washed over you like a tidal wave. Venus, by his measure, was "as nervous as nervous gets" about making the Olympic team, and Harry, who worked long hours in his liquor store back in Ruston, had seen fit to be there with her in the most anxious hours of all before the team was announced.

Nobody knew for sure when they'd find out, though a USA Basketball photo shoot had been scheduled for early the next morning and a press conference was set for 1 P.M. The hours following the Russia game had passed quietly in the team's hotel. Several players went shopping. Katy and Nikki went on a double dinner date with their fiancés, both of whom had flown in for the weekend. Harry and Venus spent some quiet time in the hotel before a team meeting VanDerveer had scheduled inconveniently for 9 P.M. on a Saturday night.

An hour later, Harry was sprawled out on the bed, watching television, when Venus returned from the meeting in VanDerveer's suite. "She came bustin' through that door so hard, I thought she was going to break something," said Harry the next day. "She was jumping around and cryin' and screaming and I was like, oh, bless the Lord, she made the team."

As it turned out, everyone had made the team. Venus made it. Rebecca made it. Katy, Dawn, Jennifer, Carla, Nikki, Sheryl, Lisa, Ruthie, Katrina, and Teresa all made it. The selection committee's chairwoman, Karen Stromme, head coach at the University of Minnesota in Duluth, had given a speech, thanking them for their hard work, telling them how proud the committee was of what they'd done.

"She was talking like there was a 'but' coming," Jennifer would say later, "like she was going to say, 'Thanks but we've made some changes.'" Lisa, sitting on the couch next to Jennifer, had drawn in her breath sharply, thinking suddenly that they were going to cut somebody from the team. But Stromme wasted no time pulling out a bottle of champagne and lifting a glass. "I just want to be the first one to congratulate you all for making the Olympic team," she said. VanDerveer, having guessed that things would work out that way, presented them each with a necklace she'd ordered ahead of time, a gold charm in the shape of each player's number suspended from a delicate chain. Venus, who previously had played without a number on her jersey, was now number 14, which could have been any number for all it mattered. To Venus, who wept big, joyful tears on and off for the next two days, number 14 was "just beautiful."

They were going to Atlanta, finally and for sure, all of them together. The next morning, the twelve of them clowned through the photo shoot in their uniforms, hopping out from beneath the white hot lights between poses to strike up a song with Nikki swaying before them like a conductor, mouthing the words so they could all follow along: *Oh, happy day, when Jesus won . . . la la la la la . . . !*

Later that afternoon they gathered in a small conference room at a hotel by the airport. A number of them would stay another night in Chicago to see the Bulls-Sonics game, which the Bulls would win handily. It was Sheryl and Eric's first wedding anniversary, and they were headed off to Vegas together for a few days of blackjack and rest. Jennifer's father had driven up from Tennessee with memories of 1992 and Jennifer's failed bid to make that team, shedding tears when his daughter was announced as an Olympian at the press conference. Rebecca was staying in town to sign copies of the autobiography she'd published with her mother and make an appearance on the Rosie O'Donnell show. Dawn was off to Philly, where before a crowd of thousands of her fellow citizens she would carry the Olympic torch up the steps of the Philadelphia Art Museum, made famous by Sylvester Stallone in *Rocky*.

Tara VanDerveer was going to her girlhood summer home in Chautauqua to watch videos of their Olympic opponents and visit with her father, who had taken ill. Before they dispersed, however, VanDerveer sat at the conference table, a microphone propped before her and her team standing behind her in their red, white, and blue sweatsuits. She looked tired, the puffs under her eyes, the drawn line of her mouth betraying the weight of worry on her shoulders. When she spoke, her voice came from deep in her throat, the emotion of the moment just below the surface. "We're in the right place at the right time," she told the crowd of reporters and well-wishers, pausing briefly to glance over at the twelve players who had come so far with her, ". . . with the right people."

13

chapter

The Final Push

"You know what it's like, people coming up saying your wife is a successful lady all the time? You know, she's real good?" Eric Jackson was leaning back in his customary chair against the wall at the training center gym in Colorado, watching the team practice. It was the end of June, the sun stayed high over the mountains until dinnertime, the air was dry and pleasantly warm. The clock on the lawn outside read twenty-three days till the Olympics.

"People always want to know what I do," Eric said. "I tell people I'm aspiring to be a great football player, taking a year off to support my wife, working for the gold. I tell them that my number in high school was number six, and people in Brownfield will never forget who number six was."

These remarks were offered in the way of advice to Lorenzo Orr, Lisa's boyfriend, who had flown in to spend some time with Lisa before the Olympics. Several days earlier, Lisa had dazzled Jay Leno, appearing on the show with a new hair weave of long, delicate ringlets and the kind of composure that suggested she was born to sit in that soft green chair where all the movie stars had sat before her. She was fielding modeling requests left and right, she seemingly was the star of every game the team played, becoming as famous for her spin move as she was for her sweetness off the court. The world was loving Lisa. The night before, his first night in Colorado Springs, Lorenzo had spent over two hours waiting while Lisa smiled her way through a *Time* magazine photo shoot with Rebecca. He'd waited and waited, hoping the photographer would let her go in time for them to catch a movie, as they'd planned. Lisa finally had left the photo shoot early, feeling bad about losing time with Lorenzo, feeling bad that she was walking out, leaving the photographer angry and Rebecca alone for the last pose. It was hard, Lorenzo told Eric, to just sit there while all these people fawned over Lisa, not because he wasn't happy for her, but because he didn't know where he fit in.

Eric was an old hand at this type of thing, however. Time and again, he said, he and Sheryl made plans to see movies, or shoot pool, or grab a bite to eat, only to be forced to abandon them when photo shoots or interviews ran late, when a last-minute promotional trip was scheduled, an extra practice added, whatever. For instance, the team had one last break coming up, and Sheryl and Eric's trip home to Texas was going to be cut short so she could go to New York and be a guest on David Letterman's show. Eric, who liked New York, was going along. When he wasn't traveling with Sheryl, he usually stayed by himself in Colorado Springs, where he said he passed his time training for football, reading the Bible, and watching television. Two days earlier, Sheryl had pointedly removed herself from the ABL draft, which was taking place in San Jose. According to Eric, she was going to take next winter off. They were going home to Texas, he said. "We're going to focus on us."

"Some people look at me and say, aw, there's another guy attaching himself to a successful person," he was telling Lorenzo now. "It's hard. I've been patient. You know what? You have to ignore those people who don't respect your choice." He was shaking his head. "There are a lot of stupid people out there."

Lorenzo nodded at this, seeming to appreciate what Eric had to say. He had just finished playing a basketball player in a basketball movie, *Sixth Man*, filmed in Vancouver. He was extremely tired. Yesterday he had dozed through the team's long practice. Today he had arrived at the gym armed with a teach-yourself-to-draw workbook, over which he had been laboring for the last hour, painstakingly copying the cartoon figures on one side of a page onto the blank of the opposite page. Once in a while he looked up to nod his head at something Eric was saying or to smile at Lisa, who, having pleaded aching knees, was spending the practice off to one side, shooting baskets and doing leg lifts with the still-injured Ruthie while the rest of the team thundered up and down the court at VanDerveer's command.

The team had come back to Colorado Springs for one last visit. After a few days of training, the players would then pack their bags and lug their belongings out of the corporate apartments that had been the nearest thing to home they'd had in nine months. It was beginning to feel like the end of the road.

Even the mundanity of their routine in Colorado Springs, the practices, weight workouts, the quick drive from the apartments to the training center, had taken on the nostalgia that comes with doing anything for the last time. They had a restaurant they liked to order takeout soul food from, a little place called La Jazz Affair, and often the sweat would hardly have dried from their faces after practice when Sheryl was on the phone in the conference room adjacent to the gym, ordering up big tins of chitlins and greens and corn bread for people to share back at the apartments. The littlest things now felt sentimental.

"I'm starting to have dreams about Atlanta," Jennifer had said on her way to practice, drinking a cup of black coffee and eating a banana from the training center cafeteria as was her habit before a workout. "I can't believe it's here."

Cell phones rang continually along the sidelines during practice as the last-minute media requests poured in. Meanwhile, media director Amy Early had drawn up a precautionary list of what-ifs, imagining the carefully worded press releases she'd have to write if something surprising happened: What if somebody got seriously injured? What if somebody misbehaved during a game? If somebody failed a drug test? What if the team got eliminated in the first round of the Olympics? The team's trainer had asked the players to submit lists of everything they ate, drank, or otherwise ingested so she could go through and make sure there was nothing that might come up positive on the drug test the U.S. Olympic Committee would administer prior to their arrival in Atlanta. (Particular ingredients of everything from cold medicines to certain herbal teas to multivitamins could potentially cause an athlete to fail drug testing.) At USA Basketball's headquarters several miles from the training center, two equipment managers were industriously packing and shipping a roomful of boxed supplies—apparel, medical supplies, press materials, extra balls—to the Omni Hotel in Atlanta, which would serve as home and center of operations for both the men's and women's basketball teams and their staffs.

At the center of it all was Coach VanDerveer. Worrying, said Carol Callan, kept VanDerveer busy. She was spending nearly every waking hour fussing over the scouting tapes they'd collected on the opponents. She worried about her team's play selection, about its defensive strategies, and first and foremost, she worried about injuries.

"You need to make sure you're getting your treatment here, every day," she said to them at the start of practice one day. "It's not an optional thing. You need to take care of yourselves, now more than ever. This week, next week, the next three weeks . . . Now, let's get out there, Team one-two-three."

"Team!" The players answered, throwing their hands in the air to break their huddle.

The coach was running every practice as if it were the last, fitting endless drills into the two-hour sessions, the schedule regulated by the cryptic page of notes she carried puckered in one hand. Her timetable generally allowed little rest, and as the players finished a full-court running-and-passing drill, heaving for air, dragging themselves toward the tall PowerAde dispensers that sat in one corner, the coach's voice would often follow them with its familiar impatient refrain. "If you need a drink, jog over, don't walk . . . come on now!"

This was the final push. If they slipped up, she let them know it. If they were performing well, she backed them up with a compliment. Often she talked to several players at once, watching the action unfold at either end of the court: "Good shot, Carla, close on her, Katy, good board, Jen, box out, Venus! Be support for each other. Don't let anyone penetrate!" She sometimes joked that she had a set of eyes on the back of her head. She had hypertuned ears as well. If Lisa made a crack about the team being overworked, VanDerveer, standing at the far side of the gym with her back to her, did not even turn around before calling out, "I heard that, Lisa!" During practices her three assistants usually oversaw the drills, tossing and receiving passes as the players ran through the prescribed motions, and VanDerveer monitored from center court. When a player sent a halfhearted pass to assistant Nancy Darsch, the coach immediately fired the ball back at her, saying politely but firmly, "Give me a real pass, please."

VanDerveer quizzed the players relentlessly, as if trying to transfer every last bit of what she understood about basketball to them in these final weeks.

"Who runs this offense? Who screens really fast?"

"Australia," said the players in chorus.

"Russia too," said VanDerveer, "Cuba a little too. You gotta review these in your own mind. Think about situations you've been in and how to respond to them . . ."

"What's going to make our defense successful?" she said, posing the question and then answering it herself. "Effort and aggressiveness. If you're not aggressive on defense, you're playing into their hands. Playing hard is being able to go forty minutes all out, busting your ass. . . ."

After a day or two in Colorado Springs, she started running them through what she called "time and score situations" in which she would set the players up in a scrimmage and then experiment with different late-game scenarios. They'd had enough close games now to understand that there were teams out there that could beat them. If the Russia game had taught them anything, it was that they had to be prepared to play each game to the very last second. With this in mind, VanDerveer tested them over and over again.

"We're down three," she said to Jennifer, playing point guard, "so what are you going to run?"

Jennifer, who now wore a transparent plastic face mask to protect her healing nose, contemplated the problem briefly. "L.A.," she said, naming a play and then the player who would ideally take the shot. "L.A. Katy."

"Right," said the coach. "Now go to it."

One afternoon, as the team rehearsed its transition defense, VanDerveer could feel the players' energy ebbing. While she gestured and commented continually, her advice seemed to sink only halfway into the players' minds. She'd correct a mistake only to have it repeated. If it was done right, it was done sluggishly. They were coasting, and it was growing infuriating. Finally, she abruptly halted the action with a whistle blast and a "Hold up!" and motioned everyone to gather around her in the middle.

"You're not looking too good out there," she said, watching their heads immediately bow. "Everybody else out there is working right now. You have to work. That's your job. If you can't do it, you shouldn't be on this team." Her hands were on her hips, her voice impatient. "This is ridiculous how this practice is going. Now, pick yourselves up. We got an hour to go. If you have pride in what you're doing, you don't need someone to show you you're doing it wrong. Make the correction."

When she finished speaking, the players went back to work. VanDerveer sank her hands into her pockets and, looking tired, continued to supervise the practice from her lonely post at center court, keeping up her commentary as the athletes retackled the drills with new energy.

Watching from the sidelines, a USA Basketball employee offered a note of sympathy for the coach.

"If they lose," she said, "that's what everyone will know of Tara Van-Derveer. . . . She lost the gold medal. She had a whole year and she lost the medal."

Carol Callan, who spent hours each day with VanDerveer, acknowledged that the coach's anxiety was mounting, adding, "She's had a year to develop her reaction to pressure, though, and at some point this team has to be able to walk on the floor realizing that they've prepared for every situation, and I think that Tara's now trying to make extra sure that she's prepared them for every situation. I think as they all start to realize that they're prepared, it will relieve the pressure somewhat."

The Olympics would be a test of VanDerveer's faith in her team. Once they were on the court, with the noise of the crowds limiting her ability to coach them from the bench, confining her to time-outs and a few shouted words here and there, it would be up to the players to execute what she'd taught them, to remember the plays they'd gone over so many times, to stay calm. When Jennifer Azzi looked back on the trip most of them had taken together to the World Championships back in 1994, she remembered thinking that VanDerveer did not really trust her team. When it was over, said Jennifer, the coach had been angry at them, as if they'd personally hurt her. "She can be really really negative," Jennifer said that week in Colorado Springs. "It's kind of like a lack of faith, I think. But this time I think she trusts us. I think she believes we can win, and she knows that if we lose, we'll all lose together instead of it being a case that we didn't do something right and so we let her down."

On one of their final days in Colorado, the entire team and a few staff members piled into a few cars and drove to a small, wooded compound in the mountains for what was being called Team Challenge Day. For six hours under a canopy of aspen and pine, they examined their "personal team commitment" on an Outward Bound–style ropes course that had them strung up on belays and tremble-footing their way across steel wires thirty feet above the ground while the others watched from below, holding the belay ropes that ensured their safety. It was, as one black member of the team put it, "a very white thing to do," confronting their fears and testing their faith in one another by climbing trees, but nonetheless it served a purpose, if only to get them out in the fresh air, doing something other than bouncing a ball around for a change.

It was difficult to know how to put closure on all their months together. While a climactic finish at the Olympics would be obviously fitting, it would still be a public finish and not a private one. The dissolution of their private life as a team was about to begin anyway. Starting the next week when they went to Florida, each player would have her own condominium at a Disney-owned resort and every one of them had invited friends and family to come down to spend time there. The Olympics, they knew, would be one heady stampede, over before they had begun and loaded with distractions. Regardless of how it ended, the players would scatter quickly, each of them eager to take a break, grateful finally to have their individual lives back.

The person who seemed to be contemplating the end most was Tara VanDerveer. Over the year, she had spoken often about what a transforming experience coaching this team had turned out to be. "I'm realizing," she had said at one point, killing time in an airport in the middle of China, "that there's more to life than college basketball." Due to her contract at Stanford, she had officially restarted her job as head coach on May 15 and had written a few letters to recruits and begun planning the 1996–1997 season from afar. Like the rest of them, she would say her good-byes and leave Atlanta almost immediately after the final event, reporting to her office at Stanford, to her old and comparatively unglamorous life as a college coach, the very next day.

"There's going to be so much emotion," she told a reporter, anticipating the end. "We've been working so hard. We've been on a mission. We have a goal. Then it's going to be all over. When you've been with these people for as long as I have, it's really sad. They're family."

On the last day of practice in Colorado Springs, a sunny Saturday morning, however, the emotion among the players was an uncomplicated joy. They would all head back to their respective homes for the Fourth of July weekend, having cleared out the last of their belongings from Colorado Springs. The bags they packed to go to Orlando the following week would be the same bags that went directly with them from Florida to Atlanta.

They scrimmaged throughout most of the two-hour session that day, which was a wise choice on VanDerveer's part given the team's fidgety energy. Taking them through drills would be like trying to get fifth-graders to sit at their desks on the very last day of school. So she let them go at it, as they so loved to do—Nikki, Jennifer, Venus, Carla, Sheryl, and Ruthie versus Katy, Dawn, Teresa, Katrina, Rebecca, and Lisa. Ruthie and Lisa, both still nursing sore knees, would play only a few minutes. Lisa busied herself by mothering everyone on the sidelines, delivering clean hand towels and PowerAde when they came in for a time-out. Right off, the competition flared when Jennifer drove the ball down and Dawn immediately leapt into her path, the two of them colliding hard—Jen's head crashing into Dawn's shoulder—the two of them landing angrily beneath the net with a thump, just like old times.

Jennifer stood up and reeled for a minute before raising the protective mask from her face and glaring at the coaches on the sidelines. "Was that not a foul?" she asked, incredulous.

When the coaches remained silent, Katy and Rebecca both put hands on Jennifer's shoulders to calm her. Dawn, standing off to the side looking fed up, rolled her eyes. The play commenced and Dawn scored right away, at which point Lisa's standard diplomacy flew out the window as she started yelling, "Hell, yeah, Dawn! Hell, yeah!"

In his chair on the side, Eric Jackson was just itching to get on the road. He and Sheryl had arrived for practice in the blue Mitsubishi they would drive straight from the training center all the way across the plains to Brownfield. They'd risen early that morning and loaded the car up with their belongings, stuffing it to the gills. What wouldn't fit in the car, they'd had to ship back to Texas.

"We didn't know what to expect, moving up here," Eric said. "We didn't know what a 'furnished' apartment meant exactly, so we showed up with laundry baskets, pictures for the wall, you name it. Plus," he said, gesturing to Sheryl on the court, "she goes out and buys two, three articles of clothing at a time, plus a few pairs of shoes and a purse to match each outfit." He put his palms in the air and shrugged. "You multiply that by twenty or thirty times, it adds up. We got a lot, and I mean *a lot* of stuff."

Dawn's team won the scrimmage by three points, which prompted her to perform a one-woman victory dance around the court, shouting "Hell, yeah!" several times at the top of her lungs, swinging her arms around in a mock-cheerleading move. VanDerveer sent them on their way quickly, as a few of the players had planes to catch. They would meet up again in a week in Orlando. Most everyone disappeared promptly into the locker room to shower. Several of the men from the team they'd scrimmaged all year had come to say good-bye and have the women sign T-shirts and balls for them. "Seein' as how y'all's gonna be famous and all at the Olympics," said one. The comment delighted Dawn, who having lingered after practice, sprawled herself on the floor and dutifully wrote her name on whatever was passed to her. "For all the times I laid y'all up!" she said, jumping to her feet and returning the signed items with a gleeful laugh.

Just then Nikki appeared in the door, fresh from the shower and dressed in shorts and a T-shirt. She shook her hips in an exaggerated dance. "Whassup! Whassup! Whassupwhassupwhassup!" she shouted, turning finally to wiggle her rear end at Dawn and the men before bounding in their direction. "Y'all, I am so ex-*cited*!" she said.

One by one they lugged their bags out of the gym and into the rental cars that would carry them to the airport. Sheryl and Eric pulled out of the parking lot and headed directly toward the interstate. Katy hugged the men good-bye and took off. Lisa waltzed out into the sunshine with an arm around Dawn. Nikki joked around with the guys for a while and then headed out to find some food. Before long, everyone was gone except Rebecca, who was waiting to catch a ride with Jennifer, who had stolen off to lift a few weights. "She's a madwoman," Rebecca said with a slight smile, claiming a chair by the wall. "When Tara tells us we don't have to lift weights, she goes and lifts them anyway. It's a bad habit of hers."

The afternoon sun slanted through the windows of the gym. Amy Early took a seat next to Rebecca, and the two of them watched wordlessly as a training center employee peeled the giant-sized USA Basketball decals off the floor of the court. For nine months it had been their home gym, and now, within thirty minutes of finishing the last practice, it was being stripped clean, clearing the way for another team, another sport. Rebecca heaved a sigh.

"I wonder if I'll ever play in this gym again," she said, watching another worker start dry-mopping the floor.

When Early suggested that the 2000 Olympic team would probably train in that same gym, Rebecca laughed. "I'm not sure," she said, shaking her head and then growing momentarily serious. "I got a lot of memories here—hard things—I mean, remember October? I don't know," she said. "I don't know if I'll be back."

They screamed through the darkness, the speed rattling their bones and sucking at their cheeks, their stomachs jerky, their eyes no better open than closed, all of it a dizzying, tumultuous whirl that was delicious and terrifying at once and lasting just long enough to thrill them before the bullet-shaped car swooned to its resting place and spilled them dazed into the human current that led outside to the soft cotton-candy dusk and the bobbing clouds of children and the lit-up spired castle in the sky: Disney World!

"Cinderella! Whassup, girl?" shouted Carla McGhee, still wobbling from the roller coaster, bumping into the delicate, golden-haired princess in her blue gown, whom she greeted like a long-lost cousin, extending a fist for a soul shake, the muscles rippling straight up her arm. They were in America's favorite manufactured paradise, getting the royal treatment—a private photo op with the Disney characters on a cordoned-off lawn in the heart of the Magic Kingdom, free king-sized ice cream sandwiches, and front-row seats at the nightly parade. Cinderella, wearing a tight smile, demurred on Carla's soul shake, keeping both hands on her parasol.

It was hard not to be happy at Disney World, and perhaps this was the point. A week after leaving Colorado Springs, the team was ensconced at the Disney Institute, a full-scale resort with the requisite golf course, tennis courts, swimming pools, staff massage therapists, and skin care experts, plus a full-sized gym and weight room and plush, spacious locker rooms outfitted with heaping bowls of fresh fruit, thick white bathrobes, and scented soaps. Each player got a sunny two-bedroom condominium, a pile of meal tickets, a free pass to all Disney attractions, and a golf cart to drive the narrow paths that cut across golf greens, between blooming hibiscus and along sparkling human-made waterways, connecting the resort with shops and movie theaters and restaurants and the rest of the teeming Disney playground. Beyond that, each player was furnished with a personal guide who offered to do everything from grocery-shop to whisk her and her guests to the front of the forty-five-minute line at Space Mountain.

The star treatment was unfamiliar enough to be embarrassing, however, which meant that mostly the guides sat idle while the women went off exploring on their own. Besides that, grocery shopping, when you've

spent a year eating hotel food, was suddenly fun. Jennifer bought gour-
met cheese and coffee at a specialty shop; Dawn and Lisa cooked up
eggplant parmesan and played cards through the flamingoed Florida
sunset on the small terrace of Dawn's condo. Rebecca sat out by the pool
between practices, working on her tan.

"The great thing about Disney," said Rebecca, who boasted that she
and Dave, who had come down for the week, rode every single ride in
the park in a single evening, "is that everyone's too wrapped up with
Mickey and Minnie to recognize you."

A number of them were now sporting new hair for the Olympics.
Sheryl had gotten long braids for her Letterman appearance and then
switched to a different style, a more severe-looking patchwork of short
braids on the top of her head with her skull shaved bare above her ears.
Katrina got her braids redone, Lisa opted to keep her new curly weave,
Venus had her hair whipped up and sprayed into a high, ripply cone at
the back of her skull, one that made her look regal and imposing and
seemed impervious to the dense Orlando heat and the gallons of sweat
she produced on the basketball court. But nobody's Olympic hair could
compare with Nikki's. Over the break she'd gone home to Ohio and on a
whim had several hundred long bronze braids attached to her scalp to
glamorous effect. Her hair now fell past her shoulders in a gleaming,
iridescent swirl that made her impossible not to notice. Even with her
hair pulled back in a ponytail while she played, the braids danced and
glinted with every move.

The hair suited Nikki perfectly. Over the last month, she had blos-
somed into a top notch defensive player. Off the court, her high spirits
seemed constant. She was quick to sass her teammates or to burst into
one song or another appropriate to the moment at hand. When she
played, it was with a full-throttle exuberance that could single-handedly
boost the tempo of a game. Whereas much of the year she'd been a
relatively undemonstrative benchsitter, suddenly Nikki was stealing the
ball, rebounding madly, and making an effective nuisance of herself on
the floor. She was loud, spunky, and could sprint with the fastest of
them. If Ruthie, Nikki's best friend on the team, played with a quiet,
measured maturity, Nikki played with a youthful, uninhibited vigor. It's
possible that her new coppery hair, which indeed accented the pertness
of her cheeks and her bright eyes, improved upon Nikki's confidence and
thus contributed to the further improvement of her game. It's more

likely that the hair helped draw attention to Nikki's already fiery play, for it seemed the media who came to see the team play in Orlando started asking to talk to Nikki. When the team made a side trip to Indianapolis to play one last game in the middle of the Orlando stint, Nikki was mobbed by reporters afterward, facing down a forest of tape recorders. She was relatively unpracticed with the press, however, having been largely neglected by it all year. But she listened hard to the reporters' questions and, in answering them, seemed to draw upon the rich history of locker-room interview clichés.

"I'm a defensive stopper," she'd tell the reporters somewhat shyly. "My job is just to come in and help the team out as best I can. I'm—I'm just doing my best to get the job done."

When the spotlight was beamed on the others, though, there was nothing bashful about Nikki. One morning, as Lisa and Teresa were set up in tall directors' chairs on the front lawn of the resort, waiting to do a television interview with NBC sportscaster Ahmad Rashad, Nikki, dressed in cutoff denim shorts and a bright orange T-shirt, hurtled her golf cart into the camera frame.

Halting the vehicle, she lifted her sunglasses and sang out in front of about thirty film crew members, "Okay! Okay, girls, you tell 'em everything!" She then replaced the shades on her head, and tossing her hair nonchalantly over one shoulder, threw her cart into reverse, swerved 180 degrees, and bombed off toward the golf course.

It was now the tenth of July, nine days from the Opening Ceremonies in Atlanta. In some respects you wouldn't have known it, watching the players frolic during their off hours. The Olympics were curiously absent from the dinnertime chatter or the quiet talk that went on in the locker room. If they spoke of Atlanta, it was to wonder whether the food at the Omni was going to be good, to inquire where other people's families were staying. On an immediate level, they did not talk about the basketball games they had ahead, did not go to sleep at night anticipating what was to come. If they allowed themselves to think about winning, then they would have to acknowledge the possibility of losing too, and thus it seemed better not to consider it at all. All of them had been through big games before, and together they seemed to recognize the comfort in Disney's happy distractions. Still, they were carrying cameras with them wherever they went, throwing their arms around one another for snapshots at every turn, joking around about all the hours they were going to sleep when it was over, recognizing but not discussing the fact that for better or worse, it was indeed almost over.

While the players kept their talk to safer subjects, they had VanDerveer to wrench their attentions to the specifics of the games they would play. Another coach might have tapered the workouts down to virtually nothing in the days prior to the Olympics, but VanDerveer kept them sweating, thinking nothing of putting them through a full two-hour court workout and then sending them off to the weight room to do their lifting. Every day they kicked off practice by doing push-ups for each day left before Atlanta, beginning at eight, then seven, then six, then five, then four.

"Someone said going to Disney before the Olympics is like studying all year for the bar exam and then getting drunk the night before," said Lynn Barry, USA Basketball's assistant executive director in charge of women's programs, who had helped to arrange the trip. "But I liken it to studying hard for the bar exam and then relaxing the night before, instead of trying to cram."

If relaxation was the goal, then it was at apparent odds with the aims of Tara VanDerveer, who was far more comfortable attacking the Olympics at a full tilt as opposed to sitting around waiting for them to come. She knew the Olympic schedule by heart—they would play Cuba first, then Ukraine, then Zaire, Australia, and South Korea before the possibility of advancing to the quarterfinals—and had memorized everything there was to memorize about the opponents, able to summon a brief bio on nearly every starter on every team. Over the Fourth of July weekend, she had carted three boxes of videotape to her parents' place in Chautauqua and watched them relentlessly, knowing she was down to the wire on preparation time, which meant, in VanDerveer's universe, that it was time to cram.

Last twenty-four seconds. Last twelve seconds. Down by one. Up by two. Down three, up one. If they were going to lose, it was going to happen at the bitter end of a game, the last clawing seconds where one basket could mean everything. And thus she obsessed on what they would do should they find themselves against the wall, as they had a number of times already, with Cuba, Australia, Ukraine, Canada, and Russia, setting and resetting the clock at practice, presenting the players with every late-game scenario she could think of.

"We're running the clock down," she instructed them on one play.

"But if we get fouled, we'll get our free throws in. We're running the clock down, but we can't risk a turnover."

"Think about the Russian post players," she urged them. "You have to beat them down the floor."

She had parceled out the scouting duties carefully between players and assistant coaches. Each player was assigned one opposing team to scout, while each assistant had three or four. They had carefully edited tapes of each team they would play at the Olympics, and it was up to the responsible player to come in and give a briefing on the playing styles of her designated team. In Orlando, VanDerveer had the team sit on the hard floor of the gym in front of a VCR and television on a cart, laboriously going through scouting tapes for an hour or more either before or after a practice. Beyond that, she and her assistants met individually with each player to review film on the individual players they would likely guard and be guarded by.

There was something eerie about it, pondering the moves of some Brazilian woman again and again, studying up on how quickly she could run, whether she shot from the left or the right, learning her weaknesses, anticipating her strengths, all along knowing that the woman on the television screen was out there somewhere on the other side of the mirror, with her own coach and VCR and you flitting slow-motion across the screen as she assiduously tried to learn everything about you too.

During the team's first few days in Florida, assistant coach Nancy Darsch was absent, having gone to see the Brazilians play in an international tournament in Canada. She arrived at Disney with a full report. Australia had beaten Brazil by one point. Russia beat Brazil in a wild, highly physical game. Canada beat Russia in double overtime. The message was clear: The competition was as hot as it had ever been, with the top several teams all within a hairbreadth of one another. Brazil's superstar guard, Hortência, had been in retirement for over a year and in April had given birth to a son, spawning rumors that she would not participate in Atlanta, but evidently she had come out of retirement, and as Nancy Darsch announced ominously to them all, "Hortência is back and she looks normal. Very normal."

One evening the U.S. team scrimmaged a team of male Disney employees, which became a rough-and-tumble foul-happy game. By now, most of the players were living in condominiums full of family and friends. Jennifer's sister flew in from her army-base home in Germany. Dawn's sister and aunts came from Philly with Dawn's newborn niece. Ruthie's sister, Mae Ola, was there. Carla's boyfriend, Willie, came down with his kids. Teresa's family came from Atlanta, Rebecca's parents and Dave came from Massachusetts, Eric came with Sheryl, Harry came with Venus, Katy's fiancé, John, came from Oregon, Lisa's best friend from college showed up. Most of the visitors had turned up to watch the scrimmage, including Harry Levingston and Eric Jackson, who sat side by side, talking and watching.

When Dawn faked a guy out with a behind-the-back dribble and then dashed to make a scoop shot under the net, Eric was impressed. "Shake and bake," he said, adjusting the Nike visor on his head. "Shake and bake de-luxe."

Harry nodded his agreement. After a time he mentioned that he and Venus had a friend who was in love with Jennifer Azzi, who with her dark hair and clean-cut good looks tended to attract a lot of admirers.

"Aw," said Eric, "everybody's got a friend in love with Jennifer!"

They watched another minute in silence.

"Venus is killin' that guy," remarked Eric, watching Venus back into a guy easily twenty pounds heavier than she, bumping him out of position.

Harry smiled, seeing his wife in action. "It's that big butt of hers," he said with a good deal of pride. "That thing is mean. Sometimes, I'll be playing against her and suddenly it's like *boom!*" Harry threw both hands in the air and mocked being stunned. "That thing hurts. It's a weapon, let me tell you."

"I think they're going to win it," said Eric after a moment. "I got a good feeling."

"If they don't win," Harry said, his eyes never leaving the court, "I don't know if I can stand to be around and see what it does to 'em."

Maybe this was why the thoughts that inevitably sat inside each of the players' minds were seldom voiced. Losing would hurt badly, worse than it had felt when the U.S. lost in '92, worse than it had felt when they'd lost the World Championships. Losing this time, in front of tens of thousands of American fans, at the moment in history when they'd finally carved out a place for professional women's basketball, after fourteen months of tireless focus, after every little thing they'd given up or delayed in order to put the Olympics first, they could not fathom going home disappointed, ending with the gut-wrenching decrescendo of a loss.

"Maybe I'm selfish," Lisa had said in Chicago, "but we've worked too hard for this. If we lose, I'm gonna be pissed."

Teresa, sitting down for a television interview in Orlando, was somewhat more philosophical. "I think we're gonna win it, I don't like to think otherwise . . . but in the event that God says no, we are a remarkable group of young women, and nobody, *nobody* can take that away from us."

Winning and losing aside, they no longer discussed the league possibilities as a group either. That had gone by the wayside in Australia, when it had become clear that each person would make her own decision about the future based on her own set of values and needs. In theory, each of them, with the exception of Sheryl, who had skipped the ABL draft, had been assigned to an ABL team for the fall.

Lisa and Rebecca had yet to sign contracts, however. Venus was talking to a team in Spain and Ruthie had a potential coaching job at Auburn. Shortly after the ABL announced a thirteen-game, one-year television package with SportsChannel, the NBA had announced major five-year television deals with NBC, ESPN, and Lifetime Television, with each network set to show one game per week over the WNBA's ten-week season. While Reebok had recently signed on to sponsor all eight ABL teams, it seemed likely that Nike would eventually align itself with the WNBA. The common speculation was that only one of the two leagues would survive. During the halftime show at the national team's game in Chicago, ABC commentators and basketball Hall-of-Famers Nancy Lieberman-Cline and Anne Meyers had discussed the two leagues, both placing their bets on the WNBA's success. Bruce Levy, a prominent women's basketball agent in New York famed for his brash manners, had purchased an ABL baseball cap, announcing loudly that as soon as the league went out of business, it would be a collector's item.

Compared as it inevitably was with the NBA, the ABL was looking like a folksy, grass-roots effort, though even without sponsors or a major television deal, it was still a league that could boast of a schedule and eighty newly drafted players. By contrast, there was a paucity of details about the WNBA beyond the television deal. Not one sponsor had been announced, not one player signed, not one city had been officially determined. But television, as Gary Cavalli and the others had learned, meant just about everything. With three televised games a week, and one of them on a major network, there was little question that the WNBA would get the sponsors and the players it needed.

Among the women on the team, it was becoming clear who was in and who was out on the ABL. In Orlando, several players, namely Jennifer, Teresa, Carla, Dawn, and Katy had taken to wearing ABL T-shirts and baseball hats to interviews, posing for newspaper photos in them, talking up a storm about the league—doing anything they could to heighten the ABL's visibility. Questioned about the WNBA, the standard answer was the kind offered by Jennifer. "We don't want to be a sideshow to the men, playing in the summer during the off season." In private, Jennifer also griped that she and Teresa had been cut out of a segment on the NBC's basketball news show *Inside Stuff*, covering Dawn's mural dedication in Philly, because they were wearing ABL paraphernalia. When several of the players draped ABL jackets over their chairs on the sidelines before a practice, according to Jennifer, USA Basketball's Lynn Barry had turned them all around, effectively hiding them from view.

There were days when it felt like almost everyone was against the ABL. It grew exasperating. Jennifer had been in New York earlier in June when a *New York Times* writer had approached her. "He was like, 'You know this is great with the league and stuff, but what about the fact that two of the most well-known people, Lobo and Swoopes, didn't sign?' " said Jennifer. "And I told him, 'You know, I'm so sick of everybody talking about two people. Why don't you put Teresa Edwards on your cover? She's a four-time Olympian, you know. That beats winning any national championship or getting any shoe contract. You guys are so stupid to think that women's basketball has only two players. There are eighty great players in the league. You're going to see that next season.' "

Ironically, as the ABL players tried to remind the world that the absence of a few marquee names would not kill a professional league, the team was joined for the final five days in Orlando by perhaps the greatest testament to athletic star power in the world, the men's Dream Team. The 1992 Olympics had seen the incarnation of the first Dream Team, or in USA Basketball parlance, Dream Team I. Dream Team I combined the NBA supertalents of the eighties—Larry Bird and Magic Johnson—with those of the nineties—Michael Jordan and Charles Barkley—to create the most dominant and ferocious group of asskickers to ever grace the Olympic stage. Dream Team II, which went and rolled all over the same hapless international teams two years later at the World Championships, was made up less of the old gods of the sport and more of the new talent like Shaquille O'Neal and Reggie Miller.

The Dream Team "concept," as it gets called in Colorado Springs, was spawned by a 1989 vote by the members of the International Federation of Basketball to overturn the rule that previously allowed any professional player in the world to participate in international events except those athletes affiliated with the NBA. The ban on NBA players, of course, was patently unfair, but possibly it was born of a root suspicion that adding demonstratively irreverent multimillionaire demigods of American culture to the event that in the words of the creator of the modern Olympic games was designed to extol "the moral and peaceful virtues of sports" could prove to be an uncomfortable match. Reviewing the triptych of Dream Team I's Barcelona odyssey, which began with Charles Barkley decking an Angolan player in the team's opening game and ended with a hissyfitting Michael Jordan and several Nike-bank-rolled compadres draping themselves in American flags for the medal ceremony, not out of a particular burst of patriotism but in order to cover an offending Reebok logo on the official U.S. warm-up suit, one had to wonder if those thirteen members of the fifty-six-member International Basketball Federation who had voted against allowing the NBA players into the Olympics had even a private moment of smugness.

If there was any plan on USA Basketball's part to steer Dream Team III toward a more gentlemanly performance in Atlanta, those hopes were dashed shortly after the team was named in June, when a reporter asked returning veteran Charles Barkley what he'd do in a rematch against Angola's Herlander Coimbra, the victim of his 1992 flagrant foul. "I'm going to hit him the same way," Barkley had replied.

When Dream Team III arrived at Disney on July 15, four days before both the men's and women's teams would fly together to Atlanta, the change at the resort was immediate. Grant Hill and Reggie Miller had joined the golf cart traffic, Scottie Pippen and Hakeem Olajuwon had invaded the weight room, Shaquille O'Neal's movie, *Kazaam*, was premiering at the resort movie theater, Karl Malone was coaching his wife on the fitness center's treadmill, and Barkley himself was on the putting green.

Suddenly, security guards patrolled the grounds night and day. A checkpoint was set up to monitor who came and went from the guarded area where the athletes were housed. At the resort's gift shop, one could buy USA Basketball replica uniforms with Pippen's or O'Neal's name printed on the back for $52. The resort's other guests loitered in front of the gym, hoping to get a glimpse of the male stars coming and going from their daily practices. Overnight, a media center complete with pastries and coffee, fax machines and telephones, was set up to accommodate the crowd of about forty journalists who swept into town to cover the Dream Team.

In truth, though, few people in the second week of July were concerned with what kind of performance Dream Team III was going to turn in the following week in Atlanta. Nobody really cared how much or how little the team was working to prepare, what kind of team chemistry existed if any at all, or how much the athletes loved their country. The field of inquiry when it came to the Dream Team players, actually, had little to do with the Olympics whatsoever. Rather, as the pre-Olympic week happened to coincide with the NBA's free agent signing period, the question on everyone's mind was whether the now-legendary Shaq was going to stay with the Orlando Magic or bail out the L.A. Lakers to the tune of $95.5 million over seven years. Other Dream Teamers were in the throes of their own negotiations as well. Gary Payton had just agreed to a seven-year, $85-million contract with the Seattle Supersonics, John Stockton was negotiating a $4-million-per-year deal with the Utah Jazz, Reggie Miller was wrangling with the Indiana Pacers for somewhere between $6 and $8 million annually.

For power dunker Shaquille O'Neal, it was shaping up to be a very good week. When he became the number one NBA draft pick in 1992, the same year that Dawn Staley had disappeared to Spain, his agent, Leonard Armato, had announced to the world his intention to make the 305-pound center into a "one-man entertainment conglomerate." Four years later, O'Neal was starring as a gentle chubby-faced genie in the Disney feature *Kazaam*, had three rap albums in the music stores, an estimated $35 million in endorsement contracts, and was now negotiating what was shaping up to be the most lucrative contract in NBA history. In the great late-twentieth-century cross-pollination of sports and entertainment, the twenty-five-year-old, larger-than-life Shaquille Rashaun O'Neal, whose first and middle names were Islamic for "little warrior," had become the ultimate hybrid.

And the way the media was handling it, it had become a matter of national importance whether Shaq moved to Los Angeles or stayed in Orlando. With David Stern's collective bargaining agreement in place, the Magic and the Lakers franchises were scraping every last penny from their budgets and stretching the limits of the newly established salary caps to launch offer upon counteroffer. During the Dream Team's four days at Disney World, bunkered down in the resort media center, reporters tracked the bids like stocks as they climbed from $95.5 million to $115 million to finally the $121-million package that sold the little warrior to Los Angeles as the highest-paid basketball player of all time. (O'Neal would tell the press that the decision "wasn't about money," backed up by agent Armato's comment that "his decision is based on what is in his heart. . . .") In the interview sessions that followed the Dream Team's practices, the media line stretched out the door of the gym as reporters waited to storm the court, hoping to get a word with Shaq.

Arriving for practice one afternoon, Lisa Leslie and Carla McGhee found themselves pushing their way anonymously through a pack of reporters clamoring to gain entrance to the men's practice, which was winding down inside.

"Excuse me, excuse me, please," called Lisa, parting the sea of television cameras with her elbow. "I got to get to practice, okay?"

If anyone recognized them, it was not acknowledged. When the men's practice, a lighthearted, relaxed affair, finished, most every member of the media deserted the premises, leaving empty soda cans and stray candy wrappers and a few lost ball-point pens in their wake, and the women's team alone in the gym to do their work. A few reporters did linger, however, and a few seemed touched enough by the quiet integrity of a group of twelve women who could total up all their salaries, plus their endorsement deals, and together still not make half the salary of one average NBA player. Some even ran stories with headlines like "Women's Team Is the Real Dream."

The women players for their part did not comment on the effect of the Dream Team's arrival in Orlando, nor the carnival atmosphere that surrounded the men. At times, they were as titillated as the next person about the famed icons who were now sharing their condo complex and gym. Katrina had modeled her game after Hakeem Olajuwon's, Nikki confessed to having an itty-bitty crush on Grant Hill.

"We're friendly with the men," said Teresa, who along with Katrina had been chosen as the team's Olympic cocaptain, one day following practice. "We just try not to let their stuff distract us too much, taking care of our own business."

Their business, as it always had been, was actualizing the reel that was continually running in VanDerveer's mind. Houston, L.A., San Fran, Sacramento—they went through the plays again and again, working at them the way a potter preps clay, pushing and prodding until the raw material warmed and became pliant, each play unfolding naturally, everybody on the court knowing instinctively which way to run, which pass to look for, and how to make the basket. They watched their scouting tapes and did their push-ups. At night they lay down, most of them in condos packed with family, and tried to get their sleep.

All year they had worked for a conclusion, an answer to the questions that had launched this thing that had become a crusade. Somewhere along the way it had gone beyond the simple need to avenge their loss to Brazil or to feel the glory of having a gold medal hung around one's neck. They'd started by hoping for one professional league and in the end they'd gotten two. They'd aimed at winning and they had won, fifty-two games straight. And on the eve of their trip to Atlanta, the feeling was inside them now, even if it went unspoken: They could do it. But seeing the men come in, watching the little kids who'd screamed for their autographs several days earlier suddenly shove past them to get to Barkley or Malone or whoever was bigger and richer and more famous than they could ever be, they had to wonder, even briefly, how much anybody out there really cared, whether any of it would feel worth it in the end.

And so, on July 17, two days before Opening Ceremonies in Atlanta, together with the men's team, the women marched in the Florida twilight, their gym bags slung over their shoulders, to the small charter plane that would carry them closer to the answers.

14

The Olympic Games
Atlanta, Georgia, *July 1996*

She had been just a kid in Los Angeles, a few days past her twentieth birthday, standing under the evening sky during Opening Ceremonies, as overwhelmed as a person could be by the lights and the noise and the heat that seemed to collect on the coliseum floor where the athletes stood, riding a current up over the crescent rows of spectators, row upon row upon row, until it broke finally into the cooler air outside. It had been 1984, the year of her first gold medal, the very beginning of her career. What Teresa Edwards remembered in particular was the great hurdler, Edwin Moses, walking to the stage to take the athlete's oath on behalf of everyone there, speaking for the thousands of athletes and to the millions who were watching him via satellite around the world. His voice had quaked; he had for a moment appeared weak, or if not weak then thoroughly humbled by his job, which was to utter the ten-second promise that was meant to bind one athlete to another, one country to the next. Watching him up there, she had thought, *God, that must be the hardest job in the world.*

And now, twelve summers later, she was in Atlanta and the job belonged to her. The day before Opening Ceremonies, the captains of each U.S. team had come together to vote on one athlete to carry the American flag into the stadium and one athlete to take the oath. A wrestler named Bruce Baumgartner was picked for the flag, and Teresa had been chosen to take the oath—her own ten seconds with the world.

She couldn't have conjured this moment, the same way she couldn't have known the first time she picked up a basketball that it would carry her out of Cairo, Georgia, a place that for so many years had felt like a self-contained universe, taking her to college and after that to the farthest corners of the world, where she would play anonymously for nine years, only to make the most public homecoming a person could make, on the day that happened to be her thirty-second birthday no less, standing up as a symbol of all athletes with an estimated 3.5 billion people tuned in to the broadcast and a live audience of 85,000. The feeling was so big, she almost didn't know how to feel it.

Instead, she focused on the words. Forty-two of them, one long sentence, a breath, and it would be over. Throughout the day before the ceremonies, Dawn and Katrina coached her, and she repeated it for them on the elevator at the team's hotel. She practiced in her room, where she'd laid out her sneakers and basketball clothes, her Bible, and the things she would need for the next two weeks in Atlanta. Her room, which was on the fourteenth floor between Venus's and Ruthie's and across from Katrina's, looked down on Centennial Park and over toward the Georgia Dome, which was monolithic against the washed-out summer sky. She recited the oath waiting in the buffet line in the small dining room they shared with the Dream Team, where families and friends were allowed to join them for meals and where USA Basketball had set up a hospitality table to provide the athletes' guests with tickets and transportation to and from events. She practiced saying the words fast and slow, sitting, standing, and walking. She practiced them when the men's and women's teams boarded the bus finally to go to the ceremonies, wearing their official U.S.A. outfits, the men in blue suits, the women dressed in red blazers and blue polka-dotted skirts, medium-heeled pumps and straw hats.

While the Olympic Stadium swirled in a fantastical kaleidoscope of oversized puppets, kites, drummers, dancers, cheerleaders, streamers, light shows, and music, a two-hour exercise in sensory overload, the nearly 11,000 athletes sat not more than two hundred yards away in Fulton Country Stadium and watched the proceedings on giant television screens, advertisements and all, awaiting the signal to line up behind their respective country's flags and march in. Because of the Dream Team's universal fame, due largely to the NBA's international television contracts, it had become impossible for the players to commingle with the other athletes, the reason why boxers, swimmers, and fencers from Amsterdam, China, Indonesia, nearly everywhere, would forget for a moment all about the dignity and honor of being an Olympian and clamor like schoolkids to get an NBA star's autograph. And because USA Basketball had been criticized in the past for treating the women's team differently than it did the men's, in the hours preceding their march into the stadium, both the male and female basketball players and their coaches along with a select few other athletes at risk of being mobbed—

Carl Lewis, Michael Johnson, and Jackie Joyner-Kersee among them—sat in a roped-off section of the stadium by themselves. And even here Teresa kept working on the oath, while the other women on the basketball team practiced walking in their heels, played with their hats, and joked around with the Dream Teamers.

Finally, the athletes started marching, 196 countries in alphabetical order behind Greece, the mother of Olympic countries. Teresa and the others continued to wait, watching the TV screens as each new team exited the Fulton Country Stadium and entered the Olympic Stadium: *Belgium, Belize, Benin, Bermuda, Bhutan, Bolivia, Bosnia and Herzegovina, Botswana, Brazil.* The sun had gone down on Atlanta, leaving a tumescent night under a big moon. Most everyone had removed their blazers and shoes until the last possible moment. Olympic volunteers passed out water and snacks. After an hour, the television screen showed the field of the stadium less than half full of athletes as the procession marched on. *Italy, Jamaica, Japan, Jordan, Kazakhstan, Kenya.* After two hours, it was time to stand, to fix themselves up, which meant for Lisa and Sheryl and a few others putting on fresh coats of lipstick—*Puerto Rico, Qatar, Romania, Russia, Rwanda*—they adjusted one another's hair, straightened their clothing, and slipped into their shoes. Then, finally all the waiting was done and they started to walk, separated by several hundred feet from the rest of the American athletes who, it had been decided, could not be depended on to refrain from autograph-mongering themselves. Katrina, who had been with Teresa in Seoul and Barcelona before this and who in her own right was the owner of a distinguished Olympic career, had been chosen as one of six athletes to carry the Olympic flag at the very end of the procession and thus stayed behind, wishing her old friend luck one last time.

When the American delegation descended the entry ramp into the Olympic Stadium, the cheering became instantly deafening as row upon row upon row of spectators rose to their feet. Teresa had been to Opening Ceremonies four times now. Each one had been different, but the feeling, standing with one's heart pounding like that, with the flags and the music and fireworks, was always the same. "You feel like the whole world is under one roof, everybody understands what you're doing" was how Teresa had described it earlier in the week. "It's so exciting. You don't need a speech or a pat on the back. You just stand in the middle of it."

Slowly, they made their way around the track, waving into the bright lights and up toward the blur of bodies in the stands, the applause seeming to crash down on them. When the Americans came to their spot on the infield, Teresa practiced her words again as the Olympic flag was marched around the track, with Katrina holding proudly to one edge. Then came a tribute to Dr. Martin Luther King, Jr., and a swell of orchestral music, and for this Teresa let the words of her oath drain from her head. King was her hero. Read over the sound system, the old words she'd learned years earlier in school pushed a lump into her throat: "I have a dream that one day on the red hills of Georgia, the sons of the former slaves and the sons of former slave owners will be able to sit down together at the table of brotherhood . . ."

And then it was Teresa's turn to speak. She walked clumsily in her heels across the grass to the large white stage at the center of the field and climbed the stairs, the words printed on a sweat-stained card which she carried in her left hand in case she needed a cue, in case her mind short-circuited. She laid her right hand on a folded American flag to take the oath. A half-beat passed in silence. This was a moment custom-built for Teresa Edwards, the woman who wanted the ball, who asked for it when the pressure was on. And so she drew in her breath and summoned the words. "In the name of all the competitors," Teresa said, "I promise, that we shall take part, in these Olympic games, respecting and abiding by the rules which govern them, in the true spirit of sportsman- ship. . . ." It was here that the smile began to break across her face and emotion crept into the last few words. ". . . For the glory of sport, and for the honor of our teams."

Getting inside the Omni Hotel was something like getting into a bank vault. First, you were required to produce a special laminated Omni Hotel photo ID that tagged you as either a "guest" or a "visitor" for the gang of T-shirt–wearing hotel security sentinels who sat in fold- ing chairs behind a barricade that separated the street from the drive that led to the hotel's motor lobby. If the sentinels waved you through, you encountered in the motor lobby a full-sized metal detector just like the ones at the airport, whereupon you were expected to surrender all elec- tronic or otherwise suspicious paraphernalia—cameras, cell phones, tape recorders, video recorders, and so on—for the inspection of a uniformed guard while the rest of your belongings were fed through the detection apparatus on a conveyor belt. On the other side of the metal detector was a small device into which you stuck your right hand for a laser scan. If said hand had been previously approved and admitted to the security system's databank, then a green light would blink, at which point, just to be doubly assured, the device required the hand owner's four-digit personal identification number.

If all went well, you next found yourself at the elevators of the sacrosanct Omni Hotel, whose hallways were a quiet and cool refuge from the glaring sun and the crowds that jam-packed the streets from early morning until late at night every day. It was here that the basketball players could glide around more or less undisturbed, which was the goal. While most Olympic athletes were housed in a state-of-the-art Athletes' Village on the campus of Georgia Tech, a $200-million affair that featured a twenty-four-hour-a-day dining hall, a coffee house/disco, a bowling alley, movie theater, florist, hair salon, bank, and five McDonald's, it was not particularly unusual for certain well-funded Olympians to stay elsewhere, purportedly to avoid distraction. The American gymnasts had rented a group house. A number of track and field athletes had found hotel rooms. Several foreign teams had booked houses or blocks of hotel rooms as well.

The truth was, it was nearly impossible to avoid distraction at the Olympics, no matter how cloistered the environment. A sports psychologist will tell you that one of the most potentially debilitating things for an athlete going into a major competition—be it a high school championship game or the Olympics—is the sudden surfacing of family and friends, who even with the best intentions can add to the already considerable pressure. When the basketball players' guests had flooded the Disney condos, it had proved to be exhilarating and exhausting and simply one more thing to adjust to. Carla had tired her legs walking all over Disney World with her boyfriend's kids one day. Jennifer's sister had taken her on long shopping expeditions on afternoons that might have been better spent resting. Dawn was sharing her condominium with her infant niece. And while it meant everything to have their personal support networks—Dawn adored her niece, Jennifer and her sister were like close-knit twins, Lisa's best friend from college cooked meals for her, Rebecca's boyfriend ironed her clothes for appearances—the guests could also unwittingly add a degree of stress. When members of

Jennifer's family saw how little playing time she was getting from Van-Derveer, they felt naturally protective and angry. But the issue of playing time, Jennifer said, was something she'd struggled with and finally accepted months earlier. "I love my family for caring," she said one day. "I just don't want to talk about it right now, you know?"

For VanDerveer, it was a matter of keeping things as routine as possible, to focus the team inward, blotting out everything that threatened to take the players out of their game. "Keep the circle tight," she told them repeatedly. "Don't let too many new people into your lives right now. We've been leaning on one another all year, and it's worked, so let's keep it that way." They would practice one day and play the next, a game every other day right through the five games in the preliminary rounds. The twelve competing teams had been divided into two pools of six. Each team would play every other team in its pool, with the top four teams of each pool, the top eight teams total, advancing for the quarterfinals. The winners of the quarterfinal games would go on to play in the semifinal round, which would then produce the two teams that would play for the gold medal on August 4, the last day of the Olympics.

Practicing for the first time at their official practice site, a small community college gym just south of Atlanta, the coach kept the workout light and familiar—running through plays, working on the time and score situations—though every player could see the firmness in her jaw, the puffiness in her face that suggested she was not sleeping much. It was a tension they all felt, though the easiest and probably smartest thing to do was not to talk about it. Tomorrow they would play their opening game against Cuba. They practiced as usual, ending the day with a perimeter shooting contest that pitted one half the team against the other, Ruthie, Teresa, Sheryl, Nikki, Dawn, and Jennifer versus Lisa, Katrina, Venus, Katy, Rebecca, and Carla. When Ruthie's team won, they celebrated with exuberant body slams. As the players were dressing to load the bus back to the hotel, a college employee appeared carrying a box loaded with bags of pork rinds and potato chips, several of which Carla snapped up eagerly, a small perk of being an Olympian, inspecting what she was getting with a self-satisfied smile, shouting over to Dawn, who herself was eyeing the snack box. "Yeah, this is what I'm *talkin'* about!"

The feeling of being at the Olympics, particularly in the first few days, was heady and disorienting, as if preparing for these two weeks for a year still gave them no insight into what it would be like. On the night before the team's first game, Lisa decided to take a walk up the street to McDonald's. She left the hotel and jumped into the stream of pedestrians on Marietta Street, a lone tall woman in a sea of shuffling, elbowing tourists. "Hey, that's Lisa Leslie!" somebody shouted. "Hey, Lisa! Hey, Lisa!" Soon the tourists had clotted around her. "Hey! Hey! The girl in the commercials, the basketball player!" She smiled and said hello to everyone as nicely as she could, but the people were now getting shoved by the people behind them, with more and more people stopping to figure out what the hubbub was about. Soon Lisa was trapped in a tight snarl of bodies. There were people pressed up against her on all sides, stepping on her toes and knocking against her legs. Other people waved papers for her to sign, they shouted questions, they shouted in foreign languages, the whole tangle of them swaying precariously with each new push that came from behind, as if they all might topple over together.

For a second it felt as if the crowd would swallow her whole. Her heart started to beat faster. She waved at the people and gently pushed at one wall of the crowd, trying to make her way back. "Lisa! Lisa! Hey!" Soon she was pushing hard, trying to keep the smile on her face, realizing that she was actually afraid of being hurt. She hadn't understood before why public figures felt they had to hide so much. What was so frightening about people anyway? Now she understood. It took her another five minutes to fight her way back to the barricade at the Omni. Apologetically, she asked a security guy to run to McDonald's for her while she retreated back inside, the sweat sopping her face, her nerves fluttering, surprised by how much her life had changed.

As they stepped onto the court at the Morehouse arena, the venue for their first-round games, they were struck most immediately by the flags. The flags were everywhere—handheld flags, flags draped over railings and fans' bodies, the giant flag that Ruthie's family flapped and waved wildly even during warm-ups—transforming the arena into a shivering sea of red, white, and blue. The players had done nothing unusual that day, though several of them had not slept well the night before. Sleep was difficult not only because of the excitement they felt but also because the Omni overlooked Centennial Park, where each night live bands played on a gigantic stage, where the speakers were aimed directly out and over the park, sending the music pulsating right through the Omni until well past midnight. On the night before the Cuba game, Lisa had lain in bed until two in the morning, trying to sleep, then worrying that she wasn't sleeping, then trying to forget about the worry so she could sleep, then thinking about the game that was coming up, then trying not to think about the game, then worrying again that she wasn't sleeping.

The Cubans had received new uniforms for the Olympics, jerseys and shorts in a sleek powder blue. Their coach was pacing the sidelines already. The two teams finished their warm-ups and came to attention for the piped-in music of their national anthems. Then the players huddled around VanDerveer while the fans—over 4,800 in all—began to clap, first slowly and then faster, the beat of their hands picking up speed, the crowd pounding its approval as the starters for each team took their positions for the tip-off.

They had played the Cubans and won eight times now, but suddenly it didn't matter. As Dawn would say later, "You never know which Cuba team will show up. I don't mean personnel. I mean which-side-of-the-bed-are-they-getting-out-on? kind of showing up."

Today the Cubans who showed up to play were the same ones who had held the Americans to a three-point game months earlier in China. Immediately, they seized control, surprising the U.S. team with a fast-breaking offense and an inside game that was amped up three levels from before. Within two minutes, the Cubans had squalled to a 10–6 lead over the Americans. Things like this had happened before, other teams had crept out to an early lead, only to get demolished by the U.S. team before five minutes was up. But this time five minutes came and went without the usual upheaval. Going for the hoop, Lisa was fouled several times before she could get her shot off, only to go to the line and miss one out of every two free throws, advancing the score in one-point increments while the Cubans plowed forward. The score was soon 14–8.

Lisa drew another foul, took herself to the free-throw line, and missed again.

"Take your time!" somebody shouted from the stands. "Take your time!"

They were choking, not just Lisa, but the whole set of starters. Katrina had launched an improbable three-point shot that had missed. She was losing offensive rebounds to Yamilet Martinez, the Cuban forward who seemed unusually gritty today. Sheryl and Ruthie were holding their own, but neither had mustered anything spectacular. Teresa was the next to be fouled, missing one and then two free throws. The players on the bench watched anxiously, waiting for the thing that would bring the starters to life, the spark, the steal, or flash of offensive brilliance that had dependably ignited them within the first few minutes of every game all year long. This time it didn't seem to be coming, however. Seven and a half minutes into the game, the Cubans led 20–13.

VanDerveer had signaled for Venus and Nikki to prepare to go in for Lisa and Ruthie, but then changed her mind, sending Nikki back to the bench, swapping Venus for Lisa, who walked to the sidelines, keyed up and sweaty, unable to beat the jitters. Several minutes later, VanDerveer pulled Sheryl out and sent Katy in. Next Teresa and Ruthie came out, replaced by Dawn and Nikki.

All year Katy Steding had been the least assuming presence on the team. Off the court she tended to be extremely private, keeping her emotions buried, her thoughts largely to herself, neither complaining nor boasting when the situation seemed to merit it. On the court she played with a generally even keel, understanding that her role on the team was to rebound and shoot from the perimeter. Today, as the others on the team grew increasingly agitated—less by the Cuban's mounting lead and more by their own foundering—Katy stayed calm.

Purposefully, she started to play her game. First she scored on a lay-up, then she scrambled after a loose ball, which Katrina eventually converted into a lay-up, bringing the American team within three points of the Cubans. Next she stole the ball. Venus scored one point on a free throw, and Lisa, who had come in for Katrina vowing to get a fresh start, immediately laid the ball up, tying the game at 20–20. Cuba hadn't scored in three minutes. They were starting to roll now, the old momentum returning. On the next possession Lisa stole the ball and passed it up court and suddenly it was in Katy's hands. She planted her feet behind the three-point line so deliberately it seemed almost to happen in slow motion. She took aim at the hoop, shot, and scored, putting her team in the lead, 23–20.

If Katy's level head had brought them back into the game, it was Dawn's razzle-dazzle that put the exclamation mark on what would become their first Olympic victory. She fired off three stunning no-look passes. She dribbled down into a one-on-two confrontation, but rather than waiting for her team's offense to get set up, she simply split the defense and scored on a lay-up. The showstopper came in the latter part of the first half, however, when Dawn picked off a Cuban's pass and drove the ball down to the right corner, where she executed a 360-degree spin at the baseline, sending a pass behind her back, beautifully timed to hit Katy's hands as she cut down the lane. Even Magic Johnson, one of the most famous ball-passers of all times, who happened to be in the audience that day, jumped to his feet, shaking his head in disbelief.

The next day's *Boston Herald* would say "Staley's stat line: four points, seven assists, and 4,869 'Ohmygawd, did you see thats?' "

"Muy pequeña, muy rápida" were the words the Cuban player who'd tried to defend Staley would stutter after the game—"very small, very fast."

Today all the mustard belonged on the hot dog. She had played flaw-lessly, and beyond that, she'd done it before for an international audi-ence, an international media corps. Dawn Staley, the player who had never had the Big Win in her life, was making herself legendary.

The U.S. team had won its first game, 101–84. Katy was beaming and would continue to beam through the rest of the day, surfacing at dinner with a gauze bandage around her neck where a Cuban player had grabbed her. Lisa, who had come back from her early case of butterflies to score 24 points, literally skipped off the court. Following the game, Dawn was sent from the locker room to greet a gaggle of reporters—many of them general-assignment writers who did not regularly cover women's basketball—in the interview room. They waited with their notebooks flipped open and tape recorders poised, straining to catch sight of Dawn, murmuring among themselves, saying *wow* and *hey now* and *wasn't it surprising* that women played basketball like that? When Dawn appeared at the door, a bag of ice lashed to either knee, she smiled out at the group, then sat down and got to business.

As the reporters bombarded her with questions, Dawn squinted and tilted her head slightly to the side, considering.

"Nooo . . . I wouldn't say the no-look is my signature play," she said, enjoying every moment. "I would say my behind-the-back would be my signature play. . . ."

When one reporter abandoned his question altogether and just blurted out his admiration, triggering a chorus of murmured agreement from the others, Dawn shrugged her shoulders and looked nonchalant.

"I've been doing these same things for the last few years overseas," she said. "It's a shame you guys didn't get a chance to see that."

Two days later, Christine Leslie sat herself in the bleachers at the Morehouse arena and settled in for a couple of hours of cheerleading as the U.S. played Ukraine. She had a small handheld American flag with her. Her new husband, Tom, a gray-haired mustached man with a gentle face, sat beside her with a flag of his own. USA Basketball had reserved blocks of seats for every basketball game, enough so that each player could invite several guests, which meant that the friends and family of the players tended to sit in clumps. Christine Leslie had already met most everyone as they waited for the shuttle van that carried them from the hotel back and forth to Morehouse. She'd met Nikki's mom and Katy's mom, and Dennis and Ruthann Lobo. Several rows behind her today sat the Reverend Edward McClain, an African Methodist Episcopal minister in Charleston, South Carolina, and a former running back with the Baltimore Colts. After watching his daughter play poorly against Cuba, Edward McClain had gone back to the hotel and given Katrina a sermon on posting up aggressively. The Azzi family sat over to the right, along with Eric Jackson and Harry Levingston, who reported proudly that business was booming at his liquor store now that a photo of Venus in her Olympic uniform was on the wall.

Ruthie Bolton had said earlier that when it came to her family—some seventy-five brothers and sisters, nieces and nephews, along with her father had come from Mississippi—she was hoping that tickets to games would fall from the sky. ("I just hope the Lord sends some down," said Ruthie.) The Boltons had scraped and scrambled and campaigned for stray tickets, and not only did it seem miraculous that most of the clan seemed to find a way into each game but that they somehow managed to sit close together, forming a raucous cheering section that chanted and sang during time-outs, the Positive Mental Attitude cascading forth.

It took a lot of Boltons, however, to drown out Christine Leslie, who was a big, tall woman with a big, sonorous voice. Christine Leslie did not just cheer for her daughter. She cheered for everyone, bellowing out her support.

"Come on, babies," she yelled, watching Sheryl run the ball and dish it to Ruthie. "Come on!"

Morehouse was a small enough arena that even from her seat in the upper rows of the stadium Mrs. Leslie could be heard down on the floor. Whatever jitters the team had felt in the opening game appeared to have evaporated. When Ruthie, who had spent extra time stretching her stiff knee before the game, sank a three-pointer early on, the Boltons revealed themselves noisily down below in the prime seating. Katrina, appearing to have taken her father's lecture to heart, was rebounding wildly. Before it was over, she would have six rebounds, five assists, and make eight of nine shots, scoring 17 points altogether. Teresa was moving the ball well, scoring often herself, while Sheryl played great defense, passing the ball expertly inside on the other end of the court for Lisa to sink her turnaround jumpers.

As the lead built up, VanDerveer sent in her bench players, who also seemed to be at the top of their games. Rebecca scored on a no-look pass from Dawn, Nikki scored on a hook shot. With under four minutes in the half, the U.S. was steamrolling Ukraine 41–24, but this did not temper the enthusiasm of Christine Leslie, who was of the no-mercy school of cheering. "Good brick!" she shouted as a Ukrainian player missed the first of two free throws. "Now throw another one!" With this, she waved her flag at the player as if casting a spell.

Mostly, though, she saved her shouts for supporting the Americans, a job she approached seriously and tirelessly, even as the drama started to seep out of the game, even as her apparently mild-mannered husband sat by quietly, smiling gently each time his new bride leapt to her feet. "Way to go, Dawn! *Shake and bake ba-bee!*"

By the time the halftime buzzer sounded, Christine Leslie was a minor celebrity in her section of the stands, having been identified as the high-volume mother of Lisa Leslie. Holding tightly to her flag, she accepted congratulations from total strangers graciously, explaining to a group of them that Lisa had signed up for both a professional team and for a modeling career. "You heard of Wilhelmina? In New York?" she said. "Lisa signed with them."

"Is she the one in those TV ads in her underwear?" asked a man.

The tone of his voice seemed to hint that appearing on network television in a sports bra and panties would be something that would not make a mother happy, but the scene to which he was referring belonged to Sheryl, and Christine Leslie was inalienably proud of all of them anyway, correcting the man without pause. "No, my Lisa's in the skimpy black dress."

The Americans dispensed with Ukraine on Tuesday and then moved to the Georgia Dome on Thursday, where they blew past Zaire. The Zaire game was historic for several reasons, the first being that with over 31,000 people in attendance, it became the largest audience ever to watch a women's basketball game. "I think I lost some bets on this one," said Tara VanDerveer afterward. "I figured that with an afternoon game on a weekday, people would have other things to do. . . ." But they didn't, and the cheering had echoed right up into the rafters that day, sending chills up the players' spines when they first looked up and saw fans the size of photographic pixels sitting up by the ceiling.

Another milestone was the U.S. team's 60-point margin of victory, the largest ever in a women's Olympic game, a pummeling of historic proportions, though it was not one anyone particularly celebrated too vigorously, since the other significant thing was the very presence of a women's basketball team from Africa, another first. The team from Zaire had trained for only about a month in the sweltering equatorial heat, playing on a grassy field with two wooden posts outfitted with rims. At the press conference following the game, the coach, whose name was Mongamaluku Mozingo, explained that in Zaire a basketball costs the equivalent of two months' salary and thus the team's twelve players had practiced with one ball. (By contrast, the U.S. team routinely brought at least twelve balls to each practice.) "If we were able to prepare like other teams," said the coach, "I think you would see we do not have mediocre athletes."

The players' plane tickets, uniforms, and sneakers had been bought courtesy of Dikembe Mutombo, a Zairean center for the Atlanta Hawks and the new owner of a five-year, $55-million contract. When Mutombo first met with the team upon its arrival in Atlanta, he had noticed that the women were practicing in worn-out, ancient shoes, saving the ones Mutombo had purchased for them for the actual competition. Seeing this, he had taken the whole group of them out shopping, outfitting each player with a second pair of shoes. After the team lost to the U.S., its third consecutive defeat at the Olympics and this time to a team whose training budget was several hundred times larger than its own, Mutombo visited the African players in their locker room.

Later, he reported back: "I just want to let them know I still love them and I'm still supporting them, because they seemed a little bit disappointed in the locker room," said Mutombo. "Some of the girls, they acted like maybe a rock fell onto their heads so they can't get up. I told them, 'You have four more games to play. You can win maybe two of these last four games and you just need to keep your heads up and play the game.' "

With each win, the buzz about the U.S. women's team mounted. Scalpers lurked outside the Georgia Dome before the team's games. People stood for an hour in the pouring rain, waiting to be checked through security to get inside for the start of a game. Each day the headlines reporting the women's progress seemed to grow, particularly as they began to shine by comparison to their male counterparts, who having played several sloppy games were being slaughtered in the press. "Many of the Dream Teamers act as if they wish somebody would mail their gold medal to them . . ." complained *The Indianapolis Star.* "Dream Team Idea Needs New Focus" said a *New York Times* headline, with the writer observing that during Olympic events, the Dream Team players' eyes "revealed disinterest, even boredom." To make matters worse, guard Reggie Miller earned headlines of his own, trying to debunk the bratty Dream Team myth with a comment that earned him little sympathy. "I'm in the hotel room watching TV, and I look at *Extra* and *Entertainment Tonight* and there's controversies over the Dream Team," said Miller. "They make it look like we're staying at the Ritz-Carlton, when we're staying at a one-star hotel. The room service is terrible."

The only entity to receive as much criticism as the Dream Team, it seemed, was NBC, whose round-the-clock coverage of the Games was allegedly designed to cater to women viewers, who, research revealed, made up the majority of the Olympic television audience. What this translated to was prime-time hours loaded with extensive gymnastics coverage, not to mention every last Dream Team game, while relegating women's basketball to tape-delayed broadcasts in the 12:41 A.M. to 2:11 A.M. slot and virtually ignoring women's soccer and softball. "Not just unfair," a *New York Times* columnist would later chide. "Insulting. And contradictory to NBC's philosophy to rope in female viewers. Has NBC secretly discovered that women [viewers] draw the line at their gender playing sweaty team sports that were once solely male preserves?"

For the women basketball players, little of this mattered at the moment. They had cruised through their first three games but were headed into what would likely be the toughest challenge in the preliminary rounds, a Saturday night game against Australia. Michelle Timms, the Aussie point guard who had led her team through several close games against the Americans during their visit to Australia, had announced, "We aren't going to be intimidated by them like everyone else."

VanDerveer understood what they were up against. The Australians had also won their first three Olympic games. They played a stifling defense; they would run her team down until the last second of the game. The first week had been relatively easy, but those games were now behind them. Meanwhile, the Brazilians were ripping through the other pool of teams, having toppled Canada, Japan, and Russia in the last several days with what one reporter called a "withering running game," playing two games without the famous Hortência, who was resting a sprained ankle. The biggest surprise with regard to the other pool was that China, long expected to be a medal contender, had self-destructed, losing to Japan and Canada and now under threat of not advancing to the quarterfinals—a cautionary tale, perhaps, that no favorite was safe, that anything could happen.

At practice on Friday, VanDerveer reminded her players to get as much rest as possible in preparation for the next week. This meant curbing any activities that kept them on their feet, including late-night trips several of the players had made to the House of Blues nightclub, where a number of the Dream Teamers tended to gravitate after dark and where both sets of athletes had access to a VIP balcony, where they mingled with a considerable number of Hollywood stars who had come to watch the Games. Part of their job, she said, was to ignore the street noise that filtered through their windows half the night and the temptations to go out. Sleep was becoming imperative.

Every last player was in her room, sleeping, or at least trying to sleep, when shortly after one in the morning that night a noise rocked through the Omni, rattling windows and jarring a number of them awake. The sound could have been anything. Some of them likened it to a giant tray being dropped downstairs in the hotel, others said it sounded like a thunderclap. It was enough to raise several of them out of bed, and those who ignored it were soon pulled from sleep by the wail of sirens and the anxious voices in the hallway that started up a minute or two later. One by one, the doors along the team's fourteenth-floor corridor began to open. The team ended up out on the balcony of Katrina's room, which looked directly down on Centennial Park. Along the thin line of highway in the distance, they could see the flashing lights of police cars, ambulances, and fire trucks streaming toward the park from the east and west. After a few minutes, Jennifer showed up with a pair of binoculars and confirmed that there were bodies strewn across the sidewalks, that the unharmed were helping the wounded, that the frightened were running away from the park, while the shocked stood still.

It was too early for the television reporters to contribute any information beyond what they could see for themselves: There had been an explosion in one corner of the park, people were hurt, people were afraid, every emergency vehicle for twenty miles had been called in. Immediately, the players started checking up on family members. A number of their families had attended the men's Dream Team game against China that had ended only a few hours earlier, and it was plausible that they had stopped by to hear the music in the park on their way home from the Georgia Dome. For a short while, Christine Leslie and her husband were unaccounted for; Rebecca worried that her parents were still out. Eventually, though, after phone calls and room checks, everybody surfaced safely. The television crews were now reporting that the explosion had been the result of a home-made pipe bomb, causing two deaths—a forty-four-year-old mother of two from southern Georgia killed by shrapnel, and a TV cameraman who suffered a heart attack— and a host of injuries. The President had declared it "an evil act of terror."

By daybreak, the rain was pouring down on Atlanta, a warm, gentle deluge. At the Olympic Stadium, where track and field events started early, the Olympic flag flew at half mast. Centennial Park had been closed to the public. While the director general of the International Olympic Committee, François Carrard, had declared earlier that the Games would go on, it was largely left up to individual delegations to decide whether or not they wanted to stay and compete. Dream Team member Karl Malone had chartered a plane and flown his family out of Atlanta almost immediately, remaining behind himself. The USA Basketball staff met with its athletes that day to discuss the prospects of continuing to play. The women were eight hours away from the Australia game now, though the idea of competition seemed suddenly irrelevant and silly.

Yet the Games did go on, the collective idea being that if they didn't, then terrorism would win. Event-goers still crowded the downtown streets, only the boisterousness of previous days was gone as people moved from place to place in an eerie, anxious silence. In the span of several hours on Saturday afternoon, secondary bomb scares had forced the evacuation of one subway station, a Greyhound bus station, Atlanta Symphony Hall, the corporate apartments Nike had rented downtown, and one shopping mall. One got the impression, walking through the city streets, with sharpshooters now positioned on the rooftops and police patrolling every block, that every garbage can, every parked car or merchandising booth, was potentially explosive. At each Olympic venue, athletes and fans bowed their heads in a moment of silence—the runners at the track, the divers, the rowers, the cyclists, and finally, when night rolled around and they took the court so, too, did the basketball players, the Aussies and the Americans, their eyes tightly shut as they said their private prayers, cleared their minds, and prepared to play.

The world could have collapsed around them, though, and the Australian women would still battle for every rebound and loose ball. The lead flip-flopped back and forth several times—with the U.S. ahead by four at 12:21 and the Australians suddenly brawling their way back, taking the lead 31–25, with 8:39 to play before the half. Every nerve ending in Teresa Edwards's body was tingling. She knew that the Australians had it in them to beat them.

"I'm scared of Australia," she would say later. "It's a respect/fear thing. Some teams, you can break their backs, but not Australia. You can't tell them anything. They're the fighting type. They'll fist fight you. They're never going to quit, but I thrive on that, it's just how I am. It's like, if you're tough I'm going to show you I'm tough, too. I'll show you I'm tougher." As the U.S. slowly started to close the gap, Teresa swooped for a defensive rebound and sent a long baseball pass to Ruthie, who scored to tie the game at 35–35.

The problem with Australia in particular was that they had their own version of Teresa in Michelle Timms, the pert blond point guard who was capable of single-handedly rescuing a game. The game began to take on an anything-you-can-do-I-can-do-better quality, as Timms scored to put Australia ahead and Teresa immediately answered by scoring once to tie, then after a turnover, faking and driving to the hoop to put the U.S. ahead 39–37. The back and forth continued, with Timms intercepting passes and Teresa ferociously driving to score as the crowd of 33,000—another record-setting turnout—slowly kindled out of its mesmerized stupor and started to chant. "U-S-A! U-S-A!" When the halftime buzzer rang, the U.S. had eeked out a three-point lead, 46–43, and the fans were at full roar. The Olympics were on again.

In opening minutes of the second half, however, the Americans still could not shake the Australians. Timms was playing a prolific game, having scored 17 points total before the second half was even four minutes old. The score was tied again, 56–56. But while Timms was unstoppable, the rest of her team was starting to fade. Point by point, the U.S. edged away, going on a 16–4 offensive run led by Teresa, Katrina, and Sheryl that finally put the nails in Australia's coffin, winning the Americans their fourth game, 96–79.

Teresa Edwards had passed for 15 assists and scored 20 points, two more than she'd scored in the last three games combined, earning her a women's Olympic record for single-game assists, hard-won praise from VanDerveer and rival Michelle Timms, who seated herself at the postgame press conference and declared good-naturedly, "Edwards absolutely kicked my butt." And finally there was the deep peace of mind that came after she'd gone all-out. When the court had cleared and the stands had emptied, while her teammates joked around in the locker room and the cleanup crew worked the aisles of the Georgia Dome, Teresa slipped back out onto the floor and stood there for a moment all by herself, soaking it all in, not so much replaying what had she done that night but casting ahead to what was still to come, what she still had to do.

Throughout the Olympics, Tara VanDerveer was unswerving in her workout routine, jogging every other morning promptly at seven with Carol Callan regardless of how little sleep she'd had, regardless of the humidity or the rain showers or the traffic blockades that made the city a maze of closed streets and alleys lined by merchandising booths. Along the route, a roughly five-mile jaunt, there were three hills to climb, each one requiring a slightly greater effort than the last.

For the coach, who liked to view the small things in her life as symbolic, the hills and the short, intense bursts of energy required to get up them had come to represent the three challenges remaining: the quarter-finals, semifinals, and the gold-medal game. The team had won its final preliminary game against South Korea on July 29. They would play the Japanese team in the quarterfinals and then, provided they won, would match up against either Australia or Russia in the semifinals. Neither team would be easy to beat. On the other side, Brazil would have to beat Cuba and then either Ukraine or Italy in order to advance to the finals—easier games to be sure. If the U.S. and Brazil were on a crash course to play each other for the gold medal, it was likely that the Brazilians would arrive at the final game less exhausted by the previous games.

For VanDerveer, the challenge would be to use her players exactly as much as she needed to in order to secure a win without pushing them into fatigue. Ruthie, who had been one of the team's most consistent players, was still nursing her weak knee. Everybody on the team was playing through one type of pain or another. It was a matter of being smart and focused—attitude and effort, as she'd told them back in October—until the very end. These were the types of things she thought about when attacking those hills every morning, visualizing the competition and the kind of game her team would need to play to be successful, then pushing herself over the crest of the first hill, then the second and finally the third, the heat blooming in her cheeks, her lungs catapulting as she visualized the final goal, her body feeling a shade lighter with each one conquered.

Walking the short distance from the Omni to the Georgia Dome for the quarterfinal game against Japan on Wednesday afternoon, Ruthann Lobo, Rebecca's mother, was practically bouncing with excitement. "I'm nervous," she said. "This is for real . . . it's like the Final Four now." Japan was a team with a ruthless three-point ability and a love of the fast break—the only team aside from Brazil that the U.S. team had not played and defeated prior to the Olympics. It had been Japan's upset of China in the early rounds that had in part handed China its abrupt departure. Despite the hours of scouting tapes VanDerveer and her players had reviewed, it was hard to know what to expect from Japan. And Ruthann Lobo was right about the pressure: If they lost now, they'd be eliminated.

And the distractions continued. The day before, the Omni had been evacuated due to a package that set off the security staff's detection devices, forcing the players, staff, and other hotel guests to sit around for two hours at the nearby CNN Center before they were called back and told the scare had been a false alarm. The rumor, though unconfirmed, was that the suspect package had contained a Nintendo game ordered by one of the Dream Team players.

VanDerveer directed her team to focus on its inside game and set her guards to work on shutting down the Japanese team, which starred a player named Aki Ichijo, who shot 200 three-pointers a day in practice and was known as "the Flamingo" for shooting flat-footed but then kicking one foot up behind her. While the Flamingo bolstered Japan's perimeter game, its diminutive forwards, all under six feet, were no match on the inside against the likes of Katrina, Venus, Katy, and Carla. The game belonged above all to Lisa Leslie, however. She scored 35 points, shooting from everywhere in the paint, connecting on seventy-six percent of her field goals, the smile that crossed her face at the final buzzer seeming to give notice that nothing—not noise, not bomb scares, nor nerves—could bother her now.

A mere two games and two practices were left on the schedule. They'd gone from scouting twelve Olympic teams to scouting two, from having to visualize three hundred days ahead to only three. Following the Americans' game against Japan, the Australians and Russians had duked it out for a last shot at the U.S., with the tenacious Aussies finally winning in overtime. VanDerveer, who had watched the game from the edge of her seat, admitted to switching loyalties several times, initially hoping the Russians would win so she could prove to the world that the one-point game back in Chicago had been a fluke, then hoping for the Aussies, since they'd played so hard throughout. Finally, when the two teams went into overtime, she was too wrapped up in the game to care one way or another. All she knew was that either team was going to knock itself out to beat the U.S. team.

Her practices had become entirely about finesse, light enough so the players hardly broke a sweat but still tightly regulated by her whistle so that not a moment was wasted, so they could run through the plays again, taking time to focus on strategies for dealing with specifics like Australia's trapping defense or Brazil's perimeter play. Over the course of the last week, the team's media following had about doubled in size. On the day prior to the semifinal against Australia, a small mob of about thirty journalists and television cameras—roughly the same number who turned up for the men's practices—waited by the gym doors for VanDerveer to release her players for interviews.

Most of the players knew better than to exude too much confidence. Not only was it ungracious, it was also premature. Twice before—in Barcelona and in Sydney—the Americans had lost in the semifinal round when nobody expected them to. "We're not there yet," Teresa cautioned one overly optimistic reporter. "We've got a ways to go still." Dawn, who after her two close brushes with championships at Virginia and the bitter memory of the World Championships knew well enough not to count her chickens early, offered a similar sentiment. "It ain't over till it's over," she said, adding, "though I can't wait till it is."

Restraint was, however, not a quality that came naturally to Venus Lacy, who stood at the opposite end of the practice court from Dawn and Teresa and most of the others, jabbering away to a newspaper writer from her childhood hometown of Chattanooga, Tennessee, thumping one hand energetically on her chest as she spoke.

"Three days," she was saying, the smile broad across her face. "Oh, man, it's three days till they gonna hang that gold medal right here, right around my neck, where it belongs. I tell you, I want it so bad. I just want it *right now*."

For fourteen months the gold medal had been an abstraction, no more than a full-color photo in their team notebooks, an idea they all shared. To imagine it as Venus had, as something particular and concrete, was for most of them still unfathomable, as was the idea that finally they could see the future beyond August 4, even though they'd just received their final airline itinerary from USA Basketball, a one-way ticket home on the fifth.

Later that day, several of the team's Nike-sponsored players made an obligatory appearance at a press conference at Nike's media center, part of a large hospitality center that the company had outfitted with pool tables, plush couches, large-screen televisions, and a catered buffet for its athletes and employees to enjoy during the Games.

Sitting in a row of stilt-legged chairs on a small stage, Lisa, Ruthie, Katrina, and Dawn passed a microphone back and forth, answering questions from a large press audience, most of which concerned the possibility of a showdown with Brazil on Sunday.

"It was heartbreaking when we lost to Brazil two years ago . . ." said Ruthie.

"But when we lost to them," said Lisa, taking the microphone, "our team had been together only a few weeks. We're two years stronger now. We're smarter."

"Brazil is mainly a perimeter team," added Dawn. "Our strength is going inside . . . no team in the world can beat our inside players. Besides, we've watched so much scouting tape on Brazil. We already did an hour and fifty minutes of scouting today."

"We know so much about Brazil," said Lisa, reclaiming the mike, "we could probably run their plays."

When someone asked how they'd feel if they lost the gold medal, Katrina, who was dutifully dressed in a purple Nike turtleneck, black denim Nike shorts, Nike socks, and Nike running shoes, took the opportunity to answer. "It would be a big letdown if we didn't get the gold. . . ."

Dawn, who herself wore a white woolly-looking cap pulled low over her eyes, added her two cents. "Silver's a bust for me."

"Where will you all be a year from now with regard to professional opportunities?" a reporter asked.

There was a brief pause.

"I'm not sure," said Katrina, passing the microphone to Ruthie.

"I'm not sure," said Ruthie, handing it off to Lisa.

"I'm not sure," said Lisa, giving it to Dawn.

Dawn grinned devilishly at the audience, her convictions the same as they'd always been. "I'll have an ABL championship under my belt," she said.

If attitude was everything, then the Australians were destined to topple the house of cards that the Americans had built for themselves over the last year. So what if the crowd of 33,000 stacked into the Georgia Dome on Friday afternoon for the semifinals was overwhelmingly American? So what if Lisa Leslie & Co. had won every single game that year, including a handful against the Aussies? As Tara VanDerveer herself had been saying recently, the record meant nothing whatsoever. It came down only to what each team brought to the floor for forty minutes right now, and the Australians were a right-now kind of team. Pumped up on adrenaline after the overtime victory over the defending gold-medalist Russian team, they warmed up almost emphatically, leaping and driving through their half-court drills as if the battle were already on, looking with their blond hair and ropy muscles and glossy green-and-gold unitards like a bunch of hungry cyborgs.

They were not humbled by the Americans, not afraid. In fact, the way the Aussie women utterly ignored the baggy red, white, and blue team warming up downcourt was hardly part of a psyche job; it was almost as if they felt the game had already been written somewhere and that they'd been given a glimpse of their victory. They were that sure.

By this time, VanDerveer's team had some sense of how a game like this could be lost. If the U.S. could run up a lead early, they might break the other team and put them away. On the other hand, if the Australians came out and sank their teeth in fast—like they had so many times in the past—if Michelle Timms got her shot going and the others rose up behind her the way they had against the Russians, there'd be trouble.

And so with the crowd screaming and the pregame music playing beneath the noise, the game tipped off, and it quickly became evident that Michelle Timms was as hot as hot got. Down in the lower sections of the Georgia Dome, a small sea of Australian flags had unfurled, and a group of men were on their feet shouting *Ozzieozzieozzie!* as Timms threw up one three-pointer then another, while the Aussies double-teamed Lisa to limit the U.S. team's scoring.

Before the first two minutes were up, half the U.S. bench was on its feet, Rebecca, Venus, Carla, and Jennifer screaming encouragement to the starters on the floor. Australia had leapt to an instant 12–5 lead. Timms then seemed to switch her focus to the inside, scoring on a lay-up and adding another point when Sheryl got in her way for a foul. Before long it was an 18–10 game and VanDerveer was sending in her subs, looking again for the player or players who would click at the right instant and reverse the game's tempo. Nikki came in for Ruthie, immediately got called for a foul, and within a minute Ruthie was in again and Nikki was on the bench. In the meantime, Katrina scored twice off offensive rebounds, bringing them within four points. Teresa and Timms were in each other's faces on defense. When Timms stripped the ball from Teresa, Teresa's arms flew out and snatched it right back, immediately dishing it to Lisa for a lay-up, putting the game at 18–16. Moments later, Katrina intercepted an Aussie pass and sent it to Lisa, who lost it when Timms flew past her from nowhere, grabbing the ball as she went. It was beginning to look like a free-for-all, Timms versus the U.S. team, and ten minutes into the game, Timms was winning by three.

It was here that VanDerveer swapped out Teresa for Dawn. Dawn was exactly the kind of person who could unsettle an unsettling team with her blinding fast break; she was also the kind who could razzmatazz herself right back to a seat on the bench. Unfortunately, for a moment anyway, it looked to be the latter Dawn on the court. After Ruthie shot three and Venus scored inside to put the U.S. ahead by two, Dawn sent a horrendously aimed no-look pass right into the hands of the omnipotent Timms, who then sank a jumper to tie the game again, 22–22.

Then the Australian coach took Timms out of the game for a brief rest, which turned out to be the kiss of death for his team. Without Timms in the way, Dawn and Lisa started to groove, as if it were a flashback to the first time they'd ever played together at basketball camp five years earlier, to the thing their friendship was built on, Dawn bringing the ball down to find Lisa waiting under the net to score. It happened once, then twice. By the time Timms was back in the game, less than two minutes later, the damage had been done. The U.S. was ahead by six, then eight, and then nine points, and for Dawn Staley it was payback time. Instantly, she stole the ball from Timms, went coast to coast for a lay-up, and drew a foul on her approach. Three points. The American fans, having watched Timms make mincemeat out of their countrywomen earlier, were wilding in their seats as Dawn pouted and posed down below, loving every second.

Timms would play a valiant, up-tempo game right through to the bitter end, scoring 27 points, but it was not nearly enough without her team behind her. The closest another Aussie had come to matching Timms's performance was a forward named Michelle Brogan, who'd had just nine points. It seemed the overtime game with Russia two days earlier had sapped the last of their energies. And while the Americans hadn't necessarily looked spectacular, they'd done enough to win the semifinal 93–71. As the U.S. players stormed the court at the buzzer, leaping into one another's arms, accepting bear hugs from Venus and high-fives from Sheryl and a slap on the shoulder from VanDerveer, a number of the Australians retreated to their bench, dumped their heads into their hands, and sobbed. Exactly as the Americans had on this same day in Barcelona four years earlier. Exactly as the Ukrainian team would do just a few hours later on the same bench in the Georgia Dome as the Brazilians danced in a circle at center court after an 81–60 blowout.

It was to be the U.S. and Brazil playing Sunday for the gold medal, just as VanDerveer had dreamed it on August 4 a year ago, sitting at home in Palo Alto with the earliest pangs of worry about how things might play out. So far, she could not have hoped for better. That night, she would call to reconfirm her flight home to California.

"It's like I see the egg timer and there's just a little bit of sand left in it. We've got one more practice, one more game . . ." she said.

Already she was looking back and questioning whether she'd driven too hard at moments, whether she might have tried to control the team's fate less. Already she was getting wistful about the whole experience. "I want August fourth to be the happiest day of my life because our work will pay off," she had said on several occasions, "but it will also be the saddest since this will all be over."

"Today's my last day to holler at you," she told them when they gathered for the last practice Saturday, her voicing sounding emotional for a passing instant before she sent them into their normal routine— some last-minute work on defense, a run-through of the plays they would most likely use the next afternoon.

The players were feeling it too. When Nikki put on a Monica CD during stretching, several of them had felt their throats tighten, under- standing that this was the last time Jennifer and Ruthie would lead them through the stretching, the last time Nikki and Carla would bop around to the music, the last time they'd be summoned by the familiar notes of the coach's voice.

Emotion, however, could louse up their concentration. Emotion was what separated the Americans from the Brazilians, and this, some of them acknowledged, was both good and bad.

"The Brazilians have a certain confidence and freedom about the way they play that we don't have," said Jennifer, recalling the World Cham- pionships. "The way their culture is, it's so loose. Sometimes I think that if anything, our problem is that we're tight sometimes and too disci- plined, whereas they're free. . . . They just go out on the court, and if they miss a shot, who cares? It's a gamble, because sometimes that atti- tude can kill you, but for Brazil it just gives them energy and enthusiasm and that's what won them a world championship."

Teresa also admired the other team's passion but saw it ultimately as a fault. "They celebrate every single basket," she said. "But when we score on them, we take a little bit away from them. The more we score, the more we take away. If you play on emotions, it's like when you're up you're up and when you're down you're down. . . . It's going to go one way or another."

In the final day leading up to the gold-medal game, the memories of Brazil's semifinal victory over them at the World Championships in Sydney stewed in their minds. "I haven't forgotten that game," said Dawn. "Anytime you're left with a sour taste in your mouth, you want some kind of revenge, and this is our chance to get it."

Katrina acknowledged the high stakes. "If we don't win, the whole year has been a waste."

For VanDerveer, the image that stayed with her was the bitter bus ride they'd taken in Sydney, the Brazilians singing and celebrating their coach while the Americans sat in the dark, fingering their bronze medals. "It was kind of like we were uninvited guests at their party," she recalled. "It made me want to figure out a way to beat them so that we could be the ones celebrating."

With this in mind, she had scheduled each player for a last video session, arranging for most of them to review game tapes with one of her three assistants. But VanDerveer scheduled to do Teresa herself, requesting that she report to her suite that evening. Outside, the daylight was beginning to fade, turning the sky a deep orange. Teresa showed up as scheduled, dressed in a red sweatsuit. She and VanDerveer, she would later say, would forever have their differences. They would not go on to become friends. But they did feel the same way about winning, and for fifteen minutes that night the two of them went through video on the Brazilian players Teresa would be guarding the next day, discussing what their habits were, breaking down some individual plays, working over Teresa's strategy.

"I think she had to have a feeling of where I was in my mind before that big game," Teresa would recall. "I knew I was there, though I don't know if I relayed it to her well. I think she was a nervous wreck."

When they'd finished with the scouting and Teresa stood up to leave, VanDerveer had led her to the bathroom of the suite, where she pointed to two color photographs she had taped to her mirror. One was a copy of the photo they all carried in their notebooks, the print of Teresa's gold medal from 1988. The other photograph was from the day on the ropes course they'd had back in Colorado Springs a month earlier. There had been an exercise called the "high lean on me" in which two people stood on opposite wires thirty feet in the air, holding on to each other's hands, edging sideways out along the wires as the wires began to diverge, forcing the two partners to lean a bit more forward into each other with every step. That day, sizing up the wires, VanDerveer had volunteered to go first and she'd chosen Teresa to go with her. They had almost made it the whole way, with Teresa coaxing VanDerveer through it—*Look at me, don't look down, come on now, we got it*—until they finally wobbled and fell, just a few feet from the end, caught by the belay ropes held by the rest of the team.

The photo on VanDerveer's mirror at the Omni was of the two of them, palm to palm, their bodies making two sides of a triangle over thirty feet of open air while the others watched from below.

"This has been my motivation," the coach told Teresa as the two of them stared at the picture in the cold white light of the bathroom. "This was a turning point for us, I thought."

The moment would confuse Teresa somewhat. She and VanDerveer had spent little time talking throughout the year, and most of the time they had disagreed. The high-wire incident had been special, she agreed, though looking at VanDerveer, who looked worried and slightly haggard, she couldn't think of what to say.

"I didn't know what she was getting at really," Teresa would say later. "I kind of just wanted to get out of there. I guess it was a turning point though. I guess in her own way, she was trying to say that she liked me better."

The Olympics had now spanned nearly three weeks, but it had felt like forever. Kerri Strug had landed the vault heard round the world on an injured ankle. Amy Van Dyken had swum to four gold medals and smiled shyly through four national anthems. The U.S. women's softball and soccer teams had taken gold, too, in highly charged emotional victories. There had been a bombing that claimed two lives and nearly killed the Olympics. And even as sharpshooters had taken their places on building tops around Atlanta, there'd been Michael Johnson and his golden shoes and Dan O'Brien and Gail Devers and Jackie Joyner-Kersee remarkably composing her injured body to salvage a bronze in the long jump. The Dream Team III had inevitably won. And the women's basketball players had found inspiration in each one of these stories, had endlessly rehearsed in their own heads the possibility of such moments, and now it seemed everyone had had their final epiphanies, except them.

They took the court four hours before Closing Ceremonies, the women's gold-medal basketball game having replaced the marathon as the traditional last event due to Atlanta's afternoon heat. With another sellout crowd of 33,000 packing the Georgia Dome, and tens of millions watching worldwide, the players went through their rituals: taping and stretching, joking to stay loose and shooting around. They sipped water to moisten their dry mouths and stole an occasional glance at the Brazilians. There was nothing left to do now but play.

The game was being touted as a battle between the American frontcourt and the Brazilian backcourt, the inside game of Lisa and Katrina versus the outside game of the legendary Brazilian guards, Hortência Marcari Oliva, who at five foot eight and 127 pounds was inch for inch and pound for pound one of the world's best along with Maria Paula da Silva, or Magic Paula, as she was known. The two of them, at ages thirty-six and thirty-four respectively, had a combined national team tenure of nearly four decades, and had over the years been largely responsible for giving the Brazilian women their air of invincibility. They were like two Michelle Timmses, backed up by forward Marta de Souza Sobral, who in Atlanta had been averaging 16.7 points and 7.7 rebounds per game.

Teresa, Sheryl, Ruthie, Lisa, and Katrina took their places on the floor, wiped their palms on their shorts, offered a hand to the Brazilians, adjusted their waistbands, and the ball went up. If they had dreamed this moment, it was real now. The waiting was over.

Brazil struck first. Marta, a rangy six three, rambled down the lane and was immediately fouled by Sheryl, then hit one of two free throws. When Teresa brought the ball back up court, she passed off to Ruthie, who was set at least two feet outside the three-point line. The Brazilians, anticipating a pass, floated back into their zone. Though it wasn't what anyone quite expected, Ruthie looked up and simply let it heave. It was almost a question: *Are we here to play or not?* The shot seemed more like a moon rock falling from heaven, hanging in the air for a short eternity, then shuddering the net for three points, as the Dome let out its collective breath and exploded.

On Brazil's next possession, Sheryl, by prestidigitation, ended up with the ball, breaking full-speed back toward the American hoop, then pulling up, letting the ball roll from her fingertips, and beaming a jump shot.

When it fell cleanly Brazil answered right back. Hortência hit from outside and then Marta scooped inside and banked the ball off the glass, the two of them moving fluidly, comfortable, it seemed, with the already lightning pace of the game. It was 5–5.

Before the U.S. would reach six points, not even two minutes into the game, Sheryl had two fouls. Too wound-up and a bit unlucky, she flopped down on the bench, disgusted with herself. Where a month ago VanDerveer would have looked to a seasoned player like Katy to replace Sheryl in as big a game as this, she motioned Nikki in and charged her with shadowing Hortência, who could make a certain percent of her shots blindfolded anyway but who might fluster in the face of a hopped-up twenty-three-year-old dervish who could scamper the court tirelessly. Meanwhile, Lisa seemed to be battling a case of the jitters again, letting several minutes slip by before she'd even attempted to score.

In the fracas of the opening minutes, after Teresa took a drive to the hoop, hitting a left-handed lay-up, then followed it with a field goal on the next possession, one thing had become clear. Both the Americans and the Brazilians were playing at a near boil. For every basket the Americans found, the Brazilians, namely Hortência and Marta, found one too. And yet the U.S. team's leading scorers through the Olympics, Katrina (14.4 points per game), Lisa (18.1 per game), and Sheryl (12.8) had so far been unusually silent. If Teresa, the floor leader, sensed as much, she started by trying to move the ball inside more.

On the next play, Katrina thrashed for position, Teresa looped a pass to her, and Katrina dropped it in. But Marta turned around and drove the lane again for two points. Ruthie hit another three; Hortência answered with three. It was 14–12 and it felt like the third quarter already.

Searching for more control beneath the basket and perhaps more emotional charge, VanDerveer had replaced Lisa with Venus, who growled and grunted as she fought for the ball. Something in her presence on the floor—both obstructive and spontaneous, ferocious and uninhibited—seemed to match the Brazilians' emotional intensity and undermine it. While at the same time, Teresa, ever calm and fluid, kept the game moving at breakneck speed, almost taunting the Brazilians to stay with them. As it was, though, Marta was still driving the lane, once and then again, and Janeth Arcain, who also had been averaging 17 points a game in the Olympics, had started to slip open for the Brazilians and hit her field goals.

At 26–22, Ruthie and Alessandra Oliveira, at six five, a head taller than Ruthie, scrambled for a loose ball, both clamping on and then both tumbling to the floor, Alessandra's head smacking hard. For a moment there was a worried silence in the Dome, but then both women popped back up on their feet, looking dazed but ready for a jump ball. When it came down to it now, their bodies had become second to their desire. *Got to have that ball.* And still every time the U.S. inched ahead, the Brazilians tagged along. With 9:30 to play in the half, the U.S. led 31–27.

With Lisa back in the lineup, however, the Americans went on a run. Catching the Brazilians off balance, Lisa hit a jump shot on the perimeter. Then Sheryl knocked down a three, Nikki got two points on a lay-up, and then Sheryl hit for three again, from almost the identical place. At the other end of the court, Lisa defiantly swatted away a shot by Magic Paula. At 46–39, after another missed Brazil shot, Katrina rocketed off the ground and retrieved the rebound, elbows switchblading two Brazilians away. She cleared it to Ruthie, who instantaneously hit Teresa on the run, who fed Lisa at the other end of the court, who laid it up and in. It was the definition of flow, and a nine-point lead became ten, then finally eleven at the half, 57–46.

Not only were the Americans scoring, shooting a remarkable seventy-two percent from the field, going five for seven on three pointers, but the defense, led by Ruthie Bolton's spectacular job on Magic Paula and the hustle of Nikki and Sheryl, was shutting down Brazil's potent backcourt. Still, in the locker room, VanDerveer let her troops know that the game was far from over. The Brazilians were explosive and dangerous, and they were outrebounding the Americans 10–2 on offense. Not good at all, especially if they were to improve their forty-nine percent shooting in the first half. If Magic Paula, one of the world's deadliest three-point shooters, woke up, it'd be a tie game in a blink. She urged them to pick up the already blistering pace since the U.S. team, thanks in large part to

Teresa's ball-handling and aggressive defense, was leading 17–2 in fast-break points.

As the second half started, the Brazilian fans, who had turned out in thrumming droves of green and yellow, were going berserk. Not to be outdone, nor wanting anything to be left to chance, the American fans met the Brazilians' mania with their own. When one Brazilian in a lower section produced a bugle and started to blow the thing at full blast, the Americans overwhelmed him with their riotous cheering. The American women were twenty minutes away from everything they'd worked for, ahead by eleven points. With any other team but Brazil, the lead might have been comforting.

On the floor, not a flicker of emotion showed on Teresa's or Ruthie's or Lisa's face, nor was there a glimmer in Sheryl's or Katrina's eye to indicate that they were playing the game of their lives. After the tip-off, Ruthie stole the ball and went the length of the court, passing to Sheryl, who banked it in. After another Brazilian turnover, Ruthie led the fast break and sent a bullet pass to Katrina for a lay-up. It was 61–46 and the feeling was starting to seep into them now. Katrina celebrated her bucket by throwing two hands in the air. Next time down the court, Lisa, who was now well on her way to a game-high 29 points and seemed suddenly unstoppable, took a pass from Teresa and spun from the base-line, then unfolded her body toward the hoop, finishing the shot with her left hand. When it dropped in, she leaned her body back and punched a triumphant fist into the air. The crowd rose and punched back, screaming wildly. It was happening and it was happening flaw-lessly—the Americans, who'd already elevated their game, were suddenly elevating again. On the bench VanDerveer was still looking grim, still keeping the starters in the game to protect the lead.

With the score at 71–54, the coach finally subbed Dawn for Teresa, the two of them exchanging quick smiles as they passed. In nine minutes of play in the second half, the U.S. players had pushed the pace so hard, they'd run the Brazilians ragged. Marta, who'd gone out midway through the first half with three fouls, had returned simply human again. Ruthie sent up a shot from what felt like miles past the perimeter, and watched it rip the net for three. Sheryl buried another from just inside the key. But for flashes from Janeth Arcain and Hortência, the Brazilians were folding. Or perhaps they were being subsumed by the Americans, for now the U.S. players, who for nearly a year had harnessed their emotions under VanDerveer, were playing with their hearts on their sleeves, just as the Brazilians had in 1994.

Somewhere in those first five minutes of the second half, with Teresa at the helm and Ruthie and Sheryl playing suffocating defense and the whole team shooting impeccably, they had also seemed to add a last dimension to their game: perfection.

They jacked up the lead to 80–57. Magic Paula shot an air ball. Hortência had finally been silenced. When Lisa was fouled on a lay-up, Venus, who'd come in for Katrina, started to howl.

And then it dawned on them: They were going to win. The game had passed out of the realm of competition and into the realm of show. With eight minutes to play, and Jennifer now in the game for Ruthie, the Brazilians missed a three-pointer. In the scramble for the loose ball, Jennifer beat out Magic Paula, then broke over center court and bounced the ball down to Dawn, who was streaking for the basket. On a dead run, without seeming to have to think but just seeming to know, Dawn bounced the ball back behind her, where Katrina, invisible until then, simply snatched it and laid it in. There was sheer bedlam in the Dome, the screams pulsing through the players—all as one—and Dawn's expression, the wonder and cocky delight, said it all: *Live it up.*

The NBC commentators were already dubbing it the best women's game they'd ever seen, and these Americans the most spirited team they'd ever witnessed. In the final four minutes, Katy, Rebecca, Jen, and Carla all rotated into the game. As if scripted, they each had their gold-medal points too. Katy got a lay-up. Carla drove for the hoop, hoisting the ball up and in. Rebecca banked a shot after a pass from Jennifer, and finally, just before the buzzer, Jennifer scored on a lay-up. As the final seconds ticked down, Lisa melted into tears on the bench. Sheryl had both arms around Ruthie. Teresa and Katrina smacked each other five triumphantly and Dawn stood at the end of the bench and jumped up and down for joy, running her mouth without realizing that nobody was listening.

And then it was over, in the largest purest rush they could imagine, the scoreboard set at 111–87, the Americans weeping for joy, the Brazilians weeping for what could have been. The U.S. players circled the court in a victory lap, "Celebration" blaring over the Dome's sound system. They danced and cartwheeled, skipped and held their arms outstretched, pointing up at the crowd; they hugged each other and held on. When they accepted their gold medals, they almost seemed stunned, placing their hands over their hearts as the flag was slowly raised to the rafters of the Georgia Dome and the national anthem began its familiar refrain. Half of them sang, half closed their eyes. VanDerveer and her coaching staff stood on the sidelines, emotionally spent, but proud as mothers. Lisa bawled through a television interview. Ruthie went into the stands and gave her medal to her sister, Mae Ola. Jennifer led another victory lap, just for the heck of it.

Going back to the hotel later, they would celebrate at a lavish USA Basketball party for family and friends, and late late at night, even as dawn started to break over Atlanta, they would still be together, the medals still hung around their necks, lingering in the lounge of the Omni as Ruthie's brother played the piano and Ruthie and Nikki sang a few last songs. Sheryl stood watching, her arms draped around Eric. Teresa, Dawn, and Katrina laughed raucously at the bar. The night wouldn't feel like night, the same way the end wouldn't feel like the end, until their airport times arrived and one by one they dragged their luggage through the lobby, hopped into taxis and shuttles and, too tired almost to say good-bye, the team dissolved and each player went her own way.

The Season Beyond

Shortly after the U.S. women won the gold medal, Katrina McClain announced that she had accepted an offer to play professionally in Istanbul, Turkey, for $500,000, making her the highest paid women's basketball player in the world. A week later, Ruthie Bolton revealed that she had signed for $150,000 with the same Turkish team, which traditionally offered high salaries to two premier players each season. Several weeks after the Olympics, Katrina and Ruthie moved to Istanbul, both breaking contracts with the ABL.

Jennifer Azzi left the Olympics and went directly to Palo Alto, California, to run a week-long basketball camp for girls. Similarly, Katy Steding spent the month following the Olympics working full-time at her own girls' basketball camps and preparing the September launch of the Katy Steding Basketball Academy, an afterschool program in Beaverton, Oregon, where to date fifty girls regularly train. Teresa Edwards took a week's vacation in Hawaii and then returned to Atlanta to help ABL organizers prepare for the season ahead.

On Friday, October 18, in San Jose, California, Teresa and Jennifer faced each other for a ceremonial tip-off to start the first game of the American Basketball League season, Teresa playing for the Atlanta Glory and Jennifer for the San Jose Lasers. Over the course of the next several months, Teresa would set league records for single-game points (42) and assists (14, tied with Dawn), and was one of the ABL's top three scorers. Jennifer would suffer a shoulder injury in November and be forced to sit out the rest of the season, working instead as a sideline commentator for the ABL's televised games. Carla McGhee joined the Atlanta Glory, Katy Steding played with the Portland Power, Dawn Staley moved to Virginia as the point guard on the Richmond Rage, becoming teammates with Marta de Souza Sobral, the Brazilian center who had proved so stubborn in the first half of the Olympic finals, and Olympic heptathlete and former USC basketball player Jackie Joyner-Kersee. Kersee signed with the ABL in September but withdrew from the league after several months of sitting on the bench with the Rage, deciding to focus her efforts on her track and field career. With the help of Nike, Dawn has started the Dawn Staley Foundation in Philadelphia, which she describes as a "community service program to help inner-city youths develop academically as well as athletically."

Nikki McCray became one of the ABL's leading scorers, playing for the Columbus Quest in Ohio, a team that went undefeated for the first eleven games of the season before being upset by the Seattle Reign, which starred Venus Lacy. Venus, however, sustained a knee injury that required surgery, sidelining her for the second half of the season. Sylvia Crawley signed with the ABL shortly after her trip to Australia with the national team and spent the season playing for the Colorado Xplosion. Val Whiting was hurt in a car accident in California on August 3, the day before the gold-medal game, and spent six weeks rehabbing an injured knee before joining Jennifer Azzi on the Lasers. She pointedly did not watch the broadcast of Tara VanDerveer and the national team winning the gold medal, saying later that the memories of her three attempts to make the team were still too painful.

Rebecca Lobo says that she did not touch a basketball for three months following the team's victory in Atlanta. Instead, she spent time with her family and boyfriend in Massachusetts, played a lot of golf, and then signed on as a television commentator for the UConn Huskies home games, working for Connecticut Public Television and ESPN2. The continued success of the women Huskies and the legacy of Rebecca Lobo has helped to make Connecticut and western Massachusetts an epicenter of the growing support for women's basketball in this country. The Hartford/Springfield-based New England Blizzard, the ABL team that had hoped to have Rebecca on its roster but instead featured Rebecca's close friend and former teammate Jennifer Rizzotti, drew more spectators, an average of nearly 5,000 per home game, than any other ABL team.

On October 23, five days after the start of the ABL season, Rebecca joined with Sheryl Swoopes at the All-Star Cafe in New York to announce that they had signed two-year contracts as the charter members of the Women's National Basketball Association. "What you people have to understand," Sheryl told the group of assembled reporters when questions were raised about her earlier commitment to the ABL, "is that when the ABL was first announced, we were just so excited to have a league to play in. We didn't even know that the NBA was thinking of forming a league. The NBA had a lot to offer. This isn't personal. I don't think people should get mad with each other. To me what this means is that there is a lot of interest in women's basketball."

When asked why she, unlike the others on the national team, had delayed signing with the ABL, Rebecca said this: "I was not going to jump in headfirst without knowing what I was getting into. Teresa had an emotional commitment. The WNBA had a television contract. That's important." Later, she would add, "It was basically a two-part decision. I was too tired to start playing a month after the Olympics, when the ABL's training camps started. I also knew that the NBA would do a good job with women's basketball, and it just felt like the right choice for me."

In the weeks that followed, the WNBA announced that it would field teams in New York, Los Angeles, Charlotte, Cleveland, Phoenix, Utah, Sacramento, and Houston, and that teams would be operated by existing NBA franchises. Commissioner David Stern predicted that expansion will be "immediate."

In November, Ruthie Bolton became the third national team member to sign with the WNBA. Sheryl, Rebecca, and Ruthie would eventually be joined by Australia's Michelle Timms, the Russian center Elena Baranova, Zheng Haixia of China, and Janeth Arcain of Brazil. They are all scheduled to begin the WNBA's 28-game season, which opens on June 21, 1997, with the exception of Sheryl Swoopes, who woke up one morning in December and ate two sweet pickles, a sour pickle, a Popsicle, and cereal for breakfast and realized that she was pregnant. As a result, she has announced that she will begin playing for the WNBA's Houston franchise as soon as possible following the arrival of her child, a boy, expected in June. She spent the months following the Olympics traveling for Nike, promoting an updated version of the Air Swoopes. Eric Jackson, her husband, played his first full college football season as a running back at Angelo State College in San Angelo, Texas.

Finally, on December 11, dressed in a lavender pantsuit custom-made by a Beverly Hills designer, Lisa Leslie had a press conference of her own in Los Angeles, where she, too, announced a two-year deal with the WNBA. "The ABL started just a few weeks after the Olympics, and I was exhausted," she said of her decision not to follow through with her original intentions of playing in the fall league. She reported that her mother, Christine Leslie, had essentially made the decision for her. "I told her I could play in the ABL, which had no team in L.A., or the WNBA, which does," Lisa said. "So my mom said if there might be a chance I could play here, it would mean she could see me play. And since she's my number-one fan, that's what I did."

Three days after the gold medal game, Val Ackerman was appointed president of the WNBA. She says she has monitored the ABL's season from a distance and is encouraged by what she sees, adding that she has never considered her organization in competition with the ABL, given their different seasons, nor is it likely the two leagues will ever combine. "The ABL is off to a good start, they're averaging about 3,500 per game, and that helps all of us in women's basketball," she told the *Los Angeles Times*. "It's important to us that they do well. But no one is talking about a merger."

At the end of June 1996, Bobby Johnson abruptly withdrew from the ABL when the second part of his investment came due, citing personal and professional reasons. As the Olympic team went undefeated in Atlanta, Gary Cavalli and Steve Hams scrambled to make up for the sudden loss of league capital, campaigning for new sponsors and, according to Cavalli, "waking up at three A.M. many nights in a cold sweat." According to a February 1997 article in the *Atlanta Journal Constitution*, Johnson and a business associate are under investigation for allegedly skimming over $5 million from Georgia State Medicaid programs in conjunction with two nursing homes Johnson owns. Neither man has been charged.

With Reebok as the league's national apparel and footwear sponsor, the ABL has drawn the corporate support of Nissan, Lady Foot Locker, Phoenix Insurance Group, and others. Still, Cavalli predicts that the ABL will lose roughly $4 million in its first season, though he is quick to add that plans for the 1997–1998 season are already underway. Games will be shown on SportsChannel and Black Entertainment Television. With regard to the lost deals with ESPN2 and Nike, as well as the loss of Sheryl Swoopes, Lisa Leslie, Ruthie Bolton, Katrina McClain, and Rebecca Lobo, Cavalli says simply, "We're doing great. We don't need to look back."

Still, as the ABL finished its inaugural season, several of its premier players hinted that they might leave the league in order to play for the WNBA. "I'm realizing that basketball is a business," said Dawn Staley at the end of the season. "I have to look out for me." Carla McGhee and Venus Lacy have also expressed indecision about whether they will play another season with the ABL.

In the meantime, both Katrina and Ruthie returned home early from their season in Turkey, saying that the team was months late in paying them. "Generally, I don't like to complain," said Ruthie from Istanbul the day before she left for the U.S. in February, "but it's been tough over here. They're unprofessional. Women don't have a voice: They think we shouldn't complain if they don't pay us. There are no black people here, so you get stared at all the time. My bags are packed. I'm ready to come home."

Following her decision not to sponsor the ABL, Sue Levin was promoted from manager to director of the women's sports marketing group at Nike. When the ABL's Portland Power played its first game on October 19 in Portland, Levin was one of 8,704 to attend the game, sitting anonymously in the stands with what she says were mixed emotions. "I still wish that something could have worked out," she says of Nike's involvement with the ABL, "but I think it was a sound decision [not to sponsor the league] on my part." In mid-February 1997, as the ABL moved into the last week of its regular season, Sue Levin together with Val Ackerman announced that Nike would join Lee Jeans, Bud Light, Champion, and Spalding in becoming an official marketing partner of the WNBA.

Tara VanDerveer, who is at work on an autobiography, says that she misses coaching the national team. In addition, she has said in the press that she would consider coaching a WNBA team at some point, that returning to her beloved college team has been in moments difficult. She still thinks often of the medal ceremony at the Olympics, through which she cried openly. "It was really strange," she told a reporter in the fall. "I never thought about it being over. I never planned. I knew I had a plane ride back home, but to me there was nothing beyond August fourth. I didn't even know what to do with myself. I thought, 'It's over,' and I never really thought that day was actually coming because all I pictured in my mind was that flag going up, that anthem being played, that team standing on that podium. And after that, it was just like, well, now what?"

The day after the game, VanDerveer returned to Palo Alto to start the next chapter in her coaching career. In the weeks following the Olympics, she personally answered some two hundred congratulatory letters and then departed at the end of August for a two-week competitive tour in Italy with her new team, which was also her old team, the Stanford Cardinal. On December 17, 1996, Tara VanDerveer lost her first basketball game in over a year to Old Dominion University by a score of 83–66. Her team did not lose again during the regular season. Headed into the 1997 tournament, VanDerveer and the Cardinal were ranked number two in the country, just behind Geno Auriemma's UConn Huskies.

The 1996 women's Olympic basketball team was selected as the U.S. Olympic Committee's Team of the Year in December, voted upon by the Olympic Committee members and the national media, beating the gold-medal U.S. gymnastics team by one vote. The top four vote-getters, interestingly, were women's teams, with the U.S. softball and soccer teams falling just behind basketball and gymnastics. The 1996 Atlanta Olympics will be remembered largely as the games that belonged to female athletes, who participated in record numbers, helping to dispense with the notion expressed by the founder of the modern Olympics, Baron Pierre de Coubertin, who in 1896 declared that the Olympics should be an "exaltation of male athleticism" with "female applause as the reward."

In December 1996, *USA Today* reported that according to a survey by the American Basketball Council of equipment makers, the number of girls ages twelve to seventeen playing basketball rose from 39 percent in 1994 to 46 percent in 1995, a rise the survey attributed directly to the success of the women's national team in its fourteen-month, high-profile march to the Olympics.

Teresa Edwards has now played ten years of professional basketball and has four Olympic medals, three of them gold, to her name. The medal that means the most, she says, is the one from Atlanta. She says she is considering retirement. Looking back over her long career and its very public culmination at the Georgia Dome on August 4, she adds, "It amazes me that people really saw me, since in the past people never did. That's big. I can't describe the feeling. People come up and say, 'You're Teresa Edwards, I remember you.'"

ACKNOWLEDGMENTS

I am deeply indebted to the twelve members of the U.S. Olympic women's basketball team and their coach, who let me into their lives during a time when privacy was already at a minimum and the demands on their time enormous. For the six months I tagged along with the team, the players and coaching staff treated me with warmth and generosity, teaching me a lot not just about basketball but about faith and tenacity as well.

The staff at USA Basketball was equally as accommodating. I owe special thanks to Carol Callan, Lori Phelps, Carla Jennie, and Caroline Williams. Above all, I am tremendously grateful to Amy Early, who has given hours of her time and energy in helping me with my research and interviews for this book and whose friendship I value greatly.

Coming into this project without a lot of background in basketball, I also have relied heavily on a number of people I met along the way, namely the group of writers who regularly covered the team. Their reporting and thoughts informed this book, and I thank each of them for their help, companionship, and insight: Alexander Wolff of *Sports Illustrated*, Chuck Schoffner of the Associated Press, Mike Spence of the *Colorado Springs Gazette*, Celeste Whitaker and J. C. Clemons at the *Atlanta Journal-Constitution*, Steve Wieberg of *USA Today*, Malcolm Moran at *The New York Times*, Earl Gustkey at the *Los Angeles Times*, Mel Greenberg of *The Philadelphia Inquirer*.

There are also several magazine editors without whose help and support I could not have written this book: Pamela Miller at *Self*, who originally assigned me to write about the team, Shelley Youngblut of *ESPN Total Sports*, who made my trip to China possible, and Lucy Danziger at *Condé Nast Sports for Women*, who has been a believer from the very start.

In addition, I'd like to thank the many people in the sports world who gave of their time and wisdom: the organizers of the American Basketball League, Steve Hams, Gary Cavalli, Anne Cribbs, and Bobby Johnson, welcomed me as an observer as their league took shape. At the NBA I'm grateful to David Stern, Val Ackerman, Carol Blazejowski, and Sandi Bittler for the time they spent with me and their considerable support. Special thanks go to Adam Silver of NBA Entertainment, who was particularly helpful in allowing me access to his organization's video archives of the women's national team, and to the various NBA producers whose work aided my own. Sue Levin at Nike has continually broadened my thinking about women's sports and given freely of her time for this project. Teri Schindler of KTM Productions was an adviser and friend throughout. Susan Lyne at Disney has been an enthusiastic supporter as well. Thanks also to David Lee of Nike China and Natalie Stewart of Basketball Australia for their help with my international travels, and to Jill Jameson of Virginia Tech for taking time to track down obscure basketball trivia for me.

There are two outside sources which deserve particular mention: *Playing Nice: Politics and Apologies in Women's Sports* by Mary Jo Festle provided excellent background on Title IX and the history of women's professional basketball. Ruthann and Rebecca Lobo's memoir, *The Home Team: Of Mothers, Daughters, and American Champions*, was also a significant help to me.

Amy Goldwasser and Miles Harvey, two of the most trustworthy and smart editors/writers I know, each gave a first draft of the book an incisive and thorough read on a tight deadline, for which I'm extremely grateful.

I was lucky as well to have a number of dedicated helpers and friends, including Kate Raley, who tirelessly transcribed tapes, Tim Dilworth, Greg Netzer, Daven Lee, and Julie Greenberg for their research help, and JR Romanko, who researched and fact-checked the book diligently and energetically. My grandmother, Margaret Fulton, spent hours videotaping games and clipping newspapers for me. My parents, Chris and Peggy Corbett, helped with this book and supported me in countless ways. I'd also like to thank Dick and Marianne Paterniti, Peggy Orenstein, who came into my life at exactly the right moment as a friend and mentor, and Clare Hertel and Susan Casey, who are like teammates to me.

My agent, Sloan Harris, lent everything he had to ushering this book from rough idea to finished project and whose enthusiasm I could always count on. I am thankful for his friendship and hard work on my behalf.

At Doubleday, Bill Thomas was a patient and thoughtful editor whose good humor and insight made the prospect of writing a book far less daunting than it otherwise would have been, and Jacky LaPierre went to great lengths to take care of the book's photos and loose ends. I'm grateful to them both.

Finally, my best friend and most ardent believer is Michael Paterniti, who understood that there was a book to be written before I did, and who gave and gave up a great deal to see me through it. Truly, I couldn't have done it without him. This book is dedicated, with love, to him.

DATE			
APR 3 0 2001			